Vanished Act

The Life and Art of Weldon Kees

by James Reidel

University of Nebraska Press Lincoln and London

Publication of this volume was assisted by The Virginia Faulkner Fund, established in memory of Virginia Faulkner, editor-in-chief of the University of Nebraska Press.

"Prologue: July 18, 1955" and "Epilogue/Ellipsis" were previously published in different form in *Verse* 14.3 (1998): 65–77.

The excerpt from "The Evening of the Fourth of July" by Weldon Kees, from *New Directions Annual 5,* copyright © 1940 by New Directions Publishing Corp., is reprinted by permission of New Directions Publishing Corp.

Poems by Weldon Kees are reprinted from *The Collected Poems of Weldon Kees,* edited by Donald Justice, by permission of the University of Nebraska Press. Copyright 1975, by the University of Nebraska Press.

The excerpt from the November "Reviews and Previews" by Milton Gendel on Weldon Kees's one-man show is reprinted with the permission of ARTnews LLC. Copyright © 1949, ARTnews LLC, November.

Library of Congress Cataloging-in-Publication Data
Reidel, James
Vanished act : the life and art of Weldon Kees /
James Reidel
p. cm.
Includes bibliographical references (p.) and index.
ISBN 0-8032-3951-3 (cloth : alkaline paper)
1. Kees, Weldon, 1914–1955? 2. Authors, American – 20th century – Biography. 3. Artists – United States – Biography. I. Title.
PS3521.E285 Z86 2003 700'.92 — dc21 [B] 2002032351

To my family

The tragic view of life
Requires a degree of health that seldom persists
After forty.
    —Lindley Williams Hubbell, "Angelology"

CONTENTS

ILLUSTRATIONS

Following page 192

Weldon Kees at seven

John Kees

Sarah and Weldon Kees

Weldon Kees in double-breasted suit

Dale Smith and Weldon Kees

Weldon and Ann Kees in Denver

Weldon Kees, June 1941

Norris Getty, June 1941

Paramount Newsreel staff party

Weldon Kees, studio portrait

The Studio, 1948

Weldon Kees on the Brooklyn Bridge

Gallery invitation to Kees's first
one-man show

Hans Hofmann, Karl Knaths, Fritz
Bultman, Cecil Hemley, and Kees in
Gallery 200

Weldon Kees in Gallery 200

Ann and Weldon Kees with their
Lincoln

Weldon Kees under one of his
paintings

Weldon and Ann Kees in Berkeley

One of Kees's "data" photographs

Weldon, Ann, and John Kees

San Francisco Films staff

Preface

There is an old water ring on my copy of *Benham's Book of Quotations*, left, perhaps, by its former owner resting a tumbler of whiskey and ice. "San Francisco" is written in ink under his name. Little else distinguishes the book as once having belonged to Weldon Kees other than the postcard of Magritte's *Le Thérapeute* that sometimes falls out. The image I have of him from this worn, stained book is not of the man staring into the churning water of the bay under the Golden Gate Bridge. Instead, I see Kees sitting with his legs crossed, dressed in chinos and a white oxford with the sleeves rolled up, with that iced drink in hand. He has that "serenity" Donald Justice saw in the book that he edited, *The Collected Poems of Weldon Kees*.

Justice's preface is where this book begins. There he hoped that more could be done for Kees by someone who "had known the poet." Justice meant an expanded or critical edition of Kees's poems. But I apprehended this more broadly, for it pointed toward a greater void left by Kees and the need to find someone to put something in its place. The suggestion stayed with me after I received the *Collected Poems* as a graduation gift in 1979. So did the dark beauty of Kees's verse and the uncertainty surrounding his disappearance in 1955. At first, of course, I fully expected to find his biography written and his mystery solved in the library. It seemed his story would not have sat around long waiting for its author. But I found no book.

Now there is one, and it comes after a twenty-year wave of scholarship and interest in Kees that was started by individuals working unknown to each other at first but all inspired by Justice's two editions of the *Collected Poems* and a few anthology appearances that kept Kees's name alive after 1955. Their efforts, including some of my own, resulted in collections of his short stories, letters, and critical writings and the publication of his satirical novel, *Fall Quarter*. A fine bibliography now exists, and there have been symposiums, essays, a monograph, a festschrift, exhibitions of paintings, a television documentary, even a CD of his jazz. Many of these efforts became cooperative and collegial in nature and gave rise to the existence of a small and dedicated group of Kees scholars. His photographs and films—of recent interest to the Department of Linguistics at Georgetown University—may soon be reclaimed and reappraised as well.

This is not a "chapter book," as children call their more formidable reading assignments. Life, as Kees saw it, came in "fragments, odds and ends," which is how this work came together over nearly two decades of research and writing. To give such a life shape, I have arranged this book using the cities in which Kees lived, rather than parceling it out into traditionally numbered chapters. What we see then is the bell curve of his unfinished life and the way each city represents Kees's transitions from aspiring novelist to poet, from poet to painter, and from painter to jazzman. Kees the poet is the core of all these vocations, but so is Kees the cultural adventurer, with his incredible range of contemporaries, and the culture's harsh critic.

Some who come to this book will have to decide for themselves if there is any mystery surrounding Kees's disappearance. For me, the case is closed and long has been. While working with the BBC on a Kees documentary, the Nebraska newspaperman Paul Hammel asked me if I thought Kees might be alive or might have lived out the life implied in that question mark after his dates on old library catalog cards. This was in 1993, when those apocryphal stories about old gringos playing ragtime piano in places like Quintana Roo were still circulating. I hedged on my answer. I was already finding out that Kees did not have the patience such an afterlife required. He may have titled his first book of poems *The Last Man,* an allusion to the Romantics' idea of the man who sees the Apocalypse. But Kees's disappointment with midcentury civilization suggests he had already seen one, had seen enough of it, and had decided his last man would be the first to go.

I was also asked what it was like to be Kees's biographer. It was, I replied, more like working with shattered glass than with the picture of a body hitting the water. I said this because it was overwhelming then to piece together his life, with only that partial collection of papers Kees's mother had entrusted to the public library in Lincoln, Nebraska, an act that had a kind of small-town, civic-duty flavor to it even as it preserved the memory of a son who once lived in New York, whose Robinson poems personify the city in its black-and-white postwar years. (How could I refuse her? I sometimes asked.) Looking back now, I also have to say that working with Kees provided me with a strange combination of peace and restlessness, like that of the art restorer, and with the sense of mission the detective has in those B-movies Kees loved. At times, I worried that there would be no outcome to all my work. Two others had attempted biographies and stopped cold. I worried that I might not have enough here, that I had told too much and taken away from that experience of private discovery that draws people to Kees. Now, however, I feel I have done something that will make it possible at last for others who will now know Kees to do more in their own way.

ACKNOWLEDGMENTS

I would like to express my gratitude to my friend and volunteer research assistant Laura Lacy, the former curator of the Weldon Kees Papers, deposited in the Heritage Room of the Bennett Martin Public Library in Lincoln, Nebraska. Without her help, this book would not have been possible.

Bill Heick, Kees's friend and photographer, also deserves my special gratitude for providing his incredible images of Kees, as does my friend and photograph researcher Todd Tedesco, who obtained and selected the other images used to illustrate this book.

The Stein Gallery's owner, Gertrude Stein, and her niece Joi Grieg deserve the same gratitude for making available to me the materials that John Kees entrusted to Michael Grieg, who had the care of Kees's paintings, letters, library, phonograph records, tape recordings, films, manuscripts, and photographs.

Nina Duvall Anderson of Omaha, Nebraska, I thank as well for supplying me with the baby book, photographs, and news clippings that Sarah Kees kept to record the childhood of Weldon Kees.

There is something special to say for every one of the people who follow. They should, if they can, for some are no longer with us, look for their contribution in this book. Each provided me with some kind of assistance or piece of information over the last twenty years that shaped my work: Simon Armitage; Sanora Babb; Judith Barrett; Anne Becker; Marvin Bell; Saul Bellow; Arthur Berger; Dr. Jack Block; Joseph Brodksy; Chandler Brossard; James Broughton; Byron R. Bryant; Fritz and Jeanne Bultman; Christopher Busa; Herbert Cahoon; Bernice Wells Carlson; Nancy Casey; Carol J. Connor; Malcolm Cowley; Jordan Davies; Peter De Vries; Phyllis Diller; Manny Farber;

Lawrence Ferlinghetti; Harry Ford; Stephen Foster; Norman Geske; Ervin Getty; Kahlil Gibran Jr.; Daniel Gillane; Allen Ginsberg; Robert Goodnough; Daisy Goodwin; Pamela Gossin; Esther Gottlieb; Robert Greensfelder; Jim Gulick; John Haines; Donald Hall; Daniel Halpern; Linda Hamalian; Paul Hammel; Robert Harper; Bob Helm; George Hitchcock; Sidney Hook; Richard Howard; Philip Hoy; Ron Hull; Jean Johnson; Donald Justice; Pauline Kael; Alfred Kazin; Hugh Kenner; Robert E. Knoll; Vicki Elliott Krecek; Seymour Krim; Leighton Kunkel; Hal Lainson; James Laughlin IV; Toni LaSelle; Eleanor Barrett Lawrence; Ketty Lester; Chris Lewis; Jennifer Liese; Frankie Lowry; Robert Lowry; Ruth Lowry; Robert S. Marvin; Annette Mattoon; Gerard B. McCabe; Harvey and Miriam McCaleb; Robert McDowell; Burgess Meredith; Toni Meredith; Howard Moss; Robert Motherwell; Anton Myrer; Howard Nemerov; Robert Niemi; Timothy Nolan; Walter J. Ong, S.J.; Virginia Patterson; Virginia Pauker; Robert Pierce; Merlyn S. Pitzele; Constance Hammett Poster; Mary Reidel; Betty B. Replogle; Janet and Charles Richards; Laureen Riedesel; Dr. Jurgen Ruesch; George Schaefer; Nancy Schoenberger; John Schuller; John Schulman; Horace Schwartz; Steve Shively; Daniel Siedell; Daniel Simko; Roy Simmonds; Jan Davis Spalding; Robert Swan; Barry Thorpe; Rudolph Umland; Penny Vieregge; Jean Waddell; Barry Werth; Ray B. West Jr.; Marian Weston; Dr. Joseph Wheelwright; Robert and Lorraine Wilbur; Joyce Wilson; and Kent Wilson.

Several institutions should be acknowledged for providing scholarly access to source materials, namely the Bennett Martin Public Library, Lincoln, Nebraska; the Rare Book and Manuscript Library, Columbia University; the Clarion University Library; the Beinecke Rare Book and Manuscript Library, Yale University; the Manuscripts and Archives Division of the New York Public Library; the Harvard Library Poetry Room; the Caliban Book Shop; University of Washington libraries; the Gage County (Nebraska) Historical Society; the Huntington Library; the Federal Bureau of Investigations; the Whitney Museum of American Art; the *San Francisco Chronicle;* the city of Lincoln, Nebraska; Doane College; the Provincetown (Massachusetts) Public Library; the *Partisan Review;* University of Nebraska Libraries; the University of Iowa Cultural Affairs Council; Watershed Associates; the Brown University Library; the Sheldon Memorial Art Gallery and Sculpture Garden; the Rocky Mountain Bibliographical Center for Research; the Grinberg Film Library; the Yaddo Corporation; and the British Broadcasting Corporation.

Finally, I would like to thank Dana Gioia and David Wojahn for reviewing the manuscript of this book and for their kind, helpful, and insightful remarks.

Prologue
July 18, 1955

Pick up the pieces,
Throw them away,
Say amen,
Because like Humpty Dumpty,
I can't be put back together again.
　　　　　—Weldon Kees song

It was Monday morning, the beginning of a new week, and Michael Grieg waited for his business partner and friend Weldon Kees to answer his phone. Grieg knew about an overseas job that would interest him, that would make up for his not having said something helpful Sunday night, something that did not sound stupid and pointless to a poet. Kees was, after all, the kind of man who wrote with such alacrity about deciding between Toynbee and luminal. Now he was deciding between jumping off the Golden Gate and going to Mexico.

The last evening had been like others that Grieg had spent with Kees during the past weeks, when his friend began to talk calmly and resignedly about what he was going to do next with his life. It seemed that Mexico was the choice when Grieg accepted Kees's invitation to come over for drinks that Sunday. Indeed, Grieg wanted to raise a glass to Kees and his will to live and found a fresh bottle of Jack Daniels Kees had purchased as if to toast this very decision.

Both men poured drinks and drank them slowly while sitting across from each other in Kees's pair of Knoll butterfly chairs. They had two or three and probably listened to records from time to time on his blond-wood phonograph. As the liquor took effect, Kees, at some point in going over the setbacks of recent months, admitted to trying to jump off the Golden Gate Bridge the week before. He had lost his nerve, however. He could not get his foot over the rail.

Though Kees was more quiet than normal—he usually dominated the conversation—he was coherent. Grieg only half-worried at what he was saying since suicide was like a professional hazard for Kees, given his poems and this new money-making book he had wanted to write with Jim Agee and now wanted to do with Grieg, a book of famous suicides subtitled *How-Not-To-and-Why-Not-To-Do-It*. Despite the amusing title, Kees was serious about the project. He worked at the Langley Porter Psychiatric Clinic and had amassed a file of suicide notes from there. He also had typed up celebrity profiles of the poet Hart Crane, the actress Lupe Velez—and Alexander Berkman, a figure dear to Grieg since he was an anarchist, too.

"It's a hell of a useless way to go about getting research," Grieg said among the other ironies he hoped would comfort and settle his friend.

Kees then responded with a smile that suggested the crisis had passed. The two men went on and discussed the notion that suicide was a statistical whim. It happened most often in summer months. It could be triggered by a poor diet. After all, since Kees's divorce, he had sometimes not been eating well or regularly. But this had just as much to do with his taking Dexedrine, which made him so gaunt that sometimes, from certain angles, he seemed almost to be bodiless inside his clothes.

Kees turned the conversation over to what he would need to do if he went to Mexico. He should sell his paintings and books, he said. He had many first and rare editions of modern novels and poetry, such as *The Knife of the Times* by William Carlos Williams and *Harmonium* by Wallace Stevens. These books would bring a handsome price. So would the yellow Hans Hofmann, one of two that had been gifts of the painter, that had once hung in the bedroom he shared with his former wife, Ann. Somewhere in this talk, Grieg remembered, Kees quoted from Rilke's "Archaic Torso of Apollo," repeating the last line about how you must change your life completely.

As they finished their whiskey, Kees returned to the subject of Mexico. That country had held a fascination for him ever since he read a biography of Hart Crane, who spent his last, happy, bohemian year there. It was the same Mexico he found in Malcolm Lowry's *Under the Volcano*, a book he had read twice, the Mexico alluded to in that first novel he had edited and midwifed for his friend Tony Myrer: "All that avant-garde crowd down there then, terrifically wild parties, everyone doing impossible things and sleeping with everyone else. Really emancipated. Imagine it, just imagine."

Kees asked Grieg if he wanted to go with him, but Grieg could not see leaving his family. His problems, he said, did not require such a "desperate solution." Then both men left for an Italian restaurant, where they ordered spaghetti dinners, ate heartily, and later parted.

When Kees answered the phone the next morning, Grieg sensed his friend was occupied with something. He gave him the information about the overseas job and said he would call back later. He finally did so the next evening. There was no answer, though, and Kees was not at home when Grieg came back to check his friend's Filbert Street apartment. The door was locked. Grieg listened at the door for a minute and then left.

The next day, Grieg received a call from the California Highway Patrol. His friend's car had been found on the north end of the Golden Gate Bridge in Marin County. The keys were still in the ignition, the police said. A lab coat belonging to the Langley Porter Clinic was neatly folded on the rear seat of the 1954 Plymouth. No note was in the car, nor was it the only car abandoned in the sightseers' parking lot. The other belonged to Joseph R. Eppler, a salesman, aged fifty-nine, who had left a note admitting to a business failure and including the usual request that he be forgiven for what he was about to do. These two cars and the lack of a note—and body—from Kees made for a bureaucratic problem: Which of the two men would be the official eighty-eighth person to jump from the span, and had there actually been an eighty-ninth?

With two police officers and another Kees friend, the printer Adrian Wilson, Grieg entered Kees's apartment. Little had changed from the Sunday before. The Jack Daniels had not been touched. Sheet music was spread across the upright piano. There was a pile of reel-to-reel tapes that Kees had made with his musician friends. Grieg took the top one, which contained two of Kees's torch songs that he had recorded with the Purple Onion club's singer.

Dostoyevsky's *The Devils*, which Kees had been reading, was placed near his bed beside another book, Unamuno's *Tragic Sense of Life*. A note lay on the telephone table; on it Kees had jotted down some of the details about the job Grieg had spoken of. In the bathroom sink, two red socks were still soaking. In the kitchen, beside a bookcase that Kees kept there, stood a plate of congealed milk for his cat, Lonesome, which turned out to be the only living thing in the apartment.

The phone rang. One of the policemen answered. Then he put the handset back down on the cradle and told the others that no one had been on the other end.

Beatrice
1914-1931

The porchlight coming on again,
Early November, the dead leaves
Raked in piles, the wicker swing
Creaking. Across the lots
A phonograph is playing Ja-Da.
[. . . . .]
And I am back from seeing Milton Sills
And Doris Kenyon. Twelve years old.
                    — Weldon Kees, "1926"

In her last year, in the months after the assassination of President Kennedy, Sarah Kees lived in a retirement manor that resembled a motel, that may have been a motel. She kept a number of family photographs in her small room. Among them were images of her missing child. They show a smiling, small-town boy a lifetime and several cities removed from all that remained of him: three slender volumes collected into an already fading paperback edition of his poems. The many private and individual acts that it would take for Kees's work to be rediscovered and for the story of his life to be reclaimed had yet to happen.

The smiling boy in the photographs does not resemble the child in the damaged world of the poems. There is a picture of an infant Kees sitting on the floor splay-legged in little hard-soled, high-topped button shoes. He is dressed in a white baby gown. It is his first Christmas, and by him there is a Scotch pine. The tree is not very full or overly decorated. A few glass balls hang in the boughs, along with paper Santas, bells, English setters, and what could be an angel at the treetop. A thin tinsel rope forms a crazed pattern. The gifts around the child are simple and plain, too. A cast-iron terrier, slightly out of focus, and a stuffed Pomeranian have been placed near Kees for him to play with — or they have been *posed*, for it is a kind of Americanism to have dogs in photographs. They lend an air of contentment and normalcy to an image that people alone cannot. The contentment and normalcy in this Christmas photograph look incongruous if one knows that the adult Kees had more affection for cats named Flowerface, Daughter, and Lonesome; that such animals are esteemed in his poetry; and that pet dogs are pariahs and emblems of dystopia, of the "gray world / not without violence" that is described in his signature poem, "Robinson."

After looking harder at this picture, one sees more than just the dogs. There is a jack-in-the-box. There are two tin drums and balls that have been rolled across the floor to the delighted child. There is even a string of lights in the Christmas tree emitting colorless white specks of light, certainly a novelty in 1914 and indicative of the Kees family's feelings of comfort and prosperity in the new century.

In contrast is the portrait of Kees at one year. Here the studio photographer has used lighting and a pose unchanged since the daguerreotype. Weldon's white, lace-trimmed frock and the locket that hangs from his neck reveal how he started life in one century and lived in another. Placing this same antiquelike baby portrait beside a snapshot taken of him in 1955, in which he holds a Budweiser and sits in a modern Sonoma County kitchen, makes for another impression of Kees's chronology—that his life seems to have covered more time than the forty-one years it actually did.

Living in the heartland did not inhibit Kees's parents from posing him in a sailor suit for another studio photograph, taken in 1921. In this image, one that would seem to have been his mother's favorite, he looks like a Nebraskan tsarevitch or a Prince of Wales wearing the yachting togs of some imperial navy. The iconography speaks for its time and for the heightened middle-class aspirations that Sarah and John Kees had for their family and their only son, whose sly faint smile suggests that he enjoyed pretending to be a landlocked nautical dandy.

This photograph and the others from boyhood show Kees's distinctive features. The full lips and the soft, intelligent gaze of his dark eyes would change little, save to be hardened by the thin mustache he wore after 1940 in the style of Clark Gable and other Hollywood debonairs. The meticulous dress and grooming, which friends of the adult Kees noticed as much as they did the craft in his poems, are very much present in the old photographs, too. Kees in knickers, in a tartan-patterned necktie, in a double-breasted summer suit and two-tone wing tips, even when wearing an open-collar shirt, always looked like he had jumped out of the department-store advertisements in the *Beatrice Daily Sun*. This was how his mother liked to remember him until she had saved enough of the sleeping pills her nurse gave her, until some visitor who would sign her out came to ask about her son who was almost so famous and successful.

Harry Weldon Kees was born on February 24, 1914, into an "existence of subnormal calm." This is how he described Beatrice, Nebraska, thinly disguised in one of the many short stories he wrote before he moved to New York and became almost exclusively a poet. Yet on the same day the newspaper reported the birth of John and Sarah Kees's son, it ran stories about the worst winter storm of the year, trains trapped in snow, and a farmer freezing to death in his farmhouse.

These were not ominous signs but normal weather—and life—in Nebraska. To accept such weather is a kind of freemasonry, Willa Cather wrote, and for a new baby on the plains it simply provides a reason to wrap him up well and make him a portent for good and wholesome things to come. So that he might "rise in the world," the infant Kees was carried up the staircase of the Mennonite Deaconess Hospital by Sister Agatha Haarus and taken back down and returned to his mother. After this folk rite, he was given his first bath.

The new baby represented such promise because he was the first of a new generation of the Kees family, prominent in what people would have modestly called "society" in Beatrice. Their wealth came from the F. D. Kees Manufacturing Company, a manufacturer of hardware and various kinds of farm implements, machines, and other metal objects that ranged from corn-husking hooks to skates for frozen ponds and town sidewalks. The company, the oldest of its kind in Nebraska, had been founded by the family's patriarch, Frederick Daniel Kees, forty years before the birth of his first grandson.

A German gun- and locksmith, Weldon's grandfather—known as Fred or F.D. to the townspeople and as Daniel at home—had come to America aboard the *Weser* on a combination one-way ship's passage and railroad ticket, which was offered by the German steamship lines. Other members of the branch of German Keeses to which Daniel belonged had immigrated to America before him. Some had settled in Gage County, Nebraska, and Daniel, seeing that they had prospered, followed them there in the early 1870s. He soon bought a lock- and gun-repair shop and hardware store for a twenty-dollar gold piece, from which he began his manufacturing enterprise in November 1874, producing husking hooks and pegs from his store and workshop on Court Street and converting army cap-and-ball muskets into needle guns.

The business diversified and expanded the range of its products as the railroads brought more homesteaders and more business than one man could handle. During the 1870s, Daniel met and married Emma Zimmermann, a smallish woman who had also emigrated from Germany. Her petite form is still evident in the exhibit made of her silvery blue silk wedding dress, displayed on a headless dressmaker's form in the former Burlington Railroad station, which became the county historical society's small museum.

As Emma's husband's business grew, he turned his store over to his brother Fritz in 1910 and moved to a redbrick building at 24 High Street. The resulting factory became the town's major employer, bringing Daniel the wealth and the social prominence that came with success in America. From the turn of the century on, members of the Kees family were officers in the German Baptist Church and, later, in the First Presbyterian Church. Ice cream socials, bridge parties, dances, and other events held in their homes were recounted in the newspaper.

Daniel and Emma Kees had three children. Weldon's father, John, was the eldest, followed by Weldon's uncle Dan and his aunt Clara. Both sons attended college. John graduated from the University of Nebraska at Lincoln in 1899, and his brother attended school in Wisconsin. Their free-spirited sister, who never married, camped and fished in Minnesota during the summers with her brothers, as well as taking part in all the other healthful and manly outdoor activities that were popular during Theodore Roosevelt's presidency. She considered herself a fine singer, and she often was heard singing hymns from her front porch well into her eighties. From the time she was a teenager, she favored the progressive ideas of her day. In this way, she was like her brother John, whom she physically resembled—one of the rare Democrats in largely Republican Gage County. Since she was a woman, her politics made her even more of an oddity in the small Midwestern town. There is a photograph of Clara in the costume of the suffragettes, the leader of a handful of women who marched through the town in 1910. The spinster aunt would have influenced her nephew as a model of nonconformity and through the constant mystery she posed, with her eccentricities and her unmarried state. (He would later manifest this continued influence in finding lesbians both attractive and repulsive.) There is a suggestion, too, of a closer, nurturing bond between Aunt Clara and Weldon: the French dictionary she gave him for his high school graduation. He kept it close at hand all his life and used it for reading Proust and staying limber for the dialogue in the Renoir films he loved.

Like that of the other wealthy families of Beatrice, the Keeses' importance and prosperity rose as the town became the junction for three great railroads that ran along the Big Blue River and the economic center of the farmland around it. Beatrice was where the farmers came for their loans and to sell their crops and livestock.

Even with its vital connection to the farmland, visible in the flatness all around it, the townspeople of Beatrice had the amenities of a larger city and even the illusion of living in one. A small trolley car ran from one end of town to the other. Touring plays, operettas, and musicales staged their shows in the town's theaters and auditoriums. There were modest buildings that had just enough scale to impress the farmers and the town's children, such as the courthouse, the fine hotel where large parties were often held, and the Carnegie Library, a stone Beaux-Arts structure intentionally designed to be the working miniature of a much larger public building. There was even a copy of the Statue of Liberty, life-size in that it was proportionate to a real human. Another large building, the hardware store that the Kees family opened on Court Street, was the most prominent structure in the hand-colored post-cards one could buy in the town's two railroad stations.

Weldon Kees considered Beatrice to have been at its height during his early childhood and in a fallen state by the time he grew up, a kind of capitalist's mistake. In the entry for Beatrice in *Nebraska: A Guide to the Cornhusker State*, the Federal Writers' Project guide that he edited during his communist phase in the mid-1930s, Kees's disparagement is like that evident in descriptions of the Nebraska towns of his stories. Beatrice is not named for the muse of Dante and the Pre-Raphaelites. It is, however, named for a poet—the daughter of the town's founder, Judge John Kinney, who read some of her own verses at its ground-breaking ceremony in 1857 and saw the town only once or twice. Its river is muddy and slow-moving. Its manufacturing plants are grimy. The landscape is one of severe droughts, dying trees, and gaps in the industrial scene. One of the only points of interest is the Institution for Feeble-Minded Youth. Even before the Depression, Beatrice's prosper-ous age—a golden time when the silent-film comedian Harold Lloyd sold popcorn on its streets as a boy and when screen idol Robert Tay-lor was known as Spangler Arlington Brugh and Weldon Kees's play-mate—had run its course.

The brief profile of the F. D. Kees Manufacturing Company in the guidebook is colored in the dark sepia tones of Kees's memories of his first visits to his grandfather's factory. The building's length and width are described as larger than they actually were, as they would seem to a child. The lathes and their belts, the tool templates hanging on the walls, the metal shavings, the wooden boxes of scrap are listed in a way that is almost romantic compared to the other prosaic descriptions of Beatrice. So are the finished things the workmen piled on tables and every other spare surface: the hooks, housings, blades, and other pressed-metal specialties that the Kees family made—along with the contract work they did for others. The odd shapes of machines lined together in the factory suggest the mysterious and wonderful processes that went on—from the shaping of curtain rods to the counting of ball bearings for roller-skate wheels—and their deafening clatter, which made it possible to hear only one's thoughts.

The F. D. Kees Manufacturing Company, along with the other industrial institutions of the town, prepared splendid exhibits for the state fair in Lincoln in 1908, about the time that John Kees became the youngest man to ever serve as the president of the Nebraska Manufacturers Association. Each year, the company expanded its line of goods that came after the original cornhuskers. Window hinges, eave-trough hangers, woven-wire window guards, trellises, desk railings, and other articles of hardware followed, including more sophisticated devices, such as furnace regulators.

In January 1930, two months after Black Monday, the *Daily Sun* reported that the "Kees Company is Prospering." Its sales in 1929 had increased 50 percent over the previous year, and the company kept adding new articles, like the Kees Frost Kleerer, a windshield defroster that attached to the dashboard with suction cups. The eclectic imagination behind the many different products would seem to have manifested itself in Kees's many talents and in the concatenations of objects and trivia he turned into poems and abstract expressionist collages.

John Kees's seat on the library board reveals that he preferred his prominence and participation in town life to be exercised in quiet, understated roles. He was a small, reserved man, with a wide, thoughtful forehead where a shock of dark hair held its own against a receding hairline. He sometimes wore a pince-nez like the new president, Woodrow Wilson, which may have corrected farsightedness and aided reading. He read histories and biographies when he came home from work and counted Thomas Hardy and Cervantes among his favorite authors. Yet he had an open-mindedness about him as well, one that allowed for reading the James Joyce his son recommended and for taking the little avant-garde magazines that published his son, one that suggests he had literary ambitions of his own before he entered the family business—and before he laboriously cataloged the work and papers of his missing son. John was tempered by the progressive and liberal magazines of his day, such as the *American Mercury,* H. L. Mencken's journal of social criticism and literature, and the *New Republic.* And these he shared with his son, which makes for a compelling image of the young Kees poring over the work of the World War I pacifist–essayist Randolph Bourne, whom he later revered. How deeply he read such serious fare can be seen in the way he scolded his aunt Sylvia for reading popular magazines and made a list of "Things for Aunt Sylvia to Read," which included philosophy, history, and religion. His aunt, however, got the upper hand when she reminded him that both she and his mother had studied these subjects in college and taught them in high school.

The woman John had chosen for his wife determined that his social rank would rest on something more than the new wealth of his father's hardware factory and store. Sarah Lucy Green considered herself to be from the Middle Atlantic colonies of pre-Revolutionary times and not the prairie, where she had been born, like her husband. The daughter of Stephen Warren Green and Mary Weldon Odell, settlers from Royalton, New York, she was born in 1880, near Oconee, Illinois, a farming community in the middle of the state, roughly sixty miles east of Saint Louis. Sometime before 1893, the year her mother died, the Green family returned to the East, perhaps because of homesickness or the failure of their farm or business. Sarah subsequently spent the rest of her youth in Medina, a small town in Niagara County along the Erie Canal. Called "Sadie" by the townspeople, she did not marry immediately but instead went to college in order to be a schoolteacher—as did her sister, Kees's aunt Sylvia Ferrell. After their education, they moved to Nebraska, where they had relatives on their mother's side. In 1908, Sarah accepted a position at the public school in Beatrice. There, at one of the enlightening programs, picnics, or dances held at Chautauqua Park, along the Blue River, she met the young businessman who would become her husband.

Their courtship lasted for a year. It was conducted mostly through the mail, for Sarah had gone back to New York. Sometime in 1909 she accepted John's proposal of marriage, and on September 20, it was reported in the *Daily Sun* that John had departed over the Burlington route for Newfane, New York. They were married in the presence of Sarah's relatives, and they traveled through the East on their honeymoon before settling in the home the groom had prepared on North Ninth Street in Beatrice.

Sarah, despite her humble background and circumstances, made up for these deficiencies by her search for a more impressive pedigree. She became an amateur genealogist and discovered she was a descendent of someone who had sailed over on the *Mayflower*, which allowed her to join the Sons and Daughters of Pilgrims. Unrelenting, she was even able to prove herself related to the Plantagenets and became a member of the Americans of Royal Descent and the Society of Magna Carta. After Sarah had traced her lineage through British prison ships, the graveyards of Atlantic County, New Jersey, and old family bibles, the Elizabeth Montague chapter of the Daughters of the American Revolution made her a member in 1913. That she accomplished all this before she allowed herself to become pregnant and have a child is indicative of her ambitions.

Photographs reveal that Sarah looked the part of the schoolmarm and of her office, for she appears as serious and unsmiling as the D.A.R. sisters in Grant Wood's famous painting. Yet she loved flowers such as zinnias, especially rows and rows of them, and would have her husband stop the family car to admire them—a side of her that Kees would re-create in one of his "Weston" short stories about the strange normalness of Beatrice life. Indeed, this "smallish, plain, expensively, tastefully dressed woman with blue-gray hair," as she was described by one of her son's friends in later life, seemed hardly as dangerous as her son—and her daughter-in-law, Ann—made her out to be. She had more the sweet, Martha Washington, candy-box charm of a "typical American mother of an only son."

Sarah gave her family the Anglo-Saxon respectability it did not get from the Kees side. She chose names for her son that diluted his German background and connected him to his distaff English and Presbyterian roots. His first name came from Dr. Harry E. Diers, a general practitioner in Beatrice, and it would seem to mean that Kees's birth had been a difficult one. Such naming was the custom, especially if the doctor had saved the baby's or the mother's life. Sarah was thirty-four when she bore her son, and her age and the fact that she and John conceived no more children hint strongly that another pregnancy would have posed a risk.

Weldon, who was always referred to by his middle name that his mother had borrowed from her mother's family, became the focal point of his parents' love and attention. Sarah entered all the significant events associated with the birth and progress of her son in the baby book that John had presented to her after she left the hospital. Sarah noted how his proud father read the first letter their son received, written by Great-Aunt Libby in Florida. In September 1914, Weldon received his first pair of shoes. They were "white kid with three pearl buttons," his mother noted. He wore them, with a white ruffle-trimmed dress made by Aunt Henrietta Kees, in the photograph that illustrated his parents' Christmas cards that same year. In the photograph, he is depicted as the doll of the family, providing his services to the ironical, lighthearted verse his father had printed on every card— a verse that hardly makes the association one can now make between the baby and the lines he wrote as an adult, in which Christmas greens "smoulder in an empty lot" and the "erubescent Santa Claus" features sawdust running out his side.

On New Year's Day 1915, John and his brother-in-law, Edward Green, pulled Weldon in a sleigh around the snow-covered yard of their home at 415 North Ninth Street. It was after dinner, Sarah wrote in her baby book, and the light was failing. During the previous year, she had recorded her son's milestones and miseries: the first step, the first words, the colic, and the teething pains. She described taking him to the Buffalo Bill Show's street parade, where she had held him up to see the Indians and cowboys as they entered Beatrice in August 1914. "The calliope was a little too loud," she noted, "for Weldon put his hands up to his ears." Two months later, his parents took him to his first football game, at which Beatrice beat Grand Island, thirty-two to zero—which mattered more in the newspaper than the faraway war in Europe.

After her son learned to walk, she pinned a piece of his creeping gown to one page. On another page, she taped down locks of her son's pretty dark hair to memorialize his first trip to the barber. Inside a printed border of azaleas, when Weldon was at twenty-one months, Sarah recorded his first "cute saying," an imitation of the women of

Beatrice who came to the screen door of the porch and cried, "Mrs. Kees, Mrs. Kees." His mother would say, "Play a little tune and sing," and he would then "make his little fingers go and hum."

The baby book eventually evolved into a scrapbook that contained mementos of Kees's early childhood. His mother glued down pieces of newspaper and photographs—or saved the birthday cards her son received from his Sunday school teachers. A yellow clipping from 1924 reported the celebration of his Grandpa Kees's birthday—and included the birthday poem Weldon wrote and read before a roomful of adoring family and friends. The little rhyme expresses affection for this remote old man whom Kees remembered in his long poem "The Hourglass" for not having left him his "old silver Waltham."

The absence of siblings intensified Kees's relationship with his parents, whose love and attention were undivided. He thrived in this environment and developed quickly, learning to talk earlier than most children. By watching his parents, he even learned how to operate a Victrola before he was three years old and could find his favorite records. When his mother asked him how he did this, he pointed to the words on the label. Recognizing his giftedness, for she was a teacher, Sarah taught him to read well before he entered the first grade. She also taught him to play the upright piano.

Her success at making him a little man had its price. Many neighborhood children considered Kees a bookworm and a freak for the way he talked and played like a grownup, for his never wanting to get dirty because Sarah made sure his clothes were always clean and pressed to the point that it became impossible for him to see himself otherwise. This was so even at four years, when Aunt Sylvia made him a fine coat from one of his father's old topcoats and then bought him new shoes that buttoned down the side to complete the ensemble. Weldon was so proud of how he looked that he felt like one of the doughboys home on leave. He even saluted all the big people he passed until he accidentally stepped in a puddle and muddied his coat and shoes. He cried that day. He also cried on the day he turned six, when the neighborhood boys at his birthday party refused to sit in the living room and carry on pretend conversations. Instead they flew from the divan and chairs to run and play and get away from the one they called a "momma's boy." This opprobrium he took so much to heart that as an adult he always

tried to distance himself from his mother even though he knew he had
been imprinted to please her:

> My mother came
> To the grayish river where the children stared:
> "My son, you have honored the family name."
>
> I was happy. Then a parade went by
> Near the shadowy river where the children waved,
> And the uniforms made me shiver and cry.
>
> — "River Song"

Kees was not a loner, however. He certainly played with Robert Taylor and probably performed duets with him for their mothers since he
played piano and Mrs. Brugh's son played violin. Kees also loved to
skate on Beatrice's frozen ponds in the winter with the other girls and
boys who wore the famous iron skates made in his grandfather's factory—it was one of the few outdoor activities he loved. He also liked to
be in plays with the children of Beatrice, such as the performance put
on by the sons and daughters of the library-board members in November 1923, called "Friends in Bookland." He was Sir Lancelot, one of the
storybook characters who come to life in the dream of a girl named
Ruth who refuses to read good books. Like the children who played
Alice in Wonderland, Penelope with her distaff, Pinocchio, Undine the
water sprite, Heidi, the Prince and the Pauper, and Robin Hood, Kees
slipped from behind the girl's three-foot bookshelf to mildly present
himself and admonish her for neglecting him. He would have been
photographed in his charming suit-of-armor costume like the other
child actors, but he left early, after the refreshments were served, perhaps displaying what would be a kind of trait in him.

As well as participating in make-believe performances, Kees enjoyed the rainy-day activity of drawing and writing with one or two
friends, often girls. His cousin Bernice Wells Carlson, later a children's
author, produced her "first book" and his during their families' vacation on Michigan's Lake George in the summer of 1925. It was a collection of nonsense rhymes titled *Imbiciles* [sic], for which she drew the
caricatures of the silly personas Kees made up, and he carefully block
printed the text and stapled the pages.

∾

A fascination with Hollywood during its golden age and with motion pictures led to many boyhood pleasures that Kees never quite put aside and that he even reprised in adult forms during the months before he disappeared in 1955. Indeed, Hollywood's presence and pull were so powerful for him that his most important achievement, his poetry, can be read as a kind of film that moves from an involved socialist's nightmare of America to a coda of revelation in relieving the loneliness of the cat.

One of his earliest and most cherished childhood memories surfaced in Kees as he sat in a nightclub in 1954 and watched his lady friend dance with the still-handsome silent-film actor Walter McGrail, for he could remember being five and seeing the same man rescue Pearl White in *The Black Secret*. By the age of twelve, Kees could go by himself to the matinees and evening shows at the Rivoli Theater, only a few blocks from his front door. There he kept up with the adventure serials and the feature-length ten-reelers that had all kinds of dark characters and plot twists. His favorite actor was Milton Sills, who defined the "strong, silent type" during the 1920s. His performance in *Puppets* as Nikki, an Italian puppeteer made deaf by the falling shells in World War I, inspired Kees to ask for his own puppet theater. It was Sills's factory-floor adventure *Men of Steel*, with its scenes of molten steel being poured on him and of the romance with the working-class girl, played by Sills's wife, Doris Kenyon, that Kees would evoke in his Nebraska poem "1926."

The young Kees considered cinema actors more interesting and more important than the aviators and baseball players who towered in the lives of most boys during the 1920s. He wrote and typed the copy of his own mimeographed movie magazines, with names like the *Screenland Spy, Silver Screenings,* and *Camera Magazine.* In them he listed the stars' birthdays and their addresses so that other children could write their favorite actors or send them a card. He had his own column, "Reviews of Current Pictures," in which he rated *The American Venus,* with Gloria Swanson, "fine" and *The New Commandment* as "terrible." As a special feature, he wrote a Hollywood murder mystery that ran over several issues. It had a leading man for its hero who was a real detective in his offscreen life.

With the puppet theater he wanted—and received from his parents for Christmas in 1926—Kees directed and performed "pretend

movies" with his friend Dwight Perkins before audiences of neighborhood children. When word spread of his shows, he consented to dem-
onstrating his puppets on the stages of the Carnegie Library and the
YWCA.

Beatrice was a town in which the return of the boy scouts from Camp
Otoe was momentous news and worthy of a front-page story in the
Daily Sun. For many of the boys, camp was the first time they had been
away from home and their mothers, a rite of passage that Kees's father
was very much pleased to see his son make. Weldon's name and the
name of his best friend, Robert Marvin, the son of the newspaper's
editor, were printed in the paper. So were the games they played, such
as "The Ghost Walk," "Treasure Hunt," and "Trail." The scouts had
gone hiking, too, at Camp Otoe, and swimming, shooting, and fishing.
Bats had flown into their cabins, snakes had crawled into their beds,
and they had all come back alive. Around the campfire at night, "with
delicious marshmallows and popcorn," the boys had listened raptly to
their scoutmaster tell ghost stories.

Kees learned to tell his own ghost stories after his weeks at Camp
Otoe in 1927. He and other children gathered in the summer evenings
on the large porch of the Sherwood family's home and tried to outdo
each other with tales of horror. Bob Marvin remembered that Kees
always told the best stories. His had plenty of blood, murder, and
ghosts. He loved to frighten the younger boys and the Sherwoods'
daughter Marion, who would not have minded having him for a boyfriend.

When his porch-swing audience had grown up and chanced to read
the poetry Kees published from New York and San Francisco, some
thought they saw a continuity between the verse and their friend's
ghost stories. They did—but they had no idea that real deaths and
ghosts existed for Kees as well. His elegy about the 1927 funeral of a
family friend, the kind of young man adolescent boys look up to and
want to be like, reveals how primal his alienation and tragic view of life
were, reveals that the universe of Beatrice was not a place to feel safe
or, more importantly, real and known. Kees wrote "For H. V." when
he was the same age as the deceased, which makes it a sort of mirror
through which he saw the kind of trap of fate he learned he wanted to
elude.

Another source of continuity was the Calvinism Kees learned in the family pew at Beatrice's First Presbyterian Church, where H. V.'s funeral probably took place. He considered himself a nonbeliever as an adult. He even called himself an atheist after high school. Yet the high moral and ethical tone of his poetry echoes that of a Presbyterian minister. Its wounded composure, its renowned "serenity," partly comes from religion, from what he learned in Sunday school while memorizing the verses that counseled him that when one falls one should never cry but give a "merry laugh instead."

When H. V. was laid to rest there was another kind of death going on in Beatrice: that of its comfort-giving prosperity. Even before the Depression had undermined the American prairie town as the paragon of nineteenth-century positivism and Manifest Destiny, a corrective for "Nature's mistake," John and Sarah Kees saw the end of that "civilized, elegant, and lush world of the Wilson-Harding-Coolidge years," of the "shock-absorbing twenties," as their son would much later describe them in a review of a Wallace Stevens book.

In 1926, they were forced to sell their second home, a large gray stucco on Garfield Street, after John lost nearly ten thousand dollars in a Colorado gold mine with other wealthy investors in the town. This was a considerable fortune then, and to make up for the loss and keep his factory supplied with orders, John had to become the company's traveling salesman and go away for weeks at a time. The big house that had announced the family's prominence was exchanged for a smaller bungalow on North Fifth Street, which John purchased in Sarah's name as a precaution against foreclosure.

Their son seemed not to experience the fall in status or to suffer much from the move. The new neighborhood had the same porch-lit wholesomeness that all of Beatrice had. He was still given presents, clothes, and an allowance so that he could go to the movies. By 1930, his family had recouped much of its lost wealth and his father was steering the F. D. Kees Manufacturing Company through the first uncertain months of the stock-market crash. Nevertheless, Kees internalized an enormous sense of disappointment that may have been channeled from his mother's trying to cope with shame at the family's humbled circumstances. His lifelong mistrust of money and the American business culture and his disdain for Sarah's middle-class anxiety were also probably different sides of the same coin.

His father, however, stood for something else when his son saw him off at the train station. His business travels signified an escape into the larger world of big cities and the Roaring Twenties. Writing John and getting his letters from Boston and New York would make Kees see Beatrice as remote and small, a place that could not grow with him, that would trap him instead. This change came at nightfall, when he could pick up the AM radio stations that broadcast Dixieland music from the hotel ballrooms of Cincinnati and Chicago. It came whenever he cranked up his phonograph and imagined New Orleans as he listened to "Mississippi Mud" and "Ain't She Sweet," played by the Rhythm Boys with Bing Crosby and Bix Beiderbecke, the first jazz record he ever bought and one that he bought again in 1950 for a dime on Turk Street in San Francisco. Seeing the painted big-city sets on the screen behind Milton Sills also made him think of the world outside Beatrice.

In those summers between his freshman, sophomore, and junior years at Beatrice High School, Kees often accompanied his father on day-trips to Omaha and on longer overnight journeys to cities as far away as Chicago. Having Weldon for a companion was for John more like traveling with a close friend than with his child, which was always a boon. John even accepted the way his son addressed him as *John* and his mother as *Sarah* around this time—or as *Sadie* whenever he became exasperated with her. No one thought this unnatural or something to be discouraged.

On one of these business trips, Kees saw his first talkie in Minneapolis and wrote a review of the marvel on the train back home. His father was so impressed with his son's writing that he convinced the editor to publish the piece in the *Daily Sun* as a surprise for Weldon. This was the sort of accomplishment that John could see as the first of many in which Weldon would make him and Sarah proud—and give something enlightening back to undo how dull and little the town seemed to the young cosmopolitan they had made together. But John had shown his son the way out of town too many times. He had no idea that the knowledge and wonders given to the precocious boy would bring the adult to a poetry that looked back on Beatrice as the starting point for all the time he had left.

Lincoln
1931-1936

Instead of being the warm center of the world, the Middle West now seemed like the ragged edge of the universe.
—F. Scott Fitzgerald, *The Great Gatsby*

In Kees's sestina "After the Trial," composed in 1941, the condemned son recalls the evenings when his parents settled his "future happily forever." Certainly he knew of such evenings in his own early life. By 1927, old F. D. Kees was dead; his company belonged to his sons, John and Dan; and Weldon was not so much being groomed for the family business as he was being made comfortable with it so that he could naturally segue into a world of tools and dies when the time came. He was often seen after school in the factory office, where his father let him type his stories and rhymes and "publish" his movie magazines on the secretary's typewriter. And John always made his work interesting for the boy. He even turned his business trips into little adventures described on the stationery of different hotels. He brought home all kinds of small gifts and souvenirs.

John must have wanted his son to take over the F. D. Kees Manufacturing Company one day, but not as a consolation for having done nothing else. Weldon could also have a brilliant career outside of the company if he wanted it—something John may have wanted for himself but could not have. Talent had thus far come naturally to Weldon thanks to his mother and aunt—and giving him culture would be like giving him Presbyterianism, not so much to save his soul but to save his character. His personal library of books, his drawing paper, paint boxes, puppets, and sheet music had always been intended to deepen him early with something besides the Republican bonhomie of Gage County.

By the time he was a teenager, it seemed he wanted that brilliant career more than something close to home. Weldon produced essays and stories that could be published and sometimes were. He played the piano and other musical instruments. He acted on the stages of crowded auditoriums and told stories to small groups of friends sitting on porch swings. While attending Beatrice High School, he printed satirical pieces for the school paper. The *Homesteader*'s masthead listed him as "Censor," his youthful and rather knowing protest against the Hays Office, Hollywood's attempt at self-censorship.

He made schoolmates laugh at the "wisecrax" in his "Gab" columns, written with his good friend Leonard Thompson and bylined Mr. O and Mr. O O underneath "photographs" that were white-and-black squares. He wrote the fan mail for Mr. O and Mr. O O, too, addressed from the State Institution for the Feeble-Minded.

On the auditorium stage during his last year in Beatrice, he performed "elderly characterizations," such as Reverend Chasuble in the senior-class performance of *The Importance of Being Earnest*. At the seniors' Class Nite talent show, he recited the "Class Will" that he had written in a deep voice that protected him from being identified with the soft boys who were picked on for doing all the creative things he did. Beneath his yearbook photograph, his motto was printed in the same satirical spirit: "A little nonsense now and then / Is relished by the best of men." And beneath that his extracurricular activities ran on in small type that took up more space than his senior picture. He had edited the student newspaper and served on student council. He had sung in the operetta cast, the mixed octet, the male quartet, and the glee club and played banjo and guitar in the class orchestra.

Kees graduated from high school at the age of seventeen in 1931, and, surprisingly, he said he wanted to work for his father. He even answered the question of "What the Seniors will be Doing in the Near Future" by saying that he would try his hand as a "drummer" selling for the F. D. Kees Manufacturing Company.

He also disclosed in the *Homesteader* that he wanted to do little during the summer of 1931—except to get enough ambition to visit "various parts of the East" and New York, which he did in August with his parents, probably for his mother's Mayflower Society convention.

Kees began his freshman year at Doane College in the fall. Located in nearby Crete, Nebraska, Doane was a small, Congregationalist, liberal-arts school with an enrollment of 250 students. The train trip there followed the Blue River north and lasted long enough for only a few chapters in the book that Kees might have brought to read.

Besides the college, Crete boasted its "Tree Menagerie," which consisted of many boxwoods trimmed into grotesque animal shapes. Though Kees would one day write stories and poems that incorporated the strangeness of such Midwestern gothicisms, his going away to school was hardly an exotic change for a young man who wanted to leave Beatrice for New York and other big cities. To his parents' relief, he had been pragmatic in his willingness to go to a good college in the state. When it seemed he would do something romantic and individual, he had gone with a transition that was familiar and safe and taken by many other local young men and women.

Doane was an extension of Beatrice High School for Kees. He joined the Doane Players so that he could continue acting. He wrote satirical pieces for the college newspaper. He had several old friends at Doane. The soon-to-be-christened Robert Taylor, Arlington Brugh, had recently attended the school, as had other young men and women from Beatrice families. Bob Marvin had enrolled at Doane, too, and now roomed with his boyhood friend in a dormitory on campus.

Kees took courses in elocution, history, journalism, Latin, and philosophy. These made for a versatile foundation for someone not committed to any vocation yet, who had arrived at a point in life where he relished imagining himself in one role after another. Creating and re-creating himself and confronting the mystery of who he was eventually would become his vocation, but at Doane this searching was part of coming up with the right formula to please himself and his parents. They, of course, were already impressed that the path he was on would lead to nationally circulated magazines, syndicated newspaper columns, and the like. Though Doane offered no degree program in journalism, Kees took a double major in English and psychology in its place and styled himself "H. Weldon Kees," which hinted at more literary aspirations than a byline in a newspaper or a monthly.

Despite such earnestness, however, Kees completed only two credit hours of "Vocational Psychology." The class bored him (as did the others). It was all theory, and he wanted to hear about pathological and deviant characters. Of more relevance were his readings of *Pagany, Hound and Horn,* and *transition.* While at Doane, he discovered James Joyce, T. S. Eliot, Ezra Pound, William Carlos Williams, and the other early moderns. He also closely read such Jazz Age novelists as Dos Passos, Hemingway, Fitzgerald, and the like — and he took up smoking cigarettes, much to the consternation of his parents.

When Robert Taylor transferred to Pomona College, he had left a vacancy in Doane's little tea-dance trio. Kees replaced him and his cello with the piano and played popular jazz tunes and fox trots in the basement of Gaylord Hall. He even wrote tunes for the trio, with titles like

"Make My Dream Your Only Theme," which the school's larger dance band, the Collegians, also played.

His favorite teacher was Mary-Ellen Inglis, who taught drama and had founded the Doane Players. Kees appeared in a number of the company's productions in the Sokol Theatre during the 1931–32 school year, including *The Royal Family*, a comedy by George S. Kaufman and Edna Ferber, Oscar Wilde's *The Importance of Being Earnest*, and *A Midsummer Night's Dream*. Once again he specialized in mature male roles, such as the farmer James Mayo in Eugene O'Neill's *Beyond the Horizon*. The *Beatrice Sun*'s society reporter described his appearance in the cast of *Ladies of the Jury*, a "high class comedy" written by Fred Ballard, the prominent Nebraska playwright. "Weldon," the paper noted, "played a double role, first as Steve Bromm, on the jury; and as a court clerk. He is to be congratulated on the fine work he is doing in the department of dramatics and as a member of the Doane Players."

Miss Inglis also encouraged him to write and present his one-act plays for the company. Some were performed at the college and others at a movie house in Crete in front of the screen between features. These ranged from pathos to farce: *Strained Interval, In the Suburbs, Summer Cottage*, and *Man of Honor*. The playbill for *Pink Spiders* promised a "mad comedy" for the evening of April 29, 1932. The little play was set in a Midwestern county courthouse—on "any hot afternoon you have in mind"—its dementia further intensified by musical interludes hammered out by a student on the xylophone. Kees would not have the same fun again until 1955, when he again produced his own plays for the *Poets' Follies* in San Francisco and for his own theater, the Showplace.

With all his acting, the readers of the *Beatrice Daily Sun* would not have been surprised to find an article under the fold that reported that Kees, like Robert Taylor, would be taking a screen test in Hollywood. Several of the town's young people had already left for Los Angeles— and many of Kees's friends and teachers at Doane could have predicted his leaving for there.

Kees further reinforced the idea that he had in mind a career in the film industry in the spring of 1932, when he turned in his assignment for English 108, "The Percy Poggle Incident." This is a short story about a young comedic "discovery" who sits out the premier of his first motion picture because of his funny-sounding name, which he expected would be changed in Hollywood to something more like "Clark Gable" (whose first movie had recently played in Nebraska's theaters). Instead, however, the name "Poggle" is why everyone loves him, and Hollywood, which almost existed to undo the verbal monstrosities that Midwestern young people were saddled with, is making him keep it—this name Kees drew from the onomatopoeic combinations of German surnames and Anglo-Saxon first names that he had heard all of his life in Nebraska. Ultimately, though, the satire is more about the anxiety Kees already felt about money, success, and self-compromise even this early in his life. This theme and even his fascination with disappearance and a "new life" are present as the movie mogul Sam Glogatz pushes a pen toward an angry and rebellious Percy:

"No, Mr. Poggle—Poggle your name must be—it's marvelous—I've told you—"
"You will not consent, then, to a change?"
"No, positively."
"Very well, Mr. Glogatz. I'm thru. Goodbye."
And the comedy find of the year walked out of the door to be a newspaper man in Australia under the name of Don Cook.

When Miss Inglis looked for one of her students to play the restless, dark-eyed, and doomed hero of Eugene O'Neill's *Beyond the Horizon,* she needed one who not only looked the part but had "a touch of the poet about him." The natural choice came down to Kees. Yet the play, with its problem of whether to remain at home and marry your sweetheart or leave for an adventurous life, also would further feed the restlessness of Miss Inglis's most prized student, who wanted to leave Doane.

He was different from the other students, with his gaunt good looks; his dark brown, shoe-polish hair; his impeccable clothes; and his demeanor of the artist and intellectual, which made him seem older and more knowing than even the professors. There was a class difference, too. He was from a well-to-do family untouched by the Depression. A few young men had cars on campus in 1932, and Kees was considered one of them. Unlike the "hashers" who served food in the cafeteria, he did not have to work his way through college. He also clashed with Doane's strict Congregationalist rules and mores, with his cigarettes dangling from his lip, his taste for the communist writers in the little magazines, and his knowledge of where to find forbidden liquor.

During the 1932–33 school year, Kees described Doane as a "kind of hell" and convinced his parents to let him transfer to the University of Missouri at Columbia in the fall. He had heard that some of the faculty members of the English department's school of journalism had cultivated a circle of creative writers, even though the school itself made no claim of training anything but newspaper writers and editors. One of the faculty, Dr. Robert L. Ramsay, taught a short-story course as an elective and managed the Mahan literary contests.

Instead of joining Ramsay's circle, however, Kees came under the wing of Mary Paxton Keeley, a middle-aged journalism teacher at nearby Christian College and a passionate sonnet writer. In her basement apartment, she conducted the quaint "literary evenings" that her new, frequent young guest would later satirize in his novel *Fall Quarter.* However, during his first and second semesters at Missouri, Kees became quite dependent on his first mentor for help with his short stories and for friendship.

He was different from the other students who came to her apartment for tea, coffee, and conversation. The others would only write something to enter in newspaper contests or what had been assigned to them in class. Kees brought Mary one story after another. He did not just talk about writing the Great American Novel. He actually brought over chapters for her to read as he attempted to write a novel for the first time.

Mary felt his work was promising. The one thing that she suggested repeatedly was that he write about people and places that he knew. He objected to this, however. He put great stock in his imagination, in his ability to see through things and interpret them as if he were unaware of his own youth and inexperience.

He knew no people except those he had grown up with and those at Doane, and these were people and places he wanted to forget about, he said, not commemorate in a novel.

This aloofness was also exhibited in Kees's personal life, and he struck Mary as lonely and detached from his fellow students. He often came to her apartment after the other aspiring writers had left to discuss his work with her. When Mary saw him on campus, Kees seemed often to walk alone until she hailed him, and then he would return the wave, smile, and say, "Let's go jelly" — campus slang for having a Coke or beer together. This detachment, however, came to be interpreted differently by others. Mary found this out when she had to comfort him during what she called his "strange terrors," those times when he came to her after he discovered his unsettling power to attract homosexual men.

Though Kees did not seem conventionally handsome to her, his impeccable dress, his poise, his slight build, and his carefully groomed hair conveyed to some men that he might be gay. This impression was further reinforced by Kees's separation from the fraternity men and college athletes and his interest in books, culture, music, acting. And he was never seen dating girls. Added to the whole effect, to the stereotype, was his arresting face, in which one saw nothing but his beautiful, despairing, dark eyes, as one of the men who fell in love with him described them.

A poet's face, Mary thought in her old-fashioned way, and nothing more—the face of someone who might have walked out of her sonnet cycle, *To a Lost Lover.* She did not think Kees looked effeminate, nor did she think he was homosexual. Given the way he spoke so knowingly about "sex perverts," he seemed to know how to recognize anyone making advances on him and how to handle the classic scenario of being set up for a homosexual seduction. This false impression of Kees kept Mary from warning him about certain professors and other men who lived in Columbia, whom she called "pederasts."

Late one afternoon, during the winter, he came to her apartment breathless, as though he had been running. His white face made Mary ask him if he had seen a ghost. Then she realized he was about to faint. She pushed Kees into one of her large, overstuffed wing chairs and hurried to make him a pot of tea. He asked for a stiffer drink, the kind he knew she never served. (Kees made fun of her for this in *Fall Quarter.*)

After he had composed himself, he told her what had happened. He had been asked by a classmate to deliver a term paper to an apartment near the campus. When he knocked on the door, it was opened by a naked man wearing only a smile, a smile that conveyed the expectation that Kees understood the true nature of the liaison. Instead, Kees claimed, he dropped the term paper and fled.

He said he felt scared and foolish for having fallen for the trap. Worse still, he loathed the sudden realization of what people *really* thought of him.

Mary listened and told Kees of several men he must avoid. Then she began to confront on her own the men she knew to be homosexual. She wanted to find out why they were making passes at her teenage friend and to see if she could get them to stop.

"It's his eyes," one of them said in the bookstore where Kees was known to shop—and where men picked up other men. His eyes had a kind of sadness and longing in them, he continued. They suggested kinship, suggested that surely the boy was a homosexual himself and just needed to find out.

For several weeks, nothing happened. Mary even thought of telling Kees that his encounter might be the fodder he needed for a real novel instead of the false start he had been reading to her in her apartment. Then, however, came an incident in the early spring of 1934 for which she felt responsible.

A textbook salesman came to Columbia to take orders from Mary and other professors. She had heard from some students that he propositioned young men when he came to town, but Mary did not think the stories about Bill were true. She discounted them as simply the fantasies of minds too much taken up with sexual deviation—just like Kees's. So many of her students and young writer friends had just discovered the world of homosexuals and lesbians. She even had to sometimes take precautions about what the young people thought of her by reminding them she had been a widow since 1926. No reputable publishing house, Mary chided those who made insinuations, would send out a man like that. Bill did not look like a "pansy."

Naturally, Mary did not think it odd when Bill asked her if there was anyone interesting on campus. Since he knew about the young writers who gathered in her basement apartment, she assumed he meant one of them and immediately thought of Kees. She told Bill about her young novelist friend, thinking she was doing Kees a favor since Bill claimed to have connections in the New York publishing world. He asked some questions about the novel Kees was writing, listened to her answers, and then asked Mary where he could find the young man. Since Kees had an evening class in Jesse Hall, he would be easy to find after the class got out in half an hour.

"Let's go pick him up," Bill said casually.

Finding Kees after his class, Mary and Bill drove him to a campus pub named the Pierce Pennant. There the two men ordered beers and Mary lemonade. During their conversation, Bill asked Kees what he was doing over the weekend, which sounded strange to Mary. Bill had told her he was leaving the next morning.

Kees said he had to write a paper. Gradually, Bill came to be sitting just about on top of him. Kees was obviously nervous now, since he knew the routine, and he gave Mary a pleading look. She could see him pushing Bill's hand away under the table. Finally, he rose up and said he had to go home and work on his paper.

In Bill's car, Mary intentionally sat between the two men so that Kees would no longer have to endure the meaningful squeezes the salesman had been giving his thighs and buttocks.

Bill, however, had not given up. He was certain Kees just needed be alone, away from his chaperone. He insisted on taking Mary home first. It was no trouble, he said. But after they had driven a few blocks, Kees pointed to a house and said that he lived there and that they needed to pull to the curb. It was well before 200 College Avenue, where he rented a room.

The textbook salesman left Columbia and was not heard from again until some years later, when news came back that he had jumped from the high window of a London hotel. Kees, too, left after the embarrassing incident. He mentioned Hollywood as one possible destination, and that is where he was thought to have gone after he left Columbia in May 1934.

ॐ

Kees had actually returned home for the summer. There he arranged to transfer to the University of Nebraska at Lincoln for the fall semester. He told his parents, who must have been disconcerted over this "wandering" from college to college, that Nebraska would be a better choice for him. Not only was it his father's school—which may have been why he had not gone there in the first place—but he could now study writing under Lowry Charles Wimberly, a Nebraska-born, Harvard-educated folklorist and literature professor—and the founding editor of *Prairie Schooner,* one of the few literary reviews affiliated with an English department that cultivated younger talent and published good writing. He had already taught several young Nebraska writers, including the pulp novelist Jim Thompson, the author of *The Grifters;* the poet-scientist Loren Eiseley; and the Western historian and biographer Mari Sandoz.

As well as a new mentor with his own magazine, Kees hoped to find the literary life in Lincoln. It was a Republican city that boasted ninety-eight churches, a statistic that Wimberly himself had included in one of his satirical pieces in the *American Mercury,* H. L. Mencken's magazine. But Lincoln had a community of writers that Kees would not find in Mrs. Keeley's basement apartment back in Columbia, Missouri. With the *Schooner* as their center, Wimberly, his students, and his former students had made a kind of Greenwich Village in the college town. They had staked out booths in their favorite cafés and tables in Lincoln's tearooms, where they could discuss the politics and art of the 1930s in various shades of the period's pink, romantic communism.

Wimberly also connected his students to the world outside Lincoln. He was a member of what Kees, writing in 1949, would term "Mencken's elite," the ones who published in the *American Mercury* and lashed out at gentility, censorship, bigotry, academicism, and prudery. These were men who for the most part "regarded life as a ridiculous joke to be enjoyed at the utmost." Wimberly came across as a kind of Greek god to his students, but he also had a darker side where Kees found what he had been looking for when he took psychology at Doane: Wimberly collected real-life stories about suicides and discussed them with his students. In this way, he "rubbed off like lamp black," as one of them stated. Many thought he would write a book about suicides, one as compelling as the short story he wrote for the *Mercury* about a woman who gasses herself and her children, which may have persuaded Kees to come and seek Wimberly out in Lincoln.

Wimberly also had advance knowledge of his new student before he arrived at the University of Nebraska. While still at Missouri, in the early spring of 1934, Kees had sent him a short story for *Prairie Schooner.* Though Wimberly returned "Saturday Rain," he advised its young author to lengthen it and send it back again. This Kees did in the early summer, and Wimberly accepted "Saturday Rain" for the fall issue of *Prairie Schooner.* This story, which Kees considered his first published piece of serious writing, would be well-timed, for it portrayed the estrangement many of Nebraska's university students felt after leaving places like the fictional Barker, a thinly disguised Beatrice. Kees had learned how to fuse the spare language of Hemingway and the sentiment of Thomas Wolfe. In addition, as Wimberly must have noticed, Kees had invented a small-town orphic descent from his own experience of coming back home: "My bag felt heavy and unwieldy as I carried it up Ash Street. It rubbed on the roughness of my suit and on my leg. I switched it to my other hand and tried to hold it out away from myself. Cars were journeying slowly (as they seemed to do in Barker), their lights like sleepy eyes caring little whether they saw me or not. I wondered whether or not I knew any of the people that were driving them, and if they knew where Arlene could be."

When Kees began the fall quarter at Nebraska, he had a story in the new issue of *Prairie Schooner,* an accomplishment that made some of his classmates jealous. Some thought that publication had gone to his head already (and he did not look any the less pretentious for having dropped signing his work with the "H" of his first name). Norris Getty, who would one day become his best friend and the first reader of his poems, initially observed Kees in Wimberly's class, and his first impression was probably not unlike others': "I thought 'pale fish' and 'my God, if I have to look at that face all semester.' An anthropoid slouch under Englishy tweeds, as if he were trying to touch his shoulders together in front."

Kees was aloof. He wore a bored expression and sat quietly in one of the seats against the wall in the back with a sorority girl, Ann Swan, who had transferred to Nebraska from Pomona College (where Robert Taylor had recently been spotted by an MGM talent scout). She was from Douglas, Wyoming, a small town much like Beatrice and Getty's hometown, Waco, Nebraska; she had been born there in 1915.

Ann was the first child of Ronald Swan, a banker, and his wife, Verna. Her mother encouraged her to read books and write well. As much as Verna Swan depended on her eldest daughter to help raise her other children, she did not dissuade Ann from thinking about another kind of life. By the time Ann was in her teens, she had the quick-witted personality of what was then called a "career girl." She saw herself living in a larger city, with more to do than there was in a Wyoming town surrounded by farms and sheep ranches. Unlike most of the other girls in Douglas, she enrolled in college after high school.

In the photograph on the back of her university registration card, Ann holds up a slate board with her name written in chalk, the same slate board Kees holds in his official university photograph. The photographs reveal two young people who could almost have been brother and sister, not because of any direct resemblance but because of the knowing expression they shared. In person, Ann and her boyfriend had the same silky dark hair and clear fair skin. When they were side by side, Kees, who was a little beneath average height, stood nearly a head taller than she did. She was petite, but Ann had a "sturdy build," even though her small-breastedness made her look frailer than she was when she posed or postured to detract from her fuller hips and thighs.

How the two of them came together is uncertain. But given his unhappy experience at Missouri, Kees did not want to be perceived in the wrong way again—or not without his sanction and control over events. His story "Saturday Rain" also sent the same signal. It dealt with a sensitive, bookish college student who loses his pretty girlfriend back home to an "athletic type." Though the young man feels unburdened as he leaves her porch and walks away in sunlight, there is no mistaking the fact that he is no less a real man than the athlete. Indeed, he is someone who would find the plainer Ann more to his liking, as Kees did. She had read many of the same moderns that he had and had a sense of irony and humor that complemented his. Getty assumed they had come together because, at Nebraska, they had no one else.

Kees made other important friendships during his senior year at Nebraska. Dale Smith, another aspiring novelist, and his future wife, Margaret, were in Wimberly's class—as was Kees's closest friend during this time, Maurice Johnson. Both belonged to the same fraternity, Sigma Delta Chi, which was predominantly composed of English majors. Johnson and Kees attended many of the same courses, such as "The Continental Novel" and "Eighteenth-Century Prose." In addition, though Johnson wanted to be a scholar—his mentor was Louise Pound, the philologist and the companion of Willa Cather—his friendship with Kees stemmed from a mutual interest in contemporary novelists and poets—not Jonathan Swift. They discussed Faulkner and Joyce and the other novelists of the Jazz Age passionately and groaned together over the overrated writers of the moment. ("William Saroyan in the *Yale Review* ... again ... again," Johnson complained to Kees in one letter that preserves the tenor of what they thought of certain reputations. "Thomas Wolfe in the *N. Am. Rev. Quart.*: America I Love You.")

Kees and Johnson saw the university and even the world split between those who knew who Stephen Dedalus was and those who did not. They even developed their own private language after reading *Ulysses* and installments of *Finnegans Wake* ("rainsound," "gluesmell," and like constructions). With just as much flair, they also lampooned stream-of-consciousness writing, making up an anyone-can-do-it article with parodies fictitiously penned by Mae West, Franklin Roosevelt, and Huey Long for the *Awgwan,* the campus humor magazine. (On the cover of that issue, the two friends appear together in caricature with the rest of the staff as acrobats in a flying circus.)

When Robert Taylor's first movie, *Handy Andy,* had its run in a Lincoln movie theater, Taylor's childhood playmate had arrived in the city, too, as a published young writer with new admiring friends and plenty of self-confidence and self-awareness. He had no intention of going into the family business as more of his short stories were accepted not only by the *Schooner* but by other little avant-garde magazines as well.

His father, who sometimes came up from Beatrice to visit and drink beers with Weldon and his friends and teachers, including Dr. Wimberly, had no issue with this decision. After drinking at their favorite haunt, the Bull's Head, he left his son's boardinghouse in a fine mood, for there had been a time in his life when he probably wanted such an intellectual circle for himself. Now he could experience it vicariously through his son.

He was also heartened by his son's practical ambitions, for Weldon said he wanted to attend graduate school at the University of California. Though this was not the fallback that John had imagined should his son give up his dream of writing for a living, the choice boded well in another way, since Weldon's girlfriend wanted to live in California. The presence of the girl meant Weldon had normal inclinations—as did that description of him in the *Awgwan* as a young man who would make "a tough right wing for anybody's hockey team."

Yet the idea of being a college teacher contrasted with Kees's grim view of his mentors in the spring of 1935. He saw Wimberly as a stillborn dilettante and a cultivated provincial academic. He had the same opinion of another favorite professor, Orin Stepanek, whose comfortable home, decorated with old Czech paintings and Navajo rugs, was well-known to Kees during his senior year. It was the place where the "best brains in Lincoln" gathered. Though he certainly learned how to disport himself like a young intellectual at such gatherings, Kees also became impatient and wanted something more.

Lacking the credit hours to graduate with the rest of his class, he stayed on in Lincoln and enrolled in the summer session. The June graduation ceremonies passed, and Kees felt nothing as Ann Swan and Maurice Johnson, sweltering in their caps and gowns, listened to the high-toned commencement address ("Nebraska has given you all *she* has to offer") and received their diplomas. He had in the past year become a full-blown nonconformist and would have loathed the address delivered by the conservative president of the University of California, who assured the class of 1935 that "All Will Be Well," as Johnson reported, if they no longer had any more "thoughts of nasty things like C-mm-n-sm." Such thoughts Kees had.

He considered himself a communist, as did other educated young people who began to understand themselves as individuals in the imperfect and discredited society of the Great Depression. The party's acid doctrines against bourgeois values also gave him a way to excoriate the comfortable and familiar poles of Beatrice and Lincoln so that he would never go back, never run the Kees factory—and never give up wanting to become a writer. Cursing everything bourgeois would cut holes in his ever considering the safety net his parents had long been and still were making for him.

His writing, classes, and Nebraska's heat prevented Kees from devoting very much of himself to the Cause during the long summer. No amount of hammering on his boardinghouse's piano like Fats Waller or singing like one of Paul Whiteman's Rhythm Boys made time pass quickly enough. During the week of a teachers' convention, he indulged in a stream-of-consciousness letter to describe a typical day for Maurice Johnson:

High school superintendents in crinkly seersucker suits meet in campus washrooms and while micturating discuss higher education of the Madrid (Nebr.) publicschools, the salaries there, and the unparalleled value of a Master's thesis on "How Far Should a District School Be From the Road?": Wimberly has a doublebreasted robinseggblue suit with clarkgable pockets and a shirred back; he becomes a bit boring in

his particular brand of mysticism which he ladles out in the sweltering
Seventeenthcentury Prose class; here in the Beta Theta Pi house a poker
game runs day and night: so does the radio: [...] the sun burning: the
blank faces: the schoolteachers from Weeping Water and Hayes Center
approaching menopause slowly but surely in their darkblue eyelet dresses
with pink slips underneath: the gin (legal) cooling: the assignments long:
the nights maddening: the bed lumpy: the summer wearing on.

At the end of summer school in July, Kees traveled out to Colorado to stay in his parents' cabin for two months. There, in the peace and quiet of the mountain country, he wanted to finish the novel he had started in the spring, *Slow Parade*. It was an auspicious time to take on such an ambitious project. "Saturday Rain" had been listed in the back pages of *Best Short Stories*, where that collection's editor, Edward J. O'Brien, recognized the writing that he had no room to anthologize in his annual volume. O'Brien had even given the story an asterisk to distinguish it among the other honorable mentions. Though Kees considered these tin medals, he knew that the editors of New York publishing houses would notice.

Kees camped near the town of Drake, Colorado, where the Big Thompson River rushed down out of the Rocky Mountain National Park, passing below his cabin. He could now devote all of his time to the novel without having to earn the final credit hours he needed to graduate. In previous summers, he had come here with his parents to escape from Nebraska's dog days. Family vacations, however, were not in keeping with the subject and style of *Slow Parade*, in which Kees employed a technique he wanted to be similar to that of Dos Passos yet inverted. Instead of taking isolated characters and bringing them slowly closer and closer to each other, Kees wanted to take the members of one family and show them growing further and further away from each other.

Through August and September, he labored over the novel so that his first reader, Maurice Johnson, would have it in time, before he started graduate school. He wanted the writing to be spare and have the same economy that he had achieved in his short stories. He wanted a prose from himself that not even the famous editor Maxwell Perkins could get from one of his best-selling modernists. "It seems to me," Kees wrote Johnson at the beginning of August, "there is a greater need for criticism before books are published than after (Vide: Thomas Wolfe)."

Kees started writing and revising in the morning and broke off for lunch to retrieve his mail from the general store across the Big Thompson. This routine was utterly pleasant. "And so I work from five to eight hours a day on a screenedin porch," he wrote Johnson, "with the river flowing by making rainsound twenty feet away, with the pines behind me, with the typewriter on a stand I made out of a peachcrate." The natural beauty of the high country, the river, and the trees helped ease the doubts Kees had about *Slow Parade*. At times, when he read back what he had written or changed, he felt terrified and also convinced that the book would "amount to something," that it was not "anything to be ashamed of yet." He even felt that he had crafted a socially conscientious work, one that aimed toward reform, that was good "propaganda" despite how grim the book sounded when he read it back. Without knowing it, he began to prepare his friend for how to take the manuscript: "Isn't Faulkner trying to 'sell' us on the futility of futility? Isn't Wolfe trying to put across his 'lostness'? T. S. Eliot is the poet who sings the song of Oswald Spengler. [...] It seems to me that anyone can be a futilitarian right now: it's the easiest, simplest thing in the world—because it is *negative*. [...] But surely we should have more admiration for those writers with some guts, those who are trying to find a rational solution and are willing to fight a little, than for those pale and hopeless young men who have little more to say than Booth Tarkington and Kathleen Norris."

The only ripple that disturbed his mood of accomplishment and the perfect image of a writer at work came from Ann, whose letters may have burdened him with her insecurity and her missing him. She would have been disappointed that he had not come to California with her, that he had applied to the University of Chicago instead.

In September, Kees returned to Beatrice and learned that he had been accepted into graduate school. But he was more concerned with what to do next with his finished novel than with giving a master's degree in English literature any thought. He assumed he could do the work at Chicago with the same comfortable effort that he had given his studies at Nebraska, where he had earned mostly As and Bs.

Through the open windows of his boyhood home on North Fifth

Street, the neighbors heard him play piano during what would be the last time he ever really lived at home, for a little over a week. Then he took one of the Burlington's silver Zephyrs to Chicago, where he passed uneasily from the freedom of writing in Colorado to keeping up with his reading list and turning out papers. The transition seemed well-planned. He had given the manuscript of *Slow Parade* to Maurice Johnson in Lincoln. If the book was ready, he would use the next break from school to find an agent or just send the novel to editors himself. He had sent out a number of short stories in the spring and summer and now could wait to see which ones were accepted. *Windsor Quarterly* had already taken and printed "Escape in Autumn," a story about a man with a skin-cancer lesion on his cheek who deceives a blind man, telling him the children in the park say his face is "as beautiful as a ripe apple."

As it turned out, Kees could not put down his up-to-the-minute literary life and commit to hours of reading more Chaucer, Milton, and Dryden. Within days of his arrival, he completely upended months of planning and expectations. From his room in a transient hotel named the Mira-Mar on South Woodlawn Avenue, he realized that he would not last the quarter, that he did not have the scholarly stamina that Maurice Johnson had. Even Johnson would have found that the coursework at Chicago left no time for the little magazines and avant-garde anthologies they had devoured in their undergraduate days. He had expressed envy over how lucky Kees was to get into Chicago—but Kees now advised Johnson to be "content with his lot" at Nebraska.

Kees dragged his suitcase back to Union Station with little to show for his two weeks in Chicago save for what he brought to read on the train back to Beatrice: a two-volume set of Alfred Döblin's *Alexanderplatz* in English translation. He read almost without ever looking up and then only to see what station his train passed through—and to think ahead about what to do now, what to tell Sarah and John.

Despite the antipathy he had expressed for the teaching life, Kees came back to Lincoln and enrolled in the Teachers College at the university for the first quarter. While there, he took three courses and earned mediocre grades. He also took a salesclerk job in Ben Simon's department store selling men's clothes and there started picking up material again for the stories he would rather write than papers for English professors.

At Doane, Kees had let "Percy Poggle" pass through a number of hands, and one reader wrote in the margin of the manuscript: "I have a shrinking feeling when I think of Keyes in Hollywood." Despite the misspelling of his name, most people, from those who knew him well to those who only knew he acted with the other Doane Players, assumed he would get into the movies. Academia, and not California, had been his only real direction since 1934, however. Even when he thought about moving there after graduation, it would have only been to continue his education and to follow Ann Swan, not Robert Taylor.

Ann now lived in Los Angeles and had probably been begging Kees to come out for months. Like many good communists, he considered California a "fascist place" controlled by William Randolph Hearst and the police, who turned back thousands of unemployed workers trying to enter the state. But the labor unions held sway in Hollywood as much as the movie moguls did, and he could find employment more easily there than elsewhere in the country as the Depression began its seventh year in 1936. He could act and get bit parts or even character roles. His writing talents could land him a job working on scripts. He could play the piano or some other instrument for one of the studio orchestras. Besides, he had yet to tap that romantic, boyhood interest he had had in the movies. Reawakening his relationship with them might lead to his becoming a leading film critic or even a filmmaker.

The idea of going out to Hollywood grew more and more attractive in the fall of 1935. Robert Taylor's success had already inspired a small contingent of young people from Beatrice to seek their fortunes there. Kees, of course, had a higher purpose for himself. Whatever he would do in Hollywood would support him until he made it as a novelist or, at least, would not be incompatible with being one. F. Scott Fitzgerald and other writers, Faulkner especially, were now proving the possibilities.

When he arrived in January 1936, Kees found Hollywood split into camps of "violent" Communist party sympathizers and anticommunists. In conspiratorial tones, Kees reported back to Maurice Johnson that a great many writers, actors, and executives were communists and had to keep their beliefs very quiet. A prominent director, he said, poured half his salary into the "C.P." At the other extreme was Hearst, who Kees heard had sent "vigilantes" out to kill the movie critic Joel Faith for giving Hearst's mistress, Marion Davies, a bad notice in *New Theatre.*

It did not take Kees long to find that he had nothing in common with the other members of the "Beatrice contingent." He had little to do with them, especially after he tried to exploit his connection to Robert Taylor. In a letter to Dale Smith, he reported that his one and only meeting with the leading man had been a waste of time: "My erstwhile friend Arlington Brugh, now Robert Taylor of the silver screen, would not even see me, and you may instruct the local Bolsheviki that they are more than welcome to boycott his pictures without any denunciatory mutterings from me." Taylor's inexplicable coldness and the politics of Kees and his friends back in Lincoln suggest that communism was a factor in a falling-out that came years before Taylor admitted to the House Subcommittee on Un-American Activities that he would never willingly act beside a communist.

In the days that followed, Kees rented a room in a bungalow on South Kingsley Drive near the studios. From there, he searched for work or took the Red Line cars downtown. Being outside in January and accustomed to Nebraska's weather, he was struck by the eerily mild winter of southern California. He also spent a good deal of time in his room, working on his new novel, listening for calls on the landlady's phone, and waiting for the mail to come with news of *Slow Parade.*

The novel had gone from one New York house to another since November. That it had been taken seriously provided Kees with some mild consolation; so did, perhaps, the two kinds of reactions he would get. Harold Strauss of Covici said the novel was "unrelievedly grim" — while Donald Elder at Doubleday Doran felt "almost unqualifiedly enthusiastic." Elder's only reservation concerned not so much the book itself but getting Kees to revise it so that it could pass the "prudish standards" of his house: "The part that requires change is Cynthia's sexual aberration. There is also a good deal of the dialogue which doesn't meet the purity standards." Kees must have enjoyed the controversy and editorial soul-searching his writing had caused. Being rejected, however, was not the same thing as being the author of a banned book. One had to publish it first.

As the days in Hollywood wore on, Kees spent more time in line waiting to buy a movie ticket than he did finding steady work in the film industry. To escape the boredom of waiting for something to happen, he rode the streetcar downtown and sat in one movie palace after another, seeing *The Petrified Forest* with Leslie Howard and Humphrey Bogart, Charles Chaplin's *Modern Times,* Fritz Lang's *Fury* with Sylvia Sidney and Spencer Tracy, *The Prisoner of Shark Island* with Paul Muni—and *Camille.* The movie posters for *Camille* claimed that Greta Garbo loved Robert Taylor, and Kees would have found that alone amusing. But he may have already known, too, given his interest in such things, that the leading lady had nothing to do with men and that the leading man was rumored to be a bisexual.

Where Kees stood was still a work in progress, much like the novel waiting back in his room, for while he found no permanent place on either side of the sound stage, he unconsciously studied the tough-guy roles on-screen that would harden the poet's face and the sensitive eyes seen in Missouri. (Ten years later people who knew him would even use the term "Hollywood tough" to describe him.) Bogart and Muni were even more of an influence than seeing Faulkner sitting behind him in Grauman's Chinese Theater, for the author of *The Sound and the Fury* looked less godlike whispering intensely to his companion, a "Hollywoodlooking brunette." "The conversation," Kees wrote when he got back to his room, "was not what you imagined at all. Merely inane. She kept pawing at his lapel, and the talk was of the Scott Fitzgerald type."

When the movies were over and Kees walked out into the street, he experienced the same world Nathanael West would capture in *The Day of the Locust.* "The damned hurry," he wrote, "the noise, the goddamned lights enjoining you to mobilize your car chew Ex-lax and keep regular dine and dance without overcharge see Dick Powell subject yourself to colonic irrigation, the gasfumes, the freaks, the hurry hurry hurry, the seers, the Christian Scientists, the pitchmen, the unending rainy season, the hurry."

The wild stories heard about this "mad and terrifying region" seemed to be true. "Augment them," he advised Maurice Johnson, "with recollections of all the satires written about it, and that is the actual and genuine Hollywood. Ben Hecht's remark, to the effect that out here they're all 'either drunk or crazy' is fairly accurate." Los Angeles to Kees overflowed with "oil, orangejuice," and "the sperm of moviestars," and there were times when he came back to his rented room and thought of "chucking it all and coming back to the Cornhusker State."

Each time, however, his situation brightened just enough to keep him going for a few more weeks. He found temporary work of one kind or another, probably as a musician in different studio orchestras. This meant joining a union, which tilted him further leftward, as did the books he read, such as *In Dubious Battle* ("Even though [Steinbeck] has a totally erroneous idea of the makeup of a Communist organizer, it's one of the most exciting books I think I've ever read"). He was also gratified to learn that the Guggenheim fellowships in literature were being awarded to James T. Farrell, Josephine Herbst, Kenneth Fearing, and Granville Hicks—writers from whom he took his political cues. "The position [is] reversed," he wrote Dale Smith back in Lincoln, "you see: the Capitalists feeding the Hand that Bites Them."

In April, Kees learned that his satire "Frog in the Pool" had been reprinted in *Modern Story Selections*. This piece, however, was one of those disposable stories that he had turned out for Wimberly the year before. He did not take getting it anthologized as a sign to shift from the social-protest novel he was writing now to lighter fare. ("Frog in the Pool," with its botched frog murder, does end with the one constant readers find in Kees's fiction: a revelation of impotence that can range—sometimes at once—from a cosmic depression to one of the bedroom. The story's end also has the pestilential ominousness that would mark his poems.)

That same month, Kees continued spending much of his free time in the audience rather than writing or performing for one. He saw Lillian Hellman's play *The Children's Hour* and attended a spirited debate between Norman Thomas, the Socialist party candidate for president, and the novelist Upton Sinclair. It seemed from his letters that he was sitting by himself most of the time, but he had made a small circle of friends during his months in Los Angeles. Included in that circle were the short-story writer Sanora Babb (before she married the cinematographer James Wong Howe) and her sister Dorothy. They were also from the Midwest, via Kansas and a farm in Colorado, and had much in common with Kees. They shared a comfortable apartment in Hollywood, not far from where he lived, and they often invited him over for dinner and drinks and to talk about movie actors, screenwriters, and the hardships of writing and getting work published. They also discussed the Depression, the unemployed, social justice, unions, and Spain, for Sanora, like Kees, considered herself a communist.

Sanora and her sister were not Kees's only women contacts. Though Ann Swan is never mentioned in the letters he sent back to friends in Lincoln, she would have been a presence in his life. She had her own place on Lindbrook Drive (and later on Cynthia) that was far enough away for Kees to both enjoy her company and keep his affair with her discreet. In this way, he could avoid the "bourgeois" convention of marriage and not horrify his mother by living unmarried with a girl-friend. Ann was so invisible that Kees seemed to Dorothy Babb "un-attached," and she developed a "crush" on this most unusual commu-nist, who was handsome and as formal in his appearance and dress as a Wall Street banker, totally unlike the other young idealists who took great pride in looking "working-class."

As much as the Babb sisters found him out of keeping with their other contemporaries in dress and manner, Kees surprised them in the way he obsessed about death. To Sanora, many of his conversations seemed always to come around to some recent suicide that fascinated him or some car wreck that involved people with their "whole lives be-fore them," tragedies that happened often enough in Hollywood. He also liked to speculate about what had happened to Ambrose Bierce, who had disappeared in Mexico in 1914 and had been missing for as long as he had been alive.

Kees's morbid interests were not necessarily pathological. He needed material and that kind of discussion in which authors float their ideas rather than give anything away. The Babb sisters hardly knew about the two novels in progress he had written during his months in Hollywood. By May, he had nearly finished manuscripts of *The Dead Are Friendly* and *A Good American*. He had also sent new short stories out to the little magazines. Wimberly received "Let-ter from Maine," which he published that summer. It was another of Kees's dark takes on the kind of light story one heard in radio serials; in this one an elderly and dependent man receives hundreds of dimes after he becomes part of a chain letter that are then taken away by his daughter-in-law, "that damn Julia woman."

The *Schooner*-type story, though it brought him success back in

Nebraska, did not have the daring of the fiction he tried to write in the discarded story "Requiem." "Requiem" had the kinds of things he talked about with the Babb sisters, in this case teenagers who kill themselves "because-they-got-syph." "This Is Home," the story that broke Kees into *Manuscript*, a little magazine that took more risks than the *Schooner*, came even closer to the mark. It concerned a gullible young sailor recruited off the street to have sex with an impotent man's wife. Though Kees totally imagined the story—which features a car that dispenses lit cigarettes from the dashboard, an invention that shows the renegade creativity that nearly belonged to the F. D. Kees Manufacturing Company—it progresses naturally, as if he had experienced its events himself. The sailor goes from thinking he is being picked up by the man—that uncomfortable experience Kees had at last mastered here—to thinking he is simply having dinner with him and his wife. Then the sailor gradually realizes why he has really been brought into the couple's home. He notices that the little girl looks only like her mother, that she has none of her father in her, that the wife has a fulsome health and radiance about her that make her husband seem shrunken as he fingers the neck of a beer bottle. The nature of the service the sailor must perform, however, Kees strings out to the very end of the story, where the wife's name, Eve, and, perhaps, Kees's awareness of Freud's theories on the fear of women have the most shock value. This is when the sailor follows the wife's voice upstairs and sees her in bed waiting for him.

∾

Each of the good jobs Kees was after "blew up with a crash." Then came the loss of several manuscripts and his typewriter when fire gutted the house on South Kingsley. Instead of looking for a new room, he left Los Angeles and returned to Nebraska in June. He passed through Beatrice and saw his parents for a day and then continued on to Lincoln. There he looked for a place to live and learned from Dale Smith that there were good-paying editorial jobs to be had compiling the state guide of Nebraska, a book of city and town profiles, statistics, maps, photographs, and other information that visitors to the state could use. It was part of a nationwide series sponsored by the Federal Writers' Project, a New Deal relief program under the Works Progress Administration. Kees also learned that nearly all the directors and staff of the Nebraska guide had once been students of Lowry Wimberly, who exerted considerable influence in getting his former students desks and jobs at a time when Depression unemployment was peaking.

Wimberly also had another purpose in mind besides the welfare of his students. He believed the state guides would preserve the nation's various and vanishing folklore, legends, and cultural ways as radio and the cinema made for a more homogenized American culture. When Kees dropped by to see him in his office in the English department, it was partly this romantic idea that played a role in Wimberly's helping the younger man. He knew Kees's writing, had watched him drink beer and talk like a communist at the Bull's Head. Wimberly saw Kees, more than any of his other students, as a new type, a person whose mind was fixed in the present and the future and who saw the past as something to be discredited and discarded. The state-guide work, however, might change him for the better, Wimberly thought, might make him care about his Midwestern heritage. The favor he could do for Kees would be a kind of therapy for an obviously unrooted young man, whose transcripts showed how many schools he had passed through, who had gone from being a protégé at Chicago to living out of a suitcase in Hollywood. Wimberly made the appropriate phone call to the Union Terminal Warehouse by the Union Pacific railroad yard, where the state guide had its office.

There Kees was quickly hired as an editor by Jacob Harris Gable, the director of the project, and shown to a desk that directly faced that of a quiet and somewhat taller young man whom Kees recognized from a class he had taken with Wimberly. Gable introduced Norris Getty as Kees's supervisor and asked that he show Kees around the open, undivided loft space, where the rest of the staff worked amid the noise of typewriters and the constant shunting of railroad cars that came through the large open windows during the hot summer months.

Kees developed a reputation around the state-guide office of being a spoiled and brilliant adolescent who had read too much about art, novels, poetry, movies, and jazz and who also remembered everything that he had read. Even Getty thought of Kees as someone who had all the accomplishments, experiences, and money that young men from small Nebraska towns were not supposed to have. Still, he came to like his new friend's appearance, his "unearthly cleanliness, dark eyes, neatness of lashes and hair." He also came closer to becoming Kees's best friend: "His obsessions are the Communist Party and the stupidities of middle-class America. He is so discouragingly well read, knows and has done so much that I must feel that my lack of interest in the Cause is a serious deficiency. I have been reading the Communist poems of K. Fearing, and have tackled O'Hara, Hermann, and Dos Passos in a wistful attempt to attain some sort of even standing with him. [...] He is so much more clever than I, a better satirist. I find so little to say that doesn't sound stupid or trite; I've started fumbling words."

Some of Kees's coworkers, unemployed typists, newspaper reporters, housewives, bankers, students, insurance agents, and even an osteopath, grumbled that he had not contributed a single line to the state guide. Getty, however, knew differently, knew that Kees had deleted more than his fair share of text during those sessions between their facing desks, when one man read the manuscript in a loud, clear voice above the office din and the other used a blue pencil on the typescript. Hardly a sentence of copy, often sent in by amateur writers from places with names like Broken Bow, got by him without some slashing emendation that made for greater clarity or smoothness.

Many in the office thought Getty had let himself fall under Kees's spell, an impression reinforced by his forming, with Kees and his other friend on the staff, Dale Smith, the "Unholy Trio." Gable called the three this because they laughed at things he took seriously, including his deepest wish, to get into *Who's Who in America,* and his inordinate and insecure pride in being the author of a boy's book on exploration and one on astronomy.[1] Gable's ambitions clashed with the trio's image of themselves as unrecognized geniuses, creative writers, and social revolutionaries trying to organize the staff for the Farmer-Labor and Workers' Alliance.[2]

The other thing about Kees that bothered Gable was his sense that he was entitled to work on his manuscripts while on project time. Nebraska's pioneers, Kees said, bored him. So did the state's history. The only thing that kept Gable from firing Kees for his snickering and sneering was the fact that he was also liked in the way certain obnoxious children are tolerated more than they should be, are allowed to think and say things denied to others who are more mature. A good example of this occurred when Kees and some of his coworkers were returning from lunch and encountered a woman whipping her boy on the sidewalk. "Hit him again, Ma'am!" Kees shouted, jumping up and down gleefully. "Beat him with a stick until his teeth fall out! He's just a little fellow who can't hurt you." This was street theater for Kees and a way to shock his friends into seeing where violence came from— that good and wholesome world the guide was all about, that world Wimberly wanted him to see.

Norris Getty became Kees's confidante and the person he now showed his manuscripts to first. The earliest of these was "Noon," written a few months after Kees started working at the guide. Getty called the short story a memorable piece, and what he may have prized in this story was how Kees let on that he knew what it was like for someone who could never be open about his sexuality, who would have to endure "platonic" relationships. Kees's model for this person seems to have been Getty himself or the person he read in Getty. "*There are things going on around me all the time,*" the effeminate office manager thinks while silently putting up with his lunch companions ogling a small-town prostitute, "*things that are not part of me, things which barely touch me, things of which I know nothing.*"

Kees certainly revealed something profound about himself that summer, if not about Norris Getty. One late afternoon, Gable asked the two friends to visit a graveyard in Lincoln. As soon as they entered the cemetery, Kees sat in the shade of the nearest evergreen tree. He said he would vouch for anything Getty wanted to write about the cemetery.

As Getty wrote down names and dates from the headstones, he heard Kees talking. "More and more," his friend said from under the tree, "I think Hart Crane had the right idea."

Getty listened and did not think this odd, for the poet known as the "Roaring Boy" stood for survival of a kind. He had jumped from the ss *Orisiba* and swum away from the ship, back to Mexico, leaving his poems behind instead of a block of stone like the ones found all around them in the cemetery. This was an apocryphal story that Kees had found in Philip Horton's biography of Crane's troubled life, which he had borrowed from a friend. He had been talking about the biography for days, and his utterance was hardly ominous. Kees was turning out his own poems, inspired in part by the Crane book and a few original poems that Getty had shown him.

Kees's first poems offered him a freedom from fiction, which was expected by magazine editors to have a "finished look" and a "punch ending." Poems had something over novels, too, which Kees, in the book reviews he was now turning out for the *Schooner* and other little magazines, criticized for being "too well arranged" or worked out "with a slide-rule."

"Subtitle," one poem Kees preserved from 1936 and made the prologue to his first collection, shows that he enjoyed the freedom of poetry and its empowerment, even though that freedom came from the despair of sitting unemployed in Los Angeles theaters. Surprisingly, Kees reacted against Crane's influence, as theorized by Harold Bloom, who placed Kees in his "Western canon," for there is in Kees none of Crane's romanticism or paeans to an innocent America.[3] (The debt for this goes to Kenneth Fearing, whom Kees later sought out when he traveled to New York in 1940.) Instead one finds America's opposite incarnation, as a vast enterprise that is part studio system and part police state. "Subtitle" made a laudable debut when it was published the following year, one that made Kees seem fully arrived as a poet who promised a serious, "feature-length" performance:

We present for you this evening
a movie of death: observe
these scenes chipped celluloid
reveals unsponsored and tax-free.
We request these things only:
all gum must be placed beneath the seats
or swallowed quickly, all popcorn sacks
must be left in the foyer. The doors
will remain closed throughout
the performance. Kindly consult
your programs: observe that
there are no exits. This is
a necessary precaution.
Look for no dialogue, or for the
sound of any human voice: we have seen fit
to synchronize this play with
squealings of pigs, slow sound of guns,
the sharp dead click of empty chocolatebar machines.
We say again: there are

no exits here, no guards to bribe,
no washroom windows.
NO FINIS to the film unless
the ending is your own.
Turn off the lights, remind
the operator of his union card:
sit forward, let the screen reveal
your heritage, the logic of your destiny.

Denver
1937-1943

The intellectual life here is very saddening.
—Weldon Kees

Even with the big windows of his warehouse office thrown open, there was no relief from the heat rolling off the prairie during the summer of 1937 while Kees worked hard on the "Nebraska Baedeker," the nickname his coworkers had optimistically given to the state guide. He felt differently, however. He could not imagine anyone seriously using the book or wanting to visit its out-of-the-way places. His attention to detail was less out of diligence than it was out of a desire to vent his real feelings. Sitting at the desk across from him, Norris Getty watched as he went through the stacks of terrible copy, deleting superfluous adverbs, effusive adjectives, and clichés that aroused in him "a more immediate and destructive fury than all the goons in a Southern coal field."

Toward the end of the summer, Kees decided to enroll in the library program at the University of Denver. This change was probably designed to please his parents, who may have been gently pressing him into making his relationship with Ann Swan an honest one.

Another reason for Kees to leave Lincoln was the uncertain future of the Federal Writers' Project. Roosevelt's Republican enemies considered the program a boondoggle for communists and wanted it ended. Kees had to consider this as well as his personality conflict with Jake Gable. A library career in some large city or college would be a way out of this situation before it came to a crashing end. It would also be secure and friendly to his writing since learning to be a librarian and being one, to him, seemed to require little mental investment. And such a career could be easily discarded when success came.

While visiting his parents in Beatrice, Kees secured their help in relocating and, if necessary, paying for his tuition. Then he returned to Lincoln to obtain letters of reference and to complete the necessary paperwork. He now saw himself leaving for good, as others in his circle already had. "Somehow it pleases me," he wrote not very wistfully, "to know that people are leaving Lincoln like rats deserting a sinking ship. I wish every one of them a happier home."

In late August, Kees quit the Federal Writers' Project. When Gable told Norris Getty and Dale Smith to let Kees know that his name would not appear in the published state guide, Kees said he preferred it that way and returned to Beatrice to stay with his parents through the first week of September. Then his father drove him to the rail junction at nearby Wymore to meet a train on the Burlington's Kansas City–Denver mainline.

Malcolm Glenn Wyer, the avuncular dean of the library school at the University of Denver and head of the Denver Public Library, had once taught at the University of Nebraska. He had close ties to the teachers there, who had recommended the surprised and pleased new student. Not only had Wyer admitted Kees into the graduate program in library studies, but he had also offered him a job on the staff of the public library. This made up for any doubts Kees had had on the "unpleasant and slowmoving train" from Wymore about quitting the Federal Writers' Project. He described his smooth transition in a letter to Norris Getty after his first three weeks in Denver. He made the same amount of money as he had in Lincoln, while taking

Book Arts this year, and Cataloguing and Administration next. This relieves me of considerable anxiety as to money, and will make it possible for me—at the end of the period—to have had two years of work and experience in a firstrate public library in a good-sized town. This should be of some value, in addition to the BS degree in Librarianship, when I go after a job. And if Ann doesnt find work right off, we will still be eating, if only the fresh vegetables, reasonably priced, which Colorado offers to its residents.

Much of the work at the library is good stuff, and I like it. Of course there is the usual number of bitches. [...] There are all sorts of amusing things: the little Russianjew who is writing a lengthy letter to some friends and comes in every day to have me help him with his English. Frankly, I think the man's an exhibitionist of sorts. You should see the letter. It goes on and on, and would delight the Spirit of Ring Lardner. ... Nuns who come in, after G. K. Chesterton or H. H. Munro or some other Pope-sanctioned hack. ... Shy virgins wanting to reserve Married Love by Marie Stopes. ... The deaf-and-dumb lady who handed me a piece of paper with this legend: "goon with the wing."

Denver, however, was not such a cultural backwater as Kees first imagined. His first "arty" cocktail party, given for the benefit of the Spanish Loyalists, became a starting point for the small circle that formed around him in his new city. The host, Michael Stuart, had once served as Joyce's confidante and aide in Paris—and had published a story in the same issue of *transition* in which Kees remembered reading Kafka's "Metamorphosis." His Joyce connection, testified to by an autographed picture of "J. J." prominently displayed in his apartment, seemed utterly surreal in its Denver setting. Bob Hutchison was a member of the WPA's Art, Writers' and Theatre Projects in Denver and the "black sheep" of a wealthy Denver family. He had the money and desire to start a magazine and asked Kees if he wanted to help edit it. The writer Gilbert Neiman and his wife, Margaret, a painter, entertained him with their plans to live in Mexico among the dissolute expatriate Americans who were already there. Neiman, like Kees, wrote poems and short stories. He was now translating Federico García Lorca's *Blood Wedding*.

On the day after the party, October 3, Weldon and Ann were married. The event must have struck him as one of those bourgeois necessities, for he barely gave it mention in letters to friends. Nevertheless, there was a small church ceremony conducted by a Unitarian minister. Printed announcements were sent to friends and family.

Ann moved from her furnished room on nearby East Thirteenth Avenue to a small apartment on the top floor of a two-story house at 1119 Pearl Street that she would now share with Weldon. Their neighborhood in Washington Heights was the middle-class kind that had inspired the motto of Denver's real estate interests at that time: "The City of Beautiful Homes." Despite this setting (and the natives' way of saying "Denver, Kaleradoe"), they made the best of it and married life. If it did not resemble Bloomsbury, it was at least Bloomsbury's poor American cousin.

The Keeses furnished their apartment with tasteful, clean-lined furniture; some bookshelves; a Minipiano; and a few fine art prints, such as Georges Rouault's *The Old King*. They also bought a radio with their wedding-present money to hear jazz and classical music broadcasts. Such performances as a concert of Berlioz with Enesco conducting helped mask the whimpering of the "psychopathic dog" that lived downstairs and made it easier not to look outside at Weldon's vision of

Denver as a kind of snow globe full of "soot peacefully floating in the cold Colorado afternoon" from the city's furnaces. The apartment was also a refuge for getting tight together on gin and 7-Up—the bottler's slogan a comforting one that Kees found himself repeating ironically: "SEVEN UP LIKES *you*!"

Not long after the wedding, Ann found temporary work as a stenographer and typist for the law firm of Van Cise, Robinson, and Charlton. They would eventually hire her permanently, which more than assured that she and Weldon would live comfortably during the ongoing Depression.

Kees, however, did not feel absolutely secure. "A million people," he wrote Dale Smith, "have been fired [...] but that isnt what is disturbing these latter-day Adam Smiths: no: the money isnt coming in so fast, and theres a great flurry and lots of anger and the old talk about Mussolini and his doctrines and the good they might do here is getting under way again." The clerical services Ann provided for the lawyers during the day were also provided for her husband at night. She typed clean manuscripts from his draft typescripts and even performed as his amanuensis when he experimented with dictating parts of a novel about a childhood friend in January 1938. He had been working on it intermittently the previous year and had returned to it after learning that his friend, one of the young people who left Beatrice for Hollywood, had been killed in an auto accident. The tragedy moved Kees to write about the friend's fate, which he saw with a fusion of communist and Presbyterian morality, and the novel:

The thing that impressed me about his life, principally, was this: he attempted to meet society on its own grounds and lost integrity, dignity, and decency. I know that those are words that are suspect, but I think you know what I mean. The passage I wrote tonight was concerned with a day when he was about 11 or 12: he is chased home from school by some toughs in his school, he practices music, dreaming about becoming a great composer and showing them all. It could have been first-rate, but I'm afraid that, as it stands, it's on the level of Morley Callaghan. Which is a trend I do my utmost to discourage.

As far as meeting society on his terms was concerned, Kees was frustrated "that nobody much gives a damn whether you write or take dope or read the American Magazine." *Slow Parade* had been rejected again after coming close to publication. None of Bob Hutchi-son's promises of money for the little magazine had come through. And as Kees tried to start another novel with the artist theme, based more on "things that have happened to me," he did not get very far before realizing in a letter to Norris Getty that "you cant write about yourself, really; try it; it's impossible." He wanted "no Joycean, Wolf-esque, handling," but being so deliberately unfashionable and precious about originality made writing harder. (In this he admitted to being influenced by *The White Mule* stories of William Carlos Williams.)

Riding the number 44 streetcar as it trundled through Denver's drab north side in late January, Kees focused through the rain-streaked windows and then sketched out a poem about the unemployed and a future that would soon "explode." More exercises followed, their quality uneven, with only a few hitting the same register as "Subtitle." Some were abstract. Some were satirical. Some were propagandistic, as in the case of one published in *New Masses*. He could write them without the same expectations that he had for his fiction. The poems gave him pleasure the way music did. There were at once meter and rhyme—and flashes of the Great American Novel that had eluded him, that took the risks in taste and shock a fiction editor would not allow:

> *Squat, unshaven, full of gas,*
> *Joseph Samuels, former clerk*
> *in four large cities, out of work,*
> *waits in the darkened underpass.*
> *[. . . . .]*
> *He takes an object from his coat*
> *and holds it tightly in his hand*
> *(eyes on the stretch of endless sand).*
> *And then, in darkness, cuts his throat.*
> —"The Beach"

"It is full of excellent things," Kees wrote after poring over his review copy of *New Directions 1937,* the second issue of the annual of new writ-ing published by the poet and Pittsburgh steel heir James Laughlin IV. He found Henry Miller "a sort of combination Joyce and Wolfe" whose work was "damned exciting." He liked the Cocteau play translated by Dudley Fitts and the poems of Delmore Schwartz. Everything about the anthology forced Kees to reconsider his chances of getting published and the quality of his work, especially in light of what Laughlin wanted to print. "We need some of Kafka's phantasy and allegory and symbolism—even horror," Laughlin wrote in his preface. "Our writing has too much physical and too little spiritual horror." For Kees, the message was clear: American writing should come from a Prague insurance company of its own.

In the Denver Public Library, however, it was hard for him to think seriously about writing that would get him into *New Directions*. One cold Saturday afternoon, he observed that the snow outside drove people into the library searching for works on tatting, Kathleen Norris, tree cutting, the weaning of babies, Pareto, how to mend inner tubes, and Kathleen Norris again.[1] "I live the active life, all right," he put down in the letter he was typing.

The American public library was not that "reading-emporium" of culture and civilization, that Carnegie ideal, he continued, "but everything from a place to get into out of the rain to an investment counselor." It was from small revelations like this one that he found the kind of horror that Laughlin was looking for; indeed, he had already found it when he wrote the first of his "library sketches," which had been quickly published in the little magazine *Directions* in December 1937. In "Homage," a monstrous, thick-lipped, coarse-haired teenage girl chews her nails and shows her "appreciation" for the most iconic American poet in library property:

The girl turned to page 239 and wrote: If my name you wish to know look on page 285. *Then she turned to that page and wrote:* If my name you wish to know, look on page 304. *And on top of page 304 she printed carefully in large letters:* HA! HA! FOOLED YOU!!

She smiled, and a giggling sound came from her throat. She looked at what she had written, her smile widening, and then she closed the book quickly and held it out from her. On the back was stamped Leaves of Grass Walt Whitman.

As Kees learned the "murky atmosphere of L.C. and Dewey numbers" during 1938, he wrote a handful of stories set in a Nebraska everytown, Weston. This attempt to make another Winesburg, Ohio, however, came to only a handful of stories over the next few years. He produced a hundred pages of *But Not the City*, the autobiographical novel he had wanted to write in January, and then went "stale" on it.

He had a growing pile of poems and what he called the "library saga." This kind of sketch work, however, still did not quite measure up to the kind of writing he could send to *New Directions*. One of the stories, written outside of the ambitious groupings and novels, was an exception. It had the working title "Light before Darkness" and used what Harvey Swados would term the "diseased impressionism" of Erskine Caldwell and James T. Farrell in his introduction to *The American Writer and the Great Depression*, one of the anthologies in which the story would be reprinted. Here Kees stopped writing about the strangeness and estrangement he found in flat small-town lives and even flatter scenes. Instead, he used a darker and more textured urban setting for his fantasy of what kind of man could pimp his deaf sister.

Kees saw this story as a statement about the real American heartland (anticipating the trailer-park fiction of the 1980s and the pathos of Raymond Carver). He even submitted an early draft to Ray B. West, the editor of the *Rocky Mountain Review*, for an anthology of regional writing. West, however, reacted negatively to its shocking subject matter, his reaction actually reinforcing for Kees the rightness of his direction. On a warm summer night, when Ann was asleep and it was too late to use the typewriter, he wrote West back in longhand:

I first got the idea for the story several years ago. Originally, I planned to "prepare" the reader; that is, I "arranged" the materials of the story so that there was little "shock" to speak of. (The use of all these quotation marks is the effect of Kenneth Burke's criticism.) The story, when completed, missed fire considerably. Then I realized what I thought was wrong with it. The "point" of the story should depend upon the "shock effect." [...]

Perhaps I've been struggling around too much to make an obvious point more obvious, and consequently banal; but I think you get the point. Everyone I've showed this story to, however, is strongly affected: some are revulsed, some are very enthusiastic, a few told me "they couldn't get the situation out of their minds" (this may be crap and flattery; I don't know), and Gilbert Neiman had a slant on it that would take pages to go into. (His comments were philosophical and non-technical.)

That summer, Kees made his first appearance on KOA, the Denver radio station where he talked about new books and authors such as

Nathanael West, Robert Cantwell, Lee Smits, Katherine Anne Porter —and William Carlos Williams, whose work could not be found in the Denver Public Library until Kees came on the staff. He made it part of his routine to drop in on the library's order department to see what new books had arrived—and to convince the department's head that more collections of experimental writing and literary magazines should not be passed up "in the anxiety to stock eighty copies of *Gone With the Wind.*" Without intending to, he was a cultural missionary in a city where, as he wrote James Laughlin, there were "some good people who preferred Dr. Williams to Dr. Cronin, but they're all broke." [2]

In August, Kees faced more than just the expenses of books and little magazines and friends without money. Ann suffered appendicitis and needed an operation. At first she would not see a doctor and tried to kill the pain with a few stiff drinks, which took her husband by surprise because she was in pain. He had never considered her a "hospital-phobe." After Kees had convinced her they could afford the surgery, she relented.

After his stint as housekeeper and cook during Ann's convalescence, Kees returned to his routine at the library and continued with his courses in library science. He wrote as much as he could and, in the autumn, submitted book reviews, poems, and short stories, among them "Light before Darkness."

Laughlin, like Kees's Denver friends, could not get the story "about the girl with the broken arm" out of his mind and accepted it for publication in *New Directions 1939.* The good news lifted Kees, and he agreed to change the title at Laughlin's request.

∾

Spengler is such fun. —Weldon Kees

Kees made and unmade plans for his future in January 1939. He did not like being exposed to the public, working the main desk of the library, where seeing the patrons depressed him. He needed some kind of job and stability. Staying in school was one choice, and he applied for two fellowships at the University of Chicago, one offered by the American Library Association and the other by the university's prestigious library school. Yet, as he approached his twenty-fifth birthday in February, he could not "work himself up" to the thought of more graduate school, especially after he saw the photographs he had taken for his applications. They made him "look like the King of the White Slavers or one of the less savory characters in a novel by Wm. Faulkner"—and convinced him to grow a trim Clark Gable mustache.

When he was not accepted for either fellowship, Kees hardly felt disappointed. He did not need to go to lengths to build a library career that would support him as a writer, especially now that his job at the public library was his for as long as he wanted.

In March, he took his quarterly examinations at the library school. He complained about writing "odious" term papers on the subject of cataloging books, for it distracted him from reworking *Nothing Happens* at the behest of Donald Elder, the Doubleday editor who had been so receptive to *Slow Parade.* Kees had finished two hundred pages and wrote Gilbert Neiman in Mexico that the effort seemed worth it ("The anxiety is much greater than it is in writing short stories, but the pleasure is greater, too").

French films and a newly arrived bohemian couple provided the Keeses with diversions from their own lives in the winter and early spring of 1939. The Hiawatha Theatre had been converted into an art house that showed foreign-language, English, and good Hollywood pictures. Among the handful of Denver's cineastes, Kees was probably the most appreciative:

We have seen Carnet du Bal, *with many good actors, particularly a Frenchman who played an epileptic and who reminded me somehow of some of the sad middleclass men, gone seedy, who come to the library each day to take out works by the good grey Western writer, Zane Gray, Mr Oppenheim, and Mr Max Brand; we have seen* Grande Illusion, *which impressed me as much as any movie I've ever seen;* Mayerling; *and we are promised* Dr Mamlock, The Informer *(again),* Sous Les Toits de Paris, A Nous La Liberté, Le Roman d'un Tricheur, Chapeau de Paile d'Italie, *and the Alfred Hitchcock pictures, and perhaps some early Pabst, Fritz Lang, and the Russians. As you might know, they are not exactly packing them in, but Huffman [the theater owner] says he will keep it going as long as they dont go in the red. I imagine he makes enough from the Shirley Temples and Rudyard Kipling adaptations that are always with us to afford such philanthropy.*

The new friends were made in March, when Kees, while working at his desk in the library, looked up from peacefully worrying over some duty and saw a gaunt, amazing-looking man in a brown overcoat. The man removed his hat, revealing thin, red, uncombed hair. His eyes bulged as though he had just been told something astounding. He looked about forty. "I'm Walker Winslow," he said.

Kees greeted him affably. He knew the name. Winslow poems had appeared in *Prairie Schooner* and *Esquire*. Winslow then told Kees he had just arrived in Denver by way of Hawaii and Portland, Oregon, with his wife, Helen Anderson, whose name Kees also recognized, for she had published a lesbian novel with Doubleday Doran, *Pity for Women*. He could see that there was something odd about Winslow and used some library task as a pretext to end their brief conversation. Before he broke away, though, he made a date for lunch.

Kees's life was peopled with forgotten writers, artists, and musicians to a degree not consistent with the lives of his better-known contemporaries. They figured for him both because he saw them as self-destructive victims of a monolithic American money–success culture and because his contact with individuals such as Walker Winslow reinforced the *subtlety* with which he operated his own career—trying to be successful without the *Life* magazine fame.

Winslow was late for the lunch appointment he had made with Kees. During their conversation, he appeared distracted, which Kees would discover was his normal attitude. He learned that Winslow was on the Writers' Project and had been transferred to Denver with the aid of his wife's former father-in-law, the artist Boardman Robinson, who had illustrated *The War on the Eastern Front* by his friend John Reed and who taught at the Fine Arts Center in Colorado Springs. This connection to the American communist hero intrigued Kees, as did Winslow's news that his novel would be published by Doubleday and that he had a double spread of poems in *Esquire* for which he had been paid $275. He went on at length about his life as a publicity man for the Honolulu Chamber of Commerce and Hawaiian sugar companies, as well as suspicions about the loyalty of the Japanese minority and the conditions of the natives—all of which factored into his novel.

Despite everything, Winslow said he and his wife were now poor. So when they returned to the library, Kees borrowed money from a friend to lend to Winslow, who thanked him and walked up Broadway with his great brown coat flapping in the wind.

After turning down several invitations—fearing that accepting would mean lending them more money—Weldon and Ann saw both Winslows one evening after they had rented a nice apartment in the Keeses' neighborhood.

They were greeted at the door by Helen and the Winslows' dog, a Pekinese named Pooh, which the Keeses soon learned had once been a favorite of Sinclair Lewis and had been painted by the artist George Biddle (whom Kees would befriend ten years later in Provincetown).

Kees's first impression of Helen was that she was "arty." She wore her red hair in bangs, and her face and figure reminded him of Louise Rainer in the film *The Good Earth*. She was extremely friendly and naïve, a classic "open book." In her theatrical voice, she told the Keeses that she had been an actress and a dancer. She had had minor roles in a few motion pictures. She knew a great many people among the New York literati, including Sinclair Lewis and Thomas Wolfe. She had nervous breakdowns. And like her husband, she had a way of talking about herself without restraint, of going on and on intimately about her past. Yet, when Kees tried to recall what she—and her husband—had said, he discovered that there were alarmingly empty phases that the Winslows did not account for until they came up at some other time, such as how Walker had been committed by his first wife to an insane asylum in Hawaii for alcoholism. (Weldon and Ann had already noticed that the other couple would only serve small glasses of sherry.)

With no persuasion on the Keeses' part, the Winslows pulled out the Murphy bed and spread out their unpublished manuscripts. Winslow read one poem after another, which for Kees was like listening to two radio programs at the same time. Not one line was read without stuttering, fuzziness, repetition, mouthing, or slurring.

When it was time to leave, Helen gave Ann a copy of her novel about a young woman living in the Barbizon Hotel who discovers she is in love with another woman. The Keeses, in turn, asked the Winslows over for drinks the following Sunday evening.

That Sunday evening, Kees mixed whiskey sours. He realized too late that he should have served only one round, for Winslow drank prodigiously. When the whiskey ran out, Winslow noticed the vermouth and a bottle of muscatel on the mantel. Eventually he reached for one, worked on it for several minutes, and then switched to the other, going back and forth. Tactfully, before Winslow became too drunk to leave on his own power, Kees suggested they all go down to a Chinese restaurant he knew.

Before they left, Winslow stumbled into the bathroom and, while fumbling for the light, smashed his tumbler in the sink. Pieces of glass scattered all over the floor. He made no apology. Instead he only looked mildly surprised.

The next day, Helen called Kees at the library. She was worried about Walker. His drinking binge had already been already a day old when they had dinner on Sunday. It was now Monday, and he was still drinking heavily. She was hysterical and did not know what to do. Kees promised her that he would not serve drinks to her husband again.

On Tuesday night, while Kees worked late at the library, Helen came over to the apartment to see Ann. She had not eaten since they had Chinese noodles on Sunday, so Ann fed her and loaned her some money.

Several days later, the Winslows asked the Keeses to come over for dinner. When they arrived, though, there was no sign of a meal in progress. Walker was still drunk—and it was obvious that he had found a wealthier subset of Denver's bohemia from whom to sponge. On the couch sat Thomas Hornsby Ferril, the Yale poet of 1926 and a publicity man for Great Western Sugar whom Kees considered a "regionalist" talent and a bit of a fake.

Ferril, seeing that there was nothing to eat in the Winslows' home, asked them all to come over to his house for a dinner party that he and his date, the headmistress of the Kent School for Girls, were having. There, in front of some of the leading members of Denver society, Winslow went from being an entertaining drunk to punching the president of Great Western Sugar. After he was subdued, Helen agreed to have him committed to the Colorado Psychopathic Hospital.

A brief and uneventful few days followed before Winslow was released and caught writing bad checks. When he and Helen could not pay their rent, they moved to a cheaper apartment. Since the society people who had given them "a play" would not help, they leaned on the Keeses again.

In April, Winslow found Kees in the library again and said he had left Helen. He drunkenly confessed that she was his fourth wife and that he was sick of women. He could not write with Helen around, he said. He would only leave after Kees had promised to move him into a hotel, where he could work on his new novel, which his agent called the next *Of Mice and Men*.

Winslow soon left Denver. Weldon and Ann remained in touch with his wife, supporting her as much as they could until she moved in with her former in-laws in Colorado Springs.

Before she left, Helen gave Kees a watercolor portrait she had painted of him in profile. She had no other way of paying him back, she said, for all he and Ann had done.

In April, Kees became a contributing editor to *Rocky Mountain Review*. He was given a supply of letterhead with his name on it and encouraged to ask his correspondents in the East to submit and subscribe. Though he had wanted such an opportunity after moving to Denver, his place on the masthead lapsed into an honorific. Suffering from fatigue and eye trouble after four months of spreading himself thinly and intensely across the responsibilities of the library and his term papers — and with the Walker Winslow episodes finally over — he now rushed to complete a new draft of *Nothing Happens*.

With Donald Elder's referral, he now had a New York literary agent, Mavis McIntosh. She promised Kees that she could place his stories in good magazines and get Harcourt Brace and other publishers to consider his novel, and she seemed to him good for this. Her sympathies for experimental writing were evinced by her marriage to John Riordan, whose work had appeared in the *American Caravan* anthologies and the *Little Review*. The success of her firm, McIntosh and Otis, had come from representing John Steinbeck and other well-known authors.

Mavis received the manuscript in May — when she could also show editors that Kees was making a name for himself as a young poet in the latest issue of *Poetry*, that he had an ear for the wasted, fashionable anxiety and overflowing banality of the times and wanted nothing to do with them:

> news of the German Jews, the baseball scores,
> storetalk and whoretalk, talk of wars. I turn
> the pages of a thousand books to read
> the names of Buddha, Malthus, Walker Evans, Stendhal, Andre Gide,

[. . . . .]
Plurality is all. I sympathize, but cannot grieve
too long for those who wear their dialectics on their sleeves.
The pattern's one I sometimes rather like; there's really
nothing wrong
with it for some. But I should add: It doesn't wear for long,
before I push the elevator bell and quickly leave.
                  — "Statement with Rhymes"

The Keeses had planned for weeks to take a vacation after Weldon was done with his novel and term papers. They decided on staying in San Francisco for two weeks and then touring the cities of the Pacific Northwest. As much as a getaway, the vacation would be a scouting mission for a new place to live, since the Keeses wished to get away from Denver, which Kees routinely scorned in his letters as the "brokest place" and worse.

On June 15, they took a breathtaking train trip across the Continental Divide and arrived in Salt Lake City the following day. There they toured the Mormon Tabernacle and stood before a glass case that enclosed Brigham Young's gold inkwell, a privilege Kees recorded in the poem "Two Cities." They purchased liquor from a package store — the only way liquor was sold then in the Mormon city, a fact that also found its way into the poem — and had drinks with Ray West and George Snell, another editor of *Rocky Mountain Review*.

The Keeses arrived in San Francisco on June 19 and checked into the Hotel Biltmore. After getting settled, Weldon found the complimentary hotel stationary inside his room's writing desk and took the opportunity to answer a postcard from James Laughlin, who still needed a title for "Light before Darkness." "I'd like to have it appear as 'The Street,'" Kees suggested, "if you have no objections." He also pushed Laughlin to consider Gilbert Neiman's translations of Rimbaud — and the Lorca play *Blood Marriage* — instead of those of Lionel Abel, who Kees felt did not translate Rimbaud well at all: "He vaguely approximates the thought and tosses in so much of his own that it comes out as pretty pure Abel."

The letter made a perfect segue for getting together with Kenneth and Marie Rexroth later that day, for Kees would already be warm to discuss things that would interest the most prominent figure in San

Francisco's literary and bohemian communities. Since the Rexroths had no phone, seeing them meant taking the streetcar to Wisconsin Street and searching for the right address.

The two poets would seem to have had little in common but rivalry. Rexroth, Kees wrote in his *Prairie Schooner* review of *New Directions 1937*, was to him "often an interesting poet," but one "lost in a fog of private sources." For his part, Rexroth, the older of the two, saw Kees as a younger holdover from the Jazz Age and as too encumbered with the *Waste Land,* like other poets of his generation. Yet of all the poets who had this defect, as Rexroth saw it, Kees was the most authentic.

Authenticity, strangely enough, was the virtue that Kees saw in Rexroth after finding him at his Potrero Hill home. He was surprised to learn that Rexroth was not only a good poet but a fine abstract painter and composer of modern music. His reputation for knowing the California mountains also impressed him, along with the fact that Rexroth had spent months in them by himself, working as a guide and cook for the U.S. Forest Service. "He is a German who looks like the best type of Irishman," Kees wrote in a letter portrait of Rexroth, "volatile, anarchistic, and very witty." Rexroth struck Kees as a marvelous mimic as they indulged themselves in literary gossip and backbiting and Rexroth imitated his victims such as Lionel Abel, Ford Madox Ford—and Harry Roskolenko, who Rexroth said was better equipped to write bad poetry than anyone else of his time. Though he acted like a soapbox orator from Chicago's notorious Bughouse Square, part Wobbly, communist, anarchist, and a "hobohemian," a fusion he had coined himself, Kees admired Rexroth's commitment to "the cause."

The one thing both poets found they had most in common was their belief that the coming war was a capitalist's venture, their commitment to pacifism in the tradition of Randolph Bourne, the liberal essayist and social critic, the "little sparrowlike man" of Dos Passos's *U.S.A.* who opposed U.S. military involvement in World War I, asserting that "war is the health of the state." Like Bourne, Rexroth said, he too would take a public role in keeping America out of the war—a role Kees said, before he and Ann left, that he considered for himself as the news from Europe that summer became increasingly ominous.

Exploring San Francisco during the next two weeks made it hard to think for very long about war. Its beauty and amenities—the bridges, streets, "foreign settlements," ocean, and good food—cheered both Keeses, especially Weldon:

You are amazed at the compactness of San Francisco: that it is but a few minutes' walk from Telegraph Hill to the Italian district and from there to Chinatown, and that Fisherman's Wharf is no distance at all from Nob Hill. You grunt and puff climbing the hills, but you do not really mind because the weather is fine and cool; you are constantly being startled that even the most tawdry restaurants serve better food than it is possible to get in expensive places in other towns; you have a feeling that you are in a European city, and that the town gives the impression of having everything New York has (except the Theatre) without the monstrousness, the noise, and the hysteria of New York.

How profoundly Kees was moved by the city is apparent in the San Francisco section of "Two Cities." Here, revisiting what must be an observation deck near or on the Golden Gate Bridge itself, he at once promises to return to this place and admits that he cannot stay and enjoy the refuge it holds out. The degree of his disappointment, doubt, and even, perhaps, foreboding is transposed onto a presence in the poem that Ann would have recognized as herself when she typed the manuscript version months later:

Beside the bay, observers penetrate
Distance upon distance, cloud on cloud,
Crayons of smoke that sketch blue sky
With gray appeals. We pause, stretched side by side,
Safe for the moment from the nudging crowd,
Laughter for strangeness, and old myths crisping in the grate.

These trinkets, essences that we have saved,
Sheathed valuables that hold us here
Where gull-cry, wave-wash, dash of listening sea
Stir memory and love, are suddenly
Minute survivors, permanent and clear.
— We must go back. Your eyes are mirrors, strangely grave.

After Norris Getty left the Nebraska guidebook project, he worked first as a dispatcher-bookkeeper for the *Los Angeles–Albuquerque Express* and then as a reporter. In July, the newspaper transferred him to Denver, and he resumed his role as Kees's best friend and the willing reader and editor of his poems after taking an apartment next door to the

Keeses. He now saw the couple nearly every day, even after they moved a few blocks away in late September to 1060 Pennsylvania Avenue, in Denver's Capitol Hill district.

Poetry mattered even more for Kees after his vacation. During the long train trip through Portland, Yakima, Tacoma, Seattle, and Boise, he pored over the 1919 Knopf edition of Arthur Waley's translations of Chinese poetry that he had purchased in one of San Francisco's fine secondhand bookshops. He was especially taken by the candid reflection of Po Chü-i, the Sung Dynasty poet, and the fate of his translator, who had disappeared. Both figure in his "Homage to Arthur Waley," with its final line taken from "Arriving at Hsün-Yang":

Seattle weather: it has rained for weeks in this town,
The dampness breeding moths and a gray summer.
I sit in the smoky room reading your book again,
My eyes raw, hearing the trains steaming below me
In the wet yard, and I wonder if you are still alive.
Turning the worn pages, reading once more:
"By misty waters and rainy sands, while the yellow dusk thickens."

War also mattered for Kees in the weeks after his vacation. The hostilities in Poland were almost a month old when he and Ann started living in their new apartment on the third floor of a former Victorian mansion. The talk in Denver was already about "preparedness" and drafting young men—and Kees responded by making copies of Kenneth Rexroth's "Chain Letter for Peace" that were intended for other writers, including the most influential ones. Each copy also included a personal note that underscored his fear of a coming military dictatorship: "We can keep out of another senseless war only if we all raise everlasting hell. If we don't—I'll see you in a concentration camp."

Kees also joined the League for Cultural Freedom and Socialism along with William Carlos Williams, Joseph Cornell, Louise Bogan, Kay Boyle, James T. Farrell, Delmore Schwartz, Clement Greenberg, and Harold Rosenberg; this was the antiwar group that Dwight Macdonald had formed to counter Malcolm Cowley and others on the left who did not come out against Stalin's pact with Hitler. Macdonald had announced his organization in *Partisan Review*, where he was an editor, articulating the view, which Kees shared, that the same thing would happen to "our culture" as with the entry of America into World War I. There would be a "sharp change in literary development" again, and a generation of writers would commit spiritual suicide by supporting a president who had misled them. "Regimentation due to war psychology destroyed the movement of social criticism," Macdonald wrote, and the "liberal movement in economics and politics came to an abrupt end."

The war, and Getty's presence in Denver, saw more originality and confidence in the new poems that Kees produced with some regularity. In "For My Daughter," he departed from the fatherly sentiment Yeats expressed in his "Prayer for My Daughter" and reduced the hope for a better world vis-à-vis the symbol of the girl child. As he had done with the deaf young woman in his New Directions short story, so Kees now created a disturbing anima with his "daughter." In early January 1940, John Crowe Ransom, the New Critic and editor of the recently founded *Kenyon Review*, was moved enough to accept "For My Daughter" and several other Kees poems for his spring 1940 issue.

ॐ

Through much of 1940, poetry would be a brilliant sideshow for Kees. He still believed he would establish his reputation as a novelist who had made his debut as both a poet and storyteller. This was true even as he gathered the manuscript titled *Thirty Poems* in June for New Directions' forthcoming pamphlet series, the "Poet of the Month," an ambitious effort that flowed from his inclusion in *New Poems 1940*, the anthology edited by Oscar Williams (who called him a leading poet and included the horrible photograph taken for his library fellowship application). Still, in January of the new year, he expressed less enthusiasm for novel writing in a letter to James Laughlin and more for a new kind of short story: "Am revising my novel and cutting right and left. Have six or seven stories almost completed, but have put them aside until I have the novel in some kind of shape. I don't suppose anyone will want it, but enjoy writing it. [...] The story I'm sending for your consideration for next year's anthology is one of the best I've done, I think, and I hope you agree. I seem to be getting away from the shackles of reporting and naturalism, which I don't think should be condemned per se; but they limit one."

"The Evening of the Fourth of July" was Kees's reaction to the public demonstrations of patriotism and flag-waving that took place after September 1, 1939, which seemed all the more irrational since the country had not been attacked and was not at war. The method he arrived at shows the influence of European surrealism and the strangeness of Nathanael West in *Miss Lonelyhearts*. Kees also found it easier to write from experience with his break from naturalism, making his interrupted life of the mind part of the absurd and banal tableau of an America war-ravaged by its own Independence Day:

There were explosions everywhere. McGoin decided that it was impossible for him to concentrate any longer on the Bhagavadgita, which he had been trying to read. Putting the book down, he dressed and left his room. On the porch he unrolled the newspaper to see what was happening in the world. Deaths and injuries from the holiday celebrations had exceeded the wildest prophecies, he noticed. [...]

Explosion after explosion followed. One looked for buildings to topple over, to see passersby clutch at their hearts and fall over into the street. The effects of the day's celebration were wherever one looked: the street, caught in the light of the burned-out sunset, resembled some thoroughfare in Hell. It was littered with red fragments of firecrackers, strips of paper flags; bunting; broken cardboard horns, blown with such zeal throughout the morning that they were useless by the middle of the afternoon; paper hats of red, white and blue; crumpled cellophane; empty pop and beer bottles; and a ripped picture of George Washington, on which someone had drawn a crude Vandyke and horn-rimmed glasses. Across the street, a shaggy and bloated dog was chewing with tired persistence on what appeared to be a human arm.

Laughlin accepted "The Evening of the Fourth of July" for *New Directions 1940*, calling it "an attack on the daymare of 1940 life," and for Kees the fallout from this success took a number of forms, the first of which was a new sense of self-esteem. His deeper involvement with the publisher of avant-garde writing suppressed some of the dark thoughts that he had about missing out on the glory years of modernism. This shows in the way he responded to the April 1 issue of the *New Republic*, in which an "obituary notice" by the English writer and painter Wyndham Lewis announced "the death of abstract art." Lewis, who had been Pound's collaborator in the founding of the short-lived vorticist movement just before World War I, wrote his April Fool's Day necrology as a joke—one certainly played on the generation born too late to have created during the years "1913 to 1923," the "utmost span" of modern art. And Kees, being a member of that generation, played along, sending a letter to the editors that was representative of the mailbag contretemps that ensued. He called Lewis an undertaker for more men and movements than could be counted. Ironically, a good many of them, "with the obstinacy that must annoy him like a stray Sitwell, an eight-day clock or a copy of *transition*," were refusing to stay buried and were "giving signs of unmistakable health." As proof, he noted that Hemingway and Joyce were "still going concerns."

"With hell breaking loose," Kees wrote James Laughlin after the invasion of the Low Countries, the fall of France in May, and Dunkirk, "it's hard to think or work, but I manage to do it and I'm going to continue. The calamity-howling is terrific here."

He also began to appreciate where his pacifism might lead. "Some guys wrote Peace on the sidewalks here," Gilbert Neiman wrote from Los Angeles, "and they arrest them overnight for disturbing the peace. [...] Peace is a dangerous word." In Denver, Kees observed more of the patriotic displays he had satirized in "The Evening of the Fourth of July," including those of the retailers of alcohol, who had forgiven the country for Prohibition:

People here have quieted down considerably since the fall of France; whether it indicates a fatalistic state of mind or the quiet before the storm I don't know and don't much like to think about. However a thriving business is being done in God Bless America signs, God Bless America buttons (for gentleman's lapel), God Bless America recordings (by Kate Smith) and God Bless America banners (liquor stores are biggest purchasers of these, strangely). There is also a song out (which you surely have heard) called I AM AN AMERICAN *(and proud of my liber-tee). The Gallup poll says a substantial majority of citizens favor the Burke-Wadsworth conscription bill, but no one I've talked to wants it except for a few furious childless old ladies and some die-hard New Dealers who contend that the administration must be supported in everything they do. Senator Claude Pepper seems to want an American fascism very badly. [...] Well, I guess I'll get my* GOD BLESS AMERICA *banner out and parade around a few blocks while I hum on my old kazoo.*

Kees was appalled at the increasing number of writers coming out in support of America's involvement in the war, the poet and playwright Archibald MacLeish being the most outspoken in the press and on radio. It was against his own kind that Kees wrote the poem "June, 1940," an immediate and literary protest that *Partisan Review* published in its September–October issue. Even though the committed pacifists on the left were finding their uncompromising position increasingly academic as Hitler took more of Europe, Kees performed for them a necessary, even bardic role:

> *It is summer, and treachery blurs with the sounds of midnight,*
> *The lights blink off at the closing of a door,*
> *And I am alone in a worn-out town in wartime,*
> *Thinking of those who were trapped by hysteria once before.*
>
> *Flaubert and Henry James and Owen,*
> *Bourne with his crooked back, Rilke and Lawrence, Joyce—*
> *Gun-shy, annoyers, sick of the kill, the watchers,*
> *Suffered the same attack till it broke them or left its scars.*
> *[. . . . .]*
> *An idiot wind is blowing; the conscience dies.*

As much as the national mood swing toward war sickened him, Kees saw his work published and enjoyed celebrating his success with Ann. He sent out batches of new poems and short stories throughout the spring, including his first submission to the *New Yorker,* which resulted in a run of correspondence with Cap Pearce about one of the poems; this fed his ego, for he thought the magazine's editors only wrote letters to writers "living East of Pennsylvania Station"—not librarians in Denver. He also planned an "academic-bohemian" novel and drafted several chapters before going on a New York City vacation in the late summer.

Kees's hangover on the morning of September 3 was from drinking all night with Robert Lowry, the editor of Little Man Press, who had published two of his short stories in *The State of the Nation,* one of the unusual and original illustrated chapbooks that Lowry printed in the basement of his parents' home. Lowry, who was younger, with lots of unmanageable hair, and both exuberant and worried about Little Man's survival, had made for an entertaining escort during the Keeses' layover in Cincinnati, where they visited his Hutton Street home, read galleys, signed a special edition, and later toured the city, sampling its famous Graeter's ice cream before continuing on to New York by train.

Ann hardly contained herself from mentioning her husband's condition in the postcard she sent from the Hotel Cincinnatian. She could hold her liquor better than he could and suffer the less for it—and Norris Getty would find Weldon funny, too, for he looked quite undignified as James Laughlin's discovery from exotic Denver on his way to attend the 1940 English Institute Conference at Columbia University, an annual gathering of English professors and writers.

Ann was making her first trip to New York. Kees, who had visited the city with his father in 1931, wanted to meet people he had only known through letters or from their work in books and little magazines. He especially wanted to meet them without feeling he needed to apologize for living in Denver, something he had experienced after meeting Laughlin's plane in February, when the editor came to Colorado to ski.

In New York, the Keeses stayed at the Hotel Albert, a fine old establishment at the corner of University Place and Tenth Street, where Hart Crane had once lived in a furnished room between 1919 and 1920. From this location, they could easily walk to the secondhand bookstores on Fourth Avenue, to the subway station underneath Union Square, and to Greenwich Village.

Their first full day was spent at the 1939 World's Fair. The attractions were still open, and they dined in the Swedish pavilion, where a bird soiled Weldon's jacket. They also saw the Ford ballet and the "Gay" New Orleans exhibits and were taken on a drive around the financial district at night after it had been raining, getting out at Battery Park to see the Statue of Liberty.

During the next few days, they visited the Frick, the Metropolitan, and the Museum of Modern Art. At the Guggenheim Gallery of Non-Objective Art, they saw the Rudolf Baur show, which Kees described as "hundreds of horrible daubs." Only a few Légers, Grises, and Picassos—and the building, a former automobile showroom (and not yet the Frank Lloyd Wright–designed museum of 1959), which struck Kees as a "wonderful place physically"—made up for the other art.

They ate at Luchow's and at Swiss, Italian, French, and other assorted restaurants. They heard a "swell girl" singing risqué songs at a place called Number One on Fifth Avenue and took in several Broadway plays and French movies. For a romantic moment, they went up to the sixty-fifth floor at Rockefeller City and had a drink at dusk, looking far down Manhattan Island.

Philip Rahv and the other editors of *Partisan Review* took the Keeses to Jack Delaney's bar on Sheridan Square, where the electric horse on the marquee jumped over a neon fence—and might impress this couple from the West. Kees mixed perfectly with his new friends, while Ann observed the New Yorkers fidget after their party had squeezed around the table. The *Partisan Review* "boys" played with their cigarette holders. Dwight Macdonald played with his beard. Don Elder, the editor who had admired Kees's novels, did little to hide his hands, which shook as if he badly needed a drink. James Laughlin stared into space and rubbed his head against the side of the booth "like a friendly dog." He had arrived in a long red-upholstered coupe that, to Ann, was in keeping with his being "a very long man." She noticed he had none of the vices of the others. He neither drank nor smoked and seemed to Ann like someone always training for a ski championship. She also found it amusing that, between rounds of drinks, Laughlin often got up to make telephone calls. Ann pictured him trying to reach someone tall, blond, and dumb at the other end of the line. "This is called Hot Pants," she wrote Getty back at the Hotel Albert; in light of the sign on the men's room door, which read "Colts—Geldings—Studs," she was certain that Laughlin was "definitely stud."

Kees also had fun observing the New Yorkers and identifying their many literary factions. There was an "International Homosexual Set" that consisted of Charles Henri Ford, Nicolas Calas, Paul Tchelichev, and Parker Tyler—whom the Keeses met costumed for a surrealist ball and, as Kees noted, "getting a little pot-bellied but still very beautiful in his way." (Tyler, before he departed, asked, "Do you know anything about the surrealist movement, Mr. Kees?" Kees responded, "I've heard a little about it.") This group, however, stood apart and was considerably the lesser compared to Auden and his friends. The "*Partisan Review* bunch" included the editors Rahv, Phillips, and Macdonald, Lionel Trilling, and various contributors. The Brooklyn clique consisted of Willard Maas, Harry Roskolenko, Kenneth Patchen, and so on. There was a small Stalinist clique—and Horace Gregory off by himself, doing what he could to avoid getting entangled with any of the others.

No one, Kees noticed, had anything good to say about anyone else. "You bring up someone's name," he wrote in a letter to a Denver friend, "and someone will say, 'Him? I never see that bastard anymore.' [...] People talked about Schwartz a good deal, most of them ran him down. *Everyone* ran down Kenneth Patchen."

There were people, mostly from the anti-Stalinist left, whom Kees considered the fine company that he really missed living in Denver. Often these couples—among them Dwight and Nancy Macdonald; Horace Gregory and his wife, Marya Zaturnenska; and Lionel and Diana Trilling—invited him and Ann to small, intimate cocktail parties that seemed half opportune and half given in their honor. At the Trillings' Riverside Drive apartment, Kees found that he liked Lionel very much:

His talk is just about as good as his writing, only, of course, more casual and marked by a slightly different kind of wit than you find in his criticism. I remember that we talked about the way Mann had been translated; Mrs. Trilling got out two versions of DISORDER AND EARLY SORROW *and we read the first page of each, an exhibition calculated to display the sad shortcomings of Mrs. Lowe-Porter. And we talked about the writers who attracted nuts: Bob Ingersoll, Kant, Mary Baker Eddy, Marx, Edgar Saltus, etc. [...] His wife is nice, too; and she has a mind of her own; a good argument. I made one bad break when I said something a bit snide about Tess Slesinger; it turned out she's a good friend of the Trillings. I looked penitent and the remark was quickly forgotten, I hope.[3]*

At the Macdonalds', Kees met James T. Farrell in the company of the art critic Clement Greenberg and B. H. Haggin, the music critic at the *Nation*. Farrell was "a dumpy, vivacious Irishman with thick-lens glasses," who talked more about the bandaged carbuncle on his neck, in the manner of his Studs Lonigan trilogy, than he did about the things Kees expected would concern such a controversial writer. ("Maybe he'll write a long novel about carbuncles," Kees reflected later. "He could. Had Dwight ever had a carbuncle? Had Rahv? Had I? They were bad things, carbuncles.") At the time they met, Farrell was writing a broadside against Lewis Mumford and his theory of the organic community, which relied on "a regional culture, beautiful cities, and a happy humanity" serving, as Farrell called it, a capitalist power state. He would have found in Kees a younger writer who shared the same fear of such a society divorced from reality—and may have inspired Kees to portray the author of *Faith for Living* as a dwarf uttering a bizarre anodyne in the poem "A Cornucopia for Daily Use."

During the conference at Columbia, there were gatherings at the cafeteria at Broadway and 115th. In a haze of pipe and cigarette smoke, teachers, poets, editors, critics, and students talked about books, Eliot, Auden, the war in Europe, and the divided American front. In these conversations, the librarian from Denver used his gift for delivering a sardonic remark with a kind of subtle disdain that was not easily surpassed and was easily resented by the less gifted. Those who appreciated his kind of dark wit got to know him better, such as Cleanth Brooks, one of the Fugitives at Vanderbilt in the 1920s and the leading exponent of New Criticism. The year before, Brooks had published *Poetry and the Tradition,* and like his friend and fellow New Critic poet Allen Tate, he legitimized younger modernists like Kees as a living continuation of a tradition in poetry going back to Donne.

Tate, too, was present in the cafeteria, and he already had a high opinion of Kees. As one of the editors of *Kenyon Review,* he had recommended publishing "For My Daughter" and the other poems that Kees had submitted the year before. Fifteen years older, Tate fell between Kees's generation and the generation of Eliot and Pound. Having lived in Greenwich Village during the early 1920s and having lived the émigré's life in Paris and London from 1928 to 1930, he had enjoyed a literary life that Kees envied. With his large, protruding forehead and slight build, Tate impressed Kees as the embodiment of a man of letters. His thin mustache was as much a legend as his formidable reputation for the way it arched on one side whenever he found the work of another poet bad.

Kees considered Tate's "Ode to the Confederate Dead" one of his favorite poems. He liked "Alice," "Idiot," and "Emblems" as well. Here in a New York cafeteria, the poet was now drinking copiously alongside Tate and hearing, perhaps, about Tom and Viv as if they were a few blocks away, about the "roaring boy," Hart Crane, as if it were still 1930.

The Keeses stayed in New York for another ten days, taking in more of its cultural attractions, attending lectures at Columbia—including an "appalling" talk given by Auden, dressed in a powder-blue tie and a dark green suit—and going to the movie palaces of Forty-second Street. They left the city on September 24 for New Haven and spent a day visiting newly made friends at Yale. Then they caught a train back west via Pittsburgh and Chicago.

"I could live in it, but I don't think I could write in it," Kees said after he left New York, thinking such a life would be one cocktail party of smart talk after another—but then he loved showing off his wit and gift for irony, what his personal saint Randolph Bourne called "the photography of the soul." Ann, however, took a darker view. "This is the pace that kills," she wrote after experiencing New York intellectual life. "I wouldn't live in N.Y. if I had the gross income from Rockefeller Center. There's an undercurrent of gossip that has small towns beaten every which way."

When Kees returned to work at the end of September, he had a new title and position at the Denver Public Library. Malcolm Wyer had chosen him to be the acting director of the Rocky Mountain Bibliographic Center for Research. It was an administrative position, which meant he would no longer have to serve the public from behind the Readers' Advisor desk and work at other similar posts that he found less "serene." It also meant that he would get a substantial raise—and "considerable grief," he told himself, thinking it might now be harder to write on the job.

The center had been started several years before with Andrew Carnegie money to oversee a union catalog of library holdings in the Rocky Mountain region. With a large collection of bibliographies, trade catalogs, expensive library tools, and the like, the staff of the center could carry on reference work that small, financially strapped regional libraries were not able to do.

In a memorandum written by the former director, Kees learned of his new duties and the character of the two people who would work under him. It was imperative, Kees read, to keep Eulalia Chapman, his immediate subordinate. She had worked at the center from the beginning. Kees would be dependent on her in getting acquainted with his duties—and she would be dependent on him to keep her WPA salary from being taken away. She was also afraid of having to work in some rural Colorado library, in a town where she could not find a good school for her daughter.

Despite the inequitable terms of the male-dominated library administration, an arrangement and rapport developed between Kees and his assistant. He did not hide that he really wanted to write and did not dispute that Eulalia was really in charge. In this bargain, she could run the center the way she wanted and loyally cover for him when he stole away to work on his poems, novel, and correspondence. And when the time came, it would be impossible for Wyer to refuse Kees when he recommended Eulalia as his successor.

"Bibliographical centers and union catalogs are interesting, but not too interesting," Kees wrote three months into his new assignment. Yet he managed to learn an enthusiasm for the center's mission. The project—or "experiment," as Kees's predecessor told him to call it— was the "only bibliographical center" in the country. For the very reason of its newness and significance, much of his time would be spent begging for money for his two-person staff, writing for grants from the Carnegie foundation, and speaking at various libraries and colleges. He also had to help the two women who worked with him do the dry, monotonous, detail-oriented work of the compilation process. It required duplicating the contents of the member libraries' card catalogs drawer by drawer, with manual typewriters and a Dexigraph machine, a forerunner of the photocopier.

Kees grasped some of the importance of what he was doing. For him, however, the reward in processing so many thousands of books was the found surrealism of strange titles. Allusions to obscure works of erudition abound in his poems and fiction, some real, some fused together in the blur of card after card: *Simple Conjuring Tricks Anyone Can Do* by Wlademirus Goldwag.

"Believe you're going to find Denver a little changed when you come back," Norris Getty had warned Kees, "a matter of something in the air, getting a little more intense day by day, so gradually you could almost fail to notice it. The churches are beginning to hold meetings on the consequences of a German victory. The newspapers carry a few more pictures every day of smiling stalwart young soldiers taking off gaily for camp."

The new novel, unlike the poems and stories Kees had written since 1939, had nothing to do with the current situation. It was set in the recent past. The war, however, made that seem like another time and place and redoubled the atmosphere of isolation and insulation that he had so far achieved for his Midwestern college town, an atmosphere he had long endured.

The working title was now *Spring Quarter*, and he spent the rest of the autumn writing new chapters and revising the early ones. His dusty, depressing arrival by train into Denver and his new job helped him visualize his English instructor hero, William Clay, taking up his new post in the middle of the country after a fine education back East. The academics he had encountered at Columbia and the New York bohemian–intellectual parties he had attended would also make good material for finishing the book, especially when reduced to the absurd by being transplanted to his gritty fusion of Denver and Lincoln. He would use the misadventure of the photographer Walker Evans's attempt to find a Coke for his painter girlfriend because she could not drink the rum concoction that Dwight Macdonald ladled out. Philip Rahv's infatuation with the girlfriend would look hilarious grafted onto William Clay—already much fashioned after the bad dream Kees imagined his life would be had he become a young college professor. Thinking of Gilbert Neiman's letters, in which Neiman described his growing dependence as a member of Hazel Guggenheim's traveling entourage and the legendary Mabel Dodge Luhan, he had a model for the bizarre, drum-playing patroness character, Mrs. Diego Shanahan. He borrowed liberally from the lives of the even more strange, colorful, and thwarted types he had found in the miniature bohemias of Lincoln and Denver.

∾

In early December, Mari Sandoz finished reading the manuscript of Kees's retitled autobiographical artist-coming-of-age novel, *Passage*. Kees wanted her reaction. Mavis McIntosh could not get a publisher interested, and he was ready to put it aside. "It has," Sandoz wrote, "the sensitivities and the lucid prose of your short stories, which you know I have always liked. There seems only one way of accounting for its meandering among publishers—its location in a pre-war world."

Kees had already apprehended the war profiteering on the part of New York publishers and knew that *Spring Quarter* had the same problem of timing and context. But he could point to the debut of Carson McCullers's 1940 bestseller, *The Heart Is a Lonely Hunter*—and to a book more in keeping with the madcap of his own work, *The Day of the Locust* by Nathanael West (who died later that month in what Kees considered a peculiarly American form of divine retribution for its young and gifted artists, a car accident). Kees had another Holly-wood dimension, too, in the screwball-comedy style of his writing. He also had another recent bestseller in mind: *Tobacco Road*. In place of Erskine Caldwell's social realism, Kees used some of the social surreal-ism that gave his Fourth of July story much of its interest. In place of the rural South, he wanted to introduce a new American-type land-scape, the decadent Midwest, which was present in *Spring Quarter*'s very first paragraph, where "sun-baked and desolate farmland gave way to a village, a general store with tin signs advertising flour, to-bacco and female remedies, a bank with boarded-up windows, an un-painted church. Two dogs were fighting in the middle of the main street. The train whistle shrieked; once again he viewed the same flat land. William Clay took out his watch, a present from his uncle on his graduation from college."

In early February, Paul Hoffman solicited the novel, and Kees asked for and received a standard contract, which promised him an advance and the assurance of publication based on the acceptance of the final manuscript. Though such an arrangement was largely symbolic, he felt he had received the respect due him and his long-awaited break.

Mavis McIntosh handled the paperwork and the delivery of the first nine chapters of *Spring Quarter*. According to the reader's report that Hoffman circulated among his colleagues at Knopf, the first part of the book strongly suggested that the novel would make the firm's list and that Kees was sticking to a known formula: "This is a novel of life in a western college town, more specifically of one William Clay's. He is an English instructor of 25 who has just arrived on the scene, having only the previous spring taken his M.A. back home somewhere in the mid-West. Filled to the brim with the usual idealism about and enthu-siasm for his exalted calling, his is the old story of pretty immediate disillusionment and discouragement."

Harold Strauss was the next reader, the same man who had turned down *Slow Parade*. He had reservations about Kees's blend of slap-stick and social commentary but believed that the problems would disappear and would yield, without too much risk for Knopf, an enter-taining and publishable book:

The story had sincerity and bite, and moves right along. It is not by any means an important book, and at times I found the irony (which is Kees' chief implement) a bit heavy-handed. Nevertheless, the central charac-

ter, with his fatuous idealism and his jarring disillusionment, is very real, and Kees has an excellent eye for odd details—the offensive Peke, for instance, who sheds yellow mange powder on the boarding-house carpets, and the mannerisms of a gent who is the author of "The Boys Book of Camera Craft" and thirteen similar opera. For the fact is that the oppressive life of the college town drives the inhabitants to cherish their idiosyncrasies (to put it mildly). If you live long enough in this kind of atmosphere, you begin to take the screwballs for granted. When Kees does that, he is amusing. But sometimes he "protests too much." He becomes dogmatic about things that should be left to the reader's intuitive grasp. This is what I mean by "heavy-handedness." [...] But the book looks as if it will turn out to be a tart, amusing tale given just a tinge of seriousness by its irony.

The spring of 1941 was a time of hard work and well-earned praise for Kees. Paul Hoffman wrote Mari Sandoz at the end of March to tell her that she "was a good girl" for putting him on to Kees. He had recently discovered Kees's poetry, which seemed to be in all the important little magazines and anthologies, and proposed that Knopf might publish a collection. As Kees understood it, the novel and the book of poems were almost like an unspoken package deal, and he poured himself into both endeavors with the success of each linked to the other.

For fresh ambiance and material for the novel—and as a way to reward himself for a week of work—Kees often spent weekends at the Colorado Springs Fine Arts Center, where he and Ann took in the many lectures and readings—and the inevitable drinking parties hosted by the young artists who studied with Boardman Robinson, among them David Kennedy, the brother of M. F. K. Fisher and the brother-in-law of Alfred Young Fisher, the Joyce scholar.

It was in the center's stunning flexwood and aluminum art deco theater that they heard Thomas Mann speak on "The Making of *The Magic Mountain*," a talk that bored Kees so much he started literally to see through the German author as he studied the thinness of Mann's dinner jacket and the outlines of his suspender buttons and the spikes in the buckle on the strap of his vest. More disappointing was the way Mann "worked-in" his allusions to Wagner, Goethe, and Nietzsche and marketed his neohumanism and himself, autographing copies of *This Peace* and $1.89 editions of *The Magic Mountain*.

At a party afterward, in a stable that a young artist and his wife had converted into a home and studio, Kees watched several students get quite drunk and play calypso records. He also listened carefully as they traded different strategies for avoiding military service, something Kees knew he would need someday, such as getting classified 3D by admitting you were a bed wetter. He left that idea at the party but took back with him some of its location and energy for chapter 12 of what he would soon retitle *Fall Quarter:* "Alone, he sat gingerly on a bench and inspected the room, a barn-like affair hung with Chester Thompson's paintings. Representing the work of ten years, each painting documented the momentary enthusiasms by which the painter had at one time or another been seized. There were imitations of the Flemish school, primitive art, a portrait in the manner of some particularly unskilled R.A., a farm scene dominated by a bony and undernourished cow, three 'Picassos'—one of them from the Blue Period, one *collage,* one example of Cubism—and what appeared to be an attempt to beat Wassily Kandinsky at his own game."

The run of poems that came after his New York visit resulted in many new appearances as he sent out work throughout the winter and spring. As much as he wanted to publish in the *New Yorker,* Kees searched out new and promising avant-garde magazines that advertised in *Partisan Review* and the New Directions anthologies.

One of these was *Furioso,* edited by a student at Yale, James Jesus Angleton, the future mole hunter at the CIA. Another was *Diogenes,* edited by students at the University of Wisconsin and printed by Robert Lowry. Here Kees published "A Cornucopia for Daily Use" and drew the endorsement of Malcolm Cowley in his essay "What Poets Are Saying," in the May 3 issue of the *Saturday Review of Literature.* "Kees ought to be published more widely," Cowley wrote, because Kees's work represented a revival of poetry that came from "the critical state of this country and the world." There was not just a sense of doom in reading Kees, but rather a "sense of incongruity" that set him apart from other younger poets.

Kees also received what he called a "fan letter" from Cowley. He learned, too, continuing his Hollywood riff of self-consciousness, that Cowley was acting like his "press agent," making it known that Kees was the poet to watch.

Almost perfectly timed with the praise for his poetry that spring was the recognition his fiction earned. In January 1941, Edward J. O'Brien asked permission to reprint "The Life of the Mind," a haunting satire about the fall of a college professor who gives himself over to latent homosexuality and antisemitism. (This was a poignant honor, coming only weeks before O'Brien died and his editorship passed to Martha Foley, who routinely rejected Kees when he sent work to her magazine, *Story*.) In June Kees learned of another honor that had been bestowed on him: the dedication in *Best Short Stories of 1941*. O'Brien had made it his custom to dedicate his anthologies to the young fiction writers who showed the most promise. Irwin Shaw had been chosen for this honor the year before, as had Richard Wright in 1939. In previous years, O'Brien had dedicated anthologies to Willa Cather, Ernest Hemingway, F. Scott Fitzgerald, Thomas Wolfe, James T. Farrell, and Ring Lardner—and it was rare for a writer not to succeed or be heard from again after O'Brien's notice.

News of the dedication got back to Lincoln and Beatrice, and the newspapers there printed glowing profiles of the favorite son, even though the reporters felt compelled to mention that he had yet to appear in the "name magazines." The *Nebraska State Journal* took this line despite the praise of his mentor:

So far, the young writer has had more renown than receipts. He has been accepted generally by the "little magazines," as against the conservative, slick, quality magazines. That may be partly Kees's fault. His talent is sound, Mr. Wimberly reiterates, dependable, real, and, moreover, brilliant.

But he is an intellectual who refuses to compromise with art as he understands it. He'll stick like a burr to his ideals of writing and consider their cold perfections more satisfying than a certified check. Kees has strong convictions, which probably will get in the way of sales. He's young too.

Norris Getty took Kees's photograph as he sat on the porch steps of 1060 Pennsylvania Avenue reading the *Denver Post*. It was June 22, and he held the Sunday-morning edition pulled open to the back pages, nonchalantly letting the banner headline caption the image with the cataclysmic news: "Hitler Declares War on Russia." Getty had his picture taken this way, too, and, like Kees sent it to college friends as a kind of ironic comment on an America still at peace, expressed with the same Keesian incongruity that Malcolm Cowley saw in his poems. (Also visible in the photograph is a smaller headline reporting the suicide of a Colorado state representative in a downtown hotel.)

The photograph was also made because Kees would not see his friend for some time. "Norris is going into the army," he wrote Dale Smith. "I suppose he'll write you before long. He's going to a Negro fort in Arizona, which has caused some speculation and merriment. We will miss him a great deal. I've been classified in 3A."

Kees felt fortunate that the selective service still exempted certain categories of married civilian men from military service. However, his 3A status would be short-lived, a classification for men with dependents but not engaged in activities essential to the war effort—suggesting that he had not been quite honest with the local draft board about Ann's job and their lack of children.

Kees had other reasons to think that war would come soon as he saw public opinion being swayed, as he saw more and more of his contemporaries coming out for entry into the war. "Come! Come!" he wrote in one of his droll but worried letters from the summer of 1941, imagining what the next radio round table of writers and intellectuals would be like. "The New Republic editors will be on hand with their ever-popular act: 'How to Be a Man of Good Will and an Imperialist Too.'" The war debate even filtered into *Fall Quarter*, which suggests the way he responded to such arguments:

"I say, why should we become involved?" Herendeen persisted.
"Because something will be in jeopardy."
"What?"
"I don't know. Something."
Dorothy was still talking to the pianist.
"The American people will never stand for it," said Herendeen.
"Perhaps not," Devlin said. "Right now I need a drink."

Before Getty left, Kees had expanded the manuscript of thirty poems originally submitted to New Directions. He called it *The Last Man*, after a literary conceit of the Romantic era used in works by Thomas Campbell, Lord Byron, and Mary Shelley. Though he wanted his readers to be reminded of Nietzsche's "last man," a concept popular among intellectual anti–New Dealers such as Ayn Rand, the key allusion was to the obscure and neglected poet-suicide Thomas Lovell Beddoes and his fragmentary verse play of the same title. Kees had been reading Beddoes's poetry since his student days and wanted his new manuscript of poems linked not only to a poet who had influenced him but to another New Directions project that he started editing that summer, a selection of Beddoes's poems taken from *Death's Jest Book* and other works in the four-volume Edmund Gosse edition of 1849. James Laughlin had inspired this endeavor after he initiated the policy of devoting one of the "Poet of the Month" chapbooks to "a great poet of the past" whose work had otherwise "frightened away" readers because of the "imposing bulk of collected volumes."

Laughlin had also raised Kees's hopes that his own "Poet of the Month" title would soon appear, having announced it in *New Directions 1940*. Yet despite Kees's tactful inquiries, which became almost plaintive ("I hope that there might be a chance for me"), the publisher let the project lapse in 1941, and Kees found himself pushing the Beddoes book in its place and deciding between the Borzoi imprint for his first book of poems — and the new Colt Press, founded by the San Francisco printer Jane Grabhorn and William Matson Roth, then a student at Yale and the heir of the Matson Lines shipping family, whom Kees had met the year before at a party in New Haven.

Horace Gregory had recommended their private press as an alternative to waiting for Knopf or another trade house to perform what was an act of charity for them: publishing a book of contemporary poetry. So had Mavis McIntosh, who persuaded Kees with "the most convincing reasons in the world" not to send *The Last Man* to Knopf, given the publisher's preference for poetry that was mystical (Kahlil Gibran) and abstract (Wallace Stevens).

As *The Last Man* took shape in July, finishing *Fall Quarter* became a burden as Kees lost interest. Without Ann's encouragement (and that of Gilbert Neiman, who had written on the back of recent letter, "To Maestro Kees. The Novelist of the Future"), he was sure the manuscript would still be in the one-hundred-page state. And he was not forgetting the "encouragement" that his editor had given him, that Knopf might publish *The Last Man* or another collection of poems. So he spent every day off from the library working on the novel. "The last few pages," he wrote Getty, who was now an army lieutenant stationed at

Fort Huachuca, Arizona, "sound like Jos. Conrad at his most labored and there is no pleasure in it for me."

Kees spent August "fiddling" with correcting and revising the manuscript. He badly wanted to show it to Maurice Johnson, then passing through Denver after a vacation in the West, but a readable copy was still not ready for Ann to type. Many of the book's details about what happens to college teachers had come from Johnson, who would not see the book until a carbon was ready in September.

Laughlin also visited Denver during this time, by way of a writers' conference at Olivet College in Michigan; this entailed several evenings of socializing. At a party given by one of Laughlin's girlfriends, Kees tried to interest him in the Beddoes book but only learned that New Directions was doing Robert Herrick in 1942 and that his Beddoes selection might be considered for 1943. Laughlin, naturally, wanted to avoid making any more promises and talked more about his week at Olivet, where many of the expected guest writers had not shown up. Glenway Wescott had suffered a nervous breakdown, and Katherine Anne Porter had begged off, still trying to finish *Ship of Fools.* "All the absences," Kees later reported in a letter, "made Wystan Hugh Auden very unhappy because he didn't like the rest of the staff, and he spent most of his time playing [...] a piano in one of the dormitories. When he wasn't playing 'Indian Love Call' he was playing *Carmen,* singing all the parts." That a prostitute plays the same song on the brothel piano in one of the stranger vignettes in *Fall Quarter* suggests that Kees desperately needed texture and was still using the most immediate material available, like the parties in Colorado Springs.

In late September, William Roth wrote Kees from Yale. He had recommended *The Last Man* to his partner, Jane Grabhorn. "So it has gone to them," Kees wrote Norris Getty, "been accepted, will earn me an advance, and will be published in the late Spring or the early Fall, after they publish the collected poems of Edmund Wilson and a book by Hugh MacDiarmid." This development and being able to put his novel aside in order to visit New York again and attend the English Institute Conference left Kees upbeat (even as he worried half seriously about the condition of the tracks between Denver and Pennsylvania Station). "It has been the best year, so far as writing goes, that I've ever had," he wrote in another letter, also commenting on how much he looked forward to New York. "We had such a fine time last year and met so many people we liked that we thought we'd better do it again before Mr. Ickes [Roosevelt's secretary of the interior] or someone like him bans travel altogether."

Once again the Keeses checked into the Hotel Albert. They stayed from September 27 to October 18 and sent letters to their friends in the West, reporting on whom they met, what parties they attended, and what gossip they heard. Malcolm Cowley had news that Archibald MacLeish's influence extended beyond the Library of Congress, "his fingers in so many pies he has grown several new ones." Josephine Herbst said she intended to start a still on her Bucks County farm now that a new tax on liquor had gone into effect. At a party given by Oscar Williams, Kees noticed that the anthologist now parted his hair on the side rather than in the middle, which caused the émigré poet Ivan Goll to remark, "Oscar, now you have become a romantic." The Keeses also learned that Carson McCullers "got that nipple-cutting business from autobiographical sources."

Kees's tone changed from that of a raconteur to one of deference when it came to being invited to dinner at the home of William Carlos Williams and his wife, Florence, in Rutherford, New Jersey. "For us," Kees wrote, "it was some kind of high"—especially during the after-dinner drinks, when Williams told him how much he admired his new poem in the latest issue of *Poetry*, "Henry James at Newport," and then asked him to recite it. After Kees read, Williams took the magazine from him and read back the line "Remember the detached, the casually disqualified." He read it again and said, "That's good! That's it! There's a line!" Then Kees asked the doctor to read "The Yachts," "The Sea Elephant," and "By the Road to the Contagious Hospital," the first poem in *Spring and All*, the Williams book that Kees most admired, which had one of Williams's most extreme, gnomic statements: "The perfect type of the man of action is the suicide."

New York was less intimidating to the Keeses on their second visit. Kees himself, coming back to the city after seeing William Roth at Yale, enjoyed the experience of writing a letter to a friend on a New Haven train. It felt natural to him, as natural and as much a part of the writer's life in New York as watching Carson McCullers give a party at the Brevoort and pick up a woman. He no longer felt like an out-of-town guest—and some of his new comfort had to be attributed to a fellow Midwesterner, the radical writer Josephine Herbst, who introduced the Keeses to a number of new friends, including John and Mary Cheever in their Eighth Street apartment.

Cheever had recently become a house writer for the *New Yorker,* where he was paid an enviable two thousand dollars a year for the ten or twelve stories he wrote in a rented room above the Black Cat restaurant on Broadway. Yet what surprised Kees more was Cheever's reaction when Ann told him she and Weldon had read enough of his stories to make a "swell volume." The writer, whose first book Kees would review and praise for its "acid accounts of pathos in the suburbs," shook his head and said his stories "were not much."

Seeing successful contemporaries like Cheever made Kees receptive to Oscar Williams's suggestion that he apply for a Guggenheim, since having had a book published was no longer a consideration for the fellowship. Cheever even believed it would be easier for Kees to get one than Carson McCullers, who had published two novels. "Poor girl," Cheever said, "she's so innocent, so totally lost. She doesn't know who to get to recommend her. All she has so far are Henry Seidel Canby and Thomas Mann." For his application, Kees lined up a formidable list of poets, critics, and novelists to write letters for him. Allen Tate promised one, as did Malcolm Cowley, John Crowe Ransom, James Farrell, and Horace Gregory. Although they had met him only a handful of times, they knew Kees well enough from his letters and his work—and the air of promise about him. He was obviously a dark poet, but this was balanced by the way he entertained his contemporaries, telling disarming literary anecdotes and sometimes playing jazz if there was piano at hand.

On the way back to Denver in late October, Kees stayed at his parents' home in Beatrice and impressed them with stories about New York and the debut he would soon make with both a book of poems and the novel *Fall Quarter.* Maurice Johnson had sent a marked-up carbon of the manuscript to the Hotel Albert before Weldon and Ann had left, and his positive remarks made it easier to convince Sarah and John that their son was on the verge of success. Johnson had found the English professor and his bumbling desire for the small-town radio singer Dorothy Bruce, modeled after Faye Greener in *The Day of the Locust* and Lola-Lola in *The Blue Angel,* hilarious. The demented minor characters that peopled the novel also seemed convincing: Devlin, the dipsomaniac professor; Elliott Eliot and the loud phonograph; and the evil child, Little Raymond. "It was grand of you to read it for me just now," Kees wrote in a letter of gratitude. "If you have any afterthoughts on the book, I wish you'd write me at Denver about them. I want to get the final draft to Knopf in a month or so and I hope they'll bring it out in the early Spring."

Kees wanted Norris Getty to read the manuscript before he sent it to Knopf, for his judgment would be more reliable than Johnson's (who had once confessed to Getty that he did not understand their friend's poems). Getty had read the novel's first installments before joining the army. The early chapter drafts had left him apprehensive, especially when he saw a character or remembered a scene that Kees had cannibalized from one of his discarded manuscripts. He found it difficult to give the book a "clean read."

Working in Johnson's corrections and suggestions forced Kees to find—or imagine—other problems in *Fall Quarter* at the end of October. He was uneasy as he packed a new carbon into the stationery box that Ann had emptied typing a fresh copy and gave the package to the REA delivery man—whose somber face and dark green uniform added to Kees's sense of doom. "I hope it reaches you soon," he wrote in the first-class letter that would overtake the manuscript. "It would be fine if it would arrive in time for you to cope with it over the weekend. I know you're rushed like everything, but I'll be awfully grateful for any and all reactions and suggestions."

In a few days, he had no reason to fear that after all his work he had no novel, that *Fall Quarter* had failed because he felt burned out over the whole "business" of writing it. Getty described how much he enjoyed reading the carbon on a quiet Saturday when his company of recruits was on leave: "Well, the misgivings are quite resolved now, so there's no harm in admitting them. They were largely, I can see, the result of reading so much of the book piece by piece, over so long a period of time. Yesterday, Saturday afternoon, I read the whole novel through in one sitting. [...] It was after dark when I finished, and I felt much pleased with the work, went out to the Chinaman's for supper in quite tranquil frame of mind. Telling myself, as I have told you here, that I should have trusted you more all along. [...] Your weather is handled beautifully throughout, and helps the book a lot."

Getty's seamless reading meant much to Kees. He had achieved a modern comedy, where a common Hollywood "sight gag" like an uncooperative candy machine coexisted almost naturally with a boy dismembering a small animal or sophisticated party guests piling into a car to watch a plane crash. Relieved, Kees thanked his most reliable reader and friend: "I was awfully pleased that you liked the book. I thought all along that I was writing a 'well-made' novel in spite of steady doubtful feelings, too. [...] Now I don't want to write anything for a while, except some poems, perhaps."

Kees touched up the typescript one more time. Then he shipped *Fall Quarter* on November 7 to his New York agent, who held on to the novel for three weeks. During this time, a Japanese carrier force steamed into the northern Pacific under radio silence, and Kees received a letter from his agent filled with her puzzled response to the finished book. Still caught up in the hubris that came from Getty's and Johnson's positive readings of *Fall Quarter*, he requested that Mavis McIntosh do her job and deliver the manuscript to Knopf in spite of her reservations.

Paul Hoffman read *Fall Quarter* on December 8, 1941, under conditions that were hardly like Getty's idyllic weekend evening on an army base in peacetime. In the hours after the afternoon papers reported that the United States had declared war on Japan, the editor sat down to read Kees's academic comedy. Overnight, the late-Depression world in which Kees's story was anchored had vanished, and *Fall Quarter* became a period piece inside of a day. The Japanese torpedo attack that sank the American battleships at Pearl Harbor was merely one reason for the estrangement in Hoffman's reader's report, which he submitted to Alfred Knopf and his colleague Harold Strauss. Kees had, over the months since he sent in the first provisional chapters, taken a course that Knopf's editors had not foreseen—or wanted: "It may be that last night and this morning were not precisely the best of times to read a light novel about campus life in the Middle West. [...] At first I thought things I objected to were merely lapses in discrimination and began to make notes as cuts and revisions but as I got into the new text, I gave up. Every one without exception behaved more and more like a screwball and presently even the properties, so to speak, of the piece began to take on a look of incongruity."

Within the week, Strauss turned in his report. It agreed with Hoffman's. Strauss's reaction, however, had some rancor in it. "Kees has not only botched the job," he wrote, "he has also revised most injudiciously the part which we had already tentatively approved. Indeed, revised is too mild a word, for he has ditched the previous chief female character, who was quite an amusing screwball, and substituted for her a very ordinary gold-digging wench."

Mavis McIntosh informed Kees that *Fall Quarter* had been rejected. She also repeated what she had written him in November. Her letter was followed by Paul Hoffman's, on the day after New Year's Day 1942. Hoffman was diplomatic to the extreme in setting Kees down, and he also had some advice for him, born out of a respect for Kees's poetry and rising reputation. *Fall Quarter*, in his mind, would have suffered severe reviews. "I'm being so candid with you because I think you would want me to be," he wrote. "And [...] I think Miss McIntosh is entirely right in wanting you to put this book away and not try to sell it elsewhere. I'm almost willing to wager that its publication not only wouldn't do you any good but might hurt your future chances."

Kees read these rejection letters aloud to Ann—and quoted them liberally in letters to the friends who had read and enjoyed *Fall Quarter*. "Can you help me to discover what type of mind is operating here?" he asked Getty. "What do you make of all this? Are these people completely humorless and dense, or is the book really bad? I don't think so, and from the way you wrote, I don't think you do either. But Jesus, Norris, I just feel as though I'd told my favorite joke and nobody even smiled."

If it had not been such a defeat for Kees, Getty, from Fort Huachuca, felt he should just shake his head and forget. But publishers, he wrote in a letter of consolation, were like "two-headed calves, they inspire in me a degree of disgust, but no very intelligent comment. Just what the devil they thought they were getting to start with, I cannot imagine. What they mean by 'changing heroines' I cannot understand at all; you were almost pedantically careful, I thought, in getting your heroine introduced at the very beginning."

Hoffman, Strauss, and McIntosh had expected salable filler for Knopf's list. They wanted a kind of Corn Belt Evelyn Waugh from Kees, a post–Dust Bowl *Decline and Fall*. Instead the "incongruity" for which Kees was praised as a poet and the *humour noir* of his fiction crossed over. He now understood that he had miscalculated with his "caricatural and fantastic effects." "If you read my story," he wrote Ray West, "'The Evening of the 4th of July' in last year's NEW DIRECTIONS, you'll have an idea of the sort of thing that got them down; although such effects are much more sparingly employed in the novel."

∽

You'll never be sorry for any poem you've published. — Ann Kees

Through March and April 1942, Kees tried to market *Fall Quarter* without his agent. He sent it to Colt Press, which did not have the money to take it on, and to New Directions. Cap Pearce of Duall, Sloan, and Pearce, who respected Kees for his poetry, was the first to regard *Fall Quarter* "as a casualty of the war."

"We'll see it published," Ann promised her husband, "if we have to print it ourselves." Despite her attempts to boost his morale, however, the continuing rejection of *Fall Quarter* had an enervating effect on him. To friends Kees complained of writer's block. *Fall Quarter* had cast a pall over risking any new ventures of like size or effort. The little that he produced made him desperately open for something to fill the empty paper. He saw a man sitting in a barber's chair looking out a window through an old-fashioned sea captain's spyglass. He came up behind two strange-looking women waiting for the streetlights to change and heard one say to the other, "You're not going to kiss her, are you?" "Of course I'm going to kiss her!" the other replied. Experiences like these only went into letters describing how mad and maddening Denver seemed to him.

"Keep working," Jim Farrell advised him, saying it was necessary that writers keep working. "We are being drowned in banality, Philistinism, etc." So Kees poured himself into an anthology of modern light verse, a project that had occurred to him when he reviewed Richard Aldington's *Viking Book of Poetry* in the March 1942 *Poetry*. "Parody and nonsense verses are under no circumstances to show themselves here," Kees had complained, pointing to the overrepresentation of the so-called serious poem. This sin of omitting Edward Lear, Lewis Carroll, and the like, he decided, would be addressed in his own anthology.

Kees also read detective stories during his unproductive spring. Raymond Chandler's *Big Sleep* and *Farewell, My Lovely* proved to be good escape reading for him — and the inspiration for one poem, "Crime Club," that he considered one of his contributions to light verse:

Consider the clues: the potato masher in a vase,
The torn photograph of a Wesleyan basketball team,
Scattered with check stubs in the hall;
The unsent fan letter to Shirley Temple,
The Hoover button on the lapel of the deceased,
The note: "To be killed this way is quite all right with me."

On May Day, which had meant something when he called himself a communist, Kees received a letter from Yaddo, the artists' colony at Saratoga Springs, New York. He had been invited to spend the summer.

This offer came as a great consolation, for he had only just learned that he would not receive a Guggenheim fellowship. "Cheever pulled wires," Kees wrote Getty, "Cowley pulled wires, and I got an invitation. Wyer very decently granted me a leave and I expect to go early in June if the draft board leaves me alone."

Kees had a minor operation to remove a cyst from his right sinus, followed by an allergic reaction to the iodoform paste used to pack his wound, but he was released from the hospital in time to make a cross-country train trip to New York.

Ann could not leave her job at Van Cise, Robinson, and Charlton, where Mr. Van Cise needed her for a trial in Omaha. She also had to be the breadwinner in order to send Kees spending money. Missing out on Yaddo and giving her poet-husband advice were her chief concerns in the first of many revealing letters she wrote "Weld" over the summer he was away: "Somehow, in the scuffle I forgot that you would very likely see Dr. Williams and his wife. If you do, give them my very best and tell them my not seeing them is practically the one reason I regret not having come along. If you go over there, do take some whiskey or good wine or something along—and then probably be arrested for transporting it across the state line. But being accustomed to a long line of spongers, I am sure they would be doubly appreciative."

Ann imagined her husband learning to play pinochle in self-defense with so many men in uniform on the train she saw him leave on. She also began to agree with her best friend, Viola Young, that she was now a "widow" as loneliness set in. She stayed up late reading Mary McCarthy's first book, *The Company She Keeps*, and made plans to clean cupboards and the like. Thankfully, Viola liked to come over to drink Tom Collinses and talk, and there were random visits from people that Ann and Weldon knew. Some were pleasant, like the dinner Ann enjoyed with Harry Tarvin, a mystery writer Kees had befriended in Denver, and his wife. Some were nuisances, like the visit of L. S. Griggs, the editor of the *Colorado Review,* who came to the Kees home to borrow money so that he and his family could take a bus back to New York City after he lost his job.

Griggs came in the evening, as did the next and most unexpected "friend" of Kees who needed his help. Ann was in her apartment, listening to Viola talk about her boyfriends and her bookstore job, when the landlady, Mrs. Garnett, shouted up the stairwell that there was a Japanese man knocking on the door and insisting on seeing Mr. Kees. Ann, who was wearing her negligee, asked Viola to see him and tell him that Kees was out of town. When Viola came back upstairs, she told Ann that the man had acted strangely before going away and said he expected to see Kees before he left for New York in order to get "something" from him.

The next day, Ann tried to make sense of the situation, for Kees had gotten himself involved with a certain Mr. Omura. Thinking that the man at the door had been Omura, she searched for his telephone number and called. The first time there were various buzzes and clicks and then a dead silence; finally an Japanese-accented voice answered, "Alla-pina 0550," and she asked for Mr. Omura. Immediately, the line went dead, as it did during other calls to the same number. Ann then went downstairs to weakly explain to Mrs. Garnett that she had no idea who the Japanese man was, for now she felt she had exposed her husband to danger.

Ann knew that Weldon had agreed to be part of an underground movement to assist Japanese Americans who had been ordered by the government to enter the internment camps that had been set up for them in several Western states. Working with the Fellowship of Reconciliation, the American Committee to Protect the Civil Rights of American Citizens of Oriental Ancestry, and the Quakers, Kenneth and Marie Rexroth had started a chain of phone calls to their friends, Kees being one of them, asking each to contact five other people who were willing to help sabotage the internment order and to lessen the suffering caused by it. Unlike his participation in the "Chain Letter for Peace," however, Kees's role in helping fugitive Nisei during the summer of 1942 remained a secret necessitated by the real possibility of surveillance and arrest.

Then a bulky manila envelope came in the mail and was left outside on the porch, where Mrs. Garnett could see it. It was addressed to L. Kanai. Ann examined its contents and discovered that it contained Nisei correspondence, much of it written in Japanese, which made her afraid. She wrote her husband and asked: "Now, what the hell shall I do with that? Goddam Kenneth Rexroth. If any more of these goddam crazy things happen, I'm going to move out, and it's going to be quite a distance. I know as sure as anything that Mrs. Garnett is going to the FBI. I just wonder if I shouldn't go there first."

The following week, two airmail letters arrived at the Kees apartment also addressed to Mr. Kanai. At first, Ann did not know what to do with them, except get them back inside the apartment as quickly as possible. Then she looked up Rexroth's last letter on her husband's desk and found some instructions in a postscript: "If a chubby gentleman calls on you unexpectedly and says his name is Abraham Lincoln Kanai—take him in—bed him and feed him—he is a pearl without price, the real saint of the 'evacuation.'" Ann then angrily wrote her husband, for she felt he had left her with a responsibility that even he had not anticipated before he left for Yaddo: "And if you don't have a wife when you come back, darling, just remember Kenneth Rexroth. Knowing him, I know exactly what he told Kanai—that you and he were just like that, [...] and all he had to do was come to your door. If K. is the pearl, Rexroth is the oyster—especially during the summer months. [...] Oh well, if you were here you would know what to do, and I feel utterly unable to cope."

On arriving at Yaddo, Kees used its famous stationery to write his friends about his first impressions. "For the first time since P. Harbor," he wrote in one letter, "I feel like a human being." He confessed that until he experienced Yaddo, he had never really believed there were ivory towers. And when he left, he wrote that "something like Yaddo everyone ought to have a month or two of annually."

After getting off the train in Pennsylvania Station, Kees stayed in New York for a week and called on friends and editors. One of them, Edward Aswell of Harper's, said encouraging things about *Fall Quarter*. Kees purchased books from the Fourth Avenue stalls and saw some new motion pictures that would take forever to come to Denver. From his room at the Hotel Albert, he wrote Ann and Getty about the things that concerned him. The Colt Press was taking prepublication orders for *The Last Man*. John Cheever had been drafted. James Laughlin had not been drafted because of "psychoanalysts' reports." There were also colorful accounts of evenings spent with Kenneth Fearing (despondent over being "on the wagon"), William Carlos Williams (working on "his long poem Patterson"), and James T. Farrell and his wife, Hortense ("The boozy sentiment that Jim wafted to and fro that night seemed to me even too much for an Irishman"). And there was new gossip, like the story he had heard from Charles Angoff at the *New Republic* about Mary McCarthy's practice of going to the bathroom with any man who happened to be handy at a party "for a quick lay." Sometimes, he wrote, she took two.

Yaddo was another extreme. It had once been the home of a wealthy and cultured New York couple, Spencer and Katrina Trask. However, after Spencer Trask died in a train wreck, his widow established the artists' retreat in his memory, its centerpiece the main house. This house was a virtual copy of England's Haddon Hall, surrounded by miles of forest and formal Italian gardens and lakes. By the time of Kees's stay, however, after the Depression, the genteel days of the retreat were over. The stable of cattle and the great carriage house that had been filled with Trask family relics were now gone. Much of the pastoral farmland that had isolated the fifty-five-room mansion from the world had been sold off to developers. Triuna Island, in Lake George, which had a boathouse where John Cheever worked as a young man, had been sold as well. The large kitchen staff, trained to please the palates of the Gilded Age, had been scaled back. The silver tea service of the Trask family had been put away. Despite the economies, however, Kees found the food "magnificent" and the service "perfect." Given what he and the other guests would go back to, they were being utterly spoiled. Still overseeing them and the other guests was Elizabeth Ames, Yaddo's original director. She received Kees, gave him an introduction to the mansion and its environs, and showed him how to find the isolated forest studio in which he could now work.

The days of proletarian writers and Communist party sympathizers were over when Kees arrived at Yaddo, even though it was still under the surveillance of J. Edgar Hoover's FBI, whose agents filed Kees's presence and background because he had once published a poem in *New Masses*. Yaddo in 1942 had moved on to its "Southern period," as Malcolm Cowley termed it, which flowered with such guests as Carson McCullers, Katherine Anne Porter—both of whom Kees encountered during his visit—and Eudora Welty. He made most of his new friends among the other younger men, however, such as the critic Alfred Kazin, then writing his influential first book *On Native Ground*.

Though so many of the guests who were there that summer would go on to become much more well-known than Kees, Kazin, in remembering what impressed him most about his stay, found that it was not just the mansion's grand staircase or the pre-Raphaelite painting of Dante meeting Beatrice. Yaddo, he wrote, was where one "mingled with up-to-the-minute writers like Weldon Kees."

He also befriended the composer David Diamond and Nathan Asch, the *New Yorker* storywriter and the son of Sholem Asch. He met Newton Arvin, professor of literature at Smith College and a member of Yaddo's board; Alfred Young Fisher, the James Joyce scholar and another member of Smith's faculty; the writer Michael Seide; and Peter Busa, a painter. It was often in their company that Kees discovered Yaddo's other benefit, nearby Saratoga Springs, which had not yet left the Jazz Age or felt the full impact of New York's new Republican governor, Thomas Dewey, who had promised to clean up its many vices. There were still plenty of bars, and the ones connected to brothels proved to be Kees's favorite stops on tours arranged by David Diamond. Each had its own historical background, lore, current trends, and clientele, as described in an omnibus letter about his time at Yaddo:

Two blocks of Commercial Street, in the downtown district, are lined with whorehouses; since people develop thirsts along with erections, there are bars sprinkled amongst them. The Asches and David Diamond and Al Fisher and I went to the Hilltop, one of the most lively bars, one night and drank beer and played the jukebox, which was of the automatic hostess type, untouched, it would seem, by the Effort. All the whores on Commercial Street are negresses, and they wander in and out between assignations for a quick drink. David knew the place and its lore forward and backward. He invited one tall, very light negress named Ginger over to have a drink with us; and she told David later that she certainly did go for Al Fisher. And a few nights later Al took his two dollars and paid her for a visit. But not, mind you, before he had tried to talk himself on the free list. (We all got a little tired of Al before the season ended.) Then the day after, David brought Al a cigar that Ginger had given him to give to

Al. Evidently he had made the little bell ring. Al smoked it after dinner, but reported it a rather poor weed. But he took the butt up to his room with him.

On another occasion, Diamond invited Kees to the Worden Hotel bar, where John Cheever "practically lived" and the "smot" Saratoga set gathered, including men who played the horses, corpulent ladies from Bensonhurst and Manhattan who seemed to be the mothers of wealthy Saratoga physicians, even students from Skidmore—and people taking the cure, whom Kees would later describe in a poem:

Iron, sulphur, steam: the wastes
Of all resorts like this have left their traces.
Old canes and crutches line the walls. Light
Floods the room, stripped from the pool, broken
And shimmering like scales. Hidden
By curtains, women dry themselves
Before the fire and review
The service at hotels,
The ways of dying, ways of sleep,
The blind ataxia patient from New York,
And all the others who were here a year ago.
　　　　　　　　— "Saratoga Ending"

Prostitutes also drank at Worden and talked shop within earshot. There Kees overheard a peroxide blonde who worked at one of the "Aryan whorehouses" say to her lesbian girlfriend, "Now that this war's on and men are being killed and everything—hell, I aint dietin." He also enjoyed Diamond's generosity. With the money he had received from winning the Prix de Rome, the young composer ordered round after round of a wonderful concoction called "Black Velvet." It consisted of half champagne and half ale, served in champagne glasses. Although the drink did not sound very good to him, Kees quickly became a confirmed enthusiast: "Three or four of them and one floats on a fleecy cloud."

Yaddo also provided Kees with plenty of interest after Carson McCullers appeared on the scene in July. He kept his promise to describe her close up at the request of Norris Getty, whose special interest in her sexuality and her new army-base novel may or may not have been fully apprehended by Kees.[4]

You wanted to know about the author of REFLECTIONS IN A GOLDEN EYE. I'll try to give you a McCullersgram, but she only arrived a few days ago and I haven't talked to her much. Well, the first time I saw her she was wearing a rather tacky looking blue serge suit with a boy's white shirt (not too clean) and blue wool socks that stopped at her bare knees. You have to realize that Carson is a big tall girl, but thin as a rail: she must be about 5'9". She's been very ill most of her life, her nose is much too large and her eyes immense; her hair is reddish brown and straight and in disorder; she looks like an overgrown child. No makeup contributes to this general effect. [...]

David Diamond and Newton are both very fond of Carson. There for a while last year David and Carson were thinking of getting married. Sounds sweet until you know that David is queer and Carson vacillates between normality and lesbianism in much more rapid fashion than D. Himalstein. There's a story about a party Carson gave in New York. She would greet each guest at the door holding a bottle of champagne, and then she would take said guest into a corner and say, "You are my dearest and most intimate friend. I want to tell you about the astonishing thing that happened to me." The astonishing thing was the story of the woman she had picked up on the street and gone to bed with. She regarded it as something of a Beautiful Relationship.

Kees too could be the center of attention, often in Yaddo's music room. There he had a Steinway concert grand to himself and banged out Fats Waller for his new friends, along with his own renditions of "What Is This Thing Called Love?" and "Saint Louis Blues." The music room also had a working phonograph—and buried under the Bach and Shostakovitch records, he found a rare album of Bix Beiderbecke 78s.

Some guests at Yaddo that summer found Kees exotically Midwestern. He came from that mythical country where the farms gave way to ranches and cowboys. That he had once played with a big Hollywood star seemed authentically American, a tall tale hardly out of keeping with his small-town origins. The New York Jewish intellectuals felt this way about him especially. To them Kees had risen from the boondocks. He seemed as impossibly cultivated and cosmopolitan as one of their own who had come up from the Lower East Side. He resembled them as much as he seemed different—and he seemed to share their ambitions, their need to flex literary muscles, as Alfred

Kazin noted: "At Yaddo in 1942 he was a brash young librarian from Beatrice, Nebraska. [...] He was unbelievably well informed on the smallest details of modernist literature, eagerly presented himself as a walking encyclopedia on every little magazine ever published between Reykjavik and Pinsk. He was a poet who desperately wanted to be 'up there,' as he used to say, with Eliot, Pound and other stars in our firmament."

It was for this reason that Al Fisher and Newton Arvin wanted to bring Kees back to Smith to replace the retiring college librarian. Kees, however, did not think they were serious and did not follow up on the offer, which would have placed him in a position to one day lend books to such young women as Sylvia Plath. There were also other reasons for his lack of enthusiasm for such a plum job, a job that would have established him in an Eastern milieu of liberal intellectuals, fellow travelers, and pacifists such as he wished he had in Denver. One of these certainly stemmed from the crucial difference that Kazin picked up on—Kees did not really belong in the time where he thought he belonged and was decidedly uncomfortable in his own:

Weldon, born a year before me in 1914, was born too late for the literary modernism that flourished in the first decades of this century and became academic business to our generation. Despite his frantic ambition to become a 1920s man in the 1940s, Weldon lacked the gaiety, the sporty independence that distinguished American writers when we were growing up. He was mysteriously unhappy in his personal life. Despite the stupendous amount of material he had churned up about the modern movement, Weldon also lacked the radical insurgency, the naive but necessary political idealism that marked our generation, so deeply marked first by depression and then by Hitler's war. An admirer of Weldon's poetry said that he found everything in the outside world inimical, that he specialized in the "pathos of objects."

Even Ann saw this in the letter her husband sent back from Yaddo. "Your letters seem to come from another world," she wrote him, "the world of the twenties for instance."

Kees did not get much writing done at Yaddo. This may have been one source of the personal unhappiness that Kazin observed in his new friend. Another source may have been the news in Ann's letters. She admitted to drinking more after the Nisei affair, and it showed in her writing not so much as anger or fear, but more as mental imbalance. She was also more insecure and lonely. "I miss you terribly," she wrote, ending her letter of June 14. "If there is anything wrong between us, please say. When you aren't here I lose my sense of proportion." This hurt tone, however, is in the same letter in which Ann casually informed Kees that she would be dating a soldier: "Viola was up late last night. I've been seeing a good deal of her and whenever I do we usually have drinks. As a result—in the last week we've already killed her quart of bourbon. I'm going to stop drinking so much—I hope. But it is a swell soporific. She's trying to fix me up with somebody from Lowry Field—at least I think that's what she has in mind. A sculptor from Chicago who ran a bookstore there for three years."

The Keeses did not have what was even then called an "open marriage." Like other temporarily unattached women—married or not—Ann was simply complying with the innocent and patriotic duty to dance or have a drink with men in uniform, and it was not until July that she finally met her soldier.

"Sex," she wrote Kees, "seemed to Rear its Ugly Head for a few minutes, but you will be glad to know that I escaped practically unscathed. It was probably too much Henry Miller or something." She promised her date that they would have dinner together—and promised her husband that it would "probably be very dull."

She also met another soldier, while drinking with Viola in one of the booths of the Edelweiss bar, who reminded her of Harold Rosenberg. Art Camper turned out to be a friend of Saul Bellow and an avid reader of *Partisan Review*. When he found out that Ann was the wife of the Weldon Kees who had written "June 1940," he responded: "Jeez this is wonderful. Imagine finding anybody to talk to in this wilderness." They agreed to meet again, and after the last time Camper left a note in the Kees mailbox: "Tell your mate he writes goddamn good poetry. Bourne was right."

Kees chided Ann about her encounters with GIs, asking her how things were going with her and her "soldier boy." What mattered more to him was her honoring his requests for money—and a fresh supply of clothes—and she reminded him that they had only $146.73 in the bank and told him not to drink their money away in Saratoga bars. "I hope you don't need any, or much anyway," she wrote about the need for thrift. "I've been a very good girl while you've been gone, even while I was working, I came home to eat—not from a sense of martyrdom but because I preferred to."

The issue of money was also a factor in whether Kees would see his parents on his return from Yaddo in August. There was evidently a *crise en famille* in July that centered on Ann and some indiscretion on his part. Such events were not uncommon, since the elder Keeses sent their son money and rarely felt their attentions reciprocated by him:

Speaking of money, I enclose a money order for $20, which I do hope will last you, but don't try to stretch it to too thin a point. I mean if you need more don't get a conscience about it. It probably wouldn't be a good idea to show up in Beatrice strapped. Please do go there, darling, if you possibly can without retching. What I did undoubtedly wasn't very nice although I never think about it unless you write it in your letters. Their letter must have really been a lulu if you haven't answered yet. Please do write them. I can't bear the thought of your being estranged from your family on my account, no matter what they are like, because I know how it makes you feel. Blood, after all. [...] You probably think about it more than you like to admit because you hate to have anything in your life messed up. And this whole business of course is very futile because it didn't solve anything, just made a bad situation worse.

As the weeks went by, Ann looked forward to Kees's return. He had wanted to stay until September. However, the new arrivals did not come close to replacing the fun he had had with David Diamond, who had left in early July, and he had grown bored of watching a "spooky" Carson McCullers carrying around her thermos of what she called "tea." Kazin still remained at Yaddo. He had offered to read *Fall Quarter* after Harper's rejected the novel—a disappointment that may have at last driven Kees to one of the isolated cottages on the estate to get back to writing fiction. He sent two stories back to Ann.

She liked "The Tower Shines like Polished Silver," a story that is now lost. "It's short and bitter and says everything it has to say and doesn't waste even a comma," she wrote. "And besides you've got one beautiful title." The other, which is also lost, was an unusually long story about Hollywood, an installment in a cycle of Hollywood stories from which only one, about a homosexual bar owner trying to pick up a young actor, survives ("Do You Like the Mountains?").

The Denver draft board's bureaucratic hunger for men began to increase in the summer months of 1942. Ann mailed off a questionnaire to Kees that had questions slanted in such a way as to expose the respondent's occupational status as not crucial to the war effort. She glanced hurriedly at it. There were no jobs that seemed to apply to her husband — and it had to be mailed back to the draft board in ten days. She reminded him to hurry lest he arouse suspicion: "The draft board might get nasty if it gets mailed from Saratoga Springs." Yet this problem paled in comparison to the financial difficulties of the Colt Press. Jane Grabhorn and William Roth did not have the money for paper and distribution. Kees used the word "bankrupt" to describe the unhappy situation. *The Last Man,* though it had been set in galleys, was put on hold indefinitely.

Ann tried to make things better, sending advice and twenty-dollar bills. "Don't run too short," she wrote. "You know your weakness." She also thought of ways for him to avoid seeing his parents in Beatrice; she was even willing to sacrifice her own well-being if Kees wanted to stay away from Beatrice and Denver for as long as necessary: "It's too bad you can't stay at Yaddo all winter. Has Mrs. Ames asked you to? If I could go to S.F. and get a decent-salaried job I could probably send you the $25 a mo. plus drinking money. What do you think? The thought of returning to Denver must be as horrible to you as the thought of staying here is to me."

Any thoughts her husband had of staying on at Yaddo, however, were tempered by the need to return to his duties at the Bibliographical Center. His assistant, Mrs. Chapman, started her vacation on August 12. So Ann stopped volunteering plans for him and prepared for his return, advising him to take a Pullman car and an express train, not the hellish Exposition Flyer, which she used to take from Lincoln when she came to visit him in their pre-Denver days and which had "no diner, no club car, no nothing." She paid all the bills, including the surgeon's fee for Kees's cyst operation, and delivered the bad news in her last letter to Yaddo that their cat Flowerface had fallen off the roof. "Such is Life," she added wistfully.

Kees had wanted to look up Saul Bellow during his layover in Chicago. Instead, he first took a train to Beatrice, where he patched things up with his parents, and then continued on to Denver. By August 13, he had taken up his duties again at the Bibliographical Center.

"A nice raise," probably prompted by the rumor that he had applied for a position at the Kansas City Public Library, made coming back easier for Kees, and he started crossing out the word "acting" from his office stationery. This change may have come as a result of pressure from his mother to have a career—and he knew that if he did not get better rooted in his job, he risked leaving himself open to being drafted.

Being director of the union catalog project also gave Kees something to center himself with as he experienced a kind of post-Yaddo letdown, for he was no longer being pampered or treated as a member of a conspicuous elite. Yaddo's afterglow also colored his feeling that his career had actually suffered a setback. He had hoped to have a parcel containing freshly printed copies of *The Last Man* to show off at Yaddo. Now, in the cover letter to some new poems he wanted Allen Tate to read, he could only say that the Colt Press kept "piddling around." Then, in November, he received a letter from Jane Grabhorn that promised *The Last Man* would be out before Christmas.

While Kees remained anxious and disappointed over this new delay, he took stock of his short stories and novels, as critical of himself as he was in the book reviews he turned out for Alfred Kazin at the *New Republic* and *Partisan Review* (which included a one-sentence pan of Muriel Rukeyser's *Wake Island*). He discarded the long Hollywood story that he had written at Yaddo. He left *Fall Quarter* to be handled by his new literary agency, Russell and Volkening. "They seem to go in for screwballs," he wrote Getty a little self-disparagingly; "they handle Wyndham Lewis and Henry Miller and Eudora Welty, and like writers to be a bit off-the-beam." Henry Volkening, who represented him, had asked his client to write a new novel, since *Fall Quarter* seemed more like a "second book," but Kees would not take the advice. He now would only write a novel if he could get a contract based on a synopsis, a practice that other writers enjoyed; this was more a sign of his estrangement from writing fiction than his willingness. Given this, he could hardly be encouraging to Dale Smith, who had asked him to read a novella about Lincoln during their college days, a subject that Kees could no longer warm to. "Publishers," he wrote, "hate these short books like poison." He even admitted to Getty that he had stopped writing fiction, claiming to no longer have the vocation. "'The only true writing that came through during the (last) war was in poetry,'" he wrote, quoting Hemingway. He now applied this to himself and enclosed for Getty the draft of a poem titled, "The Contours of Fixation." Its five tercets depict a street scene as stark, forbidding, and abstract as any painted by de Chirico, Kees's setting for a meditation on the intellectual catastrophe of the war:

> Their pain soaks eyes on every balcony.
> "Forbear, refrain, be scrupulous"—dogs' admonitions,
> Sad and redundant, paraphernalia of goodbye,
>
> Hang in the sulphured air like promises of girls.
> Then silence. Down the street the lights go dead.
> One waits, one waits. And then the guns sound on another hill.

By the autumn of 1942, pacifism as an articulate force in American society had been drowned out by the overriding necessity of winning the war. Allen Tate, Dwight Macdonald, and others felt increasingly isolated for continuing to express their opposition, as did Kees, who saw his new poems as the kind being viewed "with more and more suspicion and alarm."

In the weeks after he returned from Yaddo, Kees changed toward Ann. Her letters from June to August had been stressful for him to read. His absence had had a bad effect on everything from her self-esteem to her mental state—and she was drinking more than usual. As she felt his distance and tried to correct herself, doing everything to seek his approval, as she had in her "good girl" letters, she only made things worse, her behavior becoming increasingly bizarre—indeed, almost scripted from his poems.

By the end of January 1943, it was clear that she was delusional. In a fantastic letter to Norris Getty, she revealed that she had her own pariah dogs to deal with, and they were not like her husband's. She had written surreal letters before. There was the one she had sent to Kees in June about sitting next to Abraham Lincoln Kanai during a bus crash and one about a flying umbrella. She called these "good letters." The recent letter to Getty, however, revealed a troubled woman:

> Is it significant, I wonder, that I am afraid of the dogs? My fear has no significance, but the dogs are important. They are acting strangely and I feel that if I knew the reason a great many things would be explained.

No that's not right. Just because I got drunk with a mystic [her Catholic friend Jean Johnson] Saturday night, do I have to be a goddam chameleon? Besides she isn't afraid of anything she just worries about the state of the Mortal Soul and she has explained how it cannot possibly be honorable to commit suicide.

I heard them first when I was washing the dishes in the kitchen and I thought to myself facetiously that someone must have thrown some horsemeat in the garbage can and the dogs didn't approve. Later when I was sweeping the floor I thought perhaps there were some gypsies going down the alley on the lookout for an unlocked backdoor. But then I remembered there aren't gypsies anymore, just a few gypsies' grandsons who are in the army. After awhile I realized the barking was still running in the back of my mind and I went to all the windows to look for the dogs, but I couldn't see them.

The long strange letter continues in this way, with the dogs moving in formation, turning and wheeling like birds in a vacant lot. There are odd bits of news and worry about the selective service, the breakup of David Rose and Judy Garland, and a pregnant army wife who killed herself and her husband when she learned he was going overseas. A police dog humps a "bright dog" from behind and heaves ridiculously as an old man in "decent black" stops and watches closely until they have finished. He then takes out a white handkerchief and wipes his mouth "as one would after eating something juicy." The dogs never stop barking to Ann, and they seem "intolerably evil": "Weldon thought I made up the part about the dogs, but I didn't. I haven't that much imagination. Finally, late in the afternoon, they went away and I was able to go to the store. The vacant lot where they had been looked trampled as a battlefield would, and there was a nervous little fox terrier running back and forth frantically to sniff out what had happened that afternoon. Occasionally I see one of the dogs that was there and it is rather shocking, like seeing one of your friends who only the night before had been engaged in mystic rights."

As Ann fell apart more, her husband wrote letters restricted mostly to literary matters and poems. "Some kind of whirlwind started blowing," he wrote Newton Arvin in February, "and when it finally died down after a few weeks, I discovered that I had written ten poems. [...] Such a thing has never happened to me before, and I don't expect it to happen again." All of these poems, like the villanelle that begins,

"The crack is moving down the wall," suggest that he was cannibalizing a well-hidden domestic crisis and the chilled relationship that had grown between him and Ann:

> *There seems to be some doubt. No doubt, however,*
> *Of the chilled and empty tissues of the mind*
> *— Cold, cold, a great gray winter entering —*
> *Like spines of air, frozen in an ice cube.*
> — "The Patient Is Rallying"

Kees finally made Ann agree to a separation — his decision going hand in hand with his decision to live in New York, where his literary work might reach print sooner than it would from Denver, before the draft took him. New York was also the best location for him to be declared 4F, for there he could count on seeing a real psychiatrist. He also gave notice at the library and began to pack in the evenings, surrounding himself with string, boxes, suitcases, piles of books, and brimming wastebaskets. With only the barest hint of sentiment, he admitted to Getty that the winter had been a maddening time for him ("Rat's Alley was never like this") and that he was going to New York and Ann was going back home to her parents in Wyoming. He asked his friend to write her and, in a footnote to his letter of February 22, asked him to "please say nothing of this."

Getty complied. Yet he responded a few days after reading this news with all the depth of feeling that his friend lacked. The loss of Weldon, Ann, and their apartment in Denver left him feeling orphaned and terribly sorry that there would be no "two of you there, and the piano and books and lamps, and the French windows and the porch." He may have tried to make Kees see what he was letting happen, what he was giving up by leaving "the setting for just about every remaining thought I have about reading and writing, music, painting, or merely civilized living, including certainly food and drink. This is no exaggeration at all, believe me. At any rate, my own regrets are of small importance, considering what a change it means for you and Ann. I'm still considerably bewildered, of course, on a number of scores, but one thing continues clear: it's a damn dreary world just now, and getting drearier."

New York
1943-1948

He is Robinson Crusoe, utterly alone on Madison Avenue, a stranger and afraid in the world of high-paying news weeklies, fashionable galleries, jazz concerts, highbrow movies, sophisticated revues.
                                    —Kenneth Rexroth

For Weldon Kees's black-and-white publicity still, taken after he had lived in New York for three years, the photographer had him pose with a cigarette in his right hand, held in a rakish manner, like that of a movie actor in a glossy magazine endorsing a particular brand of cigarette. Kees wears a button-down oxford shirt. His right elbow rests on his knee, and his long fingers are held loose and unclenched, his arm forming a sharp angle that frames the solid darkness of his necktie. The gloss of his parted and combed-back hair, his carefully trimmed mustache, and the intent look he gives the camera are signs of a serious man, caught at that age when no intellectual challenge seems formidable. He could be the personification of New York *Burggeist*, the kind of man Saul Bellow met at a party in Greenwich Village, whom "the French call *sympathique*, very tense, but charming." In the early spring of 1943, however, Kees saw himself as only passing through the city and hardly as the image he would become in this photograph. He had not even brought his typewriter with him since the army would not let him keep it.

On his first day in the city, Kees found the Hotel Albert mobbed with soldiers. There were no vacancies, and even if there had been, the genteel bohemia of Hart Crane's Village could hardly be relived in wartime New York. Its Golden Age had already devolved into what the essayist Milton Klonsky called the "The Age of Lead." Kees, however, who would later make Klonsky into his hipster bête noire, could sense the presence of Henry James in Washington Square Park as the double-decker bus drove under the arch. He could look up at the same buildings Crane had seen and understand what he meant by the "faded romance of *La Vie Bohème*."

With so many men in uniform around him, Kees worried about the draft as he had in Denver. He now heard stories, any one of which could be his in a matter of days or weeks.

Kenneth Rexroth had recently entered a federal prison after declaring himself a conscientious objector. The army had taken the poet

Stanley Kunitz. The critic Clement Greenberg had been drafted in February. He was now at some remote training camp, from which he had mailed a postcard to the offices of *Partisan Review,* where Philip Rahv handed it to Kees to read its message: "Save yourselves." The opportunities to do so, however, were fading. Revisions to the Selective Service Act had just reclassified him as 3A.

Kees wandered uptown to the Brevoort but found it jammed with Jewish refugees from Europe. The other hotels he tried were also filled. So he went back downtown to the Chelsea, since he knew some of the people who lived there, among them James and Hortense Farrell. Yet at three dollars a day, he could not afford the Chelsea for very long.

Kees was an exotic around the offices of *Partisan Review,* at once the ex-cornfield communist from Nebraska, the Denver librarian-who-wrote, and someone so culturally informed and urbane as to suggest there could be a lost tribe of New York Intellectuals across the Hudson. The interest he attracted resulted in many invitations to dinner, including Mary McCarthy's after she found he shared a vice with her: detective novelists.

Though Kees had heard about her intellectual (and sexual) formidability, he soon felt at ease with "La McCarthy," as he called her in letters to friends. The gossip about her and her marriage to an older man, the writer Edmund Wilson, had given him a false picture. They resembled an ordinary couple to Kees, and this caught his attention as he described to Maurice Johnson arriving at the Wilsons' large and rather dingy apartment near Gramercy Park—in an atmosphere borrowed from Wilson's novel of Village life, *I Thought of Daisy:*

It was snowing as I got off the bus at Union Square and walked east on 15th street. When I rang the bell, "the electric clicking began—with its quick and ready profusion, plucking distinctly the string of excitement which was still capable of vibrating in my breast at the prospect of meeting new people in Greenwich Village"—I had gone inside and had begun to climb the rather rickety stairway when the front door opened and I heard my name called. It was Wilson, easily recognizable in the glum light of the hallway, his hat and overcoat snow-covered; he looked up at me and said, "What are you doing in town, Weldon? Awfully glad you're here, awfully glad you could come." And I passed some pleasantry, and we shook hands and went up the stairs together.—Mary came to

the door, very dark, very young-looking, wearing a green wool dress,
and said (to Wilson) "Hello, darling," and he said, "Hello, dear"; and we
were introduced and very soon were drinking old-fashioneds [...] then
Edmund said he thought he'd better shave, and took his drink in the bath-
room with him and talked occasionally through the door while Mary and
I talked about Graham Greene and Eric Ambler and Raymond Chandler.

When Wilson took his place at dinner, Kees found him incredibly articulate as well. There were "no pauses or lapses or stuttering at all." He did not show the infamous "touchiness" that Kees had
heard about from Kazin and his other Yaddo friends. Wilson eventually broached the subject of Kees's *Anthology of Modern Satirical
Poetry,* giving his approval to Hardy's "Are You Digging on My Grave?",
Robinson's "Miniver Cheevy," and newer selections such as Theodore
Roethke's "The Academic" and Louise Bogan's "Evening in the Sanitarium." Then he tried to see if Kees had left a poem out, becoming
"piqued" when he could not think of one until he found that Kees had
not yet thought to include Arthur Waley's "No Discharge."

Not only did the Wilsons' marriage seem ordinary, but so did their
family life. At one point, the Wilsons' four-year-old son passed through
the living room on his way to the bathroom. After he had attended
to "his small need," he ran back through the room completely naked,
utterly happy with his accomplishment. McCarthy finally got him into
his pajamas, remarking, as she did, that she had inadvertently bought
girls' pajamas for him instead of boys'.

Two nights later, Kees accepted another dinner invitation, from the
Philip Rahvs. Lionel Abel made an appearance—followed by Mary
McCarthy without her husband, which allowed Kees to resume getting
to know her after the gathering had ended and he found himself out
on the sidewalk with her.

She announced she was "starving," so he offered to go with her to
the Village. After finding an all-night diner on Eighth Street, they sat
down in a booth and ate hamburgers. They put nickels in the jukebox
and just talked, even when one of the coffee boilers overheated and
began to hiss violently.

McCarthy confessed that she had "lost God" at the age of twelve.
She gave her new friend a preview of what was to come in her memoir
Memories of a Catholic Girlhood. She told him she wanted to write a
story called "4F"—which, of course, he could relate to given his pre-

dicament, given that he would not have minded such a selective service classification for himself.

Kees was not the kind of man to discuss whether or not his encounter with Mary McCarthy had continued after the diner episode. He certainly would have paid their tab, however, and McCarthy would have given him advice on what to do in the city, if no other favor.

He had, of course, been sounding people out about what kinds of jobs were available, for he knew that the money he had brought with him would not last long. Several friends at various gatherings suggested that he get a job with the Office of War Information, where his writing skills could get him out of combat duty. The only thing stopping him was being perceived as the type the O.W.I. already hired, who seemed to him to be "former contributors to *transition*" and "arty" homosexuals talking about whether their psychiatrists were *really* doing them any good.

Nevertheless, Kees turned up at cocktail parties where gay and bisexual men were well-represented—and he found himself listening to how *they* were avoiding frontline military service. One could teach at a boys' school, work the night shift at a factory, hide out in rural Vermont—or see an analyst and thus come to the selective service as mentally unfit for duty. At one such party, whose attendees included Willard Maas, Paul Goodman, José Garcia Villa, William March, and other gay men, he found George Barker "better than his poems," a "Noel Coward type of fairy," as he wrote Norris Getty, whom he found more likable than other members of the "third sex."

As Kees grew more accustomed to being around gay men, they too took notice of him, observing that he mixed well with them, that he was "svelte," as the composer Arthur Berger said of him.

Berger met Kees in the company of the poet and translator Charles Glenn Wallis, a member of Paul Goodman's circle. He assumed Kees was homosexual, too, simply Wallis's new boyfriend, an impression reinforced on the numerous occasions that Berger saw him and Wallis together before Ann reappeared on the scene.

Wallis had qualities that Kees liked in some of his closest friends and that may have reminded him of Getty. Wallis had the same classical, scholarly interests as Getty—the same kind also found in characters from Kees's fiction. He translated the Latin texts of Copernicus and

Keppler—as well as the French of *Fleurs du Mal*, by Baudelaire, a poet whose work was never far from Kees's own. Wallis also had a new book of poems coming out with an ironic title more obvious than the one Kees had given *The Last Man*, when apprehended with a gay sensibility: *No Mortal Blow.*

This friendship is not mentioned in the Kees letters that survive, and the only trace of it is a signed copy of *The Last Man* that Kees gave to Wallis. Berger took this book from Wallis's library not long after the young poet's death at a *Partisan Review* party in Greenwich Village, an event that also went by without remark in Kees's letters, even though it had the kind of macabre detail that Kees liked to recount. Wallis, who had been sitting on an open window sill, began to laugh uncontrollably at something someone said. Who this person was remains a mystery. But what happened to Wallis turned into an obscure Village legend, for as he laughed, he leaned back and then fell to his death on the sidewalk below.

Kees moved that March from the Chelsea to a furnished apartment at 31 East Thirtieth Street, close to the Fifth Avenue offices of Russell and Volkening, where he had been taking his mail and using the office typewriter until he borrowed a good secondhand one from a friend—possibly Charles Wallis, who lived nearby on East Twenty-ninth Street.

Alfred Kazin gave Kees some book-reviewing assignments for the *New Republic.* Though these did not pay much, they would help him establish himself as a writer in the city and lead to a more permanent job.

The first review was of John Cheever's first book, *The Way Some People Live,* giving Kees an opportunity to praise one of his new friend's works and to warn him about assuming that finished, *New Yorker* quality. "Mr. Cheever is not alone," Kees wrote. "He bathes in that same large municipal pool where all *New Yorker* short-story writers swim and sink. As Lionel Trilling remarked, one feels that almost any one of them might write another's story."

The apartment on East Thirtieth Street also gave Kees a base from which to promote his anthology and a place to come back to when he met with disappointment. He prepared a new outline for his anthology—with Edmund Wilson's emendations—and circulated it first to Scribner's and then to Reynal and Hitchcock. But three weeks into

March, he found that his book would be a much harder sell than he had imagined. Readers at Scribner's thought that his tastes "were a little 'special'" and made him add Dorothy Parker and Ogden Nash. The war, too, frustrated the anthology. He was told there was a paper shortage, and then there was the matter of how "so many satirical poets have the annoying habit of satirizing such matters as war, patriotic piety, and missionary zeal—and I somehow have unfortunately included such poems."

Of more interest to publishers were books like *Guadacanal Diaries* and "lastmantosee singapore items"—or novels that servicemen would want to read. Even Kees was persuaded and began discussing with different editors a new novel that, after his brush with Mary McCarthy's high-minded enthusiasm for detective fiction, might be a literary mystery. At Scribner's, the editors liked his idea enough to "reopen the case" on *Fall Quarter,* only to let the war again play into their excuse for not taking either book. Then he suffered a further indignity when his manuscript was sent by mistake to an author in California. He made more rounds and found more interested publishers and more reasons to feel let down. "Everyone," he wrote Getty, "is 'interested.' You know. The writer may be drafted and do another Pvt. Hargrove. Do you agree that that young man should be thrown to the lions, along with Pvt. Saroyan? It is really getting quite bad."[1] Only the acceptance of a few poems, by *Accent, Partisan Review,* and the *American Mercury,* gave Kees some sense of movement in his writing during his first month in New York.

The Cheever review appeared in April. Had he still lived in Denver, Kees would have gotten reactions from Ann and a fellow librarian or two. In his new city, he could be buttonholed for what he wrote on the sidewalk or while drinking at Jack Delaney's or George's Bar— or while having coffee and pie at the Life Cafeteria, Stewart's, or the Waldorf, where other writers, artists, intellectuals, and their hangers-on gathered. In the Village, a piece of literary journalism in the latest issue of the *New Republic,* the *Nation,* or *Partisan Review* came to life and mattered. It was the tearoom in Lincoln writ large, something Kees impressed on Maurice Johnson, bivouacked at the commandeered Lazy U Motel on a stretch of Wyoming highway, and Norris Getty, on maneuvers in Shreveport, Louisiana.

Kees's number had yet to be called in April, and his money continued to run out. He wrote at the beginning of May that "3A men are about as popular as lepers," describing what it was like to look for a job. "One is looked at as already in khaki."

Malcolm Cowley, however, interceded again on his behalf, recommending Kees to his old friend T. S. Matthews, the managing editor at *Time*. Though many of his contemporaries said that Matthews, who had been at the *New Republic* during the late 1920s, had long ago sold his soul to publisher Henry Luce, his sympathies were still largely in the right place, and he took on many writers who had written for liberal and leftward American journals, especially if they had an Ivy League background.

Though Kees lacked this credential, his reviews in the *New Republic* and *Poetry* proved that he had the irascible wit, authority, and concision that made a good *Time* man — "the monkey-glandular hackman," in Marshall McLuhan's words, "who wrote to emasculate cultural figures down to the level of the Dagwood readership, affecting the tough-guy pose."

Matthews hired Kees in early May, and he soon started working on the twenty-ninth floor of the Time and Life Building, where the magazine's back pages were written and edited. He first reported to Wilder Hobson, the editor of the various cultural departments on the magazine, who assigned him as one of *Time*'s staff book reviewers. His weekly salary of one hundred dollars he considered an amazing sum and more than he expected to make, and letting his parents and Nebraska friends know that "lean, gangling Weldon Kees" was now a reporter for *Time* provided him with as much real thrill as the tongue-in-cheek kind. Writing for *Time* did have an "upside-down glamour" to it, as one of his friends noted. One could have the cachet of working for the largest and most influential news magazine without suffering the consequences since *Time* allowed for a convenient anonymity with its no-byline policy. There was also the camaraderie of working with other writers who were similarly "selling out." Kees found that other poets were on the payroll in the books department, among them Reuel Denney, Nigel Dennis, Howard Moss, and Harvey Breit.

James Agee, the author of the text to Walker Evans's book of Depression photographs, *Let Us Now Praise Famous Men,* also worked for *Time,* writing the weekly movie column, and had made an impressive crossover from being a Yale poet to developing an intelligent style of popular-culture journalism—one that Kees wished to emulate. Since both men shared a lifelong fascination with Hollywood, it did not take Kees and Agee long to talk and share ideas.

Another former poet was Agee's nervous, corpulent friend, the translator of *Bambi*, Whittaker Chambers. Better known now as the Soviet-agent-turned-patriot who accused a young State Department employee named Alger Hiss of espionage in 1948, Chambers immediately struck Kees then as a cipher.

With such personalities around him, the twenty-ninth floor reminded Kees of a college dormitory. People were always wandering around the halls and dropping into his new office to talk. Initially, however, he took advantage of his schedule, which allowed him to work at home. There he could better juggle writing his poems and *Time* reviews. He had only to show up two days a week: once to attend an editorial conference and again to turn in his copy. Still, he wondered how long his "happy set-up" would last.

All the writers in "Books" had to show their copy to the department's chief editor, the novelist Robert Cantwell. When Kees started, Cantwell had only been back on the job a few days after his release from a psychiatric clinic.

Conversation with Cantwell soon proved to be painful. Kees limited himself to yes and no answers and occasional harmless comments as he found out that his boss was more than just stressed. The Cantwell he had read in the 1930s had undergone a transformation. He had become a frustrated writer who had lost his creative spark. His fiction had once exhibited a certain humanity and social consciousness, but that, to Kees, had "gone out the window with his radicalism." And instead of editing, he made his staff rewrite their reviews, often expanding them on their own time, and then "hacked" them to pieces the next day so that nothing of any value got into the magazine after crossing his desk. "He has become a pious Episcopalian," Kees wrote Gilbert Neiman, "and refers to Tobacco Road characters as 'the proletariat.' The bridge from the C.P. to the Republicans would appear to be a short one indeed." Within a month, Cantwell went back on leave again.

Where one stood politically at *Time* often meant where one stood with regard to Henry Luce and his personal interests in such issues as

General Chiang Kai-shek, whom Luce considered a hero on the same scale as a Colonial patriot. Chinese Nationalist personalities of any distinction merited special treatment by Luce's employees—as Kees soon found out for himself at a luncheon engagement with Lin Yutang, the novelist and former professor of English philology at the University of Peking who had devised a plan to romanize the Chinese language.

Accompanied by Whittaker Chambers and fellow poets Nigel Dennis and Harvey Breit, Kees endured an "interminable horror" at the English grill of Rockefeller Center as Dr. Lin's anticommunism became increasingly more animated and his pronouncements became more bizarre. He pounded the table and called Karl Marx a moron. He said, "If World War III comes, I'll go to Africa and talk to the monkeys!" Then Lin expressed similar objections to Picasso, Hemingway, and Proust.

The more treacherous ideological drift of Whittaker Chambers was not so obvious to Kees, though he knew, as he confided to one correspondent, that something was different about him: "Saying nothing, just watching us and thinking and thinking."

When Chambers relieved Cantwell in early June, after returning to *Time* from his own month-long convalescence for stress, he was seen as only a slightly less intense version of Cantwell. He also seemed to be hiding something, something his conversion from communist journalist to the Quaker religion did little to allay. Chambers by this time had already unburdened his soul to the State Department, supplying the names and events that were ultimately used against Alger Hiss.

His encounters with the FBI were really the cause of his poor health. Yet to Kees, Chambers's paranoia, nervous exhaustion, and heart trouble seemed only to be the norm for someone working at *Time*, a transition that Kees now made in much the way Chambers described it in his memoir, *Witness*, and, perhaps, to his new writer. Chambers wrote of the inevitable "*Time* curve" "that most writers suffer and all experienced editors expect, dread and allow for. The curve graphs the rise and fall of a writer who begins by writing more or less naturally. Then he becomes conscious of something extra that *Time* requires. He tries to achieve it by writing '*Time* style,' which he invariably succeeds in parodying because his predicament proves that he has not yet grasped the fact that the style is a discipline of expression."

Kees found some escape from this dictum, helping James Agee draft a review of *The Four Quartets*, a piece that was a considerable departure for *Time*. It appeared in the June 7 issue with a piece that Kees finally claimed as his, a short notice about a new Mark Twain biography squeezed beneath the long, eloquent piece on Eliot.

∾

Your back turned to me, quite alone,
Standing with one hand raised to smooth your hair,
At a small window, green with rain.
                                                        —Weldon Kees

"Ann and I are together again," Kees wrote in a letter on the last Sunday in July 1943. The news was couched matter-of-factly, several paragraphs into a letter about his work at *Time*. "[We] have a remarkably cool apartment on lower Fifth Avenue & 10th street," he continued, adding that Ann had taken a job as Jim Farrell's secretary.

On the outside, the Kees marriage resumed as if nothing had happened. Ann just started appearing with Weldon at gatherings where he would usually have come alone or with one of his male friends. Some of his newer friends were startled to be introduced to her, for he had spoken neither of Ann nor of his life with her in Denver. Friends who had met the Keeses in the past just assumed that the couple had quietly patched the marriage, for they had remained in contact during their sixteen weeks apart.

During that time, Ann had lived on her own, moving from Denver not long after Weldon left. She first stayed with her parents in Wyoming and then took a train to San Francisco, where she stayed in a succession of San Francisco hotels until she found an apartment on Washington Street. She bought a small imitation-leather address book for her new life and entered the several New York City addresses her husband used, as well as the names of new girlfriends she made. It was not long, however, before she started using it to record what she would need or need to do for her train trip to New York: cash a check, buy cigarettes, insure her baggage, pick up timetables, and bring a copy of Dostoyevsky's *The Possessed*.

It is possible that Ann, before leaving San Francisco, checked on the progress of *The Last Man* at Weldon's request, for Jane Grabhorn wrote him several letters during the early summer, updating him on the printing and binding of his first book of poems. The sheets were now folded into signatures. Soon they would be sewn into a dark green binding of cloth and decorative paper-covered boards.

At *Time* Kees enjoyed a respite of security and professionalism in books (though he complained his assignments left him with little time to read what he wanted). He wrote lively and enjoyable book reviews, including a piece on *The Joy of Cooking* titled "One World, One Cook-book," marking the week that Mrs. Rombauer's book outsold Wendell Wilkie's memoir. He often worked collaboratively with Whittaker Chambers and Harvey Breit—and his way of telling himself that he had mastered the house style was to confide to James Laughlin that he thought his *Time* writing was "ghastly."

Chambers would not allow him be too negative, but from time to time Kees's signature made it past his boss. In a review of Vincent McHugh's novel *I Am Thinking of My Darling,* there is some approval for the plot about *hlehana,* a tropical laughing disease that spreads through New York and results in the breakdown of society, and then Kees begins to write in his own voice: "Others may surprise Author McHugh by developing a stubborn immunity to the laughing virus the longer they are exposed to this somewhat overlabored fantasy."

That summer, Kees called his workplace the Grime and Strife Building. "The pace is rather terrific," he wrote Gilbert Neiman, "and working here lends credence to all the stories one hears about the psychotic crackups. People drift in and out from such spots as Bellevue." The commonplaceness of such breakdowns in the next office or on the next floor assured that the same atmosphere in the world seen through his poems would be authentic. It would also give him more license to intensify that atmosphere in his New York–written poems. How could the verisimilitude of his work not be *right* given the *Fortune* writer who, with piles of notes, transcripts of interviews, and hundreds of books and pamphlets on the railroads, had set out to write a piece about the Union Pacific and then jumped from his chair, screamed, and tossed everything out the window?

In early August, Kees replaced the vacationing Winthrop Sergeant in the music department, for he had impressed his colleagues with his knowledge of popular music and jazz. Some had even heard him play James P. Johnson's piano rags at parties. There would be only one article to write before Sergeant's return, but it was an important one: an interview with the great stride pianist-composer Thomas "Fats" Waller and his lyricist, Andy Razaf.

The two men were staying at Razaf's mother's Asbury Park home, writing a new Broadway show to follow up the success of their *Early to Bed* and the motion picture *Stormy Weather*. Kees met them in rehearsal at Nola Studios in Manhattan and went back with them to New Jersey for a drunken evening that resulted in the only *Time* piece for which Kees saved tear sheets to show to family and friends, "How Tom is Doin'." It would be one of his only pieces of jubilant writing, especially where he described Waller's ability to "set the telephone book to music"—and his legendary appetite: "Keeping Tom Waller away from bars is a difficult feat. His capacity for both food and drink is vast. A Waller breakfast might include six pork chops. It is when he is seated at the piano that he most relishes a steady supply of gin. When his right-hand man, brother-in-law Louis Rutherford, enters with a tray of glasses, Tom will cry, 'Ah, here's the man with the dream wagon! I want it to hit me around my edges and get to every pound.'"

It is rare that we become what we pretended to be as children, but this happened to Kees when he became *Time*'s cinema editor in August, taking over much of Jim Agee's beat. His mother and father would have remembered—and may have reminded him—when they heard the good news that he had once reviewed movies for the little magazines he made in his father's office as a boy.

Kees continued to report to Whittaker Chambers, who had now been promoted to oversee the back pages of the magazine, and jokingly referred to himself rather comfortably as "a Luce lackey."

The workload now changed from reviewing a couple of bad books a week to viewing several films a day. Most were "stinkers," to use his word, and he soon tired of the privilege of seeing more movies than he would otherwise "have seen in a lifetime." Nevertheless, he had more opportunities to write as himself, for he was allowed more tart remarks for actors and directors than book authors. Too, there was that intangible perquisite of self-importance that came from visiting the projection rooms at the RKO Building, the RCA Building, and the New York headquarters of other movie studios and theater chains. "They have very comfortable leather chairs," he confided to Getty; "oh, hell, they all have lovely chairs; if only the pictures were up to the chairs."

Around the office, after three or more feature pictures a day, Kees would say things that differed little from what he wrote his friends. "Diana Barrymore" seemed to be in every movie, "with what looked like peanut butter on her chin, and Noah Beery, Jr." The copy he turned in also had the same annoyed candidness and color: "*The Phantom of the Opera* (Universal) contains more opera than phantom, more trills than thrills. In this it differs from the original *Phantom,* which Universal produced in the shock-absorbing twenties as a shivery vehicle for the late multiform Lon Chaney. The 1943 Phantom is bantam-sized Claude Rains, who attempts to terrify by sheer force of character, scar tissue, and Technicolor. Scuttling about in a robin's-egg blue mask, Cinemactor Rains scares nobody but his fellow cinemactors."

Lillian Hellman's *Watch on the Rhine* had become a play and a film as "alike as two swastikas." Joan Crawford displayed her "saucer-eyed talents" in *Above Suspicion* but without her "endless array of hats" was "reduced to a bare subsistence level." Conrad Veidt, however, in the same film, which was his last, gave Kees the chance to both pay homage to the actor who personified German Expressionism—and to stick another pin in Hollywood. "Women fainted, men screamed, children chortled," he wrote, thinking back to his boyhood days when *The Cabinet of Dr. Caligari* and *The Hands of Mr. Orlac* were shown. "By 1926," Kees wrote, "when Veidt went to Hollywood, audiences had got hold of themselves pretty well, but his adroit villainy was always good for a hiss."

Weldon and Ann went on a short vacation during the first week of September. He had borrowed a car for the drive to Provincetown on Cape Cod, which he wanted to experience for the first time before its summer season ended after Labor Day—and while friends such as Edmund Wilson were still there. Although Hans Hofmann had yet to set up his art school, and the other abstract expressionists had yet to arrive en masse, there was still that ambiance of the old artists' colony that had once included Eugene O'Neill, John Reed, and other members of the Village literati, who started summering at the Cape in 1915.

When Kees went back to work the following week, he found himself "suddenly canned." Initially, he blamed himself for having told Whittaker Chambers and some other senior editors that he might be drafted, triggering a secret policy to get around the patriotic duty expected of all employers of hiring people back after they had served their country, a duty that necessitated firing their replacements.

As Kees learned more, he found that he and several other writers had experienced what he likened to a party purge. Harvey Breit and the novelist Jimmy Stern were also dismissed. In Kees's case, however, there were other extenuating circumstances. He had fallen out of favor with Chambers, who had grown disenchanted with Kees's tone around the office—for he had been listening to Kees and had secretly arrived at the decision to put him in his place. "Our readers," Chambers told Kees, "don't want to hear you groan."

The four-hundred-dollar severance pay Kees received helped him to recover from the onus of being dismissed without warning. So did talking to Malcolm Cowley and writing Horace Gregory to confess he was glad to be through with the magazine. "It isn't worth it," he wrote, meaning the stress of writing his copy and dealing with the inscrutable Whittaker Chambers, "even for $100 a week." Jim Agee also met with him to commiserate. "The people at the top are as bewildered as the people at the bottom," he told Kees, who thought that would make a good Kafkaesque story about working at *Time*. "What if K. got to the Castle and found the hierarchy just as baffled as he had been?" Kees posed to Norris Getty. "Somehow, though, I don't like to dwell on Mr Luce in these terms."

With the loss of a regular paycheck, the Keeses moved temporarily to a less expensive apartment at 152 Seventh Avenue South, at the corner of Charles Street, near Sheridan Square. They began to search for new jobs and for a more "commodious and quieter place" that would not shock Weldon's parents when they arrived from Beatrice for a week's visit in early October—and that would help them get over the disappointment of not having their son at *Time*. Then came the final brush with the "selective service boys."

Kees had taken a blood test in May, and the results—"unsyphilitic"—and paperwork led to his being reclassified 1A.[2] He was then subsequently ordered to report again, certain he would be inducted without the deferment offered to married men without dependents. In the company of friends such as John Pauker, one of *Furioso*'s editors, Kees exchanged many amusing stories about what to do to avoid the draft. He joked about becoming a Jehovah's Witness or feigning an "epileptic fit" like the one in his novel *Fall Quarter* with a mouth full of soap flakes. He told Pauker's wife, Virginia, that he knew a doctor— one who did not want his name passed around—who administered a cocktail of drugs that foiled the draft board's physical and mental tests.

On September 24, Kees reported at Grand Central Palace, the site of New York City's selective service office, and was "lovingly placed in classification 4F." Whether he used the concoction of the mysterious physician or some other tactic is not known. In all likelihood, he was simply himself, a man with a slight build who said that he wrote poetry.

"What is psychological classification 72B?" he asked Getty in a letter written that same day; "that's what I'm in." In all likelihood, 72B was linked to one of the military's dubious and poorly administered psychological tests in 1943. At that time, millions of other young men were also being rejected for "defects above the neck," causing a national scandal. Editorials and political cartoons excoriated General Lewis B. Hershey, the head of the selective service; new tests were not in place until early 1944, well after things had gone in Kees's favor.

The week Kees celebrated his good fortune for having avoided the draft, a package arrived from Colt Press with a finished copy of *The Last Man*. Its dark green covers, its lack of a dust jacket, its watermarked pages hardly resembled the wartime paper-shortage productions of the trade houses. *The Last Man* looked like it came from another time, even though it was the debut of a new poet. Norris Getty, ever perceptive when it came to his friend's poems, noticed this when he received an advance copy in Fort Benning, Georgia, in late September. "I'm greatly pleased with everything about it," Getty wrote, "as good as anything since CATHAY [or any other] collection of Pound's."

To him there was a feeling "that the poems have been waited for." *The Last Man* had none of that "cool & fluent stuff that suggests immaculate conception." The kind of thing "most of the old SOUTHERN REVIEW boys would be likely to whip together. Your book belongs rather, I'm glad to say, in the company of Joyce and [Thomas] Mac-Greevy, Crane and early Eliot, and offhand I can think of no better praise."

Kees agreed with his friend and editor, savoring the notion that he was both a throwback and a step forward, one of the "important" young men, as one reviewer would call him: "I must say I feel too little sense of 'belonging' with my immediate contemporaries, with the exception of four or five guys. It's so easy, don't you think, to feel a sense of identification with the men of the Pound-Eliot generation, or even the Hart Crane-Tate-Horace Gregory generation, rather than the present gang, with its Rukeysers and Shapiros and John Frederick Nimses."

To assume Getty felt "a sense of identification" belied the fact that Kees subconsciously—or even consciously—knew the stake his friend had in the book, a debt Kees acknowledged in the dedication to *The Last Man,* which also included Maurice Johnson. Johnson deserved the dedication, too, although someone had to be added so as to avoid suggesting the wrong nature for the sentiment.

Throughout the autumn, reviews began to appear, for the most part noting that Kees had come up with a voice that balanced Thanatos with a sardonic will to live.

In the *New Republic,* William Poster, whom Kees knew as "Willy" and whose friendship with Kees had begun with an enthusiasm for *The Last Man,* noted that this new poet overcame the "discords of experience" with an "indistinguishably blended grief and wit." In *Sewanee Review,* Horace Gregory acknowledged the finished character of these same qualities and Kees's "unfaked" worldview. He also observed that the gloom in Kees's poetry might stand "in the way of its receiving greater notice." Gregory saw *The Last Man* as a movement toward a "new school of satire." Yet he preferred Kees in his ironical mode and picked "The Smiles of the Bathers" as his favorite poem.

Less enthusiastic reviewers watered down Kees's first appearance with lists of poets who had influenced him. Or they observed the obvious: that he was depressed, like his poetry. "One is more aware of the writers whom [Kees] has pored over," Babette Deutsch wrote in *Common Sense,* "Eliot, Auden, MacNeice, Fearing, along with Baudelaire, Rimbaud, Henry James, Arthur Waley, Ogden and Richards, than his personal evaluation of experience." A "young man with a conscience" is how Katinka Loeser described Kees in *Poetry:* "We have here the unmistakable symptoms of that popular *malaise* of the twenties, that is, of the postwar before it became the prewar world—disciplined despair. You've missed the Disney and you have to sit through the Dreiser."

Loeser saw Kees as out of lockstep with the war effort, too, stating that his poetry was not progressive in spirit or in style. "Some rather pleasant things will happen to many of us," she posited hopefully, "if we are as realistic about the postwar world as we are about the present catastrophe."

Kees was hired in October by Paramount News Service, "The Eyes and Ears of the World." Now his work would appear in countless theaters, albeit as anonymously as his articles in *Time,* since he would be writing scripts for newsreel narrators. He would also make comparatively good money: seventy-five dollars a week.

When he started at Paramount's uptown studio, the newsreel industry was undergoing a respite from a period of decay. It was now a propaganda organ of the Army Signal Corps, an arrangement facilitated by a lack of competition and journalistic independence since Paramount, Pathé, Movietone, and Hearst's News of the Day already shared footage and unionized cameramen, which made it easy for the Signal Corps to take over production of all war-related footage in 1942. The newsreels that resulted followed a formula and required little imagination. In this way, Paramount became a vast improvement over the madhouse of *Time.* Kees could write poems on the job again and continue enjoying the lifestyle of an uptown professional, such as dining at Diamond Jim's at 42nd and Broadway ("delectable pot roast and potato pancakes") or at Marnell's on East 47th Street. The Hapsburg House on 45th Street, Ludwig Bemelmans's restaurant, featured murals of the little girls from his Madeline stories for children. Having published a poem such as "For My Daughter" must have made this atmosphere ironic for Kees, who also found enchanting the lesbian clientele that included Marlene Dietrich and Greta Garbo.

Kees often lunched with Martin Andrews, a former bomber pilot whose desk sat near his. Sometimes they bought sandwiches from a bar at the end of Forty-second Street and then took the Weehawken Ferry back and forth while eating lunch, smoking, and blowing off steam over Paramount's brass, Albert J. Richard, the editor-in-chief, and the makeup editor, J. Seegar Heavilin—whose Republican politics clashed with theirs. The younger Andrews helped soak up Kees's disdain for them and his newsreel work. He even helped write Kees's copy, like he did when footage of a rodeo at Madison Square Garden came in. Kees was charged with writing the script since he was from "out West," but when Heavilin walked away, he turned to Martin and said, "Andy, I can't write this shit. You write it."

The Paramount workday, however, did have responsibilities. As a member of the newsreel makeup staff, Kees began work in one of the showing rooms, viewing films from "Rotapool," the government service that provided footage taken by armed-forces cameramen and distributed to newsreel companies on a rotation basis, as well as lighter fare from Paramount's own cameramen. The raw newsreel was then edited and cut. Titles were written, printed on film stock, and spliced into the footage. Soundmen added music and special effects.

Ann also found a new job in October as an assistant editor at *Antiques*, a sophisticated magazine written and illustrated for wealthy collectors and dealers. Her income and Weldon's made them seem "affluent" to friends such as Manny Farber, the film critic of the *New Republic*, then married to Janet Richards, the memoirist, who knew the Keeses in both New York and San Francisco. It could be said that they represented the "special type of people," as Arthur Koestler called the working intelligentsia, the "liaison agents between the way we live and the way we *could* live."

Another benefit came from Ann's new job. A correspondent for the magazine had stayed in England after the war broke out rather than risk making the dangerous Atlantic crossing, so the Keeses sublet the woman's handsomely furnished apartment at 129 East Tenth Street, on a block between Third Avenue, where the El ran, and Second Avenue, which had the feeling of a "decayingly elegant cul de sac," as described by Janet Richards, "with mossy houses from the Eighties." Inside the Keeses' new home, she found it intimately suited for them. The windows looked out toward Saint Mark's and had inside them trailing vines and ferns. There was an alcove "just big enough for a little Jacobean dining table. There was a kitchen that was only a short hallway between the alcove and the bathroom and, like me, Ann washed the dishes in the bathroom sink. In the living room there were two single beds, covered with faded brocades, one against the wall, the other in the middle of the room, since there was no other place for it [...] and all of the furniture, the chairs, bookcases, little chests and tiny tables were relics of the eighteenth century, inconspicuously maintaining their unalterable perfection of design. On the floor was an ancient Oriental rug."

The Keeses moved in during the same October week that Weldon's parents came to visit—in time to impress them, along with the Broadway shows and Carnegie Hall concerts that they attended with their son and daughter-in-law.

James Agee was a regular guest. He was known for his nighttime visits, when he might leave a Village bar and look for other company—and another source of drink, even if that meant ringing the doorbell of the Keeses' apartment late at night. There whiskey and gin poured freely, and the talk centered on films, the gossip inside *Time*, and the occasional book ideas that Kees and Agee never carried out.

Harold Rosenberg could also be found at the Keeses', for he lived in one of the apartments upstairs with his wife and infant child. Kees had met Rosenberg during his summer at Yaddo. They had exchanged letters since their poems appeared together in the same Writers' Project publications. Rosenberg, however, was now known as an art critic, and his enthusiasm for the new American painting—and his being in the same building—soon contributed to Kees's growing interest in abstract art. It was not uncommon for Manny Farber, Clement Greenberg, Rosenberg, and Kees to be in the same room together, sharing—and shouting over—the artists and paintings they championed.

The novelist William March also frequented the Keeses' apartment. Kees had met March through their mutual friend James Farrell in the spring and had attended some of March's legendary cocktail parties in the living room of his "swank" Central Park apartment. A brilliant raconteur, March told stories about his native Mobile, the trenches of World War I, and his peregrinations around Times Square with plainclothesmen on the lookout for such characters as hair fetishists who secretly snipped off locks of women's hair from behind.

Friends thought of Kees during this time as a social being. He seemed to always have something ironically dry or funny to say—like at a party given by Dwight and Nancy Macdonald, where he made fun of his host's penny-pinching. Late into the night, when it became clear that absolutely no food was forthcoming, he cupped his hand to his ear and announced sharply, "Hist! I thought I heard a cracker snap!" Nevertheless, the way he spoke and moved from one guest to the other at such gatherings conveyed, as Janet Richards saw it, an "implicit desire that they not come too near." To her he became a Nebraskan Strindberg or a man like the English poet William Cowper, who "lay down in despair and rose up in horror." For all his warmth, he had "a touch-me-not quality" now often associated with closeted homosexuals of the period. Ann, however, did not behave like the traditional "beard." It amused her that Weldon attracted women as well as men, like the time she and Weldon had dinner with William Carlos

Williams at the Sevilla, a well-known Spanish restaurant in the city. Williams had brought along his sister-in-law, who, despite being over fifty, took an interest in Weldon and during the course of the meal felt him up under the table.

∾

Louise Bogan told Kees that she would rather be a scrubwoman than a book reviewer—and leave New York for Spokane, where her lover, Theodore Roethke, now taught. "But twenty dollars a week from *The New Yorker*," she confessed, "was too good to pass up."

Kees did not disagree with her about the drudgery or money. However, he saw book reviewing as cultural journalism and saw cultural journalism in terms of saving what and who—especially in the American experience—would otherwise be neglected, misunderstood. He even, after leaving *Time,* made his own opportunity to review books again for the liberal monthly *Common Sense,* where he became the magazine's unofficial poetry reader in early October. He approached Richard Rovere, the editor, and asked if he could review Louis Filler's new biography of the liberal essayist and pacifist Randolph Bourne, who wrote for the *New Republic* during World War I. *Common Sense* frequently ran pieces that questioned the war effort, and it seemed the right venue until Rovere showed him the galleys of Babette Deutsch's review of *The Last Man.* Taken aback by the review's harshness, he withdrew his Bourne manuscript before Rovere could run it, perhaps because of more than disappointment. Miss Deutsch had written in a spirit out of keeping with what Kees wanted to achieve in praising the tragic figure of Bourne, a figure with whom he certainly could see himself identifying: "'It makes me wince,' Bourne wrote later, 'to hear a man spoken of as a failure, or to have it said of one that he "doesn't amount to much." Instantly I want to know why he has not succeeded, and what have been the forces that have been working against him. He is the truly interesting person, and yet how little our eager-pressing, on-rushing world cares about such aspects of life, and how hideously though unconsciously cruel and heartless it usually is!'"

Soon after his falling out with *Common Sense,* Kees placed a shortened version of the Bourne piece in the *New York Times Book Review* for October 31, under the title "Champion of Failures." He also earned a semiregular venue on Sundays when the *Book Review*'s editor, Robert Van Gelder, began sending him more books to read for potential reviews (as did the *New Republic* and *Partisan Review*).

What would have evaporated as bright talk during his East Tenth Street gatherings or as an acid thought while he was walking on Astor Place or the other streets that led to the Village, the El, and the subway now found an outlet in his reviews. He could reveal another sign of his generation's lackluster contribution to literature in the warmed-over Thomas Wolfe he read in a new "jazz novel." He could point to signs of cultural health in the critical regard given to Negro folk music. In reviewing a history of the little magazines, he could miss the "sense of fresh explorations perpetually going forward, the dissidence, the experimentation, above all the international spirit that animated the little magazines of the twenties"—and point to how things were in 1943, when the editors of *View* took risks by printing poems on pink paper, when the gifted editors of another time were dead or "have assigned themselves roles in disappearing acts—Ford (Ford Madox, not Charles Henri), Margaret Anderson, Harriet Monroe; have given up editing (Eliot, Wyndham Lewis); or are wanted by the Allied police force (Pound). As for writers, a whole generation of 'promising talents' examines its graying hairs and pouchy eyes in the cubicles of the O.W.I., the Time and Life Building, and in the scenario department of MGM. Many of them have not only succeeded in making complete adaptations to these realms, but have reconditioned them into closed worlds of value."

Kees, in the same *Partisan Review* piece, saw Cummings, Eliot, Stevens, Williams, and others as still the most gifted avant-garde contributors—indeed as the poets he wanted to be "up there" with. If they were the "Lost Generation," he asked, "then what is this moldy milieu in which we find ourselves; and what are we?"

Kees, however, was hardly set back by thinking he had been born too late, as his letters, reviews, and some poems suggested. That autumn, he assembled a chapbook of new poems to submit to James Laughlin for his "Poets of the Year" series—and he reworked the poems that Laughlin had already accepted for *New Directions 8*, the annual for 1944. He discussed with Jim Agee the possibility of collaborating on a selection of soldiers' letters that, if "carefully edited and cut with an eye to surprise, would make most current fiction look even duller than its worst detractors say it is." And he continued to find his place among the New York intellectuals and to liberally report back to his Nebraska friends in letters that bring to mind an actor, intimately turned to his audience, describing the overreaching of his contemporaries—such as the banter from an evening at the Rahvs':

"I think everyone in New York is crazy." This was said, as I recall, at some point between Mary McCarthy's explanation of who the real heroine of The Golden Bowl *is (I never found out: Natalie Rahv was telling me, rather irritably, what all was wrong with Dwight Macdonald) and an argument about the proper way to pronounce Randall Jarrell's last name. (Accent on the last syllable, says Edmund Wilson, adding that Jarrell is "essentially an adolescent and only interesting in his poetry when he is working off his infantile obsessions." In connection with this, you once mentioned the bevy of bears that turn up in Jarrell's work. I think now that these are all, to the last one, teddy bears.)*

Since coming to New York, Kees had often thought about writing a new novel. When he was still getting his mail at the offices of Russell and Volkening, he even discussed this possibility with his agent. But he was moving away from writing any more fiction. He had finished one or two short stories at Yaddo and published only two in 1943, both of which had been written in Denver and followed previous formulas. "Every Year They Came Out" was another of his regionalist pieces, featuring two unmarried sisters from Nebraska trapped in an unsatisfactory hotel room. The suggestion of repressed, incestuous lesbianism could have been developed further had he followed Carson McCullers's example. "The Sign" was a throwback to the library stories. It dealt with repression, too—that of a woman who places all of her desire into authoring and hanging up a sign to keep patrons out of the stacks. For some reason, however, Kees did not pick up this direction and explore it further. Perhaps it meant tapping into a place in himself where he did not want to go. Several of his late short stories have homosexual or female themes, and more of these would have been at odds with the masculine image he had been projecting since the arrival of Ann and his being declared 4F—and reinforcing with the only fiction he talked about writing: a detective novel.

The tie that people made between the author and his novels, however, was not made with his poetry. There Kees was not under the same constraints, and the female personas that appeared in his newer poems represent advance and maturity where their sisters in his fiction do not. "Girl at Midnight," written during his last weeks in Denver, has Kees assuming a young woman's voice, perhaps even Ann's, admitting that "Love is a sickroom with the roof half gone." He could also see himself and put in relief things he had probably actually said to her:

> — Your face is never clear. You always stand
> In charcoal doorways in the dark. Part of your face
> is gone. You say, "Just to be through with this damned world.
> Contagious fogs blow in. Christ, we could die
> The way deer sometimes do, their antlers locked,
> Rotting in snow."

In November, Kees obtained tear sheets of "The Evening of the Fourth of July" for Henry Volkening to show to publishers. "If there was interest," Kees told him, he would consider a new novel.

When no offers came, Volkening, in February 1944, convinced his client to write a synopsis that he could circulate along with the tear sheets, and Kees typed out a synopsis for a literary potboiler about the shadowy life of a minor poet, one part detective novel and one part *Citizen Kane*.

Kees invented a biographer's search for a vanished poet, his biographer one Carl Ellis, a scholar at "loose ends" who finds a volume of poems by a writer named Fredric Shore Strandquist. The book is fascinating and little known — the stuff of a literary discovery. Yet it is Strandquist's mysterious life that "greatly excites" Ellis's curiosity, for he learns that this family black sheep has not been seen for fifteen years and that his family is "not sure (or willing to tell) whether he is alive or dead."

The plot, as Kees imagined it, would have had the same chase excitement as Alfred Hitchcock's *Thirty-nine Steps* or Graham Greene's screenplays of *The Orient Express, This Gun for Hire,* and *The Ministry of Fear.* As the details of Strandquist's life snowball, a trail leads toward a climax in which Ellis learns that Strandquist is still alive. The reader would have been confronted by the uncertainty of being, by the notion that there is no real or secure contingent art of interpretation to undo uncertainty. Carl Ellis's search for Fredric Shore Strandquist would have revealed that the task of fully discovering and understanding another human being is "an impossibility."

On the single page he finished for Volkening, Kees emphasized to prospective publishers that a "moving picture version would, by necessity, concentrate on the shock effect of Strandquist's appearance and the contrast between his expected personality and 'real' one."

In the early months of 1944, when he left an ellipsis at the end of a decade of novel and story writing, Kees began to paint "abstract things," as he called his first gouaches in one letter.

His new friends critics Harold Rosenberg and Clement Greenberg preached aesthetic dogmas about abstract painting in *Partisan Review*. In the *New York Times* and on the radio, the painters Adolph Gottlieb and Mark Rothko discussed their art and began the abstract expressionists' assault on academicism and the "befuddled" art establishment. "Our work," they wrote, "must insult anyone who is spiritually attuned to interior decoration, pictures for the home, pictures over the mantle." In the loft-rat studios of Arshile Gorky, Willem de Kooning, and other artists, the modern idioms of Cézanne, Picasso, Miró, and émigré European surrealism were being adopted and cross-pollinated on canvas. At the evening sessions of Hans Hofmann's school on West Eighth Street, one could visit a real European atelier. Students and visitors alike could listen to Hofmann's impromptu lectures and interpret his ideas about painting, which were delivered in a thick German accent and with a rather tricky command of English, adding the authority of mystery to what he said as much as clarity. The new art spread via the webs of personal contacts that ran back and forth inside the Village. When people drank beer together in their studio lofts and small apartments, when they met for hamburgers at Riker's or drank endless rounds of coffee at the New China Cafeteria on Union Square, they began to talk more and more about art.

Kees found himself at the beginning of the New York school before the art historian Dore Ashton gave it that name. Through Rosenberg, Greenberg, and Manny Farber, and on his own, he learned what was going on in the studios of Jackson Pollock, Robert Motherwell, William Baziotes, and the others. He knew they were becoming the center of an exciting controversy that had not yet come to a head and that their "artists' talk" was more alive than the tiring "destructions" of poems by the New Critics. Like Breton, who had a generation earlier chosen to settle among the artists of Montmartre rather than the poets of Montparnasse, Kees believed there was more latent dynamism among the New York painters and their allied critics than among his writer contemporaries. And he was willing to buy, for now, the idea that these Americans, who called themselves abstractionists, nonobjectivists, or, with as much conviction, nothing at all, were the logical heirs of the European cubists.

He set up a makeshift studio in his apartment, and the only reason that he gave for his painting was that it was "wonderfully satisfying." Initially Ann did not take her husband's painting seriously and only mentioned his new vocation matter-of-factly when Norris Getty, on leave that summer, had dinner with her at Café Society Uptown. Weldon had no formal art training, and on the surface his interest in art seemed no deeper than that of other cultured people who visited New York's galleries or purchased a few tasteful modern reproductions for the walls. One of his poems in *The Last Man*, however, suggests that he did think more deeply about painting and being a painter than even his wife knew.

"On a Painting by Rousseau," Kees's only contribution to the tradition of *ekphrastic* poetry, is after *The Cart of Père Juniet*, which Rousseau himself painted after a photograph in 1908. Like Keats, Stevens, Williams, Auden, and other poets who have "beheld" a work of art, Kees used the opportunity to express some personal vision beyond what he saw in the frame.

But his "close reading" of a painting cannot explain why Kees took up a brush. Still, he must have appreciated the fact that Henri Rousseau, whose reproductions hung on the walls of so many Village apartments, was an untrained amateur like himself, the model of the outsider artist that he would become. He only had to hear some of the pronouncements of the New York painters themselves as further encouragement. "Hell," Clyfford Still said of the *Zeitgeist* that Kees now breathed, "it's not about painting—any fool can put color on a canvas."

Kees had lunch with the writer Ernest Brace in August. He had first encountered Brace's short stories in the *American Caravan* anthologies of the 1930s—and had recently read a carbon of Brace's new novel, *Buried Stream*, which Henry Volkening, who also represented Brace, had given him to review. Kees enjoyed the story of the disillusioned public-relations man who saves his protégé, a poet, from jumping from a window and is then haunted by the mental image of having pushed him instead during an affair with the younger man's estranged wife. The book, however, had not been taken seriously, as Kees learned from Brace, who had not published a novel since the early 1920s. The irony of his situation, Kees knew, was that he was the brother of a publisher. "It's been more of a curse," he said of his connection to Harcourt Brace.

Kees tried to sound encouraging. He admired the fact that Brace had dropped out of the literary gambit and now taught carpentry at a vocational college in upstate New York. (Kees would later dedicate a poem about Christ, another carpenter, to Brace.) He may have mentioned that painting, like Brace's woodworking, had become his refuge from the pressures of publishing. Still, he could not fully identify with Brace's situation. He had mail to answer from the readers of *The Last Man.*

"What you say could only give me the greatest pleasure," Kees wrote one admirer who asked when a longer collection would appear. He admitted that he did not have enough new poems for a trade book and blamed the summer for not having been a good one for writing. "For that matter, neither are the times," he added, meaning the war, which depressed him. In reality, however, painting, along with his work at Paramount, left him little time for writing. There were also the soft distractions of a prosperous young New York couple's lifestyle, which had the same contrasts as a scene in one of his poems—from seeing a Posada exhibition at the Brooklyn Museum, with its penny-dreadful depictions of lurid suicides and the skeletal *calavera* from the Mexican Day of the Dead, to escorting Sarah and John Kees around town again when they returned for the annual meeting of the Mayflower Society. "I think we managed to keep her entertained," Ann wrote of her mother-in-law, thinking of the shows she and Weldon had found for her. Most had Russian ballerinas, including the Broadway musical *Follow the Girls,* with Irina Baronova and newcomer Jackie Gleason, and the opening night of the Ballet Theatre. There they watched *Swan Lake, Pillar of Fire,* the world premiere of *Graduation Ball* by David Lichine with Tatiana Riabouchinska—and the society people in the Met bar such as Mrs. Harrison Williams, who appeared in Pond's ads, Cecil Beaton photographs, Dali paintings, and Cole Porter songs, and the actress and dancer Vera Zorina.

While he wrote little poetry during the autumn and winter, Kees had literary make-work to fill in. He read and reviewed Vladimir Nabokov's translations in *Three Russian Poets* ("fine piece of work") for the *New York Times Book Review* and tried to obtain an advance copy of the New Directions edition of F. Scott Fitzgerald's autobiographical essays, *The Crack-Up*—as well as his check for the poems he had published in *New Directions 8*. James Laughlin, in turn, asked him for a list of the best experimental writing published since 1936. Kees mentioned poems and stories that he personally liked such as, among his contemporaries, Elizabeth Bishop's "The Fish," John Berryman's "Winter Landscape," Randall Jarrell's "Death of the Ball Turret Gunner," Kenneth Rexroth's "The Phoenix and the Tortoise," and Delmore Schwartz's "The Statues." He also recommended William Carlos Williams's "Burning the Christmas Greens" and Wallace Stevens's "The Men That Are Falling" for Laughlin to use in his "10-years book" (published in 1947 as *Spearhead*).

With the increase in newsreel footage that came after the Allied landing of D-Day, Kees spent more time at Paramount. No longer could he tarry for long at the open stalls of "Books 'N Things" and the other secondhand booksellers along Fourth Avenue before he caught the train uptown to West Forty-third Street. Ann worked harder, too. Her name now appeared on the *Antiques* masthead, and she had moved from doing mostly layout to writing as well. In December, she wrote an article about the Greek Revival houses on Washington Square North for the March 1945 issue. Illustrated with a Berenice Abbott photograph, the article looked back to *The American Scene* and protested the wave of "Post War Planning" that would demolish a number of fine old brownstones to make room for high-rises that would overshadow the heart of Greenwich Village, which was now the center of the Keeses' lives, a bohemian refuge away from their workday lives that broke up the time her husband spent painting or starting a poem. Ann described that world in gossipy letters that, in this case, brought to life a February party on the Village's west side given by Jim Agee's sister, at which Weldon played piano and Wilder Hobson trombone, entertaining guests who included

Jim Agee and Mia Fritsch. Manny and Janet Farber. Bob and Virginia di Nero, both painters. Clem Greenberg and his new girl—not, thank

God, Margaret Marshall. Helen Levitt, photographer. A couple of anony-
mous young men in sharply-tailored lieutenant's uniforms and about six
anonymous and personable girls. Nigel Dennis. And about six middle-
aged people who left at 11:30. Late in the evening Helen Levitt spent a
good deal of time trying to get someone to dance with her. She said to
Jim Agee, "Please dance with me Jim. I have had lots of fun dancing with
you." Poker-faced, A. Lincoln–like, Jim said, "And I've had fun dancing
with you, Helen. But it wasn't because I was dancing with you."[3]

Back home on East Tenth Street, the color of Village life took on
other interesting shades. Wolfgang Born, the brother of the physicist
Max Born, had been coming over to work with Ann. As a noted art
historian and authority on American still-life and landscape art, he
had met Ann through his contacts at *Antiques*. This kind of painting,
though, was only one of his interests. He had illustrated the first edition of Thomas Mann's *Death in Venice*—and, with Ann's help, was
now editing his new monograph, *The Art of the Insane*. Naturally, this
project attracted Kees, whose abstractions were on view in the apartment; Kees also enjoyed talking to Born, who was a German Jew not
yet accustomed to his new country.

On one occasion, after returning from Jim Farrell's, Kees found
himself explaining *Studs Lonigan* to Born as the life story of a young
man growing up on Chicago's South Side. Not quite understanding
that Kees meant a novel, Born asked what had become of Lonigan.
"He became a drunk, got sick, and finally died," Kees answered, giving
possibly the shortest synopsis possible for Farrell's trilogy. "Oh, I am
so sorry to hear that," Born replied.

Born was probably the inspiration for the refugee Mannheim, the
"white-faced man with sad enormous eyes" in "The Bell from Europe,"
which Kees wrote in March or April. In that poem, Kees obviously
found something deeper in his connection to Born whenever Saint
Mark's of the Bowery struck the hour, interrupting their conversations
long enough for one man, from Europe, to feel at home and the other,
from Nebraska, to feel differently:

> *Reader, for me that bell marked nights*
> *Of restless tossing in this narrow bed,*
> *The quarrels, the slamming of a door,*
> *The kind words, friends for drinks, the books we read,*
> *Breakfasts with streets in rain.*

The bell tolling for Kees is a pall of smoke; "the sound of a dead Europe" hanging in the streets shows that his insomnia, his trivial arguments with his wife, their cozy life on East Tenth Street, are ironically part of a world war, a war that was as graphic for Kees as it was for the Americans fighting it.

The battle on Iwo Jima held the nation's attention during February and March 1945. At Paramount, the makeup staff put in long hours editing and reediting the raw film flown back from the Pacific. More than ever before, Kees and his coworkers found themselves challenged both by the standards of taste and censorship and by the need to honestly portray the harsh reality of total war. The Marines had suffered enormous casualties taking the island, a fact that could not be glossed over. The resistance put up by the Japanese had resulted in death on a scale heretofore unimagined—and undocumented. The time Kees spent working with the grisly content, in shifts that ran from nine in the morning until six in the morning the next day, left him sickened and exhausted.

Jim Agee, who learned about the making of the newsreel at his sister's party, reviewed it in the March 24 issue of the *Nation*. He called Paramount's *To the Shores of Iwo Jima* "one of the best and most terrible war films" and praised its use of flat silence, still photographs, and such touches as a camera moving slowly down a wall, a poetic touch that shows Kees's hand in the way it borrows, as Agee noted, from Jean Cocteau and the early experimental filmmaker René Clair.

As the Allied victory in Europe and the Pacific became assured, Kees reacted differently than other Americans to the good news. He produced new poems as the war ended that were not at all celebratory. They reminded readers instead that violence and war went on insidiously and bloodlessly.

Kees saw, with his handful of poems, a bigger picture even than what was now being planned in Moscow and Washington after Yalta. In his introduction to *New Directions 8,* James Laughlin referred to several poets and writers, identified only by initials, who represented the ways in which the war had affected their lives. "D" is Delmore Schwartz, who taught English to sailors and had to deal with seeing "F—the Jews" on his blackboard. "R" is Kenneth Rexroth, the "leftist-pacifist" who had to work as a male nurse in the psychopathic ward of a San Francisco hospital. "K" is Weldon Kees. "His hatred of violence," Laughlin wrote, "which the money system produces, is deeper and more instinctive than that of anyone I know and in [him] the pain of this war, even at the remove of New York, has induced a psychic-physical response reaction, a nervous condition that has him stiffened up like a mummy and flat on his back."

∾

During the early spring of the previous year, in March or April 1944, Kees had written a poem titled "Robinson." He had been living in New York for a year, part of that time alone. He had been in the city long enough to reflect back on how things had changed since Denver. He lived like one of the New York intellectuals. He had a good job. His wife had a good job. He painted. He reviewed books. He had a nice apartment. He had stayed out of the war and kept his dignity. He had also stayed out of publishing's commercialism and kept his dignity, setting aside his unwritten novel about a biographer and a mysterious poet without regret. He had not, however, set aside the intriguing philosophical problems his unwritten novel posed about the impossibility of understanding another human being and the contrast between an expected personality and the real one, which is not real in the first place, but simply a construct. This dialectic found its way into his poems, which always came easiest for him when the weather changed.

The premise for "Robinson" was simple enough. Kees used himself as the template for a refined man living in New York and then described the man when he was away, using his vacant room and various personal, commonplace effects as pieces for a self-portrait without the self. The poem must have been one that came quickly to him, the kind he wrote on the job at Paramount. He only had to let his mind wander back downtown, around the apartment on East Tenth Street, to see how strangely the room reflected his presence and absence, to see how every day that room was the stage for a small, personal vanishing act, for the scene as a detective would find it before filing his missing-person report:

The dog stops barking after Robinson has gone.
His act is over. The world is a gray world,
Not without violence, and he kicks under the grand piano,
The nightmare chase well under way.

The mirror from Mexico, stuck to the wall,
Reflects nothing at all. The glass is black.
Robinson alone provides the image Robinsonian.

Which is all of the room — walls, curtains,
Shelves, bed, the tinted photograph of Robinson's first wife,
Rugs, vases, panatellas in a humidor.
They would fill the room if Robinson came in.

The pages in the books are blank,
The books that Robinson has read. That is his favorite chair,
Or where the chair would be if Robinson were here.

All day the phone rings. It could be Robinson
Calling. It never rings when he is here.

Outside, white buildings yellow in the sun.
Outside, the birds circle continuously
Where trees are actual and take no holiday.

Norris Getty had usually seen Kees's poems before he submitted
them to a publisher. However, in the summer of 1944, Kees put off
sending "Robinson" and the other new poems that he had promised
to send in June. He missed the old days in Denver, when he could
get Getty's immediate reaction, but since then, since the publication
of *The Last Man*, his apprentice thinking had been replaced with the
confidence of a mature poet. It was not until October that Getty, now
stationed in New Guinea, received a manila envelope filled with new
work, and by then Kees could already report that "Robinson" had been
accepted by the *New Yorker*.

He was "astonished," for so many poems had *almost* been taken in
the past. He was also surprised and nearly disheartened by how long it
took for the poem to finally appear one year later in the October 6 issue,
a few months after the happy sailors, soldiers, and smiling girls in
Times Square on V-E Day, after Hiroshima and Nagasaki had already
been bombed, after the war.

The first readers of "Robinson" recognized the connection to *Robinson Crusoe*. Other readers would have seen the lineage of other Robinsons, too, distant European cousins derived from the same myth.
Kafka's *Amerika* and Céline's *Journey to the End of the Night*, books
Kees would have known, have American characters named Robinson.

Like Kees's, theirs are troubling, inauspicious confreres. They drift in and out of lives in an alien and alienating New York, especially Céline's Robinson, who would have provided Kees with a precursor originating in the French existentialism he assimilated in translation from the pages of *Partisan Review*. And Kees very much considered "Robinson" a satire, categorizing it as such in a new manuscript he titled *The Fall of the Magicians*.

Kees entered the poem in Houghton Mifflin's poetry contest in the summer of 1945. Though he learned he did not win, one of the judges wrote: "This is intellectual art with a strange emotional impact characteristic of some contemporary painting. I find in it brutality and violence and salt."

Like other young people at the war's end, the Keeses dealt with a new set of conditions as the competition for jobs and living space resumed in New York.

The woman from whom they had leased the apartment on East Tenth Street had returned from England, and they needed to find a new home. Fortunately, the poet Howard Nemerov tipped them off to an apartment at 227 East Twenty-fifth Street when he and his new English bride were also apartment hunting.

In the working-class neighborhood where the Keeses moved in November, the clatter of the Third Avenue El kept time instead of the bell of Saint Mark's. Street life replaced the quiet and charm of East Tenth. At first, Weldon likened the Twenty-fifth Street apartment to an oppressive "noisebox," which "combined the poorer features of Grand Central Station, Ebbetts Field, Bellevue and the Chautauqua Bell Ringers." The local color, however, soon fed the increasingly New York–centered and apocalyptic poetry now written from his new address:

> *I live. The Elevated shudders to a stop*
> *At Twenty-Eighth and Third. Among*
> *The nuns and crippled Negroes, we descend*
> *The stairway to the street, to red-cheeked chromo Christ,*
> *Hung with the bloody calves' heads in the butcher shop.*
> —"Testimonies"

Despite the jarring change fifteen blocks north had made to their lifestyle, the Keeses made do with the good company of their neighbors the Nemerovs. They occupied themselves with furnishing their apartment to their own tastes. Robinson's favorite chair and the other antique fixtures of his old rooms on East Tenth Street gave way to post-war tubular steel chairs and tables in the International style. "So here we are," Kees wrote Maurice Johnson on Thanksgiving Day, "with our Flents, our frayed nerves, our new Hans Knoll furniture, none too securely held up by the floors that look as though a herd of large, solid-hoof herbivorous mammals had once used them for hourly stampedes, but very glad to be out of the cold we are."[4]

In December, Kees escaped his noisy apartment, nerves, and lowered circumstances by attending a number of sumptuous holiday parties. Paramount News rented out the upstairs party room of the Italian Garden for its cameramen, management, and a few of the scriptwriters, including Kees, who posed in the company's group photograph with a drink in his hand. At the townhouse of Henry James Jr., his first publisher, Bill Roth, who now worked for Prentice Hall, and Gorham Munson, the editor of the little magazine *Secession* in the 1920s, hosted another holiday gathering.

Junior, Kees observed, had the high-domed forehead of his grand-uncle the novelist, if not the intelligence, and his home in the East Seventies possessed at least some of the literary opulence of *The Golden Bowl,* with ancestral portraits in gilded frames on the walls. The poignancy for Kees, however, did not come from admiring them. It came when the real Jamesian namesake, the businessman Henry James Sr., appeared to mix with the younger guests (many "women who came and went, speaking in low tones of Prentice-Hall's trade department," as Kees eliotically described them). Joining in one conversation, Senior left the impression that the family name had devolved on people who had no idea of its significance, for when someone asked him what he thought of his relative, whose novels were being reprinted by New Directions, he could only think to say, "Quite a boom he's having."

The separation of Janet and Manny Farber saddened the Keeses as they began their fourth year in New York in 1946. It would have reminded them of their own situation back in Denver, which now seemed further in the past than just three years ago. In New York, Ann had changed for the better, and Weldon soon acknowledged this when he dedicated *The Fall of the Magicians* to her. There were other reasons to feel secure, too.

Kees had been promoted to makeup editor at Paramount. He had nearly one hundred newsreel scripts to his credit, ranging from the uncovering of a Nazi spy ring to Japanese kamikaze missions to the eruption of the Paricutín volcano in a Mexican cornfield. His hours at work had been increased, too, and though this had an impact on how much time he could spend writing and painting, he still found this job "as good a way of making a living as any I know." He even took more professional pride in work that he only did to pay the bills. Later in the year, he wrote his father and told him he considered his newsreel about the atomic bomb tests at Bikini Atoll to be his best work so far: "Its power and relation to the current world crisis is so marked that the state department ordered prints to be rushed abroad; they will be screened in Moscow and at the Paris Peace Conference."

Kees would also produce other Paramount newsreels like this one, such as "Hiroshima (One Year After)" and "Atom Bomb City." Their raw poetry, of a devastated city, searing light, and soaring mushroom clouds, would also find its way into his poems—as did, perhaps, the comfort he took in Ann: "We made love while the bombers roared on by, / Gone seaward. The room rocked and the world closed in your eyes" ("The Locusts, the Plaza, the Room").

During the early months of 1946, Kees sent *The Fall of the Magicians* to smaller publishers such as James Decker in Iowa. He still believed the trade houses were not interested in publishing poetry. This perception, however, changed in May as the scene in poetry publishing "took on more glowing hues" with Karl Shapiro's *The V-Letter* winning the Pulitzer Prize in 1944 and Allen Tate's being named poetry editor at Henry Holt. The "free hand" that Tate would have there, Kees assumed, would result in his book being picked for Holt's new list. But this good news, as he reported to Norris Getty in July,

coincided with a move on the part of Reynal & Hitchcock, where Albert Erskine was pointing out to his colleagues that Stinky Shapiro had taken them out of the red ink as far as verse is concerned. Suddenly there were two houses "vitally" "interested" in "poetry." (As I write this, I have a sinking feeling that this all means next to nothing.) What has actually occurred is this: Tate wanted my new book of poems for Holt, and so did Reynal & Hitchcock. Tate didn't appear on the scene quite soon enough; so R & H got it and it should be coming out sometime this winter. Erskine

does such a good job of designing that I'm pleased they're doing it. Hell,
I'm terribly happy it's coming out at all.

Kees had other reasons to be elated. Reynal and Hitchcock was a prosperous company that paid well. Its list included Antoine de Saint-Exupéry's *The Little Prince* and Georges Simenon's Inspector Maigret series, along with his recently published *The Man Who Watched the Trains Go By*, a psychological thriller that made Kees's name already familiar around the editorial office, for it was the name of Simenon's Dutchman who, at forty, disappears from his old life and starts a new one in France.

Having *The Fall of the Magicians* published by a trade house also put Kees in a league with his contemporaries Robert Lowell, John Berryman—and even Randall Jarrell, the poetry critic at the *Nation* and the *enfant terrible* whom Kees considered "oddly childish" for writing too many poems with bears and reading too much Georg Groddeck. What made Kees different from them, however, was that he had no interest in the prizes and academic sinecures that his book opened for him. He felt more free from what he had done than beholden to a template, which publishing meant for most poets.

In June, the Keeses moved back to East Tenth Street, subletting from Dwight and Nancy Macdonald, who were at the Cape for the summer. Unlike the Twenty-fifth Street apartment, this one had "wonderful quiet," more room, a tank full of tropical fish, and a fine library "topheavy on Marxism." There was also an untuned Steinway grand that allowed Weldon to relax, as he imagined in one of the poems in *The Fall of the Magicians:* "A good chord on a bad piano serves / As well as shimmering harp-runs for the nerves."

It was an apartment in which Robinson could feel at home. However, with the Macdonalds due back at the end of September, the Keeses had to search for a new place to live. This time they looked in Brooklyn Heights, since they had heard that the neighborhood, with its handsome brownstones, was quiet and affordable; it also had some literary ambiance that Weldon found appealing, since Hart Crane had once lived here with a rooftop view of the span that inspired his long poem "The Bridge."

The Keeses found an apartment at 144 Willow Street, a street with several landmark Federal-style homes, and made arrangements to have their furniture taken out of storage. Their move from East Tenth Street, however, did not go uneventfully. While the Keeses were away in Brooklyn, the Macdonalds' apartment was burglarized. "We couldn't discover that they had taken anything of yours," he wrote the Macdonalds. "They took our alarm clock, my fountain pen and two pairs of Ann's nylon stockings."

The Willow Street building was prewar, yet it had modern lines that appealed to Kees. The apartment itself was on a floor high enough for them to have a view of the harbor if they went out on the balcony. The living room provided a hospitable setting for the Knoll furniture and the other pieces that "dribbled in" during October, following a truck strike. As a finishing touch, Kees hung one of his abstract paintings over the sofa (where it caught the eye of the artist Romare Bearden on his first visit).

The Keeses also hired a "colored handywoman" named Rose to do the housecleaning. It was a small extravagance, but they both had jobs uptown, and it was pleasant to come home to a clean apartment, even when Rose scrubbed the wood floors and left white spots that reminded Weldon, with his cosmic eye for ironic signs of decay, of a "skin ailment."

Kees set up a small art studio in one of the side rooms of the new apartment and resumed his painting. He now frequented the art gallery of Samuel Kootz, one of the most important entrepreneurs of new American painting. Kootz, who had once written art criticism himself, readily saw that Kees had a gift for sounding his views about art and like Kootz held the American imitators of Piet Mondrian in low esteem for their work's susceptibility to exploitation by advertisers and linoleum companies. These artists, Kootz said, had eschewed spiritual values. He preferred the messier struggle of that group of New York artists whom he considered the descendants of the German Expressionists, who used their "psychology of color" to express a moody, mystic *Weltschmerz*. Among them were Mark Rothko, Adolph Gottlieb, Hans Hofmann, Robert Motherwell—artists Kootz had written about or whose work he had sold in his gallery—and Weldon Kees, who, though he did not paint with the dramatic—and sometimes glandular—heroics attributed to these men, personified another of Kootz's ideals. Kees embodied a collaboration, a linkage between modern literature and avant-garde art that Kootz had imagined in his writings by quoting or referring to "modern poets"—and he could articulate his ideas about painting without sounding like he was using some secret code for Stalin's fifth column, as many artists and critics did when speaking to certain members of Congress.

For this reason, Kootz asked Kees to write a note for an announcement of a November exhibition of paintings by Byron Browne. Browne was of the generation of Stuart Davis, John Graham, and Carl Holty, all early practitioners of abstract art in America. The note, though brief, would give Kees the chance to make his first mark as an art critic and to express his own rationale for painting: "Browne has marked himself off from those artists of the fixed idea—their number has always been enormous—who stake out claims on molehill-sized areas and plow until well after numerous sour harvests are in. He is a painter who moves on restlessly to problem after problem."

Though he considered himself an apprentice, his work still derivative of Picasso, Miró, and his friends, Kees started to think of himself as a serious artist in the last half of 1946. While living at the Macdonalds', he took his canvases to a frame shop in the Village, where the proprietor, Lou Pollack, encouraged him to sell his work after hearing that Weldon was giving his paintings away, including two gouaches to the novelist Robert Lowry for helping to carry some work to be framed. These Kees signed outside the shop, in their upper corners, with words more in keeping with a book signing.

∾

"Henry Wallace and Company," Kees wrote Gilbert Neiman in January 1947, had taken over part of the same floor where Ann worked at *Antiques* and turned it into the campaign headquarters for the self-described socialist and Democratic aspirant to the 1948 presidency. In the same letter, he reported the table talk at a Chinese restaurant, where George Davis had tried to help James Laughlin as the latter tried to order something not on the menu and finally said he wanted sweet-and-sour pork again: "So the preparation was ordered and at length arrived. The waiter removed the cover from the steaming dish. Laughlin frowningly examined the contents and then addressed himself to Davis with the following immortal query. 'Which,' he said, 'is the sweet and which is the sour?'"

The letter continued in this vein as if it were a foretaste of the new year. Kees also shared his enthusiasm for *Under the Volcano,* by "an Englishman named Malcolm Lowry," with Neiman. Although it would not be published until February, Kees had already read an advance copy obtained from his editor Albert Erskine—along with the promotional materials, which he included in his letter: "This is the blurb: read it. I think it's wonderful, densely, thickly, and completely written: one of the best things that's happened to narrative prose in some years. I should think that it would be of special interest to you because it's 'about' 'foreigners' in Mexico. Anyway, this is hat's off as far as I'm concerned."

Kees also recommended that Neiman show his translations of Paul Éluard's poems to Harold Rosenberg and Robert Motherwell, who had started a large-size review of the arts called *Possibilities.* Though he thought the new magazine was "rather flossy," he suggested that Neiman use his name with the editors. The favor did not seem out of the ordinary to him. He had known Rosenberg for years. It does, though, point to a reserve of influence Kees had developed in New York with only smart conversations and uncounted ephemeral moments at bars, cocktail parties, galleries, editorial offices, and cafeterias. Though one friend said that he pulled no weight in the world of New York's "ferociously competitive" artists and intellectuals, others realized he had weightlessly risen above it, without ever seeming to be out of it, while sitting and talking in the booth of a Chinese restaurant, at the piano in a Village apartment, or next to a painting by Arshile Gorky. For example, Kees shared a pleasant lunch and walk with Theodore Roethke in January, when he offered to push Roethke's poems, the greenhouse ones that would be published as *The Lost Son,* on the *Nation*'s Randall Jarrell (who sometimes asked Kees to review poetry). "Please don't go to any special trouble," Roethke wrote in February from Penn State, knowing that Kees probably wanted to smooth things over, given the bad blood that existed between Jarrell and Roethke's lover, Louise Bogan.

Reynal and Hitchcock published *The Fall of the Magicians* in May. Its green, white-lettered dust jacket, gray cloth binding, and typography—it was the first book designed by Harry Ford, the book-designer-turned-Knopf-poetry-editor—pleased Kees, as did the reviews, which appeared throughout the spring. Milton Crane, the author of a new hagiography of the Roosevelt administrations, reviewed *The Fall of the Magicians* for the *New York Times* in a way that made it part of the reviewer's disappointment in the new Republican Congress. Kees's version of the Waste Land was not so much fashionable as it was authentic and perceptive, a way not to lose sight of the values and warning signs learned from the Depression and the war: "These poems by Weldon Kees form a chapter in the history of the disintegration of our world, written by an intelligent, witty, and detached mind. Mr. Kees has obviously felt it necessary—like many a contemporary and ancestor—to take refuge from chaos in irony. But the refuge is only temporary at best, and the destruction that will at the last be universal begins, as the poet well knows, in the drawing room."

"The Conversation in the Drawing Room," "The Heat in the Room," and "Crime Club" skillfully portrayed a "mounting horror," Crane continued. Yet what pleased most was the observation that Kees had achieved "his own kind of lightness," even though "what grins in *The Fall of the Magicians* is most often a skull."

Kees experienced a similar understanding of his work in Ambrose Gordon's review in *Furioso;* Gordon especially saw the importance of rooms in Kees's work. He listed the poems' variety of subjects: winter afternoons, ghosts, road signs, haunted drawing rooms, a parrot's death, dogs in a devastated city, turncoats, sickrooms, scientific experiments, the room imagined in the absence of its occupant, cripples, blind men, detectives, death, murder, and so on. In them he found a single thread of meaning, each poem a variation on the "theme of death and disaster and decay in our society." This theme was certainly "fashionable," but Kees had "enlivened" it with "the naturalness with which difficult and artificial verse stanzas are made to perform for him."

Gordon, in praising Kees's formalism, also apprehended the far more profound use of such difficult forms as the villanelle and sestina to convey entrapment:

For, if the book may be said to be composed of variations on a single theme, it also has a single controlling metaphor: the imprisonment of the individual within cracked and decaying walls. The book's title is appropriate, The Fall of the Magicians; *one remembers that the wizard Merlin was in the last days of the Round Table bewitched and immured in a hollow oak tree—the seer's fate in a time of disorder: "Nailed up in a box /*

Nailed up on a pen, nailed up in a room / ... you write, / 'Finished. No more. The end.' ... Beasts howl outside." This is also the modern predicament; only, instead of a tree, Kees' individual finds himself enclosed in a room slightly too small, somewhere in a house that is rather too old.

H. R. Hays, in *Poetry,* absolved Kees of being derivative in his review. "Kees' bitter wit is particularly his own," he wrote, seeing an ability to extend the modernism of the past into the present and future. "Above all, [Kees] upholds the standards of taste established by an older generation of American poets before the Auden influence crept in."

The critics now started to list Kees with Robert Lowell, Elizabeth Bishop, and other younger poets who had recently published collections of poems. *Poetry* even featured his name with Carl Sandburg, Robinson Jeffers, Wallace Stevens, Kenneth Fearing, and other notable contributors in advertisements for its thirty-fifth anniversary issue. Based on the reception of *The Fall of the Magicians,* Howard Nemerov and the other editors of *Furioso* founded the Poetry Book-of-the-Month Club to meet the popular demand that books such as Kees's would set off. They even made his new collection their first selection and found that they could not meet orders because the book was selling so well that Reynal and Hitchcock fell behind in their shipments.

Kees made *The Fall of the Magicians* a special gift to his wife. The spare dedication "For Ann" was not some romantic gesture, like Kenneth Patchen dedicating every one of his books to his wife. It was intrinsic to the poems and their irony. The dedication anticipated the lovemaking in the last part of "Eight Variations"—and counterpointed the world in the other poems, where "there isn't any love, there isn't any love" ("White Collar Ballad"). The dedication even lent to an Orphean reading of the book. "He is burning both of us. / He is burning up our lives," the woman thinks in "The Heat in the Room" as she watches a man burn papers, something Ann had seen Weldon do with his novels that she had read and typed.

After the reviews, and the immediate praise of friends such as Robert Lowry, from whom it was enough to hear that the book was "terrific," the afterglow of *The Fall of the Magicians* began to fade for Kees.

Harcourt, Brace, and World bought out Reynal and Hitchcock, which interrupted plans to keep the book in print. The modest royalty checks stopped coming.

Eventually, Kees gave away his personal copies until they were gone. One copy, which he gave to Conrad Aiken, resulted in a letter from the top of the American Parnassus. It made up for the spring and summer of 1947, when it seemed he was the most important poet alive: "You're embarrassingly and rewardingly skillful and use the light touch sometimes quite murderously, and if I have any complaint (meaning of course that I have) it's of the pale red current of vin audenaire that now and then stains your own aqua pura—or if not the vin audenaire, the professional dye that came to be made of it, if you know what I mean."

Even as *Life* featured spreads on the Nuremburg trials, death camps, atom-bomb tests, refugees wandering through the bombed-out cities of Europe, the violent birth of Israel, and ambitious Republican congressmen vigilant for communists, it also showed debutantes, bulging cars, television, modern kitchens, ranch houses, and babies. Sarah Kees, like other American mothers, could look away from the magazine left open in her lap and feel a pleasant rush of emotion that life was going on, that young people would marry, have children, buy homes. Her son, however, almost seemed to dive under this current as his subway slipped under the East River, taking him to his job at Paramount News Service. There he read his books, thought out lines for his poems (continuing to write in the workplace as he did in the Kees factory front office), and bought new art supplies during his lunch hour. Yet when Sarah and John met Weldon and Ann for a weekend at a resort in Peekskill, New York, in late July, they could only be reassured. He had published. The newspaper back home in Beatrice had praised his newsreel work. He seemed to his parents just as accomplished as his college friends. Norris Getty now taught English and history at Harvard, and Maurice Johnson lectured on Restoration literature at the University of Pittsburgh—their classes filled with G.I. Bill students. Weldon was not part of this trend either, even though the friends he had made in the East were also teaching. Nemerov was the resident writer at Hamilton. Tate was at Princeton again. Roethke was at Penn State.

In New York, Kees noticed that the people he knew were tense. Edmund Wilson had dropped out of his life for the most part and only reappeared briefly one day, on the corner of Sixth Avenue and Forty-fifth Street. There Kees heard from Wilson that the new Lionel Trilling novel, *The Middle of the Journey*, was "shocking and dreadful" before they parted outside the offices of the *New Yorker*. During another sidewalk encounter, with the young essayist Seymour Krim on Fifth Avenue, he heard the names of the people who were summering at Yaddo and felt estranged rather than informed or reconnected. When he saw "the old familiar sights" at a party given for Stephen Spender, it seemed like "full-blown hideousness" as he watched the poets Allen Tate getting drunk, H. R. Hays experiencing facial tics, and Janet Flanner taking medicine for her flatulence. And the other guests looked uncomfortable to him or even distressed. The novelist Jean Stafford appeared "more ravaged and nervous than you had thought possible."

Kees felt more comfortable in the company of painters. This was especially true after his vacation in Provincetown during the first two weeks of August. There he and Ann stayed in a rented house at Land's End, a wooded point that opened on dunes, with a view of the ocean and a lighthouse. Ann relaxed for the first time in weeks—being exposed to her in-laws at Peekskill required drinking more bottles of "nerve remedy" than usual—while Weldon assumed some of the posture of the painters' robust egos and heady individualism. He began to believe what they believed, that they were on the verge of assuming a kind of leadership in the international art world.

Yet his new friends liked him because he was so unlike a painter. He was both intellectual and literary and offbeat at the same time. He amused them with his artist's talk gleaned from afternoons spent in the main reading room of the New York Public Library. There he would pore over such arcanum as the works of the German psychoanalyst Wilhelm Stekel, the pioneer of dream interpretation and pathological psychology, whose case studies of pedophilia, wandering mania, dipsomania, kleptomania, pyromania, and other impulsive behaviors informed conversations with Sam Kootz and the painter William Baziotes—before informing some line or nuance of a poem.

Kees left Paramount in the autumn. He had come back from his vacation to find that one of the scriptwriters had quit. Others had already left, too, going over to television, which now competed directly with the declining newsreel industry. He learned from management that, "like some unavailable spare part," his departed colleague would not be replaced. Soon the shortage of help turned his job into more of a "rat-race than usual." His boss, Sig Heavilin, had asked him to come in at nine o'clock every morning—"with some gratuitous gobbledygook about noses to the grindstone and shoulder to the wheels," he wrote Ted Roethke. "I suggested that they take my job and proceed with movements of insertion." (He could depend on Ann's paycheck for now and the occasional largesse, such as the ninety-six-dollar honorarium for a poem in the *Tiger's Eye*, a new cultural review.)

Paramount and overwork, he felt, had given him skin rashes and a stomach ulcer, for which he had seen a doctor, worn a "Dr. Kildare gown," swallowed barium, and stood before an x-ray machine. He had always thought of the job as a joke, a necessary evil as well as a window on what he considered real evil. During the war, his job had intensified his already cynical view of leaders and the anguished consequences of the proud and irreversible decisions they handed down from their seats of power. He had learned how the world worked in what was cut from the newsreels and what the audiences actually saw. FDR's return from Yalta had especially opened his eyes. The footage Paramount had of the president was so fearsomely revelatory—FDR was so gaunt and ill—that Paramount's brass had killed it.

Kees, naturally, told many cocktail-party stories about what went on behind the scenes at newsreel companies. However, he would not write an exposé of the industry, even for the sizeable advance that one magazine editor dangled in front of him. As he told John Pauker, who wanted such a piece for *Furioso*, he did not want the onus of such an article since he might need to work for the newsreel people again—which turned out to be the case.

In October, Weldon started freelancing at Louis de Rochemont's documentary-film service. In December, he went over to Paramount's competitor, News of the Day, where he achieved the near goal of his life, "a two-day week." His salary was also doubled; he now made $150 a week. (He was less happy there, though, than he had been at Paramount. The management was even more conservative, and Kees found himself arguing with them more over the slant of particular stories.)

Another source of income that Ann and Weldon counted on came from the sale of the F. D. Kees Manufacturing Company. Neither he nor his cousin Dan Jr. wanted to carry on the family business, which had become a burden to their parents. The company had sold its patented ice- and roller-skate interests to the Chicago Roller Skate Company in the 1930s, and the regional markets had dried up for the small production runs of inventive specialty products with which the firm had prospered over the years and survived the Depression. During the war, the company subsisted on subcontract work and made field kitchens and radio equipment for the armed forces. Fearing another postwar depression like the one that had followed World War I, John Kees decided to retire in the spring and ran a classified ad in the *Chicago Tribune* putting his business up for sale. With their share, Ann and Weldon hoped they could summer in Provincetown longer next year. They even entertained the idea of buying a car, which was a must if one wanted to get around the Cape. "I'm going to try to stay away from a regular job as long as I can," he wrote Getty, "unless something so tempting that I can't resist comes along."

With the time he had freed by leaving Paramount, Kees painted every day in November and December and wrote "more than I have in years." He now planned his paintings, creating studies first in pencil, charcoal, and India ink. For a painting titled *Madrid,* he even used collage to visualize the final canvas, tearing up sheets of brown kraft paper and placing them together in different ways to achieve the desired effect in bold reds and yellow, suggesting a rearing bull—not a political statement about the Spanish Civil War. Painting, even as he became more conscious of craftsmanship and professionalism, was still escapism for Kees. Poetry was still the venue where escape was not possible, as in the closure of his *Tiger's Eye* poem, "The Furies," where a clown shudders and suddenly "Is a man with a mouth of cotton / Trapped in a dentist's chair."

Kees also started "a long siege of prose" in December, writing book reviews for the *New York Times* while he and Ann were snowbound in Brooklyn Heights. "For once the newspaper reports on this unspeakable winter," he noted for Ted Roethke, "have been unexaggerated; you've been well out of New York at its worst." To make matters worse, there was no heat in the Willow Street building for several days, and the roof of the building threatened to collapse from the weight of the snow. As he and the other tenants slowly turned "blue, numb and outraged" at their landlord, Kees left his teeth marks in new books of poetry, including Norman Macleod's collected poems, which he dispatched using his knowledge of filmmaking.

When Weldon and Ann did get away from their apartment, they

bought record albums "like drunken sailors" for their new Victor phonograph, among them Lee Wiley singing Harold Arlen songs—which counted as research for another of Kees's writing assignments in January 1948, a "long piece on the state of popular music and jazz" for "the *Partisan Review* boys."

"Muskrat Ramble: Popular and Unpopular Music" begins with a Jamesian epigraph that flags both an aesthetic ideal and a bitter irony braided into the essay. "In the ripe olives," Kees quoted, "the very circumstance of their being near rottenness adds a peculiar beauty to the fruit." By this he meant the final phase of the traditional modern American popular song and New Orleans jazz, which he elevated over the onslaught of canned, sanitized, and inauthentic big-band music and other "cleaned-up" forms:

It is midafternoon. I come away from the window and the rooftops and turn the knob on the radio that sends a thin line cutting across the rows of numbers. I would like to hear, say, Jelly Roll Morton playing "The Crave," but will settle for a Lee Wiley record; except for a station on which a voice not easily distinguishable from Miss Margaret Truman's is singing "At Dawning" and another on which a program of "light classics" by a feeble string group emerges oppressively distinct, all the other stations are playing record after record by big dance bands. Claude Thornhill, Kay Kyser, Tex Beneke, Charlie Spivak, Vaughn Monroe. I switch off the radio and go into the other room to pour myself a drink.

Kees went on to describe the divisions of American culture with a broad view and made glib yet unobvious associations among New Criticism, comedy, architecture, and the like, so that popular music fit the same lapsarian context into which he and his *Partisan Review* readers—the art and idea makers—believed they fell along with their beloved Cole Porter, Bessie Smith, Bunk Johnson, Fats Waller—and, for Kees, Lee Wiley:

High Culture, although it has been subject to the same accelerated tendencies toward decay that kept Henry Adams awake and put the world to sleep, still has a kind of life, however spasmodic its successes and however hemmed in by the all but completely victorious Middle Culture that takes what it can assimilate both from High and Popular Culture for the purpose of mashing them to death.

But Popular Culture is completely at the mercy of the laws hastening corruption and decay. Popular Culture must go along. No other road is open. Unlike High Art, it cannot fall back on attitudes of recalcitrance for survival. Lloyd, Hamilton, W. C. Fields, Buster Keaton—comedians of wit, humanity, and situation, for instance, give way to verbalizing gagsters: Bob Hope, Milton Berle, Red Skelton. The comic strip evolves into a series of continued stories that are linear replicas of soap operas and the pulps; and similar patterns tiredly repeat themselves in every field of Popular Culture.

More threatening was the posturing new jazz of younger black musicians coming down from Harlem to play in the clubs on Bleecker Street. Bebop was not so easily appropriated by white audiences and white intellectuals, for its composer–performers could not be turned into producers of background or dance music. With the phenomenon of improvisation, they remained central and in control not only of the music but of how it was explained. For Kees, who saw some role for himself in the last gasp of New Orleans jazz, it was incredibly disappointing, and his reaction to bebop would, despite the candor and accuracy of his social commentary, be out of step with his younger peers in the Village. It dated him:

Here is a fullfledged cult. Its more orthodox devotees even model their appearance on that of Dizzy Gillespie, bebop's pioneer and bellwether, a goateed trumpet player who wears a beret, horn-rimmed glasses, and neckties with his own not very appealing countenance painted thereon. Iconoclastic and compulsive types, many bebop cultists extend their interests beyond music—to drug addiction, abstract painting, and the theories (and for all I know the practice) of Wilhelm Reich, philosopher of the orgasm. Some beboppers are interested in the close textual critics of poetry; I learned from a friend whom I believe to be reliable that one such fan announced that Cleanth Brooks is "definitely hip"—a term of warm approval. [...]

I have been listening to bebop on occasion for several years now, and lately, as I started work on this piece, listening with more strict attention; and I can only report, very possibly because of some deeply buried strain of black reaction in me, that I have found this music uniformly thin, at once dilapidated and overblown, and exhibiting a poverty of thematic development and a richness of affectation not only, apparently, intentional, but enormously self-satisfied. Whole-tone progressions and triple-tongued runs are worked relentlessly, far beyond the saturation point. There has been nothing like this in the way of an overconsciousness of stylistic idiosyncrasy, I should say, since the Gothic Revival. Although bebop's defenders reserve as their trump card this music's "element of the unexpected," it is precisely bebop's undeviating pattern of incoherence and limitation that makes it predictable in the extreme, and ultimately as boring as the projects of Gutzon Borglum.[5]

In early March, at a party given in honor of Jean Malaquais's return from France, Weldon and Ann were suddenly introduced to the real "Boris" in *Tropic of Cancer.* At first Kees was a little uncomfortable. He had, in November, published a harsh review of Henry Miller's memoir *Remember to Remember* in the *New York Times Book Review,* titled "Unhappy Expatriate": "[The party] throbbed with people from splinter Marxist outfits, Sidney Hooks, Dwight Macdonalds, etc., and turned up an intense and rather handsome little man who turned out to be Michael Fraenkel, the guy Henry Miller exchanged so many letters with on *Hamlet.* He seized my hand with marked avidity and told me that that review I did in the *Times* on Miller was just the ticket, which rather took me aback, since I had thought that he and Miller were still bosom pals. Not at all, said Fraenkel: Miller's old cronies think he is a sell-out and getting terribly stuffy to boot."

Well before Miller appeared as the dirty old man playing ping-pong with a naked blonde in *Playboy,* Kees had isolated "the occupational disease of the established literary man," seeing in Miller the "merchandiser" — indeed, the opposite kind of artist that Kees could and would never be. For him, there was a "pervasive extinction of personality, willed and unwilled," in Miller's career, while some observed in Kees a deliberate anticelebrity. At another party, at the home of George Davis that same evening, one of the most perceptive believers in celebrity for its own sake, Truman Capote, could even see this in Kees: "Here one entered another world: smooth publishers' young men, Nancy Walker, Josephine Prémice, Truman Capote, Dawn Powell, several very creepy fairies, and an appalling woman left over from *Nightwood.* Capote said to me, 'Why don't you want to be a *success?* I can tell from the way you act you don't want to be a success. You're like Newton Arvin. Why, you're a much better poet than that old Robert Lowell. I just feel terrible. Nobody likes my novel that I want to have like it. All the wrong people are praising it.'"

That Kees reported this to friends reveals a secret pride in, perhaps, a third way for his talent to be recognized, some gray area between neglect and fame where people—all the *right* people—could go to find him rather than he finding them, like the quest he imagined for his fictional biographer or for his own voice trying to penetrate Robinson. In other words, success without its democracy.

Though Kees did not address the ideal form that an artist should take, he may have had in mind something that mirrored the work itself, as he, around this time, expressed in his profile of Robert Motherwell, who had "pushed the major emphasis of abstract painting to one kind of Ultima Thule." The piece had originally been written for an illustrated book featuring the artists in Sam Kootz's stable. The text of the book would consist of poems, articles, and manifestos by writers the gallery owner favored. While the project proved to be too expensive to produce, Robert Goldwater, the editor of the *Magazine of Art,* took the Motherwell essay that Kees had written and made it a kind of statement piece to show the magazine's new emphasis on contemporary American art. With his usual economy and clarity, Kees simplified what Clement Greenberg, Harold Rosenberg, and artists had been saying about painting in exponentially hermetic mantras and mythopoeia that did not travel well uptown, beyond the smoke-filled lofts of the Lower East Side:

Painting should be music. Painting should be literature. Painting should be propaganda, an anecdote or an arrow pointing to a path of salvation. Painting should be a vertical or horizontal window that opens on a world of ladies with parasols and appealing children, cows in gently flowing streams, a bunch of flowers, or a bowl of fruit good enough to eat. These were, on various occasions, the beliefs of the past. They are also the beliefs of your Aunt Cora, the people next door, half Fifty-seventh Street, and Mr. Truman.

The beliefs to which the most advanced painters of our time give their allegiance were foreshadowed by Flaubert, who, interrupting himself from his torments with the world-haunted manuscript of Madame Bovary, parted company with his own century to set down this unfulfilled desire: "What I should like to write is a book about nothing at all,

a book which would exist by virtue of the mere internal strength of its style, as the earth holds itself unsupported in the air. [...]"
"A book which would exist by virtue of the mere internal strength of its style. [...]" This is the literary equivalent of the canvases of Robert Motherwell.

When he wrote this, Kees tried to make Sam Kootz deliver on a promise to lend him a large and still unsold Motherwell collage. But he did not need to hang it in the living room of his Willow Street home to arrive at his discovery of a new kind of subject matter (adapted from his artist and critic friends): "It is paint itself. The paintings are quite simply 'about' paint."

Even though Norris, Ann, and his parents had worried that Weldon was giving too much of himself to painting—and now art criticism— he could only have reassured them during the first months of 1948 that he was first and foremost a poet, an ambitious poet given the parameters of his different take on fame. He produced new poems, including a third Robinson poem, "Aspects of Robinson," written in late February, shortly after his thirty-fourth birthday.

Kees sent it in early March to Getty, who then made suggestions that enhanced the poem's best moments and removed issues Yvor Winters and other imaginary readers might find, readers a good poet had to bear in mind as Kees realized:

It was damned pleasant to hear that you liked "Aspects of Robinson"; about half way through the writing of the first draft of it, I began worrying about the possibility of its turning chi-chi and pure New Yorker; and my attempts to rescue the poem from that quality set up a lot of odd divisions and strategies. — I thought all your suggestions excellent. "A thin" now concludes the first line; the "Toynbee or luminol" change has been made; and Robinson is now in the shucks with a Mrs. Morse, poor fellow. (I saw Mrs. Purdy go with real regret.) But you have a point there; don't know why exactly, for Winters on pseudo-reference has always given me a pain. Never had the slightest objection to Princess Volupine, Sir Ferdinance Klein, Mrs. Cammel, or Fräulein von Kulp. Has anyone ever mentioned that Eliot uses people frequently as objects? But such mention would just bring on a fresh tizzy from Yvor. — I can see yr. point about staring at the wall, and am almost convinced, even though I have em-

pirical proof that this happens frequently enough: often you get seated at a crummy table where there is nothing else to stare at except a wall — and sometimes when very tired and too much involved with people and things, a wall is just the ticket. I need that all sound at the end of the stanza, too, since I'm building up l's there — elephant, Herald, Hello, love, well, alone, Longchamps. Time will tell. I'm still undecided about the change. You may be right.

In late March, Peter De Vries took "Aspects of Robinson" for the *New Yorker* "like a shot." Harold Ross, the magazine's legendary editor-in-chief, even suggested minor revisions and contributed to the decision to run two Robinson poems in close proximity for his readers. "Robinson at Home," accepted in June of the previous year, appeared in the April 10 issue, "Aspects" in the April 24 issue.

In "Robinson at Home," the interior is now a gothic setting. The delineation between the persona and the poet-narrator-anima has changed in this poem. Robinson is present now, and the one who describes him does so with a cinematic and disembodied voiceover, like that of God in *It's a Wonderful Life*, but is unwilling or unable to help as in the 1946 film:

Curtains drawn back, the door ajar,
All winter long, it seemed, a darkening
Began. But now the moonlight and the odors of the street
Conspire and combine toward one community.

These are the rooms of Robinson.
Bleached, wan, and colorless this light, as though
All blurred daybreaks of the spring
Found an asylum here, perhaps for Robinson alone,

Who sleeps. Were there more music sifted through the floors
And moonlight of a different kind,
He might awake to hear the news at ten,
Which will be shocking, moderately.

The comforting, ambient music, which could be the soothing, sultry, late-at-night songs of Manhattan from Kees's own record player downstairs, is insufficient to wake Robinson from his deep, REM sleep. He dreams of idealized, detached, and hermetic roles for himself. But as Robinson restlessly turns and changes, these faces run together as if encountered one after the other on a New York sidewalk or in the terrible halls of Bellevue. They would almost form the crowd that sees him exposed in self-revelation. This takes place in rooms that once offered an asylum in the first Robinson poem. They now become the flashpoint of the Unreal City:

This sleep is from exhaustion, but his old desire
To die like this has known a lessening.
Now there is only this coldness that he has to wear.
But not in sleep.—Observant scholar, traveller,

Or uncouth bearded figure squatting in a cave,
A keen-eyed sniper on the barricades,
A heretic in catacombs, a famed roué,
A beggar on the streets, the confidant of Popes—

All these are Robinson in sleep, who mumbles as he turns,
"There is something in this madhouse that I symbolize—
This city—nightmare—black—"

He wakes in sweat
To the terrible moonlight and what might be
Silence. It drones like wires far beyond the roofs,
And the long curtains blow into the room.

The *New Yorker* had Kees change only one line. Instead of a generic catacomb heretic, Robinson had been a "Priscillian heretic," Kees referring to an obscure fourth-century form of Gnosticism that condemned marriage and procreation and practiced free love. "The New Yorker people felt their readers wouldn't understand the reference," Kees wrote, "'in spite,' as I was told in a curious communication from them, 'of the familiarity of many of our readers with early Church history.'"

In "Aspects of Robinson," the *New Yorker* readers arrived two weeks later to the day after the night of "Robinson at Home." He now wears his fine clothes. His accouterments, pastimes, preferences, drugs, drinks, women, books, and death wish are cataloged and could almost be the precious, fragile, ironic layers that protect the anima within (whose sisters could be the girl in "Girl at Midnight," the daughter in "For My Daughter"):

Robinson at cards at the Algonquin; a thin
Blue light comes down once more outside the blinds.
Gray men in overcoats are ghosts blown past the door.
The taxis streak the avenues with yellow, orange, and red.
This is Grand Central, Mr. Robinson.

Robinson on a roof above the Heights; the boats
Mourn like the lost. Water is slate, far down.
Through sounds of ice cubes dropped in glass, an osteopath,
Dressed for the links, describes an old Intourist tour.
— Here's where old Gibbons jumped from, Robinson.

Robinson walking in the Park, admiring the elephant.
Robinson buying the Tribune, Robinson buying the Times. Robinson
Saying, "Hello. Yes, this is Robinson. Sunday
At five? I'd love to. Pretty well. And you?"
Robinson alone at Longchamps, staring at the wall.

Robinson afraid, drunk, sobbing Robinson
In bed with a Mrs. Morse, Robinson at home;
Decisions: Toynbee or luminol? Where the sun
Shines, Robinson in flowered trunks, eyes toward
The breakers. Where the night ends, Robinson in East Side bars.

Robinson in Glen plaid jacket, Scotch-grain shoes,
Black four-in-hand and oxford button-down,
The jeweled and silent watch that winds itself, the brief-
Case, covert topcoat, clothes for spring, all covering
His sad and usual heart, dry as a winter leaf.

Getty could easily see why the "figure of Robinson showed such interesting possibilities" to the *New Yorker*. His relevance, he told Kees, was "pretty much urban," and the *New Yorker* was a highly appropriate place for him. Having two Robinson poems published nearly one after the other elated Kees, but success also warned him away from writing more. He told his friend Charles Addams that there was a "law of diminishing returns more exacting on poetry" than on the cartoonist's "family." Robinson would have to be put away for now.

During cold, snow, and illnesses of the winter, the Keeses committed themselves to renting a house at the Cape and staying for more than just two weeks during the summer of 1948. To offset the expense, Weldon had already asked Norris if he would be interested in sharing the rental, an offer made in January, when Kees came to Harvard to make a glass disk recording of his poems for the university's Woodberry Poetry Room. To Getty, the house and the summer would be a relief from Cambridge and his studies in Greek and Roman literature, a chance to be close to the Weldon and Ann he had known in Denver. There were now more differences between Kees and Getty. Getty was teaching, and he had been in the army.

In March, Kees found a "swell, big place" in Provincetown, with a large studio, three bedrooms, a fireplace, and a piano. "It has a pretty steep rental," Kees wrote Getty, "$500 to $600 for two months; but I am in a shoot-the-works mood." He then went up to Provincetown to see the house on 25 Brewster Street, staying for a few days at the home of the poet Cecil Hemley, who lived year-round at the Cape.

Any second thoughts he had about spending so much money were offset by feeling the world could end anyway. Gandhi had been assassinated in January over the partitioning of colonial India. The alleged suicide of Jan Masaryk, and the Moscow-directed coup that placed the Communist party in power in Czechoslovakia, deepened the cold war fissures further. Every day in the headlines Stalin challenged his former allies, and the provocations that led to his June blockade of Germany and the Berlin Airlift could not be misapprehended. In Palestine, the approaching independence of Israel was certain to trigger war between Arab and Jew. What troubled Kees more, however, was what haunted President Truman, too: the question of, not if, but when the Soviet Union would have the atomic bomb. Writing Ray West in early April, on the day after Congress passed the Marshall Plan, his gallows humor could not cover a real anxiety about the future: "Now that humankind is getting ready to liquidate itself on a really grand scale, having bungled the job during its last puny attempt, I am going to absent myself from a job—at least until Fall—to see if I can't get more writing and painting done. Took a place in Provincetown for the summer and shall hope for the best. After that, I don't know."

Provincetown
1948-1950

Here is where you can turn your back on America.
—Henry David Thoreau

The Keeses made a long train trip in May 1948 to see Weldon's parents in Beatrice. It would be the last time he would visit his boyhood home on North Fifth Street. Seeing John and Sarah depressed him, and it showed in the photographs Ann took of him, not smiling, standing underneath his old bedroom window. The same camera and the same roll of film would next be packed when they left Brooklyn for Provincetown in the last week of June.

In Boston they could either take the Boston and Maine's "Cape Codder" or board the ss *Steel Pier*. The train had a bar. The ferry also had a bar belowdecks—and a little "orchestra," as Getty charitably called it, composed of saxophone, xylophone, and a piano player who could read the *Boston Globe* between a few tired chords of "Jalousie."

Getty was already drinking with Bill and Ethel Baziotes when the Keeses arrived at their Brewster Street house, which was just a block from Cape Cod Bay. After more drinks and an exchange of news on who would be at the Cape for the season, Ann, Weldon, and Norris left and fetched the keys to their own house, a few doors down from the Baziotes'. Save for the painting and writing Kees wanted to do, the long summer days of July promised "a state of uninterrupted sloth."

The house had an old piano on which he and Getty could bang out "Nice Work if You Can Get It" and "Someone to Watch over Me." With Ann, they walked the dunes, swam in the Atlantic, and combed the beach for shells, sea glass, driftwood, and friends. They played ping-pong at the Tennis Club.

Provincetown looked less crowded to Kees than in other years. The weather was fine to a fault. Soon he had to nurse a case of "ultraviolet poisoning" from lying out on the beach when he was not immersed in the "weather" of writing his first poem of the summer. "Wet Thursday," which he dedicated to one of his New York Public Library Reading Room friends, the poet Lindley Williams Hubbell, whose own poem "The Cats" was a Kees favorite and starting point for this one, cast a colder, more Nebraskan eye at a summerless New England vista under a winter and a "freezing sun" in keeping with the world-view of his verse:

A stiff wind off the channel
Linking the chimney's mutterings
With rain; the shaken trees,
Mile after mile, greening the sand.

This seascape prefigures the arrival of a stray, a talking cat that becomes the poet's familiar, a projection of Kees's otherness, which he carried with him even as he enjoyed the society of his vacationing friends, "good liquor," and playing his piano. Here the sound of the Cape is thunder that shakes the sky to usher in

A monstrous cat that seems
Far older than the oldest carp
In the waters under the earth,
Moving like a shadow over the floor
To warm its frozen paws
Before the fire. He turns,
Smiling in the woodbox,
And says, "Felis libyca domestica
They call me, kept by man for catching
Rats and mice. Of Eastern or
Egyptian origin. Now to be
Your spiteful and envenomed shadow. Here
Will I live out my nine and evil lives
Before your very interesting fire.
And the days, months, years, are endless."

Kees sent his new poem to the New Yorker. The editors bought it quickly. "Wet Thursday" would put a little irony into the holiday spirit of their Thanksgiving issue. This success, however, did not assuage Kees's disappointment over failing that July to write a long poem, conspicuously missing from The Fall of the Magicians. Though no critic had chided him for this lack of a virtuoso performance on his part, the kind Robert Lowell and other serious young American poets were publishing, Kees must have felt his sin of omission keenly enough. He hoped that with the uninterrupted time the Cape afforded, he could begin his own "Paterson" or "The Bridge." But all he had was a ten-page false start, which he discarded as he focused instead on producing enough paintings for a one-man show.

Quite calmly, and with none of the self-doubt he expressed about his writing, Kees, over the summer of 1948, came to believe that his apprenticeship as a painter was over. He had none of the worry he had over his poems, none of the questions he posed to Getty: What order should they be in? Are they clear-edged and erudite? Is there enough sardonic underlayment to counter the nostalgia and historical allusion?

With painting, which was impulsive, unreflective, noncerebral, and unconnected to tradition save only immediate historical antecedents, Kees felt freer than he did as a poet. He could be that demiurge he imagined Motherwell to be, pitting "recklessness, savagery, chance-taking, the accidental" against "refinement, discrimination, calculation, taste."

As a painter, Kees could be the magician who had not fallen. He could now change his shape in stretching canvas, squeezing pigment from lead-foil tubes, and scissoring scraps of paper for collages.

Fifty-seventh Street mattered as much as Random House, Scribner's, Harcourt, Brace. The folding of Sam Kootz's gallery and the imminent closing of Julian Levy's mattered. Kootz would have given him a show, and he felt as if he had been "left high & dry" as the painters Kootz represented, many of them his friends.

Among the painters at the Cape, the Keeses grew very close to Hans and Miz Hofmann and to Fritz and Jeanne Bultman. Bultman, the son of a New Orleans undertaker, was Hofmann's most promising student. He liked Kees's strong opinions about art, the way he put things, such as his saying that Arshile Gorky's painting and suicide were courageous in the face of his fatal disease. Jeanne shared with Kees and Getty the distinction of having left behind a small town in Nebraska—by way of burlesque theaters and the chorus line at Radio City Music Hall, however.

Bill Baziotes became a closer friend, too, that summer. He had a "horror of being easily understood," which is what he had in common with Kees in addition to their pure enjoyment and occasional intellectualizing of mysteries and detective stories. Kees did encourage Baziotes not to lose sight of Baudelaire and other poets, since they had more utility when it came to talking about one's own art than Mickey Spillane.

The underesteem Baziotes endured gave Kees a paradigm for how he might behave in the future. Baziotes was already being left in the "dust" and "dreams" he talked about in his artist's statements by Rothko, Motherwell, Greenberg, and others aggressively establishing abstract expressionism. He was already considered a transitional artist, still producing "hybrids" of surrealism and abstraction with too much of the "fanciful and fantastic"—terms Kees actually used to praise him in his review of one of Baziotes's shows. Other critics saw this as "softness" and "whimsy," even when he painted biomorphs—shapes suggesting animals and plants—drifting unimpeded through a hostile world; Kees saw them as survivors. This insight informs "Turtle," the poem that he dedicated to the painter:

> *Something inside me moved,*
> *Sluggish, torpid, dry*
> *As air from a closed-up room*
> *That drifts through an opened door*
>
> *When the wind is right—*
> *Moved as a turtle moves*
> *Into the covering grass,*
> *Far in the woods, at night.*

Even with the painting, the social highpoint that summer for Kees was a very literary cocktail party given by Edmund Wilson and his new wife at their place in Wellfleet. There the children Wilson had collected over three different marriages, including his son by Mary McCarthy, spilled over, with all the attendant distractions for Kees of having to exercise the obligatory politesse of a forced interest in the host's children. Fortunately there was recompense—and entertainment value for the thankfully childless—in Waldo Frank's baby, whom Frank spoon-fed from his Tom Collins. And Kees, Getty, and Wilson could still engage in their rich book talk, dissecting Thornton Wilder's *The Ides of March* and its bad translations of Catullus. On this count Kees held his own thanks to Getty, who had plied him throughout the year with the right modern translations of classical literature and the right opinions on such works as Pound's "Sextus Propertius." Wilson's satirical poems also became a topic of conversation. "No one wants to publish them," Wilson said ruefully, knowing Kees had during the war.

Weldon remarked to Ann how cool Brooklyn felt in mid-September when they came back home, having lingered after Labor Day ended the Cape's season. He had shipped back many new paintings and had film to develop with pictures of him and Ann standing in front of their Brewster Street rental, beachcombing with their friends, and the like. He had more ideas for new poems than anything typed up, including "The Clinic," which may have come from contact with the analysts who rivaled the artists in taking over the Cape during the summer:

> *Light in the cage like burning foil*
> *At noon; and I am caught*
> *With all the other cats that howl*
> *And dance and spit, lashing their tails*
> *When the doctors turn the current on.*

The Keeses found that their apartment had "soaked up all the heat of summer," forcing them to leave the windows open for a few days. Groceries were purchased. A new bottle of crystal-clear gin took its place inside the monitor icebox. Weldon visited the post office and had the mail delivered again.

One of the first letters Kees opened promised a visit next month from Kenneth Rexroth, who was in the middle of a reading and lecture tour on D. H. Lawrence. He bragged about making "$25 a crack." There was also a nice letter addressed from Jeanne Bultman thanking him and Ann for the use of their bicycles that summer. And there was a letter from his parents, who were traveling around the country — "and Christ knows where besides," he thought, finding out that he had just missed them at the Cape, that they were on their way to New York.

When Sarah and John arrived, Ann and Weldon escorted them on two short trips into the city that proved nerve-wracking for both of them given the burden of finding suitable entertainment for his mother, Sarah. He wanted to take them to *Sundown Beach,* the first Broadway production performed by members of the Actors Studio, which would soon evolve into Lee Strasberg's method-acting school. It was a serious slice-of-life play set in a café near a military hospital, staged by Elia Kazan and starring such young hopefuls as Julie Harris, Cloris Leachman, and Martin Balsam. But the play had closed after seven performances, so they saw *The Heiress,* a stage adaptation of Henry James's novel *Washington Square.* Kees liked the play. He even named one of his paintings after it.

Having his parents in the city would have reminded Kees of the income he derived from them. Even though he did not want a part in the family business, he was concerned about the sale of the F. D. Kees Manufacturing Company and came to believe that the new owner had cheated his father, that the sale could have been handled better. This was another reason for the dark look he gave the camera in Beatrice in May—and for why he now began to worry about finding work again after coming back from the Cape. This worry was fed by stories his friends told about their dire straits. (Bill Baziotes realized how bad things were for him when he found only ninety-three cents in his pocket.)

The Keeses were careful with their savings through September and October. Ann returned to *Antiques,* where she earned a little more by writing articles such as her piece on the Quaker painter Edward Hicks. Her husband considered freelance offers in New York and even in Philadelphia, where he interviewed for a documentary film to be shot in South America, its exotic locales and people then attracting American filmmakers such as Orson Welles. Kees also typed up a Guggenheim application that required a bibliography of his published work, a task that he found irksome.

While waiting at home for a new film assignment, he had time to compose new poems. In addition to "Turtle" and "The Clinic," he wrote "Land's End" and "1926." He mailed them to Getty, who liked "the particular vein" that his friend had struck and hoped that it would hold out for a long time. The run of poems, however, turned into a run of letters in which both the poet and his editor reworked lines with a jeweler's precision, so as to remove the "Eliotic." "You're probably wishing you'd never seen a turtle," wrote Getty, who was having some fun at Kees's expense with the lines "Something inside me moved, / Sluggish, torpid, dry": "If a reader wants to be facetious, those lines can so easily be taken in a sort of biological, scatological sense, especially in view of the association of 'sluggish' with the laxative advertisements."

Kees wrote "1926" in the wake of his parents' visit and being in Nebraska that spring:

The porchlight coming on again,
Early November, the dead leaves
Raked in piles, the wicker swing
Creaking. Across the lots
A phonograph is playing Ja-Da.
The porchlight coming on again.

An orange moon.

The poem encompasses a world very different from the one on North Fifth Street, seen through this golden haze. The next stanza is the future that is also *remembered* in this poem, "mapped and marred" in wars, in the madness of "R. / Insane," and in the murder of "B. with his throat cut, / Fifteen years from now, in Omaha." Nevertheless, the poem does let the reader get comfortable with this black nostalgia that then flows backward into a time capsule, where Kees shows himself in a cone of light:

I did not know them then.
My airedale scratches at the door.
And I am back from seeing Milton Sills
And Doris Kenyon. Twelve years old.
The porchlight coming on again.

Though Kees seems to create a spontaneous memory from his childhood, he came close to spoiling this small masterpiece. He had to visit the Museum of Modern Art's library and check *The Film Yearbook* to make sure that Milton Sills really had starred in a film with Doris Kenyon in 1926. "Couldn't make absolutely sure," he admitted to Getty, "but some of the alternatives I've tried don't sound quite right, such as: And I am back from seeing Evelyn Brent / In *Smooth as Satin.*"

The poems were almost side jobs given the time Kees devoted to painting—and the politics of painting. His friend Clem Greenberg had said "the fate of American art was being decided—by young people who lived below 34th Street in cold-water flats, existing from hand to mouth." That demarcation extended to Willow Street in Brooklyn, where Kees painted in one of the side rooms. Like his painter friends, he was waiting to see the October 11 issue of *Life* and its first "Round

Table on Modern Art," "in which fifteen distinguished critics and connoisseurs undertake to clarify the strange art of today." He was naturally suspicious of this effort to pry into the avant-garde. He joked that it had to do with Henry Luce's having purchased "an Arp or something."

Kees needed a gallery. He spent much of September and October trying to interest Charles Egan—and other gallery people—in his work. Egan had been a young salesman in the art gallery of Wanamaker's department store during the 1930s. From that position, he assiduously sought to introduce contemporary American artists to his upper-middle-class clientele. In 1945 he opened his own gallery with Willem de Kooning's first one-man show, an exhibition that drew museum representatives, generated a number of sales, and turned into abstract expressionism's first media event. This kind of groundbreaking success was what Kees wanted. He even wanted to cross the line at Thirty-fourth Street: "I am standing on one foot and then the other, waiting for one of the 57th Street gallery boys to come over and look at my paintings to decide if he wants to give me a show. I have got to have a show because I have room for no more canvases in the closet."

When Kees had given up hope on Egan, Louis Pollack offered him the opportunity to exhibit his work in the gallery that Pollack had added to his frame shop in the Village. Kees would be the second artist to exhibit at his new Peridot Gallery. Since the time Peridot opened as a frame shop, Kees had brought his work there. As a matter of course, Pollack had developed a good rapport with Kees and a familiarity with the steady development of his painting. The gallery at 6 East Twelfth Street, just off University Place, occupied the space of a red-brick, Greek-revival row house's long living room. It still had a natural, Jamesian intimacy—the wood floors and the fireplace and the brass firedogs had been preserved—yet, with its freshly painted white walls and spotlighting on the ceiling, the gallery showed Kees's paintings to their best advantage.

Artist and gallery owner soon came to an agreement about the date of the opening; the prices of his work, which ranged from three hundred dollars for *The Circus* to twenty-five dollars for a watercolor titled *Rooster;* and the gallery's percentage. As one of Peridot's artists, Kees now joined Pollack's modest stable, which included James Brooks, Philip Guston, Esteban Vicente, Melville Pierce, and Alfred Russell.

Getting his one-man show and being "represented" pushed writing even further aside. Kees even begged off his promise to write a Cézanne book for William Phillips. He busied himself with preparations, which Ann described to Getty on Election Day 1948: "Weld's out stuffing ballot boxes for the vegetarians. At $2 a stuffing, if he travels fast enough, he figures he should end up with about a four hundred dollar profit — The truth of the matter is this show has him all tied up. He was at the gallery all day yesterday and will be again today, putting new stripping on all the canvases. [...] This place looks bare without the paintings."

Kees arranged and hung his paintings on the walls of Peridot Gallery himself. Pollack found a unique way of showing eight drawings in a fishnet bin.

Many of the paintings now bore titles: *Seated Woman, Flight, The Circus, Versailles, Game, Amused Bird, Chameleon, Weatherbird, Study in Red and Black, Madrid.* Where other artists would have insisted on a rationale for the titles, numbering them like symphonies or having some other profound "system," Kees was not so obsessive. As he explained in the *Brooklyn Eagle,* if the titles meant something else to others, he was "not at all disturbed." *Madrid* took its title merely because the "hot" colors he had used suggested Spain and the form of a toreador (though he must have known others would try to read an homage to the famous siege of Madrid during the Spanish Civil War).

The reporter portrayed Kees as "one of the nation's foremost young poets," an exotic, cultured resident of Brooklyn by way of Nebraska and Manhattan who now called the borough of the Dodgers, Coney Island, and the Navy Yard his home, too. The *Brooklyn Eagle* also printed his philosophy, that he believed painting and writing complemented one another: "Shifting from one to the other I don't get into the periods of absolute sterility that are often experienced by writers who just write, or painters who just paint. [...] They get over-specialized. They're in a trap and they can't get out."

"In my own case," he continued, with an afterthought to take the edge off of sounding deep, "I find the change from writing to painting a joyous, spontaneous experience."

The one-hundred-dollar check he received for winning *Poetry*'s Oscar Blumenthal Prize paid for the liquor served at his opening, held on Halloween. And though the post office mailed out the announcements late, 125 people came.

Kees heard praise that evening, but he was also learning that being a painter was "an ordeal," as he confided to Ted Roethke. Just standing in one spot for four and a half hours was "no picnic." Some of that time was spent explaining his work and not cooperating with fashionable Freudian interpretations, like the one preserved in Win Scott's review in the *Providence Journal:* "Those forms of mine aren't phallic: it's just that I've been deeply influenced by such shapes as those of the summer squash, cucumbers, and by test tubes."

At one point that evening, he spotted Martin Andrews on the other side of the gallery examining *Flight.* Coming up from behind, Kees, with drink in hand, asked his friend from Paramount News what he thought. Andrews, having been a B-17 pilot during the war, turned from concentrating on the black, suspended block shape that dominated the canvas and confessed that he had a different take on "flight," one that was more "aerodynamic." Kees laughed warmly, holding back the fact that what had inspired the painting and title were the dead chickens hanging in New York poultry shops.

In the days after the opening the self-taught Kees received a note from the teacher of painters, Hans Hofmann: "You are as great a poet as you are a painter. I found your exhibition [...] poetry in color [...] what painting should be." The first review appeared in the *New York Times,* stating that Kees had "already secured himself a place as one of the more conspicuous and interesting young American poets," that he was "assimilating the idiom of a number of abstract painters — Browne, Baziotes, Pollock come to mind. This he has done with intelligence and taste and with a natural instinct for texture and decorative opposition." A number of the small, more spontaneous oils, the reviewer felt, "held promise of a more arresting individuality" to come.

Clement Greenberg visited Peridot a few weeks after the opening. For Kees, what "Clem would say" mattered the most. After going from painting to painting and taking many notes, Greenberg told Lou Pollack that Kees's paintings were "terrific."

"Maybe I live right, or something," Kees said on hearing this, assuming that Greenberg's review would soon appear in the *Nation.*

Getty also saw the show after the opening, coming down from Cambridge in mid-November. He took color snapshots of the gallery interior and promised he would send copies and enlargements that Kees wanted for himself and that his parents wanted for pasting in their scrapbook along with a clipping from the *New Yorker* that listed their son's show in "Goings On about Town."

Getty also spent part of the day with Weldon and Ann walking around the Heights. Eventually, it became a kind of Hart Crane pilgrimage. They visited Crane's former home and then crossed the Brooklyn Bridge. At some point Getty asked Kees to pose for a picture. He obliged and leaned with his back up against the ornate ironwork of the rail, near a red-painted salt barrel and with a view of lower Manhattan's skyscrapers in the background, seen through a web of bridge cables. With his topcoat open on a fine wool suit, and holding his fedora in one hand, Kees looked more like a young stockbroker than an abstract painter.

Three of the Peridot paintings sold: *Composition,* a watercolor, for $75; *Black Figure,* an oil, for $65; and *Red Figure,* another oil, for $180. The gallery purchased *Seated Woman* and kept several others on consignment. Kees gave *Game* to Willy Poster and his wife, Connie. The rest Lou Pollack returned; some of these, such as *Night Forms,* Kees painted over.

No museum or influential collector had purchased a painting. And that review in the *Nation* that would have put Kees on the art world's map, as Ann observed, did not come: "Clem said he wasn't going to write about the show because, altho. everyone liked it, they were saying it was a flash in the pan."

Greenberg told Kees in a note that his work was "some of the most respectable contemporary painting there is to be seen anywhere." But he urged him to paint "a lot," to have a second show. He wanted to see Kees's next five or six pictures—a request that Kees found hard to take. It made him look like he was no more serious a player than a Sunday painter, like he was being given a generous chance by Greenberg, whose profile of the painters he endorsed was left open for an artist who worked in a spare bedroom in a quiet, middle-class neighborhood across the river.

Since August Whittaker Chambers had been testifying before Representative Richard M. Nixon, a young, ambitious Republican congressman from California, and other members of the House Subcommittee on Un-American Activities at the Commodore Hotel and the Federal Building in New York. During his appearances before the committee,

Chambers accused a State Department employee, Alger Hiss, of being a Soviet spy. Hiss, though not an important official, had had access to the late president Franklin D. Roosevelt and had accompanied him at Yalta, where the Republican opposition believed that too many concessions had been made to Stalin.

Kees followed these events. His stint at *Time* had given him a small walk-on part in the life of the rumpled, unkempt Chambers, who had put on more weight, wore dentures, and now edited *Sports Illustrated*. He had no idea Chambers had once been an agent for the Soviet Union and part of an elaborate Communist underground in Washington during the 1930s.

Kees never worried about having said anything to his former boss that "could be used against him." He considered Chambers a failed writer who had found his audience at last in the government's prosecutors. Nevertheless, in November and December, when the Hiss case was turned over to the grand jury, the stomach problems that had plagued him before returned. The meander of a vein on his left temple became more pronounced. He had taken to his bed—as had Ann—with a bad cold a few weeks before, getting up only to change the Pete Daily record on the phonograph. Propped upright with pillows, he read books and newspapers. Chambers's testimony reached a climax. He produced a microfilm from his Maryland pumpkin patch that proved Hiss was an important player in a Communist conspiracy in Washington. Kees followed the case in the newsreels and the papers and took a grim view of these events, a view that later surfaced in a 1952 letter in which he reacted to the publication of Chambers's memoir, *Witness:* "I have watched Whittaker Chambers, for instance, in operation, and it is not a pretty sight." He was especially put off by Chambers's religiosity during the Hiss trial and from this time would see it as an insult to "every human being who has tried to struggle for goodness & decency without benefit of the particular dogmas."

In Kees this struggle was manifested through art and meant coping with the disappointments of his one-man show and, more recently, unexpected rejections from the *New Yorker*. It meant reading, with the intensity of a Presbyterian missionary, Ted Roethke's *The Lost Son* and listening closely to *Bluin' the Blues* for his church music. These fed Kees with as much tranquility as he had verbalizing his appreciation of Hans Hofmann's vision and aesthetics in a poem written around this time:

The scraps
Of living shift and change. Because of you,

The light burns sharper in how many rooms,
Shaped to a new identity; the dark hall

Finds a door; the wind comes in;
A rainbow sleeps and wakes against the wall.

"A Salvo for Hans Hofmann" he thought better than the poem
Auden had written for Eliot's birthday that year with its embarrassing final line: "your sixty years have not been wasted." Unlike the
Bloomsbury superman, Kees's artist-hero is understated, subordinate
to the creative process—an affirmation that Kees would have applied
to himself. The French art review *Derrière le miroir* printed Kees's little
homage to being and art and an essay by Tennessee Williams in an
issue that featured the Paris retrospective of Hofmann's paintings in
the very existential year 1949.

In January the perjury trial of Alger Hiss loomed, as did Communism's
advance. Peking had fallen to Mao Tse-tung. In Eastern Europe, Stalin
further consolidated his power with the establishment of Communist
puppet regimes and mass arrests of intellectuals. The United States
and its allies had completed negotiations for the North Atlantic Treaty
Organization, further raising international tensions.

What was now called "the cold war," with its arms race and emerg-
ing military blocs, deepened the anxiety of Americans and, of course,
the intellectuals, the artists. This was seen by the Soviet Union and its
American sympathizers, from hard-core Stalinists to the followers of
Henry Wallace, as a ripe opportunity to improve their tarnished image
and counter the bitter pitch of the anticommunists.

To this end, the National Council of the Arts, Sciences and Profes-
sions held a huge public-relations event called the Cultural and Scientific Conference for World Peace. The council, however, was quickly
labeled a Communist-front organization by those on the left, including Kees, who accepted that the Soviet Union was a police state and
that Stalin had murdered and jailed millions. Its peace conference was
just as quickly labeled a ploy.

Harlow Shapley, a Harvard scientist, the chairman, was decried as a
fellow traveler. The event's financing came from unions that still had

strong ties to the Soviet Union, notably the ILGWU, and from wealthy sympathizers in the entertainment industry, as well as unions that represented the rank and file of Hollywood and Broadway. From their number, and from many other fields and disciplines in the arts and sciences, Shapley enlisted a cast of thousands that included Berenice Abbott, Thomas Mann and his children, Linus Pauling, Ad Reinhardt, Lillian Hellman, Norman Mailer, and a young actor named Marlon Brando. These conferees were led to believe that the international crisis between the Soviet Union and the Western democracies was a cultural misunderstanding, a simple breakdown in communication that could be fixed by panels, committees, and mutual declarations for world peace.

The conference became newsworthy before it even took place in late March. Shapley had invited many writers and artists who were openly communist. Each time the State Department or the FBI denied an artist, like the Mexican muralist David Siqueiros, a visa or turned one away at the borders, it generated a potentially embarrassing wire-service story that made it hard to insist that the United States was more free and tolerant than the Soviet Union.

The most illustrious and controversial group deplaned at Idlewild Field in New York, a Soviet delegation including the Russian writers' union head, the novelist Aleksandr A. Fadeyev, and composer Dmitry Shostakovich, whose display and cryptic remarks made the peace conference all the more like Soviet theater. Kees saw the newsreel footage taken at the airport and remarked that Shostakovich's pallor looked abnormally gray as he and the other Soviets deplaned and brushed past the embarrassed representatives of the conference's American hosts, Norman Mailer and Aaron Copland.

On Saturday, March 26, the conference officially opened at the Waldorf Astoria. There the audience heard speech after speech of ritualized goodwill and pleas for international understanding. Outside, on the sidewalks around the hotel, the anticommunists equaled the intensity of the conferees with picket lines, prayer meetings, and demonstrations that included the clergy, wheelchair-bound war veterans—and those intellectuals who no longer believed the "Russian myth" of the Soviet Union as the ideal society. One of their leaders was Sidney Hook, a philosophy professor at New York University and writer for *Partisan Review*. He formed Americans for Intellectual Freedom, the group that Weldon Kees joined.

Kees, who once wrote nostalgically about long, ten-mile hikes with Hook and John Berryman in the Jersey Flats, lent himself to Hook's organization. Calling on his old contacts at Paramount and other newsreel services, he helped ensure coverage of AIF demonstrations, press conferences, and their own counterrally at the Freedom House on West Fortieth Street. Weldon and Ann even appeared briefly in Paramount's newsreel "Peace Parley Weekend of Controversy," listening attentively to Sidney Hook and a Russian woman who described the harshness of Soviet labor camps.

Kees enjoyed his small role in what would be called the "great anti-Stalinist crusade," in which he sided with Robert Lowell, Mary McCarthy, Dwight Macdonald, Irving Howe, Arthur Koestler, and others. Lillian Hellman complained about how successful Hook and his allies had been in importuning "many of us" to withdraw from the conference. Kees also revealed the irony of his situation in the poem he sent Lowry Wimberly around this time, "The Older Programs That We Falsified." He dedicated it to Rudolph Umland, a fellow state guide editor who had taken Kees to task over his politics back in Lincoln:

Some joined the enemy (forgive my smile), some dragged their fears
To psychoanalysts or into the dark,
Or shot themselves in bathrooms. Has it been ten years?

After the Waldorf conference, Kees returned to his easel and painted new oils for Peridot's next group show. He had a painting in the "American Abstract Artists" show—as did Clement Greenberg. "Clem," Kees wrote Getty, "[who] has been painting for about twenty years off and on, is for the first time showing a painting. He is nervous as hell about it, naturally. We were over at his place a week or so ago and he showed us his most recent works. They show a strong influence of Jackson Pollock."

Kees saw Kenneth Rexroth, who was on his way to Europe. Rexroth "put on a bang-up performance" the night he dined at the Willow Street apartment, telling stories about the poets on the West Coast and reading his poems. After Rexroth came Robert Lowry, returning from a year in Italy. He told Kees "gruesome accounts of the behavior of the artistic expatriates over there and in France." Sitting at an outdoor café near the Pont Royale, Lowry had encountered Gore Vidal on his way to the American Express. Vidal asked Lowry if he wanted to walk along. Lowry said he wanted to finish his drink first, so Vidal sat down and began talking about what a wonderful sex life he was having with a Frenchman—and about their game, in which they pretended to be jousting knights with their erections.

Lowry had another story: about Truman Capote confessing to having had a girlfriend in high school. Kees, too, had stories to tell: about the Yaddo affair that Robert Lowell touched off when he publicly accused Elizabeth Ames of being a Communist sympathizer and harboring a spy, the journalist Agnes Smedley, and about how doing so drove him over the edge until he was found screaming obscenities and crazy talk from the window of Allen Tate's Chicago apartment.

Kees's life, of course, was generating no gossip at all, and going unrecognized was a different problem for him. It had to do with surviving the anxiety of your own "construct," as we would call it now, the self "behaving with greater wackiness than ever before," as he said of his contemporaries. He explored this survival in "Relating to Robinson," the new poem he drafted on the evening of April 10.

Like the other Robinson poems, it read like the perfect *New Yorker* piece. The seasonal criterion had been worked in. The poem would fit nicely in a summer issue, the kind people read while getting a suntan on the beach at the Cape. The city was as much a persona in the poem as Robinson. It had a street scene that could almost be photographed by Berenice Abbott or Edward Weston. It enveloped a jarring and faithful representation of those chance, hurried, and self-involved sidewalk encounters that are so much a part of New York life, where familiarity and estrangement exist as one emotion:

> Somewhere in Chelsea, early summer;
> And, walking in the twilight toward the docks,
> I thought I made out Robinson ahead of me.
> From an uncurtained second-story room, a radio
> Was playing There's a Small Hotel; a kite
> Twisted above dark rooftops and slow drifting birds.
> We were alone there, he and I,
> Inhabiting the empty street.
> Under a sign for Natural Bloom Cigars,
> While lights clicked softly in the dusk from red to green,
> He stopped and gazed into a window

Where a plaster Venus, modeling a truss,
Looked out at Eastbound traffic. (But Robinson,
I knew, was out of town: he summers at a place in Maine,
Sometimes on Fire Island, sometimes the Cape,
Leaves town in June and comes back after Labor Day.)
And yet, I almost called out, "Robinson!"

Placenames at once hold Kees's tableau together and pull it apart. He could almost be describing Main Street as much as a fragmented world that only comes together in the vague recognition of another. The sights and sounds provide other sources of tension. Ominous birds are made less so by their counterpoint in the twisting kite. The traffic lights click but do so softly. The voice in the poem is at once alone and confronted with the prospect of meeting an old friend whose whereabouts, customs, and habits are as easy to see as one's reflection in a shop window. The chance meeting even suggests the possibility of a tryst (even a homosexual tryst at the infamous Chelsea docks), given the song that plays overhead, from Rodgers and Hart's 1936 Broadway show, *On Your Toes*. The ballad posits a boy-meets-girl idyll, where "We'll creep into our little shell." Yet, where Kees intended readers to hear in the background a couple singing, "Looking through the window you can see a distant steeple; not a sign of people," and a woman's voice asking, "Who wants people?", Robinson confronts the reproduction of the Venus de Milo, as if he, too, seeks a fusion of love and the equally delicious feeling of being alone, of having escaped the city. The goddess of love is unable to service him; she is a sight gag around which Kees has depicted the urbane madness of his class:

There was no chance. Just as I passed,
Turning my head to search his face,
His own head turned with mine
And fixed me with dilated, terrifying eyes
That stopped my blood. His voice
Came at me like an echo in the dark.
"I thought I saw the whirlpool opening.
Kicked all night at a bolted door.
You must have followed me from Astor Place.
An empty paper floats down at the last.
And then a day as huge as yesterday in pairs

Unrolled its horror on my face
Until it blocked—" *Running in sweat*
To reach the docks, I turned back
For a second glance. I had no certainty,
There in the dark, that it was Robinson
Or someone else.
The block was bare. The Venus,
Bathed in blue fluorescent light,
Stared toward the river. As I hurried West,
The lights across the bay were coming on.
The boats moved silently and the low whistles blew.

Kees could rely on how many of his readers would seize upon the phallic cigar pointing to the goddess, guided by Freud or Jung, by Sir James Frazer and *The Golden Bough,* by Sartre, or by Margaret Mead. Each thinker fed the new interest in mythology, existentialism, anthropology, and human behavior—and the new aesthetics surrounding the interpretation of abstract paintings. (Kees could have had in mind the editors of the *Tiger's Eye,* especially their issue on the Sublime.) Overly intellectual and fashionable readings would, unavoidably, sound ridiculous latching onto a Robinson standing under a cigar, interpreting it as the sign of his potency and interpreting him as Pygmalion in *Venus observa,* the position he assumed, perhaps, in his abortive attempt to enjoy the favors of Mrs. Morse in another Robinson poem.

Naturally, the first readings and critical interpretations of this poem hardly reckon with Kees's humor. Robinson's "outburst" eclipses such subtleties as the stanza Kees borrowed from the Emily Dickinson poem that begins, "The first Day's Night had come." The narrator in Chelsea does not necessarily *hear* these words—italicized in Kees's poem—as lines of poetry. By not supplying the quotation marks, Kees rendered the Dickinson as something an ordinary man could possibly speak—and as something that can be experienced with all the surprise—even for readers who recognize the lines—of having heard a dog talk.

The joke means even more if one knows that the allusion to Emily Dickinson's poetry in "Relating to Robinson" is a response to her rise in stock among academics and the reading public during this time. Getty complained that anthologists only represented her "Bees Robins & Daisies routine." So Kees represented *their* version of the poetess, the one who stood for "insensitive" tastes, an undertaking Getty developed further. When the draft of "Relating" came to him in early April, he suggested the riskier use of italics over single quotes so as to provide "an indication that the narrator recognized the words as a quotation."

Getty also felt strongly about keeping intact the "eeriness and uncertainty" needed "right through to those peaceful lines at the end." His friend had nearly spoiled the effect in the final stanza with a line that read: "The man had looked / Enough like Robinson to be his twin." "To me," Getty advised, "that seems to state pretty definitely that it *wasn't* Robinson after all, just someone who looked like him, and this lets the poem down a good deal." A few days later, Kees thanked Getty for the help: "You fixed on the very spot in the poem about which I was queasy."

∾

What you have scheduled looks like the most exciting thing in art ever to run outside of New York in the summer—or in the winter too.
— Clement Greenberg

"For some reason or other I seem to have a car," Kees wrote Maurice Johnson in early May 1949, referring to a 1938 Plymouth purchased from Mark Rothko for $175. It barely ran. Its bug-eyed headlights made it look like a Fleischer cartoon character. The mohair upholstery had so many holes that the car, to Kees, looked as if it had been used "for hauling porcupines and railroad spikes" instead of art supplies and paintings. The front seat had so many rents that it looked like "an unmade bed in a Bowery fleabag."

Kees christened the car "Tiresias" so that he and Ann could be seen driving around in a car that looked like it had been driven through the Waste Land long before the serious young people at the Cape started taking Eliot so seriously on the G.I. Bill. It would be a rolling version of a very shopworn literary allusion, a nod to the surrealism of Appolinaire and to Cocteau's *La Machine Infernal,* which such a potentially unreliable car was.

As Memorial Day approached, Weldon and Ann made all kinds of preparations for the summer, including moving out of their Brooklyn apartment. They would find a new place to live in the fall. Ann arranged for their "few sticks of furniture" to be stored for the summer, and Weldon drove them to a warehouse in Brooklyn. They advertised for a tenant to take up the remainder of their lease—someone, Ann wrote to Eleanor Scott, "who is responsible but at the same time screwy enough to pay more rent than is reasonable."

The Keeses lived off soup and crackers during this time. Ann could not fix the recipes Eleanor had sent them while they closed down their apartment. Everything associated with the process of leaving Brooklyn Heights was hurried and complicated to Ann, especially given the added responsibility of typing Weldon's manuscript of poems.

A Late History, the working title of the new book, came together in April. Kees wished Getty could have come to Brooklyn and given him a hand with the arrangement of the poems before he sent the typescript to his new publisher, Harcourt, Brace, which had recently bought out Reynal and Hitchcock. This had turned out to be a much harder book to put together than *The Fall of the Magicians.* He spent many hours "shifting" the poems around "without getting anywhere in particular." He wondered if they added up to "a unit" and if anyone even read books of poems that way anymore. He knew that he did not. The thirty-five poems that composed *A Late History* struck Kees as more personal than his earlier work. He told Getty that "1926" was "patently autobiographical." The poems also struck him as being on "a higher level" than those in *The Fall of the Magicians,* and there was, to him, "the undeniable fact" that the book was "much more somber in tone than *The Fall,*" which had a moderately heavy emphasis on satire and the exterior world." He also resigned himself to their lyrical quality and to his incapacity to write a long poem. He only salvaged a portion of a hundred-line, centerpiece poem in "The Coming of the Plague," which made up for what it lacked in length in the enormity of its approaching catastrophe:

> We could hear the sound of beating clothes
> All through the night. We could not count
> All the miscarriages, the quarrels, the jealousies.
> And one day in a field I saw
> A swarm of frogs, swollen and hideous,
> Hundreds upon hundreds, sitting on each other,
> Huddled together, silent, ominous,
> And heard the sound of rushing wind.

A *Late History* featured three of the Robinson poems, and it tapped into Kees's rediscovery of Hawthorne. To Kees he was the finest expression of "refined alienation from reality." Choosing an epigram from the preface to *The Marble Faun,* Kees suggested his program was the same as Hawthorne's: descending "those dark caverns into which all men must descend if they would know anything beneath the surface and illusive pleasures of existence."

Kees trusted that Robert Giroux and his colleague Ted Amussen would accept his new book and publish it at the end of the summer. Like a businessman who had turned a good profit, he finally believed that Harcourt owed him for the success of *The Fall of the Magicians* as much as the new book merited publication on its own. He looked forward to having lunch with both editors, who had made important poets out of Robert Lowell and a handful of the other elect, to talk about *A Late History.*

Since March Kees and Fritz Bultman had been making plans for a series of cultural events in Provincetown. They had become close again during the time of the "American Abstract Artists" group show, which had been on view at Peridot Gallery in April. Kees wrote Bultman that their paintings hung side by side along with works by Louise Bourgeois and Willem de Kooning.

Bultman was keeping an eye out for a building that had plenty of space for readings, talks, performances, and an art show that he and Kees thought would be a response to the cultural conference at the Waldorf Astoria, one that actually dealt with the culture. He was happy to report that the Provincetown art dealer Donald Witherstine had a new gallery on Commercial Street. The only drawback was that it was not a gallery yet, just a large, empty, and unfinished interior that still resembled what it had been: the garage of a Ford dealership.

The "forums" would resemble the "Eighth Street Club," the informal name for the school that Motherwell, Baziotes, Rothko, and other abstract artists had founded at 35 East Eighth Street in 1948. There, every Friday evening, lectures were given that explored "The Subjects of the Artist," the official name of the school; they focused on what it was in modern life that the teaching artists and their students painted "about."

Bultman and a new partner in the forums, the poet Cecil Hemley, made contacts and preparations at the Cape. In New York Kees promoted the idea to his friends. He spent many evenings meeting at the apartments of Dwight Macdonald and others to collect ideas for readings, performances, films, rehearsals, and exhibits that all featured some group discussion that mixed poets, artists, dancers, filmmakers, critics—even psychoanalysts. (Macdonald thought they should include the topic "The Psychopathology of Vacations.")

Kees recorded at least two radio broadcasts for the Voice of America with Bill Baziotes, during which the artist suffered from some "mike fright" as they discussed the upcoming forums and the Cape's artists' colony. The latter topic must have also included some commentary, social, ironic, and otherwise, about the lifestyles of certain groups and the reputations of certain talents. "Those who know either of us," Kees wrote Getty, "or Provincetown shd. enjoy some of our rather (necessarily, all things considered) subterranean remarks."

The Keeses drove to the Cape over the weekend of May 14 and 15 in order to find a rental. They made a layover in Providence on the first day and had dinner at the home of Win and Eleanor Scott. There they enjoyed tomato cobb and talked about the forums and traded stories about Robert Lowell, who Weldon hoped would be out of the sanitarium in time to participate in a poetry reading he wanted to put on in Provincetown.

The next day Ann and Weldon drove on to the Cape. They stayed overnight at the Bultmans' home and spent the following day searching for an apartment on Commercial Street. They found one near the wharf and close to Days Lumberyard, where the enterprising owner had converted some sheds on the north side of the main building into studios.

Taking their time, giving Tiresias's radiator plenty of opportunities to cool, the Keeses returned to Brooklyn via Newport, the site of Weldon's Henry James poem, the one he had dedicated to Ann. Instead of the fin-de-siècle twilight, which the Keeses had felt drawn to in 1943, they found a "mangy" chrome-plated roadhouse. Ann thought it featured the "world's worst orchestra." The food, too, was "quite in keeping"—as was life on Willow Street for the next two weeks. But at last a new tenant took over the lease on the apartment, and all the unfinished business got finished. Weldon met with his publisher. He had lunch one more time with New York friends he would not see for the

Weldon Kees at seven, 1921. (Courtesy of Nina Duvall Anderson)

Top left: John Kees, about 1914. (Courtesy of the Gage County Historical Society)

Bottom left: Sarah and Weldon Kees, about 1924. (Courtesy of Nina Duvall Anderson)

Top right: Weldon Kees in a double-breasted suit, summer 1930. (Courtesy of Nina Duvall Anderson)

Bottom right: Dale Smith and Weldon Kees sitting on the wall of the Nebraska state capitol in Lincoln, 1937. (Gertrude Stein Gallery)

Above: Weldon and Ann Kees in Denver, shortly after their marriage, 1938. (Gertrude Stein Gallery)

Right: Weldon Kees (above) and Norris Getty (below) reading the Sunday *Denver Post,* June 1941 (Gertrude Stein Gallery)

Opposite, top: Paramount Newsreel staff party, c. December 1945. Kees is standing in the back row, eighth from the right. (Gertrude Stein Gallery)

Opposite, bottom: Weldon Kees, studio portrait by Raymond Shorr, New York, 1947. (Collection of the author)

Above: *The Studio,* oil and sand on canvas,
1948. (Gertrude Stein Gallery)

Right: Weldon Kees on the Brooklyn Bridge,
November 1948. Photograph by Norris Getty.
(Gertrude Stein Gallery)

WELDON KEES

recent paintings

PERIDOT GALLERY

6 e. 12th st., n. y. 3, n. y.

preview monday, oct. 31, 4 to 8 p.m.

through nov. 26

Top left: Gallery invitation to Kees's first one-man show, illustrated with ink drawing. (Collection of the author)

Bottom left: Hans Hofmann, Karl Knaths, Fritz Bultman, Cecil Hemley, and Kees view artwork for the Forum 49 exhibition in Gallery 200, July 1949. (Gertrude Stein Gallery)

Above: Weldon Kees sitting in Gallery 200 during Forum 49. Fritz Bultman painted the poster for Kees's jazz lecture. (Collection of the author)

Top left: Ann and Weldon Kees standing with their Lincoln Zephyr, Provincetown, 1950.
(Gertrude Stein Gallery)

Bottom left: Weldon Kees sitting under one of his paintings in Berkeley, early 1953. (Gertrude Stein Gallery)

Top right: Weldon and Ann Kees, Berkeley, early 1953. (Gertrude Stein Gallery)

Bottom right: One of Kees's "data" photographs for *Nonverbal Communication*, 1953. (Gertrude Stein Gallery)

Left: Weldon, Ann, and John Kees, Santa
Barbara, summer 1953. (Gertrude Stein
Gallery)

Above: San Francisco Films staff, December 1954. (Gertrude Stein Gallery)

Top left: Jermayne MacAgy in 1958. (Photograph by Eve Arnold © 1968 Magnum Photos, New York)

Bottom left: Kees and "Lonesome," early 1955. (Gertrude Stein Gallery)

Top right: Michael Grieg, Kees, and the stripper Lily Ayers planning her poetry reading for *Poets' Follies*, January 1955. (Collection of the author)

Bottom right: Lily Ayers and Kees pose before *Poets' Follies* billboard designed by artist William Mayo, January 1955. (Collection of the author)

**DIRECT FROM ITS RECORD-BREAKING
ENGAGEMENT IN SAN FRANCISCO !!!**

MR. MICHAEL GRIEG & MR. WELDON KEES
present

THE

POETS' FOLLIES

OF 1955

MR. R. H. HAGAN, *Master of Ceremonies*

PREMIERE PRESENTATION! THE

 ## Giant Poetic Brain

Electronic Flashes direct from Mount Olympus!
Cybernetics Meets Iambic Pentameter! The
BRAIN Will be Fed the Works of *Alexander Pope, 'John Masefield,*
and *Yvor Winters.* Don't Miss It !!!

☛ **MISS BURLESK OF 1955**
in a Reading of her FAVORITE POEMS, and a Discussion of the
Relationship of her ART and the Art of Poetry.

☞ NEW POEMS & SONGS BY MR. ☜

 ## WELDON KEES

whose *Poems 1947-1954,* has just been published. Mr. Kees
at the Steinway. (Has tuxedo, will travel short distances.)

☛ An Inspired Reading by Mr. Michael Grieg,
Bon Vivant & Raconteur, of *Certain Passages* of Lowell
Naeve's controversial *A Field of Broken Stones,* recently
CHIDED IN MARIN CNTY.
(Mr. Grieg has cutaway, will travel long distances.)

POEMS & TRANSLATIONS from the *French* by
MR. LAWRENCE FERLING
Stormy Petrel of the Columbus Avenue Booksellers.

☛ AN EXHIBITION OF THE DANCE & POETRY BY
Mr. Dick Martin & Miss Jayne Nesmith
A Series of Dances to Poems of Ezra Pound, Henry Reed,
e. e. cummings and William Carlos Williams

BARBARY COAST 5

Featuring CAROL LEIGH, *Queen of the Washboard,* in a Recital
of Compositions of a Lowdown & Traditional Nature, Emphasizing
Ragtime & the Blues, with Horace Schwartz, Percussion Virtuoso,
& Adrian Wilson, Wizard of the Clarinet.

☞ **Mr. Walter McGrail**
Star of Stage and Screen! Songs that Touch the Heart by
Miss Tamara Lindovna

A NEW PLAY, "*The Three Bottles; or, Poison in the Poesy,*"
Dealing with Angst & Poets in Three Cultures, written by
MICHAEL GRIEG
and Starring those Stalwart Players from the Bella Union Co.
**Mr. William Ackridge, Mr. R. Martin, &
introducing Miss Phyllis Diller.**

Directed by the Producers and DICK MARTIN
Staged by WILLIAM ATLEE   Asst. Stage Mgr: Frank Craig
Consultant to the Producers: Eric Vaughn
Illumination: Marge Craig Set Design: Kenneth Nack
House Staff: Guy Nesmith, Yvonne Rainer, Mary McDonald,
James Fahl
Billboards: William Mayo   Photography: William Heick

Berkeley Little Theatre
Allston Way at Grove

TWO PERFORMANCES ONLY!
Sunday, January 30, 1955 at 2:30 & 8:00 pm
All Seats $1.00
Box Office opens at 1:45 and 7:15. Tickets available at the Door.

 Adrian Wilson Steam Press

Left: Broadside for second *Poets' Follies,* printed by Adrian Wilson. (Collection of the author)

Top right: Horace Schwartz, Carol Leigh, unidentified, Kees, and Adrian Wilson perform as the Barbary Coast Five in the second *Poets' Follies,* January 1955. (Gertrude Stein Gallery)

Bottom right: Kees in uniform reading Henry Reed's "Unarmed Combat" and dancers at *Poets' Follies,* February 1955. (Collection of the author)

Top left: Kees, Ketty Lester (Freierson), and Don
Ewell, March 1955. (Courtesy of William Heick)

Bottom left: William Heick and Weldon Kees
filming schizophrenic artist at Langley Porter
Clinic, spring 1955. (Courtesy of William Heick)

Above: The Showplace. Nina Boas and Penny
Vieregge are in the foreground. Kees and Grieg
speak to a reporter on the stage. May 1955. (*San
Francisco Chronicle*)

Announcing a Change of Date! Opening Friday, May 27th

Limited Engagement!   An Evening of Unusual Theatre!

FOUR TIMES ONE {
● "GALLANT CASSIAN"
● "SWEENEY AGONISTES"
● "THE WAITING ROOM"
● "THE BRIMSTONE BUTTERFLY"

by Arthur Schnitzler, T. S. Eliot, Weldon Kees, Michael Grieg
with the Company of "The Poets' Follies of 1955"
including NINA BOAS, PENNY VIEREGGE, BYRON BRYANT, JAN DAVIS,
FERDE GROFE, Jr., ERIC VAUGHAN, MILLIE ERICKSON

Fridays and Saturdays at 8:30 p. m.

THE SHOWPLACE

2528 Folsom Street (near 21st Street)   Admission $1.00 and $1.50

Top: Advertisement for *Four Times One,* May 1955.
(Collection of the author)

Bottom: Weldon Kees under the Golden Gate Bridge,
early 1955. Photograph by William Heick. (Courtesy
of William Heick)

summer. Soon, two weeks into June, he would write from the Cape that he and Ann were "settled, busy, getting tan, getting in some first-rate swimming, staring out now & then at beaches, wharves, gulls, old men wading at five o'clock in the morning, eating lustily."

Ann typed the leaflet announcing "FORUM 49" and its first month of programs in the middle of June. The first evening, a panel discussion scheduled for 8:30 on Sunday, July 3, featured the painters Hans Hofmann, Adolph Gottlieb, and George Biddle and "a fourth speaker to be announced," who Weldon hoped would be Clement Greenberg.

Greenberg, however, begged off the art panel, implying that it was a distraction not only for him. "Are you doing much painting?" he asked in the note declining Kees's invitation. "Don't let public affairs abstract you too much." Panels, Greenberg continued, did more harm than good and only unsettled people who were working their problems out satisfactorily in isolation. A talk by a single "personality" on modern art would better meet the "audience's resistance head-on," and that personality would not be him ("Speaking takes too much out of me in terms of fright and tension").

If Greenberg was unwilling, Kees could still rely on the pool of artists, writers, critics, and other talented people who were or would be vacationing in Provincetown, Wellfleet, and Truro during the summer. Marcel Breuer, Serge Chermayeff, Frederick Kiesler, and Anthony Smith could be tapped for a panel on modern architecture. Wyndham Lewis could lecture, for he would be visiting the Macdonalds for a few days in Wellfleet. Some kind of panel on the state of fiction or the novel could feature Howard Nemerov and Mary McCarthy, along with Waldo Frank ("as an irritant"). Other participants could be brought in from nearby, too. Conrad Aiken lived only thirty miles away in Brewster. Allen Tate would be in Cummington; Kees saw him on some August Thursday evening with "three or four poets reading their works. No more than 10 or 12 minutes for each, in order to keep the evening within some sort of bounds. I'd like enormously to have you read on this evening; we could set almost any date that would suit yr. convenience. — The programs will be held in a large new art gallery which is opening July 3d; it seats 200. I don't know yet how we are going to make out financially; so I can't make any definite promises about payment. But unless a backer is forthcoming, which isn't entirely out of the question, there'll be little money in it for anybody."

Kees prefaced his solicitation with applause for Tate's letter in the May issue of *Partisan Review,* for Tate had dared anyone to accuse him to his face of being an antisemite for his part in awarding Ezra Pound the Bollingen Prize in literature for the *Pisan Cantos.* The "topic calls for gesture, mimicry, and, here & there, a nice choice of oaths," Kees wrote to Tate. The controversy reminded him of "the curious atmosphere that had been pushing in on all sides this past winter in New York." Where Kees fell in this debate can be understood from his reaction to Clement Greenberg's letter in May's *Partisan Review.* That Greenberg could feel, as a Jew, physically threatened by the *Pisan Cantos* left Kees "gasping," for Greenberg went on to contradict himself on this ("my perhaps irrational sensitivity as a Jew cedes to my fear of censorship in general") and the other points he made. What Kees found unbelievable was Greenberg's notion that it is justifiable to demand that an artist be a successful human being before anything else, even at the cost of his art. Pound, for better or worse, had met this bitter criterion when he spoke through Mauberley and the other "voices" of the pre–crazily totalitarian Pound.

Nevertheless, Kees recognized the Holocaust and its victims. That same summer in Provincetown, Kees delivered a merited rebuke. The painter Mark Rothko said one evening that he had not felt anything when he saw the films of the Nazi death camps; they did not have anything to do with him. There was a shocked, tense little silence, for Rothko was Jewish, and then Kees said quietly, "What you mean, Mark, is that you're a moral dwarf."

Scheduling the Thursday-evening forums for July and August kept Kees and his friends busy with everything from printing stationery and flyers to reaffirming their loyalty to the United States. The Cape's sun offered no protection from the cold war.

Dwight Macdonald agreed to deliver a lecture on the Soviet Union and its influence. When the talk was advertised in the Provincetown newspaper and Forum 49 literature, Kees ran into a certain amount of hysteria he had not counted on. Some took a look at the program and took the word "soviet" in the title of Macdonald's talk to mean that "the Commies have taken over the building at 200 Commercial." Kees quickly defused a scandal with reworded fliers and press releases — and then wrote Macdonald that it would be safe for him to come up from New York: "Apparently some of the talk was helped a bit by the fact that a lot of people here in town, due to the ever-present cultural lag, still think that you are a foaming Marxist. Do you still run into this sort of thing? Anyway, I had a long talk with one man here, who is still not convinced, after all I told him about your various changes in philosophies during the past five years, that you are not a Communist. (Incidentally, most Provincetownites do not make any very subtle distinction between a Stalinist and a Trotskyite.)"

The painter George Biddle and his brother Francis, President Roosevelt's attorney general and the American judge at the Nuremberg war trials, had homes, respectively, in Truro and Bound Brook Island in Wellfleet. This was the most contained, remote, and charming part of the lower Cape, a place of nearly untamed land, its sandy roads for the most part leading nowhere, with tangled locust and scrub pine, scrub oak, and swamp alder between the little dunes on the way down to the bay. Ann and Weldon enjoyed the drive there, going through "the hot fragrance of sweet-fern and wild indigo" that Conrad Aiken described in the autobiography he was writing that summer, going "from one secret pond to another"—and ultimately going to the cocktail parties that the Biddle brothers gave.

The Biddles brought to life the Harvard of T. S. Eliot, Santayana, Maxwell Perkins, and other figures from an earlier generation. Francis had recently published *The World's Best Hope*, which argued against isolationism and for Americans to assume the full responsibilities of world leadership left by the collapse of the British Empire. Of special interest to Kees was Biddle's positivism, which, as in de Tocqueville's writings on America, did not underestimate the country's dark side: the anti-intellectualism, the racism, the inability to tolerate difference, and so on. Much of what Biddle said about America's preeminent political role paralleled its leading position in the arts, in which Kees and his painter friends fervently believed. Such a sober view was not heard in a Washington dominated by the hearings of the House Subcommittee on Un-American Activities, so Kees invited Francis to give a talk at Gallery 200—and gave Forum 49 a forward-looking political vision to complement its cultural one.

Though not purely a conservative or academic artist, George Biddle had come out against abstract art, and he provided Kees with the perfect foil for the abstract painters participating in the Forum. Together, the brothers, along with Francis's poet wife, Katherine Chapin, would open for Kees an avenue to the liberal, cosmopolitan, and cultured branch of America's patricians.

Closer, in nearby Truro, the Keeses made new friends, and Weldon kept an eye out for people he could bring into Forum 49, such as Donald Slesinger, the lay analyst, who agreed to lecture on psychoanalysis. His profession's new significance in cultural terms could be strongly felt in the sheer presence of practitioners and their patients who vacationed on the Cape.

At a cocktail party held in a barn that had been converted into a dance studio, Kees met the choreographer Todd Bolender and convinced him to present a forum on dance to be held in August. At the same party Kees also befriended Marie-Jeanne, one of George Balanchine's favorites and a principal dancer in the New York City Ballet. She, too, promised Kees that she would come with Bolender to speak and perform in Gallery 200.

In the woods around Wellfleet, the Keeses visited Dwight and Nancy Macdonald. They also visited the summer residence of photographer-filmmaker Helen Levitt, whom they knew from Jim Agee's circle and who was sharing her cottage, much to Ann's surprise, with some young Harlem gentlemen.

Levitt and her collaborators, the writer-producer Janice Loeb and Jim Agee, had won the New York Film Critics' Prize for *The Quiet One*, which had been nominated by the Motion Picture Academy for best documentary earlier in the year. Naturally, Kees wanted Levitt to contribute something to Forum 49's "Evening of Films," and he was elated when she gave him a film can containing her newest work, *104th Street: Notes for a Documentary.* A precursor to her better-known film *In the Street, 104th Street* was shot using hidden cameras and other techniques to catch the spontaneity and unpredictability of Spanish Harlem's street life during the war. To him it contained some of the most beautiful photography he had ever seen. "Drunks, whores, kids playing bizarre games with masks, dogs, women shopping, people talking on the sidewalks, accidents," he wrote Getty, "and all done with an eye similar to Walker Evans', but going a good deal deeper."

Kees collected other participants for Forum 49 from the same secluded preserve near Wellfleet, among them the architects Serge Chermayeff and Marcel Breuer, who had just built one of his stilt houses by a small lake. Both men would participate in Forum 49's panel discussion "Directions in Twentieth Century Architecture," which also featured Gyorgy Kepes, the designer and the author of *The Language of Vision,* and Peter Blake, the head of the architectural division at the Museum of Modern Art.

Besides adding speakers to the evenings of Forum 49, Kees also collected paintings for Gallery 200, as it underwent its transformation from garage to white-walled exhibition space, humbly echoing the Guggenheim's origins. For this he depended heavily on his artist friends in New York to send work. Romare Bearden sent Kees watercolors, searched for a painting by his mentor Stuart Davis, and made a call to Barnett Newman to see if he could lecture at a forum.

Kees envisioned a series of exhibitions for Gallery 200, the most important—and long-running—being the show of abstract painting. Not only did the art on the gallery walls provide the fresh cultural ambiance for everything else Forum 49 covered, but it would also provide Forum 49 with some of the buzz coming from *Life* magazine. Kees knew that its editors were planning a forthcoming piece on Jackson Pollock, and he had a Pollock for the show.

"Weld has lost 10 pounds and is practically walking around in his bones," Ann remarked in a letter to Norris Getty. One source of frustration for Weldon was dealing with the gallery's owner. "This creature Donald Witherstine," Ann continued, "is a Class A son of a bitch for my money and has managed to create an incredible amount of confusion [because] he can't wait to get in a show of dogs like John Whorf, et al."

Gathering sponsors, raising funds—and getting more than just moral support—gave Kees little time to write or paint, just as Clem Greenberg had said. Hans Hofmann helped back Forum 49 with a donation, as did Adolph and Esther Gottlieb and Dwight Macdonald. Ann noted with some relief how the Gottliebs "plunged right into Forum work and have been great comforts." George Biddle and Karl Knaths, though not regarded as abstract expressionists, also sponsored Forum 49, and their presence, as well as that of Hofmann, made it possible for Kees to approach a wealthier group of sponsors, whose names appear on the handsome Forum 49 stationery Kees printed.

These included Peter Hunt, a long-established Provincetown figure from the 1920s who was a folk artist, bon vivant, and interior decorator specializing in the "Cape look" (his clients included Helena Rubinstein); the psychologist Carl Murchison (author of a monograph on criminal psychology that interested Kees); the anesthesiologist John C. Snow; and Hudson D. Walker, the art collector and benefactor who later founded the Walker Art Center at the University of Minnesota, an important cultural institution that was partly inspired by Forum 49.

Tiresias also had to keep up with its owner's pace. One time the black Plymouth stopped dead right in front of the Atlantic House on Commercial Street, and Kees worked frantically for several minutes under the hood while the beach-bound traffic piled up behind them in a bedlam of howling horns and boiling exhaust. He told Dwight Macdonald that he had to work eighteen-hour days painting Forum 49 posters, typing press releases, and finding enough chairs (including some old pews from the Central Methodist Church that cost nine dollars apiece), as well as cleaning and painting Gallery 200, with its bare cement floors still stained from the oil and grease of its garage days.

The Bultmans helped, as did another couple who befriended the Keeses that summer, Judith Rothschild, another of Hofmann's students, and her husband, the novelist Anton Myer, whom Kees always called "Tony." They formed the center of his social life.

To celebrate the longest day of the year, the Bultmans gave a dinner party on the terrace of their home. Jeanne prepared hand-caught mussels, which caused her a little embarrassment. "I think they were caught on the sewage side [of the bay] because several people got quite ill from them," Ann wrote Getty in the bored, disparaging tone that entered her letters to him from this time. She felt that Weldon wasted too much time on the Forum and had not spent enough time relaxing on the beach — or withdrawing with her to talk about how stupid many of the Forum people seemed to her.

Judith Rothschild was surprised to find that Ann hardly participated or took interest in the Cape's lively cultural scene. This was especially disturbing given that Ann was the wife of a poet and painter. Where Kees was gregarious, Ann preferred to be in smaller groups, the smaller the better — or just alone in bed during the day reading movie magazines and getting drunk by herself. This struck Judith as odd, for she was younger than Ann and considered drinking, as it had been in college, something you did in the evening with friends. Ann drank during the day and for no particular reason, like a "mild, controlled alcoholic." (Weldon indulged, too, getting away to smoke marijuana on the beach at night with the painter Kahlil Gibran Jr., the son of the poet.)

Ann also kept to herself because she was insecure about her appearance. "The trouble with being over thirty," she told Judith, "is one's face is so puffy before noon that you really should not be seen." Ann's skin to Judith was as white and thin as tissue paper—and she wore no makeup, which intensified the milk color of her skin. She seemed more of a "Wisconsin farmer's wife, a homebody," than the wife of a sophisticated poet and painter, and this impression was intensified by her clothes: she had an English "country" look, with practical and appropriate slacks and shirts.

Judith attributed the Keeses' childlessness to Ann. It set them apart from the Bultmans—and this postwar period when so many younger couples were having babies. Ann was always vehement, even venomous about children. She colorfully detested them in front of people like her favorite actor, W. C. Fields, who Judith felt was a real hero to Ann.

While Judith observed Ann and came away with one view, her husband, Tony, developed a totally different picture of Weldon. Though a pacifist—Tony had served in the war—Kees had all the dedication of a soldier, a soldier for art, culture, ideas, and principles. In this Kees was one of the last great romantics, who genuinely believed that artistic sensibility and talent would receive its due recognition with time. He even believed that beautiful and important films could still be made in Hollywood. In Kees, there was a belief in an openhanded generosity of spirit, which was a personal obligation in a world of gentility and merit. Kees's aesthetic sensibilities were almost Proustian to Myrer— at times he patterned himself on an overidealized Gerald Murphy— and yet he liked to look on himself as a kind of 1930s tough guy, a sort of Zachary Scott–Barton McClain blend. He could drink with the best of them, but his manner was gentle, almost courtly, and he simply would not stand for boorishness or bad manners.

The opening of Forum 49 was a huge success. Five hundred people had to be turned away on the Sunday afternoon of July 3. There were not enough seats. Inside Gallery 200, the lucky ones, who had each paid sixty cents admission, moved from painting to painting in the provocative exhibition that Kees and Bultman had curated.

On folding chairs and surplus church pews the audience listened to a lively panel discussion. The applause could be heard up and down Commercial Street.

The show of abstract paintings consisted of paintings by the artists who would one day comprise the "New York school." A Jackson Pollock drip painting, *Number Seventeen,* hung beside Kees's own canvas in Gallery 200; it was the same painting that would be used to illustrate the forthcoming issue of *Life* that profiled Pollock and asked, "Is He the Greatest Living in the United States?" (In August Kees responded in kind by setting up a ballot box and slips of paper in front of Pollock's painting with a sign that asked this very question. After one week, visitors had voted 503 *no* and 39 *yes.*)

A special section of works in one of Gallery 200's smaller wings included art by the first generation of modern artists who had lived and worked on the Cape. As Kees wanted to prove, and most likely expressed overseas in his Voice of America broadcasts, as well as in the following press-release statement, "vital abstract work" had its beginnings in Provincetown not long after World War I in Ambrose Webster, Oliver Chaffee, Agnes Weinrich, and Blanche Lazzell. They were "part and parcel of the international aesthetic revolt that took its cue from the School of Paris—a revolt not unconnected with that of the poets, playwrights and novelists who made Provincetown famous in the Twenties."

The panel discussion that Sunday—on the topic of "What Is an Artist?"—featured a sparring match between the conservative George Biddle, who questioned the abstract artists' ability to communicate clear ideas, and Hans Hofmann, whose rambling discourses on how painters must speak through paint and not words more than counterpointed and tested Biddle's pragmatism and patience. The panel also included Adolph Gottlieb and Serge Chermayeff. Kees served as moderator, the job he had wanted Gottlieb to take, but Gottlieb wanted to sail his boat in a race that day, and he felt it would be too strenuous for him to sit both at the tiller and next to George Biddle with little rest between. "George Biddle is an experienced and skillful speaker for the conservative view point," he wrote Kees, "and I believe you could refute him better than I, because you think faster on your feet and in general are more articulate than I am."

As Gottlieb expected, Kees performed a solid defense of advanced art. In a colorful letter to Bill Baziotes, he recorded his impressions of the first forum from this vantage, and his friend replied in kind: "[Biddle's] description of what is an artist—(not to the public of course) is probably first, you must come from an old Philadelphia family or something similar, an *income*—a steady never-ending *income;* a bitterness, a steady never-ending bitterness; and last, the ability to concentrate for days on inventing epithets ('I would say, ladies and gentlemen, in my modest opinion, that modern art is the er-ah-er-ah the excesses of our er-ah not verrrry healthy age' (Faint laughter from the audience and three fucking days to think that one up. Gr-Gr.)"

On July 7, Forum 49 began its regular Thursday schedule with Dwight Macdonald on "The Dream World of the Soviet Bureaucracy" —in effect, a continuation of the culture war that had not ended with the Waldorf conference. Kees billed this lecture as a "new theory exposing the lies of the Russian dictatorship" to defuse any anticommunist backlash.

The choice of Thursday evenings had also been calculated. Thursday, Kees knew, did not conflict with the socializing and hedonism of Provincetown weekends. Having the forums on Thursday evenings also made the grist for the conversations that coincided with—and facilitated—the swirl of parties and sexual intrigues that occurred in the bars and at the parties and gatherings in artist studios, in summer rentals, and on the Cape's beaches.

This fact of Cape life did not escape Clem Greenberg when he visited Kees in mid-July. "It was nice to see you last week," he wrote on a *Commentary* postcard, "and it was nice—as I realize, now that I'm away from it—to be in P'town. But how the devil does anyone manage to do any work there? Don't let the general activity distract you any longer from your own painting."

Kees spoke at the third program, "American Jazz Music: The 1920's." He had typed up ten pages of lecture notes, which he had practically memorized. But they were there in case he needed them. Beside him he placed a crate filled with heavy, brittle, black 78s, which he had brought over to Gallery 200 in Tiresias's trunk, rare recordings from his own collection of Louis Armstrong, Jelly Roll Morton, Kid Ory, Bessie Smith, Johnny Dodds, and the musicians who worked with them. He had a tabletop phonograph next to the lectern, on which he would now bring traditional jazz, good-time music, and the blues to life. Like the movies, jazz connected Kees to what happiness he could still garner from his boyhood, when he had listened to faraway stations coming from a wooden radio. "Jazz is a uniquely native music," he began as the last stragglers found a seat in the crowded room, "—and the best of it today is a *buried* music in its *own* country—almost a music of the underground. What has taken over is a debased commercial popular music, cynically packaged to appeal to what we call 'popular taste,' which is almost impossible to escape if one has ears. This music has all but swamped the radio, the jukeboxes, the nightclubs, the theatres, and ourselves."

In his notes Kees used the same visual prompts for pronunciation and emphasis he used to mark newsreel scripts. There were additional prompts for looking up at his audience, too, and finding his place again on the page. He touched on the same issues he had discussed in "Muskrat Ramble," but he did not dwell on bebop or its presence in Provincetown. Unlike he had in his *Partisan Review* piece, Kees discussed the origins of jazz and recent jazz scholarship, quoting from Rudi Blesh's *Shining Trumpets: A History of Jazz* and emphasizing jazz's European roots in Irish reels, jigs, polkas, and the other dance music of nineteenth-century music halls and jazz's similarity to the antiphony and horizontal polyphony of medieval European music. Though Kees did not give a reason for this emphasis, it may have been a strategy to connect a European descent to "Negro music" so as to authenticate the white musicians who were becoming the caretakers of the New Orleans style as younger black musicians embraced bebop.

After a discussion of the parallels that could be drawn between classical and popular music, Kees moved from his intellectualizations to what he really wanted to do, lower the tone arm on Jelly Roll Morton's *Kansas City Stomps* ("made in the summer of 1928, with an exceptionally knowing group of men").

When Kees told his Forum 49 listeners that the New Orleans style could still be heard at the Cape on cool summer nights, he had his own piano playing in mind. Sometimes he performed at Wuthering Heights, his favorite Provincetown bar, with some of the "local cats." He also played at parties and dances in town and in nearby Truro and Wellfleet.

Forum 49 programs continued with an "Evening of Film" on July 21.

It featured rare and early films from Joseph Cornell's private collection and the screening of *104th Street*. The Cornell films, which had created a sensation when Kees saw them in New York, included three short illusionist films made by the early French experimental pioneer Georges Méliès, considered the first magician of trick photography for the new ground he had broken before 1900. Also of early vintage were a Pathé movie of 1905, *A Detective's Tour of the World,* and a group of brief European films dealing with magic and the dance, *The Wonderful Beehive, Hanky Panky Cards, Les Six Soeurs Dainef,* and Emil Cohl's *The Automatic Moving Company,* or *Le Mobelier fidele,* which employs stop photography with brilliant results. Rounding out the Cornell part of the evening was one American example, *The Count,* starring Charlie Chaplin.

On the evening of July 28, Francis Biddle delivered a lecture entitled "America's Responsibilities in the New World," his liberal vision of a strong America that could resist Soviet aggression in the cold war. "We cannot ignore our power," Biddle said of America's dominance in world affairs. He looked more toward Washington than at the bohemians in his audience. Yet his message was in keeping with the notions of American abstract painters who believed they were taking up where the School of Paris had left off in 1940 — an idea that inspired its own Forum 49 evening.

Certain artists and critics acknowledged the historic implications of American abstract art with a new, self-important rhetoric. Others saw their "movement" as a work in progress that should not be fixed in some definition or be wrapped in the flag of national pride. Kees would become more involved in this discourse as he pushed himself in August to paint more in his studio at Days Lumberyard. He was "one of the boys" there, even more than he was as the moderator of Forum 49, venturing on the catwalk that connected the studios to talk shop with the other painters in that Mediterranean light the lumberyard provided. He had been mentioned in the latest issue of *Art News.* Elaine de Kooning had made special mention of Kees's watercolors in a group show at Peridot. "Using simple forms and bright colors," she wrote, "Weldon Kees' festive pictures are almost indistinguishable from his oils."

As he painted, Kees waited to hear from Harcourt, where his next move as a poet was being decided. He began to think that it had been a mistake to submit his manuscript at the beginning of summer, that Ted Amussen was more likely spending "the months of July to September in air-conditioned movies or in Connecticut" instead of reading *A Late History*. Ann was also anxious for some word from Amussen. Her husband's next book should be a matter of course, a given for a younger poet whose first book had been so well-received. The business of poetry was also frustrating the literary evening he was planning for Forum 49.

Kees should have easily succeeded with his August forum of poetry readings. He had many friends and contacts. The readings, however, did not come together. Archibald MacLeish said from Cambridge that he was too busy. In Baldpate, a small private sanatorium in nearby Georgetown, Robert Lowell was still *"hors de combat"* from shock therapy and still suffering from screaming fits, this time about devils and homosexuals instead of communists. Allen Tate remained uncertain. There were other men nearby whom Kees did not want to approach: "Martha's Vineyard will be crawling with the Howard Moss–Richard Wilbur–Peter Viereck set, I am informed by my Pinkerton operatives; but I would prefer, really, to have them as purchasers of tickets rather than on the podium."

Bultman and Hemley, who rarely opposed him, voted Kees down on the readings after too many colorful dismissals of poets they had suggested. As the date of the literary evening approached, the poetry forum was hastily downgraded to a panel including Win Scott, Howard Nemerov, Dudley Fitts, and Richard Eberhart. Kees publicized the program as "What Is Modern Poetry?"—a title that made him wince because it lacked imagination and made the evening sound like a book-club meeting.

Other disappointments followed. The forum on modern dance had to be canceled at the last minute, as did the one planned for the novel. Kees almost canceled the forum on psychoanalysis, too. He even had to cross it off of freshly printed Forum 49 flyers with a heavy black grease pencil at one point.

Increasingly apparent to him was the fact that Forum 49's stationery had become top-heavy with sponsors who did not give enough money and founders who did not do enough. The one-sidedness of his effort made Kees resentful as he tried to believe in and serve the Cape's "thirst for culture." Wherever he could, he now disguised the extent of his involvement in Forum 49 as it turned into the wrong kind of one-man show, such as in his ground rules for an article to appear in the *Providence Journal:* "Wd. prefer writing the piece under no byline or under a pen name, since I've not only been on a lot of the forums in one capacity or another, but have had to take charge of the whole business of late: Bultman resigned & the other 'founder' has proved himself capable of irresponsibility past belief."

Kees looked forward to the opening of the Provincetown Players' performance of Conrad Aiken's play *Mr. Arcularis* with as much enthusiasm as he had for Forum 49. When that day arrived on August 8, he spent it in the company of the playwright, who had driven up from Brewster to drink with his friend before attending the play's American premier.

Sitting behind Aiken in the theater, with Ann on one side and the Myrers on the other, Kees leaned forward to listen to Aiken's nervous comments about how the play would be received. Francis Biddle and his wife were there. The French poet St. John-Perse had come up from Washington to see the play. Many young people were in the audience, as was Dwight Macdonald, whose presence made Aiken more uncomfortable given his reputation for being an extremely harsh critic.

Kees knew the short story on which Aiken had based the play. It was one of his favorites, so he reassured the older poet that the play would *have* to be good. Nevertheless, Aiken felt his audience was against him. The New York intellectuals had always written him off, and he held out little hope for getting much goodwill from the "drunken gangs of pansies and lesbians."

Kees nodded as the playwright spoke anxiously under his breath as if to a collaborator, for Kees had advised Aiken about the script in July and—after drinking too many Tom Collinses together—about how *Mr. Arcularis* should be marketed after Provincetown. Kees said that such a play could make it on Broadway—and that it was definitely the kind of thing that would make a great screenplay: a man under anesthesia, dreaming about his life and afterlife as he dies on an operating table. This fantasy, however, required a suspension of disbelief that was impossible for Dwight Macdonald, who sat directly behind the Myrers. Halfway through, he started to ridicule the play loudly and only stopped when Kees turned around and threatened to break a folding chair over his head.

The authority Kees had assumed as Forum 49's moderator did not have to be used so forcefully in Gallery 200. He now wanted the Thursday nights to continue through the fall. The August forums had been as well-attended as July's. Even the night of modern poetry on August 4, which in the end only featured Kees, Howard Nemerov, and the novelist Nathan Halper discussing Eliot and Joyce, still filled the room. Nemerov spoke about Eliot's poetry, Halper commented on *Finnegans Wake,* and Kees played recordings of Eliot and Joyce reading from their work.

On the following Thursday evening, "French Art vs. U.S. Art Today" touched off the summer's "warmest" controversy. Adolph Gottlieb, the chairman for this forum, attempted to assess the differences and conflicts between the painting done largely in New York and Paris, especially in the light of the pervasive influence of the School of Paris. Such an underlying concept, which smacked of chauvinism, offended Fritz Bultman. He called it "vulgar and uncharitable" and withdrew from Forum 49 rather than speak and sit on the panel, which included the painters Karl Knaths and Robert Motherwell; Stuart Preston, art critic of the *New York Times;* Paul Mocsanyi, art editor of the United Press; and Frederick Wight of the Boston Institute of Contemporary Art.

On August 18, Kees chaired "Directions in Twentieth Century Architecture," at which Marcel Breuer discussed the future of the one-family house and its furnishings, predicated on his founding of the Bauhaus school with Walter Gropius and his pioneer designs in tubular steel furniture. The Hungarian-born painter, photographer, and designer Gyorgy Kepes also spoke from the vantage of being the author of the influential book *Language of Vision* and a teacher at the Massachusetts Institute of Technology.

"Finding Yourself through Psychoanalysis," the forum on psychoanalysis, took place on August 25. Donald Slesinger, re-creating his role as moderator of the University of Chicago's Round Table of the Air, led a panel composed of Geradus Beekman, Dr. Wilfred Bloomberg, Dr. Leo Spiegel, and Dr. Clara Thompson, whom Kees had culled from the summer residents in the fields of psychology and psychoanalysis.

The last forum, "Everybody's Forum," took place on September 1 and "featured a galaxy of speakers from the world of arts and letters." Each person had carte blanche to talk on "any topic that deeply concerned him." Several participants from previous forums, such as Dwight Macdonald, appeared, as did new faces. These included Kees's friend Mischa Richter, the painter and *New Yorker* columnist; Elaine de Kooning; the painter Perle Fine; the sculptor Chaim Gross; Alex Haverstraf, the industrial designer; and several others. The next day Kees returned to the lumberyard to make the most of what was left of the summer by painting and drawing.

He spent an agonizing week trying to turn out a drawing for a *Partisan Review* frontispiece, which Clem Greenberg had asked for back in August. "You know the dimensions," Greenberg had written, "and, I hope, realize that it must be suitable for a line cut, with no washes, blurrings, or too fine cross-hatching." Kees sketched over seventy-five different versions before he executed one he liked, going through two bottles of Higgins India ink and coming through with some "horrendous" false starts. The drawing was slated for the October *Partisan Review.* Meanwhile another October deadline approached in which Greenberg figured.

Back in June, Greenberg had given some of Kees's Forum 49 literature to Margaret Marshall, the literary editor of the *Nation.* At about the same time, Greenberg had also resigned as the magazine's art critic under friendly circumstances. (The departure, Greenberg assured Kees, had "nothing to do with the *Nation.*") This set of circumstances—which Greenberg seems to have designed—presented Marshall with the idea that Kees would make a good replacement, for it seemed rather obvious that he was willing to get into the thick of the art world and that his anti-Stalinist credentials in cultural matters were in line with her own. She knew Weldon, too, as a fellow Westerner, for she was from Utah, having first met him at Dwight and Nancy Macdonalds' apartment in 1940. She had also published several of his poems and felt she could read him well enough to candidly inform him that certain lines of a poem struck her as "weak" or "not successful." (For his part, Kees simply resubmitted these poems to another publisher unchanged and continued to think of her as "Miss Margaret Marshall in her smartest *Nation* rationalization," as someone who wore her magazine's liberalism like a sensible outfit.)

Kees initially felt confident that he could handle this assignment when Marshall approached him in July with an offer. The column would appear once a month instead of bimonthly, as it had before, making it less of a burden. Soon after, the magazine's advertising department sent a memo and a notice with Kees's publicity photo to the New York art galleries announcing that the "painter, poet and critic" had joined the magazine and would review art exhibitions every fourth week, beginning in October.

Not until late August and early September did Kees worry about the practical realities of his new post clashing with his poetry, his painting, and his Forum 49 work. He also had to consider what to write for his first piece, which would run on October 1. The support Bill Baziotes and others in New York and Provincetown gave him from the onset made it hard for him to stand still long enough to suddenly feel overwhelmed or unqualified: "Sam Kootz thought you were the one to do it. Clem had told me that he had been confounded quite often by his inability to see clearly into the implications of his art period and to give proper interpretation to it. He claimed, however, he did it the best he could. He lacked this quality since he didn't create, and aside from your judgment on pictures, etc., I think it will be wonderful to see an art column based on reality instead of Marxism, or social ethics and the artistic parallel."

The New York gallery season had yet to begin, and when it did, he still would not be in the city, having decided to stay on at the Cape till after Labor Day. Kees contacted Greenberg about the transition. The critic replied that he was happy that Kees had taken over his *Nation* column. Yet he could not offer any practical suggestions, except to tell Kees that he should always be prepared to cut from twenty-five to seventy-five words from his pieces at the last minute. He also promised Kees to forward all the exhibition announcements and other art news he received. Kees wrote back, asking Greenberg what he thought of an article about George A. Dondero. This Illinois congressman, like many of his colleagues, had been impressed by Senator Joseph McCarthy, who had made a national reputation for himself as a fighter of communism by attacking Hollywood and the State Department. Dondero had picked out the art world as his special province.

Norris Getty stayed during the week of August 21 to 27, renting a room next door to the Keeses, and was amazed to find his friend so busy with the forums, the *Nation,* and his "raft of painting and drawing." He had always wanted to say something to Kees about getting too involved, spread too thin. Instead, he found himself going along with his friend's enthusiasms, promising Kees, who said he needed to "bone up" on art history, to find some new books on Juan Gris and Picasso in Boston's bookstores. But then there was, after all, nothing to suggest that Kees was any less committed to being a poet.

He talked about the bad Francis Golffing collection that Nemerov had lent him. He told Getty about the letters he had written Harcourt inquiring about the fate of *A Late History.* He had had several poems accepted. He told Getty to look for "Darkness" in the current issue of *Harper's;* "Land's End" would be in the October issue. John Pauker had accepted "Saratoga Ending" for the fall issue of *Furioso,* as well as "Round," a satirical poem that alluded to the recent death of a leading American art critic who had long been a bulwark against modern art at the Metropolitan Museum. It also suggested, perhaps to Getty's relief, that his friend was not quite sucked up by the role of art critic:

And something inside my head

Flaps like a worn-out blind. Royal Cortissoz is dead,
A blow to the Herald-Tribune.

Weldon and Ann cheated the official death of Provincetown's summer and stayed on after Labor Day. In early September they moved to Adolph and Esther Gottlieb's rental at 353A Commercial Street, over rooms rented out to some of the Provincetown Players who had appeared in *Mr. Arcularis.* Even though the young actors made "more racket than Spike Jones," the Keeses found the frequent and informal parties downstairs a replacement for their own summer circle of friends, which was now beginning to thin. Weldon also savored the end-of-season forlornness of the Cape. He worked it into the piece about Forum 49 he was writing for the cultural page of the Sunday *Providence Journal:*

At night, a cold wind blows off Provincetown Harbor, and by ten-thirty or eleven the streets are deserted. Natives, some of whom go into hiding for the summer, like dogs on the Fourth of July, are showing themselves again. New York, Connecticut, and New Jersey license plates no longer outnumber those of Massachusetts. Rents have dropped to a fraction of the summer rates. The artists, students, and innumerable and frequently bizarre camp-followers of the art world have returned to the cities. Provincetown, sometimes referred to as the country's summer art capital, is now, and will be for another eight months, merely a Portuguese fishing center at the tip of the Cape.

Another version of this scene, recounted for the Myrers, who had already left the Cape, showed that Kees was getting impatient, too. "The poison ivy and creeping hemley are turning the proper autumnal colors," he wrote. The town itself, filled with fog at night, was deserted, "except for an occasional somnambulist beagle & mysterious lone figures in black-&-white plaid wool jackets. All the fairies have gone back to Bonwit Teller or wherever they go." The escape from this, during the day, was his work: poems, correspondence, and the Dondero piece for the *Nation.*

He also finished a series of jazz album covers illustrated with abstract art for Kid Ory's band and the Library of Congress's Jelly Roll Morton collection, a "connection" record companies had yet to make. To this end, Kees produced several "maquettes" by painting or collaging over discarded album covers—or soliciting designs from Karl Knaths, Kahlil Gibran Jr., Romare Bearden, and others.

At Day's Lumberyard he followed Clem Greenberg's advice, painting some small oils for his next one-man show at Peridot and planning for a new studio in New York. To this end he had made plans with the Myrers to share a loft on New York's Lower East Side. They were now scouting for a large, affordable space on Hudson Street or nearby.

Every piece of what seemed like a productive summer was in place except for *A Late History,* and it did not fall into place until a few days before he and Ann left Provincetown. On Harcourt, Brace letterhead, Ted Amussen rejected the manuscript for reasons that should have reminded Kees of why Greenberg had not reviewed him, not *made* him a real painter. He had not done enough painting, and here there were not enough "truly excellent and good poems [...] from which to make up a book."

∾

... the end of New York as a romantic idea. —Weldon Kees

On Sunday, September 26, Kees found a newsstand in Provincetown where he could purchase out-of-town newspapers and picked up a copy of the *Providence Sunday Journal.* As the mysterious "J.F.A.," writing in Win Scott's "Bookman's Gallery" column, Kees stated that the turnout for Forum 49 had been like a subway crush. When he asked himself if he would do another Forum, however, he was less effusive. "Kees," he wrote, "is not very communicative on plans for next summer."

On Wednesday, Weldon and Ann left the Cape and drove to Cambridge to see Getty. They continued down through Connecticut to stay overnight with Win and Ellie Scott.

Tiresias got them to New York and caught on fire after stalling in front of Saint Vincent's Hospital, where Dylan Thomas would die in a few short years. "I shall always wonder what the hook and ladder boys thought they could do for an ancient Plymouth," Ann observed in a letter to Ellie Scott. "You should have seen Weld's blistered thumb when a package of matches blew up in his hand." Luckily, the paintings and poems in the backseat and trunk were saved.

The Keeses rented a furnished room near Union Square. Weldon called it a "flop house," but it would have to do until he, Ann, and the Myers could fix up an old factory they had found at 179 Stanton Street.

The building was in the "lox and bagel section" of the Lower East Side, running just north of and parallel to Canal Street. The main space was about fifty feet long, with thirteen windows. The last tenant had been a young woman who worked as a designer. She had left the place crammed with wire, gallon cans of foul-smelling fluids, beds, tables, and practically immovable containers of modeling clay. Both couples spent days getting these things down four flights of stairs. They painted the walls, ceiling, floors, and the furniture they salvaged. In late October, after much work, the Keeses took the space upstairs and the Myers the ground floor. In another letter to Ellie Scott, Ann called her new home a "barn," with "practically none of the comforts of home except hot water and a toilet, but lots of windows which I count whenever I'm feeling depressed about the gallons of paint we have slapped on this place. Hope you can come to New York soon, and see the results. *Somebody* has to admire it."

The loft did not have a phone, and the Keeses' telephone messages had to be left at the Peridot Gallery, where Weldon had a one-man show in November. In that month's *Art News,* Milton Gendel praised his new work. He called attention to the poetic elements of Kees's painting as well as to its composition and overall effect: "Generally working in sculptural forms set against flat, single-color backgrounds, [Kees] achieves an atmosphere of impending, momentous discovery through clear and vivid statement which is at the same time cryptic in suggestion. In *The Wall*, this effect is attained by the simplest means; on a light grey, granulated surface an incisive, black line defines turgid shapes of the same hue. In the more complex *Red Entrance*, brilliant red provides the background for a double-rudder shape in ocher, grey and blue, which is uneasily balanced on the point of a grey and pink pyramid, which in turn rests on two over-reaching claw-and-ball feet."[1] Even though Kees's show was very well-received, he sold nothing and came away with the feeling that people were spending their money "on Ben Shahns and television sets."

Having a painting in the Whitney annual elicited only a tired "What a thrill!" And the passion of his first piece for the *Nation*, "Dondero and Dada," faded from his subsequent reviews. Writing about a December exhibition of Adolph Gottlieb's work in the January 7 issue of the *Nation*, he could have been reflecting on his own experience: "From an economic standpoint the activities of our advanced painters must be regarded as either heroic, mad, or compulsive; they have only an aesthetic justification, and even this, one feels, has become increasingly meager. Morale has dwindled; it would be hard to name a painter who is working at a high and steady rate of intensity—here or in Europe—in a sense remotely approaching that of Cézanne, Van Gogh, or the Cubists early in their careers. One is continually astounded that art persists at all in the face of so much indifference, failure, and isolation."

Kees, however, in the same piece also touched on how success was ironically not the correct scenario either—and in this he anticipated the artist Tom Wolfe would parody many years later in *The Painted Word*:

Van Gogh could write, "Now it is getting grimmer, colder, emptier, and duller around me," while still insisting that "surely there will come a change for the better." Today we are not likely to insist too strongly on the chances of so interesting a modulation. And in these times, if we were dealing with Van Gogh as a contemporary, we should handle things differently: he would be "recognized," would show annually on Fifty-seventh Street, be stroked, complimented, sell a few canvases, go to cocktail parties, and be tamed. Not tamed too much, however. He might even find it possible to write that "it is getting grimmer, colder, emptier, and duller ... and things go along, worsening only a little."

Neither Ann nor Weldon had a job when they moved into the loft. Weldon set up his studio and did some small freelancing assignments for newsreel and documentary-film companies. Ann, who had left *Antiques* permanently, copied a dress she had seen in Henri Bendel's on the sewing machine her mother had given her for Christmas. She was also sick for much of December, due in part to her drinking and the harsh winter weather.

When it became apparent, as 1950 began, that they were living too much on their savings, Weldon took on a more demanding scriptwriting assignment in January.

"I went back," he wrote Norris Getty, "back to bleak governmental Astoria and got a contract to do a picture for the Signal Corps." The project, a documentary film about the Army Medical Department at Fort Sam Houston in Texas, promised "all the compelling & highly charged fascination of one's last days on the Writers' Project, or a long wait in the rain for a bus to go someplace where you know you're in for a lousy time."

The desultory mood Kees found himself in came not only from making a living. He felt his poems and paintings were moving in the "direction of a mess." He did have "happier efforts," however. "La Vita Nuova," a thirteen-line *sonetto* titled after Dante's book of sonnets for Beatrice, and "Farrago" showed that he could move away from the "so-so" poems that Ted Amussen had found in *A Late History*. Kees had made a breakthrough of sorts by writing less impersonally and outside of the Robinson persona. He could even be self-critical (albeit with a mild rebuke in the obvious borrowing from Auden) in a way that anticipated the confessional poetry of the 1960s:

—I sit in a bar

On Tenth Street, writing down these lies
In the worst winter of my life. A damp snow
Falls against the pane. When everything dies,

The days all end alike, the sound
Of breaking goes on faintly all around,
Outside and inside. Where I go,

The housings fall so low they graze the ground
And hide our human legs. False legs fall down
Outside. Dance in a horse's hide. Dance in the snow.

Kees may have seen his life as a death performance of madness and falseness, but he was not going to count himself with Ted Roethke, whose recent mental breakdown had caused him to observe that "poets are unstable fellows." Instead he slipped into the more mundane routine of a documentary filmmaker.

He left New York on January 9 and traveled by train to San Antonio to meet with the army colonel who was technical advisor to the film. From behind the large, plate-glass windows of the observation car, where he drank at the bar, Kees watched the countryside pass, covered in snow and ice. There he saw an America go by like the one shown in Hollywood movies that exercised a social conscience: "The casting directors who supply the personnel that one sees from one's window, on station platforms and along sideroads, are now outdoing themselves in furnishing heartbreakingly sad and lonely people; I think an old and starved-looking Negress, on a muddy road somewhere in the South, pulling aimlessly at some rubbish tossed in the weeds, was one of the most impressive. But they were all good."

In the smoking car Kees read *Under the Volcano* for the second time in the three years since it had shared a place on Reynal and Hitchcock's list with *The Fall of the Magicians*. The editor Albert Erskine had provided Kees's Robinson with a good companion in Malcolm Lowry's Consul. The fresh encounter with the novel proved more satisfying this time. Traveling by train to Texas, close to Lowry's Mexico, provided the right local color for a story that incorporated the macabre rule of Mexican railways: "A corpse will be transported by express!"

After two days of constant rail travel that left him exhausted, Kees detrained in San Antonio on January 11. With suitcase in hand, he wandered through the ornate interior of the Missouri-Kansas-Texas Railroad's station, which resembled a Spanish mission. There he purchased a postcard, a chromo of the station and its bell tower, and wrote on the back Norris Getty's address and a one-word message, "Help!"

Outside the station he hailed a taxi. It was late Sunday morning. Only the churches looked open. When he arrived at Fort Sam Houston, the base was nearly deserted. He found the officers' barracks and knocked on several doors before someone finally answered, a man dressed only in unusually clean long underwear. The man, who had been sleeping, said he would have to walk to the other side of the base to get a key.

The next day Kees tried to find a bar, but there were none in the full sense, only beer and wine joints. As he walked up and down the streets, he noticed a smell like that of a "ten-cent store" in the air, while San Antonio began to assume the sameness of Omaha, Providence, Los Angeles. He had hoped to get some good Mexican food. Yet the restaurant he settled on served only boiling-hot chili with large hunks of gristle over a "cool taco and a cooler tamale with the consistency of a candle."

His communion with postwar America had its strange appeal, though. He resumed his walk and found the absurdity of a cactus, an oak, and an evergreen "happily growing together" in some front yard, almost as if they were in a poem he could have written. He could even feel more like "Robinson alone" here than on a New York street, walking from the pages of his manuscript and in full view of the enormous cars that passed him, their occupants turning to stare at the lone pedestrian. No one ever seemed to walk in San Antonio, he thought.

Returning to Fort Sam Houston, Kees discovered there were no towels provided on the army base. So he washed and dried himself with one of his dirty shirts. He went to bed but could not sleep. The walls of the barracks were thin. He could hear a man in the next room snoring.

Kees stayed at the fort for a week, working with a team of army officers until he convinced them he could finish the script on the train. On the way back to Pennsylvania Station, however, he read Paul Bowles's *The Sheltering Sky* instead, even though he found it depressing, the characters "mercilessly badgered." The book was only interesting for what Bowles did not say, Kees wrote Getty, for the subtext of homosexuality.

In early February, he picked up the usual emotional speed that came as he busied himself with painting, drawing, and drafting a new poem. He did this while at the same time suppressing the anxious feeling that the endings in his poems were coming to life, that the porchlight coming on would photograph him against a wall with a mushroom cloud: President Truman had ordered the Atomic Energy Commission to proceed with development of the hydrogen bomb on January 31 — a day Kees *uncelebrated* by writing "Happy H-bomb day" at the top of one correspondent's letter.

Now living in New York would more than ever mean living in a Russian target. Though Kees expressed his typical gallows humor regarding the vicissitudes of the cold war, images in tune with the real fear of radiation sickness and enormous detonations seeped into poems he wrote during this time:

> *this parched skin*
> *Dries and dies and flakes away,*
> *Becomes your costume when the torn leaves blow.*
>
> *— Thus in the losing autumn,*
> *Over the streets, I now lurch*
> *Legless to your side and speak your name*
> *Under a gray sky ripped apart*
> *By thunder and the changing wind.*
>
> —"La Vita Nuova"

The impression this leaves, of course, is one of Kees completely at ease at ground zero, real or imagined. In the February 4 issue of the *Nation*, Kees praised his friend Bill Baziotes in such a way that the reviewer could have easily been referring to himself: "His shapes, which have always unashamedly called up associations with animals, rooms, the sky, the sea, have become steadily simpler, more isolated, lonely, and at rest."

Kees in the same review tried to move against the tendency of other critics to read so much into paintings that simply "give pleasure," the "implied discontent with painting *qua* painting," and the tendency to say too much, to see *yantras* of significance where there were none or to see some great advance just because it was forced and articulated as such, as in Clement Greenberg's claims that "all-over" painting was superior to all other styles.

Baziotes sent a note thanking his friend for the sympathetic analysis of his painting. He promised to see both Weldon and Ann at Sam Kootz's house for a cocktail party, which the Keeses attended during the first week of February—the same week they also saw *The Cocktail Party* by T. S. Eliot.

The play had just opened for its American premiere on Broadway, and in Kees's opinion it was the worst play "ever to get on the boards."

"It's appallingly amateurish and redolent of corn. I can't recall anything worse by a previously first-rate writer," he wrote Getty in March. "[Eliot] *uses* everything, and uses everything badly; now, instead of Swift and the Elizabethans and the French symbolists, it's Chesterton, Shaw, Evelyn Waugh and Frederick Lonsdale. A sorry affair."

Kees's giants were crumpling before him. Hemingway was a "similar comedown," badly imitating himself in his new novel, *Across the River and into the Trees*. Yet Kees hardly filled the void with his own work. *A Late History* had by this time been rejected by Harper's, Random House, and Macmillan.

Ezra Pound had fallen for him, as well, but in another way, as a kind of living parody of the method he had employed in the Cantos.

In early March, while he was in Washington for a new documentary film, a canceled appointment provided Kees with the opportunity to look up the poet Elizabeth Bishop. As the poetry consultant to the Library of Congress, she had the unofficial duty of providing Pound with little magazines and all kinds of books that fed his encyclopedic obsessions.

The task took its toll. Her poem "Visits to St. Elizabeth's" reveals the stamina it took to confront Pound, the tragic man, the busy, cruel, and cranky man who placed so many demands upon her while he was incarcerated "in the house of Bedlam." So to dilute her meetings with Pound, Bishop took other poets to see him, a practice Pound found to be a nuisance, for he wanted "Liz Bish," as he called her, to himself.

Kees arrived in time to accompany her and Pound's wife, Dorothy, to Saint Elizabeth's Hospital. There Pound had been institutionalized for the wartime "comfort" he had given Italy's government in his pro-Fascist radio broadcasts. A treason trial and a death sentence had been considered a just punishment. To save his life, however, his defenders had convinced government prosecutors that the poet was mentally unfit to stand trial, a claim more than evinced by Pound's bizarre behavior and, to certain officials, his poetry.

The debate over Pound's Bollingen Prize was less than a year old when Kees and Bishop made their way through the hospital's corridors, peopled with catatonics and victims of dementia. The prize had revived the spirit of a man who had been taken prisoner during the war and put in a cage open to the elements.

Now, Pound was more often than not in "full form," which Kees experienced as soon as he entered his room.

At first he was startled by how shrunken Pound had become. Nevertheless, his eyes went through his visitors "like knives." Despite this unsettling effect, Kees connected to one of his heroes, to a man who came from that golden time of modernism, for which Kees had been born too late, a man who ranked with the "estimable Stevens" and the "admirable Eliot"—as Pound called his contemporaries when he took questions from Kees. Somehow, as invariably happened when the younger poets came to pay their respects, Pound began to expound about "the yids" and "the Brits" as if he were broadcasting from Radio Rome again. Kees could hardly disagree with the knowing look from "Liz Bish" that signified it was time to leave.

The face of Ezra Pound haunted Kees all the way back to New York, where he found some escape in seeing Dean Jagger in *Twelve O'Clock High* with Ann. They also attended a party at Conrad and Mary Aiken's apartment—and Weldon suffered from having accepted too many of Aiken's orange blossoms. "It's idiotic," he wrote Norris Getty, "to try to keep up with Conrad's glass-lifting: he's such a rumpot of longstanding that I should know better." Ann fared better, not only keeping up with Aiken but waking up the next day "with flying colors" and "feeling no pain."

The warmth of their friends' liquor and apartments could not assuage having to wake up in their freezing loft, where they could still see their own breath in March. One day the stove would not light, forcing them to huddle around two small electric heaters, one of which they had borrowed from the Myrers downstairs. As Kees shivered, he talked to Ann about moving to Florida in the fall or, better yet, Mexico. He told her he had had enough of New York.

He wanted a change. He was losing interest in scriptwriting. Each project was "like a trip to the dentist." The *Nation* reviews now hung over him "like so many vultures."

Reaching a decision to leave New York was never far below the surface, even when the weather began to change in April—and his reputation as a poet who still mattered received some affirmation. He was asked to read on a new poetry record.

To prepare for this he did not drink gin for a day so as not to "fluff" his lines the way he thought he had at Harvard two years before. He made the recording at the old Nola Studios at Fifty-first and Broadway, where many of his favorite musicians had recorded, where he had spent an afternoon interviewing Fats Waller for *Time*.

Preparing for another summer at the Cape also kept him from thinking about New York. At this point, he only knew that he did not want to spend another winter in the Stanton Street loft—and that he and Ann would be traveling as light as possible. So he began cleaning out his files.

Over a two-day period Kees read one old letter after another from over ten years of correspondence. Many of the letter writers were friends, like Dale Smith, Erling Larsen, Charles Bradford, Clark Mills. They had started writing when he did back in the 1930s. Some had published before him. Some had shown promise and then faded— like him. Rereading their correspondence gave him such a "shattering sense of wreckage and waste and loss" about them and himself that he could only think of one way to get through it: crumpling their letters and his carbons into balls and tossing them into a trashcan. When the pile became too high, he pushed the letters down with his foot, later telling Getty that doing so had reduced him to "a pulp."

The Village scene, however, with its abstract painters, galleries, critics, drinking holes, and parties, was still a refuge from his misspent and miscarried literary ambitions. When Kees thought of himself as a painter, the defeatism that came from thinking about the letters he tossed out, the rejections of *A Late History*, went away. It would disappear for weeks as his painter friends that spring began to see themselves in a different light: as a kind of group, a movement.

This coming together was, on the one hand, a defense mechanism, for Washington and the national media had been critical of abstract art. *Life* magazine had been paying attention to certain painters and critics, feeding their egos with good press and bad. Many of them believed that something was either going to happen or *had* to happen to place them in the forefront of American art. Kees, when he let himself, believed with his friends that they were *on the verge*.

He was still showing. His canvas 4 A.M. had just appeared that March in the influential "Black or White" exhibition of European and American painters at Kootz Gallery. It hung with a Picasso, a Braque, a Mondrian, and work by Motherwell and de Kooning in a show that would inspire Franz Kline, a new talent in 1950 whom Kees admired in his *Nation* column that May. Despite his misgivings about his art reviews, he was now considered a compelling and coherent spokesman for the abstract painters.

He did not sound like Robert Motherwell, for example, in the catalog of "Black or White" ("I can bear it no longer. It is monstrous. It is unfathomable"). Kees wrote with clarity and did not hold back. Reviewing some young French artists, he called their "revolt against Picasso" a sham. And *Life* had "laid a massive journalistic egg" with its tepid selection of "art-school medal winners" to represent the best young American painters. The Luce publication had entirely missed the significance of "Jackson Pollock, Hans Hofmann, Arshile Gorky, and Richard Pousette-Dart." This remark fed the drive to recognize these and other neglected painters. It helped pressure *Life* to correct its mistake.

Surprisingly it was Motherwell who invited Kees to attend a three-day "artists' session" at Studio 35 in late April, for he thought Kees did not respect him after Forum 49. But then Kees was no stranger at the abstract artists' cooperative school. He had delivered his jazz lecture on one of the Friday evenings devoted to "Subjects of the Artists." He was the *Nation*'s art critic, a painter, still a friend of Clem Greenberg and Sam Kootz. He had earned a place at the long banquet table Motherwell set up in the school's large loft space for gathering the "advanced artists" together for the first time as a group, fueled for the moment by shared ideas and heaps of pretzels and bottles of Ballantine Ale (bearing the label that Jasper Johns would later iconize).

The moderators included Alfred Barr of the Museum of Modern Art, Robert Motherwell, and the sculptor Richard Lippold. The painter Robert Goodnough, then a graduate student, hired a stenographer for the transcript that he had been assigned to edit, for Motherwell believed the sessions would be historic.

The artists included Hans Hofmann, Barnett Newman, Willem de Kooning, Adolph Gottlieb, David Hare, Ad Reinhardt, Hedda Sterne, and others. Many held the belief that the New York artists had succeeded the School of Paris and now needed, as Motherwell stated, control over how they were being perceived by the media—and the public, which had become increasingly more interested in not only their painting but their lifestyles as well, where they stood politically in a country now split into the loyal and disloyal by such powerful men as Congressman Dondero and Senator McCarthy.

In the introduction to the book that Goodnough assembled from the transcripts, *Modern Artists in America, No. 1,* he noted "a certain pathos and loneliness" that appeared in the text, that had not been evident at the sessions, with everyone obviously gathered around a table but not so obviously far apart. He was thinking of de Kooning, who did not like being defined by any of the labels being suggested, and perhaps Kees. Even though virtually nothing was saved from his statements in Goodnough's drastically edited transcript, there is enough to suggest that not only New York's winter had left him cold. There was something in the togetherness that Motherwell had forced from the artists in Studio 35, and while they debated over such things as whether a rectangle or a straight line was more clear, Kees felt himself growing away from them, too. Their arguments sounded like dogma to a poet who saw dogma as as much a danger to art now as it was in religion. "In regard to this issue of clarity," he said ironically, "it might be interesting if we could find anyone who could say that he doesn't care very much about clarity as an element in his painting."

ᘓ

Ann and Weldon left for the Cape on May 23 in a newish '46 Lincoln Zephyr, powered by a V-12 engine and a cracked carburetor. They made arrangements for movers to empty the Stanton Street loft and store their furniture and possessions. They found a young woman artist, not unlike the one who had lived there before them, to take over their lease.

The only alliance Kees had made as a direct result of the Studio 35 sessions was with his friend Adolph Gottlieb, who had drafted the letter-manifesto that exposed the exclusionary policies of the national juried exhibition titled "American Art Today—1950," organized by the Metropolitan Museum of Art. This show was part of a trend by major art museums to redress the lack of representation of modern art at such institutions in the past. However, several of the most controversial painters who had participated in the Studio 35 sessions were being excluded. Gottlieb, in the Studio 35 transcripts, had been especially concerned about the danger of an "academy version of abstract painting"—and this aesthetic was now guiding the already conservative outlook of the five regional juries that recommended work to the Metropolitan.

With over eighteen thousand artists being approached by the Metropolitan and only a few of them Studio 35 painters, Gottlieb, with Robert Motherwell, Barnett Newman, and Ad Reinhardt, decided to boycott this "monster show." Their choice of words revealed their anxiety over how this otherwise friendly accommodation by the art establishment could be their undoing. The sheer number of invitees meant a diminution of the effect they wanted to achieve, that of being the *only* legitimate group of advanced artists. They did not want the media and public to confuse their art with work that had been chosen because it *looked modern,* because it had a little Picasso in it, some Klee, some Mondrian.

With the addition of fourteen more signatories, including Kees, Gottlieb's letter was sent to the president of the Metropolitan on May 20. The *New York Times* ran a piece on the next day's front page, under the headline "Eighteen Painters Boycott Metropolitan: Charge Hostility to Advanced Art." On May 23, the *New York Herald Tribune* responded with an editorial titled "The Irascible Eighteen," giving the letter signers their name and defending the Metropolitan Museum. After this, the letter's impact took on a life of its own. More newspaper and magazine editors saw this contretemps between the museum and the artists as the climax to the national debate over abstract art.

For his part, Kees expanded the scope of the protest in the liberal press. He commented favorably on the Irascibles' letter and reprinted it in his last piece for the *Nation* on June 3, and it may have been his presentation of the manifesto that provided what Bill Baziotes termed the "the right punch to make it effective with the Met and the public." He was certain that Kees's article had influenced the museum's decision to place an Irascible on the state jury for accepting work from New York artists and to choose Baziotes for the national jury.

As the Irascible affair succeeded in placing the Irascibles and the other Studio 35 artists in the public eye on their own terms, Kees became increasingly distant and even disaffected with the celebrity and controversy he had helped to set in motion.

Instead, he enjoyed a letter from Romare Bearden. "Romie"—to Kees—had come back from Europe, where he had studied frescoes and the stained glass of Paris, and reported that a nineteen-year-old surrealist had attempted to blow up the Eiffel Tower and that Mark

Rothko, en route to Italy, wanted to tear down the Place de la Concorde. Kees would have smiled at this, for he had just been asked to think about Paris and art in terms that were less anarchic.

Fritz Bultman had asked for his help in organizing another exhibition of abstract art that juxtaposed French and American abstract painting. Kees's enthusiasm for the project, however, was noticeably less than Bultman's. He went along with Bultman, who drove him "screwy," and Miz Hofmann in getting the Provincetown Art Association to give them its Hawthorne Gallery even though this meant pushing the association's members—the Sunday seascape painters, hobbyists, vacationing art teachers, and the like, "the Beachcombers" as he called them—from their own exhibition space for several weeks. Beyond this, Kees said he wanted to do little more. And he was against the idea of a Forum 50, for he was tired of "casting pearls before swine," tired of "going through the emotional wringers that these things add up to."

Bultman accused him of "backing out," but Kees reminded Bultman that his doing so was hardly an "original gesture," for Bultman had quit Forum 49 the previous summer. "I guess he's sore at me," Kees wrote Getty. "The Hofmanns don't seem to be, but I guess they will go along with him none too enthusiastically. A bit upsetting all around, however; but better an understanding now than grief all summer with those people at the Art Association. The rank-and-file are grumbling that they are being slipped a fast one by the Kulturbolsheviks."

The free time Kees made for himself at the cost of alienating his friends went unused for much of what he wanted to do that summer. The club where he had been promised a piano-playing job lost its liquor license and closed. He wanted to write more poems, but Howard Moss returned "The Umbrella" with a note saying the poem's length had gone against it. This left him discouraged, with no "further impulses" to write for the rest of the summer.

He did paint a few oils. He felt hopeful that some of his canvases would sell from the "Year's Work" exhibition at the Peridot Gallery, which ran from June to July. His work would appear with paintings by James Brooks and Alfred Russell—and sculptures by Lou Pollack's newest artist, Louise Bourgeois.

On Fridays, he attended the "criticism" at Hans Hofmann's school. Margaret Marshall stood with him and watched a particularly harsh session, during which Hofmann went from one student canvas to another, accusing this one of being to slavish to Mondrian or Pollock or Picasso.

Kees also read. He picked up Faulkner's *Light in August* for the second time—the first had been in the summer before he went to Doane College—and he read the Ortega y Gassett that Getty had picked up for him in Boston. He slipped inside an air-conditioned Provincetown movie house to see *The Asphalt Jungle*, John Huston's *noir* thriller. Overlooking the new actress the film introduced, Marilyn Monroe, he noticed instead the small-time Midwestern criminals played by Sterling Hayden, Sam Jaffe, and others, who wanted to escape the big city for Mexico.

There were the usual cocktail parties to attend, but given his self-imposed uneventful summer, Kees could hardly compete with Norman Mailer, still riding high on his 1948 bestseller *The Naked and the Dead*, and other writers. He had no book out. He was no longer the moderator of the forums. He had sold as many paintings as you could count on one hand. He did collect anecdotes about the new style of outsized New York literary egos that indicated—in his cocktail-party asides and letters to people whom such egos would call "nobodies"—that he was not outsized himself: "A local spy reports that he met Norman Mailer at a party. The body of the evening was given over to listening to Mailer discuss the fascinating topic of the relationship of his work to that of Tolstoi & Dostoevksy. Mailer is of the opinion, it seems, that he is more in the tradition of T. than D."

Kees and his wife looked more to people on the periphery of Provincetown society, the relaxed bohemian kind such as Robert Wilbur, a New York bookseller, and his wife Lorraine, both followers of Wilhelm Reich who had brought the first orgone box to the Cape that summer. They also befriended art students and other younger people not put off by Kees's affectations, which to them seemed from another time: the Lincoln, his piano playing. These new friends included the painter Hyde Solomon and his friend John Haines, whom Weldon and Ann picked up hitchhiking on the Cape that summer in their big Lincoln and had over for supper. Haines, not yet the fine poet he would become, had first seen Kees at an opening in New York during the winter and knew from a friend that Kees was a different kind of artist, the author of an important book of poems as well as a painter. Certainly other young people made this connection, but Kees was doing nothing to build on the compliments he sometimes heard, which suggested he could fill a classroom in a liberal-arts school had he wanted to.

Kees eventually reconciled with Bultman and helped organize a token Forum 50 at the Provincetown Art Association tied to an exhibition titled "Post-Abstract Painting 1950: France and America." He participated in a panel discussion about the direction of abstract art with Hans Hofmann, Adolph Gottlieb, and other artists and critics and contributed an unsigned note for the exhibition catalog. Its articulate presentation of the show's theme, however, contrasted with what he wrote the Myrers in a letter that made the panel discussion and the art being considered for the show, including work by many of the Irascibles, sound banal to the extreme: "Ten top Matisses wd. be necessary to counteract certain *maitres* to be included; I shan't mention names, thus providing you with the opportunity of playing a lively game I have just this moment dreamed up—called Guess What Paintings in Provincetown's 'Post-Abstract' Show wk Thinks Are the Principle Stinkers. It's fun, it's clean, it's educational—and what's more, children adore it. All you need is the kattylog, which I enclose."

As the show hung in August, Kees withdrew again from the social and cultural life of the Cape. A color photograph reveals that walking on the beach and swimming in the ocean like Dick Diver in a bathing cap were ways he distanced himself. He also turned up at fewer parties. Rumors spread that he was not to be found in Provincetown that summer or that he had left early. Other images show him smiling and posing gamely for the camera, clearly comfortable in the company of a few friends, including Norris Getty.

During this visit, Kees urged his friend to read Tony Myrer's manuscript for a *roman à clef* about Provincetown in 1947, with thinly disguised characters based on Mary McCarthy, Edmund Wilson, Hans Hofmann, his students, and many others—many of the kind who alienated him, who had sold their souls. Even *Partisan Review* would be taken to task as *Mephisto,* the journal for the hyperintellectual and competitive. For Kees it was not only his younger friend's first novel but also a vicarious experience, a return to his own novel writing, and the circumstances were right for Myrer. Albert Erskine, at Random House, wanted the book to fill the need for a bestseller about the young abstract painters who were making news and were increasingly in the public eye. "An important book," Kees assured Getty.

A poem came from one of these August beach days, ending nearly two months of silence, seeming to be Kees telling himself the Cape was dead. The first draft of "The Beach in August" was titled "6, 7, 8," after the grim count the lifeguard utters to time assisted respiration:

The day the fat woman
In the bright blue bathing suit
Walked into the water and died,
I thought about the human
Condition. Pieces of old fruit
Came in and were left by the tide.
[. . . . .]
Another fat woman
In a dull green bathing suit
Dives into the water and dies.
The pulmotors glisten. It is noon.

The Keeses left Provincetown on September 12. Sometime after Labor Day they decided to live in either Monterey or San Francisco. They intended to drive cross-country in their Lincoln sedan and see as much as they could, passing through Nebraska for one last time during the middle of their journey. They talked about visiting Jim Agee in Los Angeles.

There was still unfinished business in New York, and they returned to the city. Kees spent an afternoon at Peridot Gallery, where he showed Louis Pollack the paintings he had finished at the Cape. They also discussed Kees's future exhibitions and the logistics of sending paintings back and forth across the country.

They also would have shared misgivings about the feature that *Life* magazine's editors planned to run on the Irascible Eighteen and their boycott of the Metropolitan.

Adolph Gottlieb and the other signers of the Irascible manifesto had been asked to pose for the group photograph that would illustrate the article. Kees, however, was not willing to change his plans about leaving for California as soon as possible. He had agreed to sit for *Life* staff photographer Nina Leen. Time, however, was running out as Gottlieb, Robert Motherwell, Barnett Newman, and Bradley Walker Tomlin negotiated with *Life*'s editors on how the artists—Mark Rothko, Clyfford Still, Jackson Pollock, Hedda Sterne, and the other Irascibles—should be represented, a balancing act of enormous egos, art politics, and sensibilities—all things that now left Kees feeling numb and indifferent. It was an enormous opportunity in Pollack's point of view that his friend would not exploit. Kees, nevertheless, still saw himself as a New York art journalist during these last weeks. He met with Howard Devree about writing cultural pieces from the West for the *New York Times*—and with Margaret Marshall, who tactfully declined his fanciful idea of covering the New York art world from Los Angeles and San Francisco in the *Nation*'s art column. "I am afraid," she told him, "the column couldn't be done from anywhere else."

Another venture kept Kees from thinking too much about the loss of his art column. He had agreed to launch *Botteghe Oscure* in this country, a new international cultural journal heavily endowed—and edited from Rome—by the wealthy Countess Marguerite Caetani. Her sister was a friend of Kees made during Forum 49, the poet Katherine Chapin, wife of Francis Biddle. Chapin had asked Kees to be her sister's unofficial American agent during the summer, and he agreed, since the countess had bought one of his poems, "Speeches and Lyrics for a Play," and there was the chance that he could profit in other ways from his association with her and her journal. As soon as he could get a fixed address, he expected to get the five-hundred-dollar check the countess had promised him to launch a publicity campaign for which he had solicited blurbs from T. S. Eliot and other authors the countess knew.

For two weeks the Keeses stayed at Conrad and Mary Aiken's "slumlet" on East Thirty-third Street.

Weldon invited friends over for drinks and to say farewell. If they had asked him why he and Ann were leaving the city, both the Keeses would have told them what Weldon told the Aikens, Maurice Johnson, Fritz Bultman, and others: that their "romance with New York City was over." Margaret Marshall felt terribly sorry to lose him, but she could sympathize with his desire to get away from the city. Still, she, the Aikens, the Posters, the Bultmans, and others did try to dissuade the Keeses from leaving. They saw them as Westerners from the "cactus spaces." Weldon had even told them, one way or the other, that he would have settled for Atchison or Lone Pine, Arkansas, after he had had enough of New York.

When that time came, it was hardly such a casual decision. Kees really saw himself as "fleeing a stricken city," a "dark and dreadful place" so dire that when Ann remembered she had left some cookbooks in Mary Aiken's kitchen, he kept driving.

San Francisco
1950-1955

San Francisco must have seemed like rebirth to Weldon. It looked so civilized and easy and full of possibility.
— Constance Hammett Poster

Weldon came to die. — Janet Richards

After leaving New York in the first week of October, Ann and Weldon Kees drove cross-country in their Lincoln roadster at a leisurely pace for the next sixteen days. They were more like a couple on vacation than two people uncertainly starting new lives in California and in a city yet to be determined. The only side trip they did not make was to Florida, where John and Sarah Kees were wintering and had invited them to come.

Kees had no second thoughts about leaving New York. The image he had had of the city from Henry James, Hart Crane, and Edmund Wilson had been unsentimentally eclipsed by New York winters, dirt, and the oversized egos of his contemporaries, as he later wrote to Conrad Aiken: "Never once have I caught myself humming 'Give My Regards to Broadway,' and it is an unconfined joy not to walk ankle-deep in NY's minglement of snow, slush, banana skins, [and] not to experience that city's capacity for the type of Angst that has served Delmore Schwartz, et al."

That gift for letter writing that served him so well in starting his career from Denver would now connect him again to the East. "Good letters," as he called his entertaining correspondence, would have to replace his presence at all those Village parties he would now miss—and if he had anxieties about stretching his contacts with his friends and with editors and gallery people, he comforted himself with thinking they would tap him as their West Coast man. He even thought some would follow him to California once it became clear—through him—that American avant-garde culture had two coasts. Still, as much as he saw himself setting an example, especially to the younger, "hipster" intellectuals back in New York, he was also trying to get away from the careers, the "getting noticed," and the youth of that type represented by Anatole Broyard, Milton Klonsky, Chandler Brossard, and Seymour Krim. Though many of them looked up to him for his knowledge of modern literature and art, for the way he made the Jazz Age go on agelessly in his own person, they in turn struck him as neurotic and pot-smoking lightweights outclassed by the generation before them. (Kees still found it funny that Klonsky's wife, Rhoda, had left him for Auden—and provided Auden with his first "experience" with a woman.) One of the first letters Kees wrote from California, to Willy Poster, revealed in condescending asides how little he felt he owed to the young men he had befriended in New York and how he burned his bridges with them before they became influential in their own right:

> *Broyard's request that I introduce him to God, is, I fear, a less easy one to grant. I have contacted Him. [...]*
> *Klonsky's nickel is being sent under separate cover.*

Kees did most of the driving, while Ann tuned in radio stations and navigated the federal highway system with the maps they picked up at gas stations along the way. Much of their journey can still be retraced in "Travels in North America," the poem Kees wrote in early 1953 in which he used his contributor's copy of *The American Guide*, the last wPA guidebook, to add color to his memory of October 1950. For the first days, they took U.S. 50 west through Pennsylvania and down through West Virginia and across the river into Ohio. There the Lincoln's radio brought in music that dispelled the New York of Charlie Parker, Dizzy Gillespie, and their followers—and the road became Columbia Parkway, from which the Keeses saw the skyline of the river city John Huston had used for the opening location shot of *The Asphalt Jungle*.

The Keeses followed U.S. 50 to Saint Louis and on to Columbia, where they looked up Mary Paxton Keeley, Weldon's friend and mentor when he attended the University of Missouri in 1934. In the living room of her new home, he introduced Mary to Ann and then told her about his life in New York, about the writers and artists, the noise and the dirt, about working at *Time* and for the newsreels. Then he discussed some of his plans for California. Mary had not seen him more excited and hopeful. He wanted to make a "new kind of movie." The State Department had earmarked twenty-one million dollars for producing documentaries about American culture to be shown abroad. He mentioned that he would see Jim Agee in Hollywood and that something might come from that.

Eventually, Mary asked Kees about his poetry. He said that he had a new volume coming out. All he needed was a publisher, but he had high hopes that Harcourt, Brace would reconsider the book again; he had resubmitted an expanded manuscript of *A Late History,* now retitled *A Breaking and a Death.* As he spoke about this, Mary thought he looked more like a poet than ever.

Feeling that she had neglected Ann, Mary tried to keep the Keeses longer by striking up a conversation with her. Yet before they could exchange many words, Kees rose and said that he and Ann must be on their way.

The Keeses drove on to Kansas City, where they turned north for Nebraska. They did not have to stop or stay in Beatrice. John and Sarah had moved to Orlando, Florida, the year before. His aunt Clara and one of his cousins still lived in Beatrice, but the rest of his extended family had either left the town or were now buried in its cemetery.

On October 10, the Keeses arrived in Lincoln, where they spent the day with Lowry Wimberly, who thought his former protégé looked to be at loose ends. Kees even admitted to Wimberly that he was "just a leaf blown about on the earth by the winds" with no real prospects. On the other hand, however, he did not make up excuses for why he no longer wrote for *Time* and the newsreels. He betrayed no weakness, no defeat. Still, it was hard for his English professor and first editor to sound him out. Kees still protected himself with his old sense of humor from the Unholy Trio days. He joked that he and Ann would make a living picking up driftwood along the ocean in Monterey, shellacking it, and selling it to tourists. After hearing this, Wimberly came to regret not having offered his former student a teaching post at the university. He had the power, but Kees did not ask.

Ann and Weldon entered Los Angeles on or about October 14 and stayed at the Portal Motor Hotel, set in the hills of Hollywood. There, Kees flipped open his little black address book and telephoned people he knew who lived in the city. He was most anxious to see Nesuhi Ertegun, a friend he had made in New York through the Farbers.

Ertegun had grown up in the Turkish embassy in Washington, where his father served as ambassador — and where Nesuhi and his brother Ahmet acquired a taste for American music. After the father returned to Turkey, his sons stayed on in the United States. The eldest, Nesuhi, opened the Jazz Man Record Shop in Hollywood. "A beautiful place," Kees wrote, "that looks more like an interior decorator's office than what it is." From his shop, Nesuhi also ran the recording business that would evolve into Atlantic Records, which he founded with Ahmet. In the early 1950s, however, the Jazz Man label specialized in New Orleans–style jazz. Naturally, Kees picked up the latest discs and re-issues, even if he had nowhere to set up his phonograph, for he considered Darnell Howard's Frisco Footwarmers and Johnny Dodds and the New Orleans Bootblacks "vital in the extreme."

The Keeses spent nearly a week in the company of Ertegun and his wife, Marili Morden, who guided them through the "mazes of LA jazz activities." They also befriended a number of white jazz players who played in clubs and bars on Hollywood Boulevard and Vine Street, among them Red Nichols, Pete Daily, Skippy Anderson, Bob Zurke, and the great Dixieland trombonist Edward "Kid" Ory and members of his band, including the clarinetist Joe Darensbourg, who entertained the Keeses with stories from his carnival and medicine-show days. Down on his luck in a small Southern town, Darensbourg told them, things had gotten so bad he had to eat the grass in someone's front yard. When the lady in the house discovered him like this, she said, "Why you poor man, you're absolutely starved, aren't you? [...] Why don't you come around to the back yard, where the grass is higher?" Joe Rushton, the trumpet player for Red Nichols's band, showed Weldon and Ann his special measuring device for testing the amount of whiskey served in the shot glasses of Los Angeles. "Thus," Kees wrote Getty, "he is able to inform all & sundry about various spots. 'An excellent place, The Ebony Pig,' he will say, 'a full ounce establishment.' Or, 'Avoid Don's Olympia; a lean apportioning.'"

From Los Angeles, Kees listed all the tunes he heard for Getty, and when his space ran out on one of the motel postcards he sent back to Boston, he ended with the one-word sentence, "Fun." The music was so good in Los Angeles that the Keeses stayed for five days and could have easily stayed longer. They left for Monterey on October 21, stopping over in Buellton, north of Santa Barbara, to try the famous split pea soup at Andersen's Valley Inn.

Monterey was not the West Coast Provincetown that the Keeses had hoped for. They grew bored in their motel room, where they realized that they would feel more at home in or near a big city—especially after experiencing Los Angeles. They did not want to take the other extreme, like the Myrers, who would soon arrive in Monterey en route to

Big Sur, where they would live in a shack. As the Keeses reached a decision about where to live in California, they tried to make the best of living at loose ends, with an eye on not spending money and stretching what they had.

At the post office in Monterey, Kees picked up the new volume of Pound's letters that he had ordered through the mail. Back at the motel, even as he cringed at how they had been edited, he was still impressed by how much "trouble the man took" in the early days of modernism. If there were only a literary operator like him now, in 1950. "But things are far tougher than in 1919–25," he wrote Getty, "everything is more corrupt & tasteless & commercialized; and whether a man like Pound could today endure at all, doing the same things *he* did, is a pretty question."

Weldon and Ann rated Monterey a "dull hole" within a matter days of their arrival and made use of one of Manny Farber's friends, Hassell Smith, a painter who taught at the California School of Fine Arts. From Monterey, Kees phoned Smith and learned that he and his wife would soon be vacating their apartment in Point Richmond, a neighborhood near Berkeley on the east side of San Francisco Bay, just across the Bay Bridge and a half-hour north of the city by car. The Smiths intended to move to an apartment in San Francisco — once the tile layers' strike was over, which had disrupted home construction in the Bay Area. For the present, they still occupied the top floor at 204 Western Drive, where yet another painter, Robert McChesney, and his wife, Mary, also lived. The McChesneys intended to purchase the old Victorian three-story house and move into the Smiths' old apartment. This would leave the middle floor vacant.

When Ann and Weldon Kees arrived in San Francisco that November, the city's painters, sculptors, musicians, and actors were having an arts festival at the Palace of Fine Arts, a building designed by the famous San Francisco architect Bernard Maybeck to resemble a Piranesi Roman ruin and built to celebrate the opening of the Panama Canal. The Palace housed more than twelve hundred exhibitors in its colonnaded hall. Kees compared the setting to an outdoor art show in Washington Square Park back in New York, combined with a "counterblast by the far left-wing of the advance guard," in the first of many pieces he hoped to publish in the *New York Times* as the paper's West Coast cultural reporter at large, an assignment Howard Devree, the paper's editor and art critic, had given him back in September. The festival was certainly the most conspicuous sign of the influence of the California School of Fine Arts under its director, Douglas MacAgy, and the faculty he had assembled there from 1945 to 1950. The school featured prominent West Coast abstractionists as well as visiting artists from New York such as Ad Reinhardt, Mark Rothko, and Clyfford Still. Its reputation was such in the East that Robert Motherwell, when he published the transcripts of the artists' sessions at Studio 35, included a panel discussion on American art chaired by MacAgy that featured an "idealized audience," in the words of art historian Dore Ashton, of writers, critics, painters, artists, and composers ranging from Arnold Schoenberg to Frank Lloyd Wright. Though the school's "fabled years" were over, Kees knew that its presence in San Francisco had laid the groundwork for a cultural environment that would rival New York's.

The furnished apartment that the Keeses would live in was utterly hospitable. For sixty dollars a month, the Keeses would have considerably more than what they had paid for in New York: utilities, a large L-shaped living room, a bedroom, kitchen, bath, and a room that Kees could use as a studio in which to paint. The surrounding stands of eucalyptus trees could be seen from any window. The beachfront, with a view of the bay and its bridges, was literally a few steps from the front door — and downtown San Francisco was a half-hour drive away. The basement apartment was home to still another painter who had taught for MacAgy at the School of Fine Arts, Edward Corbett. The Bay Area offered Kees a fusion of New York and Provincetown in one place — and a better climate. He and Ann would have to wait for their apartment in yet another expensive motel, where they "were paying through both nostrils," but she had a place to cook. "After a while," Kees wrote Getty, "restaurants lose their charm, if any."

While they waited, the Keeses sampled the jazz that could be heard in San Francisco and discovered to their surprise as much going on as in Los Angeles. Sophie Tucker's former accompanist, Paul Lingle, was the house piano player at the Paper Doll, a "spooky" lesbian bar near Telegraph Hill. The Keeses became quite friendly with him and made the Paper Doll one of their hangouts. Kees felt his own work at the keyboard improved due to his exposure to Lingle and other piano players he met at the Paper Doll — and he did not feel it was a one-way transaction. He returned to the Paper Doll in December to see the opening performance of John Wittwer, Lingle's replacement. Kees had never seen him play before and went up and requested "Ragged but Right" from the piano player. While still playing, Wittwer asked, "Who're you?" When Kees told him, Wittwer said, "Oh, yeah, you're the author of *The Last Man* and *The Fall of the Magicians*."

During the "tile boys" strike, the Keeses returned to Los Angeles for an extended stay. They spent a wonderful evening with Jim Agee at a party. Agee looked healthy to Kees—with the most "enormous & quickly developed potbelly now worn by any us man of letters of his generation"—and successful, too, working with John Huston on a treatment of Crane's "The Blue Hotel," picking a cast.

A new circle of friends took the place of the ones left behind in the East, among them the publisher of Kees's first book, Bill Roth— and the remarried Kenneth Rexroth, now the father of a two-year-old daughter and "full of a lot of strange & incredible stuff about the new crop of British potes [*sic*]," such as Dylan Thomas, and "functioning at full tilt." In a letter, Kees suggested to Getty that he might "dwell" on leaving for the West himself: "California seems, if not to hold its own, to debase itself less frenetically than the East Coast. At least my nervous system has responded to it rather nicely. And the jazz, some of the painting, the landscape, the temperature, have it all over the E. seaboard."

Kees even enclosed a "pome. [...] Not a whirlwind, but some of the lines are not to be despised."

He was now "wild to get back" to his writing and his publicity work for *Botteghe Oscure,* for which he still needed the promised blurbs from T. S. Eliot, Thornton Wilder, and Edmund Wilson. He also looked for documentary-film work in San Francisco.

He first approached Douglas MacAgy, who was associated with the film company that Kees hoped might undertake a series of short films dealing with jazz and folk music. With the right sponsors, such as Francis Biddle, Kees imagined a scenario in which he could get a grant from the State Department—and combine his passion for jazz, his new milieu, and his interest in writing and directing, which was not "debased by Hollywood-Broadway attitudes."

Kees also tried to develop various kinds of writing assignments. The jazz historian, music writer, and managing editor of *Harper's Bazaar,*

Wilder Hobson, whom Kees had known at *Time*, proposed a series of pieces on California. Hobson teamed him up with the photographer Ted Castle, who had come from New York to investigate the culture and jazz scenes of Los Angeles versus San Francisco. Kees also wanted to paint again—which he could do in the days just before Christmas, when the McChesneys moved upstairs and he and Ann took the second floor. "I have the best damned place to work in I've ever had," he wrote, happy and settled into his new home. He had

a moderate-sized room at the back of the house, with a crummy floor that I don't mind dripping painting onto & good space & light. Warmed up by doing a couple of Jelly Roll Morton album covers and then fought it out on canvas, letting Mr. Miro have it in the groin, and Mr. Matisse in the old kidney, and Mr. Picasso in the nose, and it was good, and it was fine, and I said, "Daughter [the name of one of the cats on the premises], Daughter, it is good and it is fine, and this will show Mister Dubuffet a thing or two, with the Flik Quick Drying Enamel singing off my brush the way only I can make it sing, and it is good and it is fine, Daughter."

The cat, one of three the Keeses ended up sharing with the McChesneys and renaming, arched its tail. It clawed at the door to be let out of the room and away from too much art talk—or so her new master thought. Yet Kees felt a kind of high from being engaged and involved with all of his talents. As he looked out from Point Richmond toward San Francisco, he again felt that he had made the right move in coming West. Besides, he knew that he could almost be in two places at once, for one of his paintings, *The Delta*, hung in Gallery V of the Whitney and gave him some presence in New York's art scene, as described in a letter from Willy Poster: "You are treated very nicely in a small room, hung on a panel all by yourself, in between two panels slanting off it on one of which is a Hedda Sterne [*Monument*] (a lymphatic, neat affair subject matter of which appears to be bridges and entrails) and on the other an anemic Byron Browne [*Apocalyptic Image*]. Next to the Byron Browne is a Bultman [*Composition in Blue*], a very good piece, three big dark muddy geometric shapes on a blue background. As far as I am concerned, yours and Bultman's are the only canvasses in the show."

〜

In January, Weldon and Ann paid to have their furniture shipped from a storage warehouse in New York. Fortunately, the McChesneys had left them enough to make their new home comfortable: a bed, a table, a chair, dishes — and cats that would not leave their old home. To complete their household, they purchased a fine, large, old upright for $150, which Kees described to Conrad Aiken as a "Chicago bordello type," with "a majestic, mellow, and heart-warming bass." Its authentic barrelhouse sound made him happy. It was the best piano he had ever owned, he told Ann and their friends, the best thing that had ever happened to him, especially now that his playing "classical Dixieland" had so much improved. A "steady workout" on it daily often filled the void where he had once written more poetry. Life on Western Drive was idyllic except for the occasional odors that came from the nearby Standard Oil refinery — and the jejune landmarks that connected them to the world: the Fireball Service Station; the Plunge, the world's largest indoor heated swimming pool; and the tunnel under the Santa Fe tracks. As yet Kees had no desk for his Royal Portable typewriter, which his father had traded him for an old Remington ("jammed together by scabs during the 1935 Remington strike"), now balanced on the windowsill of his studio. There he typed letters — and watched the cats, Daughter, Lonesome, and Pulque, play outside.

To pay for their "daily gin," as Kees liked to put it, Ann took on part-time secretarial work in Berkeley, and he looked for work to replace the income he had counted on from writing for the *New York Times*. He had made fifty dollars for the arts-festival piece, but a disinterested Howard Devree had not even told him when it was published and was not asking him to submit anything more. Once again he met with Douglas MacAgy to discuss making documentary films. This time they did not discuss art films. Instead, MacAgy arranged for Kees to meet his friend the anthropologist Gregory Bateson at the University of California, who hired Kees to help him make a data film about the interaction of mothers and children through a grant from the U.S. Public Health Service.

An Englishman, Bateson reminded Kees of Nigel Dennis, the actor who played Dr. Watson to Basil Rathbone's Sherlock Holmes. Yet this amusing resemblance was tempered by the fact that Bateson had once been married to Margaret Mead and was an accomplished figure in his own right. (He had served on MacAgy's panel of cultural luminaries for the West Coast complement to New York's Studio 35 sessions.)

Every Thursday and Friday, Kees drove to the Langley Porter Clinic in Berkeley and reported to Jurgen Ruesch, a Swiss-born psychologist who headed the department in which Bateson worked. Kees liked him, even if Ruesch was too much "that lovable exponent of Viennese charm and a phallic symbol in every home." Kees also took an immediate liking to working with Bateson and quickly apprehended Bateson's alternative views on psychoanalysis. "If you have to work with anybody in these back-side-of-town fields (which I don't mind at all)," Kees admitted to Tony Myrer, "give me an anthropologist every time rather than a sociologist or psychologist. They don't seem to want to poke people into their own made-at-home pigeonholes quite so forcefully." For his part, Bateson enjoyed having a poet—and a polymath—for a colleague, whose conversations were always intriguing and outré. Kees also picked up on the nature of Bateson's research and learned to operate a Bell and Howell 16mm camera. His typical workday involved shooting up to four hundred feet of film of, for example, a mother "interacting" with her four children, or sitting in a cubicle alongside Bateson's at Langley Porter, editing the previous day's footage. Kees described their film as "anthropologistic–psychiatric" to friends. Later, as he became more familiar with Bateson's ideas, Kees took a certain pride in "the picture," describing it "as one of the few pure 'documentaries' ever made. Our picture is so damned documentary that the cameramen (Bateson & me) are always getting into the picture, partly to emphasize that it is a picture about people being photographed, and not something 'spontaneous,' 'that just happened.'"

In the second week of January, an editorial assistant at *Life* sent Kees a large manila envelope. It contained a glossy print of the Irascible photograph for which he had agreed to pose. But only fifteen of the original Irascible artists appeared in the image that *Life* ran in "The Metropolitan and Modern Art," published in the magazine's January 15 issue. Nina Leen had taken this photograph in late November, when Kees and two other Irascibles, Fritz Bultman and Hans Hofmann, were no longer in New York. At some point after Kees left, Robert Motherwell, Barnett Newman, and Bradley Walker Tomlin had acted on their perception that *Life* would make them look ridiculous or beholden to the Metropolitan. (One of the shots the editors intended to use had the artists standing on the steps of the museum, each holding one of his or her paintings.) The artists also did not want to "collaborate" with *Life*, since the Luce magazine had traditionally been hostile to modern art and, in Clement Greenberg's way of thinking, an organ of kitsch. It is likely that Motherwell and Newman felt that the concept of the photographs needed to be discussed and placed under their control. After some negotiation with *Life*'s art editors, fifteen of the Irascibles agreed to be photographed at the magazine's New York studio.

Newman insisted that the group be photographed "like bankers" as opposed to Greenwich Village bohemians—the image of the artist in the popular imagination served by *Life*. Since the abstract expressionists tended to dress in suits and ties for formal occasions (as they did for the Studio 35 session), Newman's suggestion was not unnatural. In all likelihood, he intended that the artists wear the faces of bankers, and the result was a collective intense stare—that of uptight businessmen to Kees, emblematic of the mercenary careerism he had seen beginning to take hold of his friends back in April, the very careerism that had driven him across the country. Instead of the "massive block (of genius)" that the art historian Irving Sandler saw in the Leen photograph, Kees saw "a full page spread of 15 of the irascible you-know-how-many, all of whom look as though someone had just tossed some pigpiss in their peanut butter. *Except* for Hedda Sterne. Hedda Sterne looks as though she just got an extra special, special reserve, on-the-house ration of the dreamiest peanut butter anybody on 57th St. ever buttered for anybody."

His remarks here, part Rabelaisian, part Nebraskan, suggest that Kees knew being omitted from the Irascible photograph would be a setback. He may have understood, too, that he had been intentionally *deselected,* for Motherwell believed that Kees was "not significant, not a player."

Another interested party to the photograph was Lou Pollack. Kees's third one-man show at Peridot was set to open on January 29, in the wake of the *Life* article. Having Kees in the Irascible group portrait would have made up for the Whitney's failure to purchase *The Delta* back in December, even though James Thrall Soby planned to use the painting to illustrate his essay on the Annual in the *Saturday Review of Literature.* Pollack hoped that his representing one of the Irascibles could translate into sales for Kees, into a measure of authenticity now that it too had become a commodity. He had small announcements printed that, when unfolded, gave the dates for the show in small, lowercase type on one side and the artist's name on the other—weldon KEES—affecting at once the kind of understatement and cachet of which Kees would have approved. But the opening, though attended by over one hundred people, was missing something without its artist. Kees's absence and the cold evening in late January contributed to the kind of atmosphere that would be found at a funereal retrospective for a dead and neglected genius. Willy Poster reported the gloom, but he also told Kees the opening was the liveliest and freshest one-man American show he had seen in ages. He had overheard all kinds of favorable comments. The paintings themselves looked wonderful together and were not "choked by gallery-consciousness" and the kind of "arid ambition that seems to be ruining most of the recent output hereabouts. The two larger black and tans and the large gaily colored one that used to hang in the left hand corner of Stanton St. seemed to me about the best. [...] [It] has a queer kind of macabre gaiety I found magical and very characteristic—like a more complex version of some of your early poems."

"I sold out of my show not one damn thing," Kees wrote several weeks later to Getty, who had seen the show himself and had sent Kees photographs of the installation. From San Francisco, though, Kees felt "less depressed" about this than if he were still in New York. For his part, Lou Pollack still had faith in his artist. There was no reason why his friend had to get drunk and carouse at the Cedar Tavern to be taken for a real artist. Soon after the show came down, he told Kees about Peridot's next show, called "Painters as Sculptors"; Hans Hofmann, Jackson Pollock, and other abstract expressionists would do sculptures particularly for the occasion, with each artist also represented by a small oil and a drawing or watercolor.

Pollack wanted Kees to contribute a piece. Though daunted at first by the request, coming on the heels of what must have been an embarrassment to Peridot's owner, Kees pulled himself back up. "I did a number of things," he wrote Getty, "working in both wood and stone, before producing a small stone & concrete figure that seemed to do the trick."

The *Botteghe Oscure* "caper" continued into February. On a good day, Kees (with Ann's help) could get out fifty cover letters to the Romance language and English departments of American and Canadian colleges and universities. Each letter had to be individually typed on special stationery and then stuffed, along with a brochure, into an envelope that had to be sealed, stamped, and hand addressed. Kees compared it to typing two novels, except that you typed the same page, the least interesting one, repeatedly. Thankfully, there were other ways to serve the literary arts besides stuffing envelopes for the countess in Rome.

Kenneth Rexroth started a series of Friday-evening poetry readings at his house in February. He asked Kees to be "opening gun" at the first of these. Tired after a long day shooting film with Bateson, Kees had dinner and arrived to discover that Rexroth's living room had been filled to capacity, even though fifty cents admission had been charged "to keep out the people who drop cigarette butts in the goldfish bowl." It was the kind of success he had been looking for in San Francisco, intimate, bohemian, taking place where he felt protected from the destructive side effects of the kind of literary career he felt he had had back East. He tried the experiment of reading all four of the Robinson poems together, arranging them in a new order—"Aspects, Robinson, At Home, Relating"—to produce a single poem or cycle. He also read thirty other poems to an audience that did not seem so "professionally solemn," like the people who came to readings in New York. Instead his Portobello Hill listeners reacted to the black comedy in his work. They laughed in the right places. Rexroth gave him the "entire gate," less the cost of the jug of wine that people passed around during the course of the evening. At least this success was not killing him the way Hollywood was Jim Agee, who had just suffered a heart attack while working on *The African Queen*.

Kees, too, found himself caught up in a film, an entirely different kind of film, in early March. Through Douglas MacAgy's wife, Jermayne, he met the poet-filmmaker James Broughton, who, in turn, showed him several of his short experimental films. One, *Adventures of Jimmy*, made Kees laugh uncontrollably. Now considered a classic American experimental film, *Adventures* was, as Broughton described, "Candide's ten-minute quest for an ideal mate," in which the hero, Broughton himself, is pulled one way and the other by both sexes. He observes costumed mermaids in the water off Sausalito with a telescope that lengthens like an inspired erection. He associates with prostitutes trolling for customers on Sutter Street. He encounters a winsome, barefoot girl, sweeping stairs, whose strong resemblance to Carson McCullers would not have gone unappreciated, especially given the movie's little irony, its little joke, alluded to in quick cuts to the sign for a Turkish bath and splices of handsome, bare-chested young men. Then there is the narrator himself, Broughton, speaking in his natural voice. Even if one did not know him, as Kees now did, this voice suggested that the hero of the story was not interested in having a wife anyway. The effect of this made *Adventures of Jimmy* a send-up of Hollywood, playing on one of its little secrets — that many leading men were homosexuals. This aspect of the film may have been why Kees surprised Broughton when he admitted that the movie was the story of his own life. But Kees meant as much that he enjoyed how *Adventures* "got back" to the silents he remembered from his childhood. The way Broughton acted in the movie, so deadpan and naïve, performing various kinds of stunts, reminded Kees of the style of Buster Keaton. Kees also thought Broughton was taking aim at the *reverence* that Kees felt cloaked "'ex' 'peri' 'mental' films," meaning the work of Maya Deren and others, notwithstanding the fact that Broughton knew and respected Deren — or that Broughton had in mind not Buster Keaton's movies, but a forgotten French film of the 1930s by Sascha Guitry called *Diary of a Scoundrel.*

Adventures of Jimmy still needed music, and for this Broughton turned to Kees, remembering the Jelly Roll Morton numbers and the "Georgia Cake Walk" that his new friend had played for him after dinner one night in Point Richmond. The tunes fit so many of the light-hearted scenes in his silent movie that Broughton had little trouble convincing Kees to score the film with a small group of musicians in the San Francisco revival movement. The trumpet players Elmer Bischoff and Bill Erickson sat in, as did the trombonist Bob Mielke. Other performers included the clarinetist and bass sax player Bunky Colman and the millionaire banjoist Roland Howes. Jack Lowe, a painter at the School of Fine Arts, played drums, and another art student played standup bass. "The Jimmy Waltz," as Kees called it, was finished in time for the premiere in late April at the San Francisco Art Museum. There Kees, performing under the name of "Papa Wel," and his three-piece band played as the film was shown — and continued to play such tunes as "Kansas City Stomp" and "Memphis Blues" at the party that followed.

A few months later, Kees fell out of touch with Broughton. For his part, Broughton wondered about his "beautiful [...] bright, curious, nervous" new friend. "I did not," Broughton wrote well after 1955, "suspect how profound the secret must have been." Soon after the San Francisco showing of *Adventures of Jimmy*, in July, Broughton had to leave for New York and Europe. As the film began to win praise overseas (where it won a prize at the Edinburgh Film Festival), Broughton felt overwhelmed by the good fortune of Kees's contribution to *Jimmy*'s success and managed to write Kees a letter of thanks aboard the *Nieuw Amsterdam*. But there was more than just gratitude. He missed Kees, too. Like other gay men before him, Broughton thought he knew more about Kees than Kees would fully admit to himself. He believed whatever drove Kees ultimately had to do with his inability to resolve what Broughton perceived as sexual conflicts. When Weldon and Ann visited him and his partner, Kermit Sheets, Broughton saw that Kees "would linger on, as if trying to stir enough courage to share some profound confidence." Broughton suspected Kees was gay from the first night that Kees had sat across the dinner table from him, looking searchingly at him with his beautiful dark eyes while ignoring his wife, sitting next to him. Ann, as she had so many others, struck Broughton as a nonentity. She was hardly as engaging as Kees—and she was hardly in the way. For a time, Broughton felt tempted to fall in love with her husband, even though he was happily paired with Sheets. He did not pursue Kees openly, however, and simply wondered what it was that Kees might be looking for. Broughton noticed that Kees enjoyed coming over to the flat that Broughton and Sheets shared as if to savor the creative life that the couple had together, printing books and making films. During these visits, Broughton also thought he sensed Kees's desire to share his longings for a similar loving friendship of his own. He even felt Kees envied him, for Kees made no secret of feeling impressed by the devotion Sheets and Broughton showed to each other.

Kees, while still working on *Adventures of Jimmy*, received as much pleasure and satisfaction from the film he was making with Gregory Bateson as it neared completion. In only three months at Langley Porter, Kees had evolved from a technician into a real collaborator.

He found ways for art to *help* science and ways to see art in what he was doing for science. When Dr. Ruesch wanted to photograph the gesture-speech relationships of schizophrenics, Kees tactfully suggested they read passages of *Finnegans Wake* instead of performing parlor games like charades. When he and Bateson assembled their film, he saw as much an art-house film he could have shown at Forum 49 as he did purely behavioral science.

In reality, however, the films that mattered most to Kees were the ones he still had to buy tickets for, such as Bogart's new feature that spring, *The Enforcer*. He called it "marvelous"—and felt some small connection in place of the larger one he had long ago given up: the presence of Ted de Corsia, who played one of Bogart's gangsters. At a low point in his career, de Corsia had almost done the narration for "How to Build an Igloo," one of the documentaries Kees had made for the Signal Corps. A *real* movie career for Kees had become a source of irony and amusement to him by this time—and the actors he befriended now were the Interplayers, a group of local aspirants whose recent performance of *Family Reunion* had done little to improve Eliot's standing with Kees. He even thought it might be easier for him to get a long-term contract with MGM than continue to write and publish poetry.

After hearing nothing from Harcourt, Brace since leaving New York in October, Kees "sicced" Henry Volkening on the publisher. His old agent had not heard from Kees in years, and he still held *Fall Quarter* in high regard. For this reason, he honored Kees's request to see what had happened to *A Breaking and a Death*. After all, Volkening felt, by doing this he might get Kees interested in revising the novel and offering it to publishers again. The war was over. The market had changed.

Volkening, however, delivered bad news. He had telephoned Robert Giroux and learned that Kees's book had been rejected. "God rot the guts of the entire staff," Kees wrote the Posters. Evidently the decision had been made months before, time that Kees had wasted waiting for an answer, thinking that *his* publisher would not do him such a disservice. "[They] wouldn't answer any of my letters of inquiry," he continued in his letter to the Posters, "which I might just as well have addressed to Edward deVere for all the response they evoked."[1] As Kees learned a little while later, in a letter from Giroux, the manuscript had been held in the hope of "convincing the higher-ups." Unfortunately, and with a great deal of regret—that sorry-old-boy regret that grated on Kees—the decision had been made to reject *A Breaking and a Death* on the basis of its "salable qualities." "The arithmetic convinces me," Giroux wrote Kees at last in May, thanking him for the "opportunity of reading and considering a superior collection of verse." This premise seemed surreal to Kees after the success Reynal and Hitchcock had enjoyed with *The Fall of the Magicians*, which had sold one thousand copies before Harcourt, Brace let it go out of print.

Even without the strong promise of a salable novel, which so many agents expected from the poets they represented, Volkening offered to push *A Breaking and a Death*. He sent the manuscript on to Knopf. In the meantime, through much of the spring, Kees refused to let himself "go under" with rage and despair at going unpublished for so long. He had no time to indulge in the "congenital Abe Northism of most poets," citing the failed composer in *Tender Is the Night*. "Maybe," Kees wondered in one letter, "we need a Byron to get the public interested in poetry again, though Byron's public wasn't any more interested in poetry than people today are: they were interested in Byron." But Kees could not be sure what the public was now interested in. All he could do was guess that it "ain't very pretty" and worry about his sinuses— and type a selection of newer poems for Willy Poster, a sign that his readers were dwindling down to a small circle of friends.

"I must confess that this time of year will always fill me with a yen for the Cape," Kees wrote Conrad Aiken before Memorial Day. He gave Provincetown three summers more, "by which happy time the queers & their followers will have taken over (a few particularly vigorously bull lesbians perhaps tolerated & allowed to remain) and the last of the artistes [will be] looking with interest at Red Hook or the East Side of Brooklyn as new and promising sites for colonies." The Cape, however, was hardly behind him during this time. He and Ann relived one of their summers there proofing the galleys of Anton Myrer's Provincetown novel, *Evil under the Sun*.

Kees had informed this book from when Myrer first considered writing about the Cape scene in 1949 to the manuscript's final form. Virtually every one of its details had in some way passed through him. He had even sent the book on to Getty, who worked as hard on the manuscript as if it had been one of Kees's, resolving certain problematic sections and some of Myrer's more stilted phrases. Kees had also written the song lyrics that are interpolated in some of the novel's passages. Myrer, with his advance from Random House nearly depleted, could not afford to pay royalties for the lyrics of well-known songs and so had gone to Kees, who had been trying his hand at songwriting and considered Myrer's problem a boon. "The greed of the music publishers may yet prove to be a blessing in disguise," he wrote his friend, "forcing producers of beautiful letters to study & emulate the outstanding lyricists. [...] Norman Mailer may thus outdo Spencer Williams; John Steinbeck may yet surpass Larry Hart; Gore Vidal may one day rank with Mitchell Parrish." When Kees saw his works in Myrer's galleys, they looked even better, in "the great tradition," the best being a pastiche of "Lover Man," a torch song sung with a Billie Holliday quaver by a millionaire puppeteer (one of the novel's conspicuously gay characters):

> *But where am I*
> *Without your lips to fill me? . . .*
> *More and more*
> *I yearn . . .*
> *. . . more and more*
> *I yearn for your touch,*
> *Longing for you to explore,*
> *My darling—*
> *Much too much.*

The novel even included significant pieces of Kees's persona, which Myrer appropriated for the character of Paul Kittering, former college swimming coach, war veteran, poet, and apprentice abstract expressionist, who, though "confronted with the ocean" of art "in all its vastness, its mammoth breakers," will "plunge in." To Kittering all that "counts is the work—the canvases and the poems," not career, not wealth, not even sex. This realization makes Kittering an outsider, a pariah to his contemporaries, for their involvement in a culture that is caught in 1950–51, in the intellectuals' "mood swing" from psychoanalysis to existentialism, is simply foreplay for appeasing baser, instinctive, sensual urges. This is the "evil" that Myrer (and Kees) wanted to expose with the novel—and Myrer made Kittering its counterpoint, drawing enough parallels to the life of Christ to make the life of abstract expressionism a substitute for religion, a path to a lost moral high ground. Kees must have considered this in giving the novel its title in a letter to Myrer, calling upon his long-lapsed Presbyterianism to help with the problem: "I don't warm to SHADOW OF A SERPENT. Sounds like Episode 5 of a Pearl White serial. [...] I throw this out as a possibility—one to which I am indebted to the Good Book. EVIL UNDER THE SUN. [...] It's from, as you no doubt recall, Ecclesiastes, chapter 9, #3: 'This is an evil among all things that are done under the sun, that there is one event unto all: yea, also the heart of the sons of men is full of evil, and madness is in their heart while they live, and after that they go to the dead.'"

Kittering's authenticity makes him the object of resentment and disdain on the part of his fellow painters and ruthless New York intellectuals, feelings that, for the same reasons, Myrer saw projected on Kees during Forum 49. With Kittering, Myrer also used what could have been Kees's rationale for placing painting above writing at one point in his life. Kittering, in the first chapter of the novel, is sick of words and literary careers, sick of the new emphasis on criticism. With "painting," Kittering says, "it's different; it's kept the old vitality." For some reason, Kees, the pacifist who sat out the war, struck Myrer as a kind of soldier with his vitality, his loyalties, and some kind of untouchable, unknowable psychological wound, which he portrayed as Kittering's shrapnel-damaged leg. As the book drew closer to publication, Kees also helped with the small details, such as the dust jacket, that could not be left to chance: "I have tinkered a bit here and there with flap copy A, just a few dinky changes, and I herewith wager it now shows the touch of the reigning flap-copy masters. When I copied yr flap, it filled a gap, when we were a couple of kids. Old song. Wish somehow something could have been done with the 'dynamically and movingly created spirit of the artist, the aging Carl Roessli,' but I passed it by after repeated trys. Albert E. (or else the Randomhaus flap-copy goon squad) will no doubt give it the old dePachman cadenza treatment anyhow, but I don't think he could ask for anything more, whether having rhythm or not, which I kind of doubt."

Evil under the Sun, Kees told Conrad Aiken and many others, would be the next Under the Volcano. He felt as concerned about its reception "as though it were something I'd done." Indeed, since the summers of 1949 and 1950, the gestation of Myrer's novel had stood in for Kees's own missed opportunity to publish a first novel. Now, as *Evil under the Sun* neared completion, having the novel to work on in Point Richmond prevented Kees—and Ann—from dwelling on the status of *A Breaking and a Death*.

In late April, Weldon and Ann learned from Tony that Albert Erskine and others at Random House "loved" the book's new title and had decided to go with it, unconcerned that one of Agatha Christie's mysteries had prior claim. The Keeses also received a set of galleys from the publisher and gave *Evil under the Sun* its last critical proofread in what Kees called "Every-Blemish-Must-Go Week." To him, the book seemed in "500 percent better shape" than the version he, Ann, and Getty had read in Provincetown last August.

The title reverberated after Kees read the book. The last half struck him as "masterly," the part titled "Walpurgis Night" transforming one of the Cape's end-of-summer bohemian parties into a Black Mass, complete with artists and intellectuals as pagan revelers. Even Satan appeared, part Delmore Schwartz and part Dwight Macdonald, taking the form of the editor of *Mephisto*, a highbrow magazine that Malcolm Cowley identified as a combination of *Partisan Review* and *Neurotica*. The Kittering-painting-on-the-wharf chapter, however, "still had a lot of goo in it"—and Kees left himself uncommented as Myrer's hero painting quietly on a canvas "naked but for a visored utility cap and a pair of khaki trousers rolled to the knees."

Signing off with "Yrs. in the blood of Bennett Cerf," Kees turned in his last corrections to Myrer at the end of April, being both tactful and firm. "I bore down very hard," he wrote his friend in the following week, "motivated by a desire to remove *anything* some hostile critic (who might dislike the book for, um, other reasons) might pounce on with joyful cries." *Evil under the Sun* had become a personal stake for him. He understood the risk that Myrer had taken in demonizing liberal New York intellectual writers, careerist painters, hedonistic and femmy gays, and other Provincetown types. Portraying them as evil, especially those who used Freud to explain and justify all conduct as the result of traumas, fixations, and drives, might be taken as the maundering of a Congressman Nixon rather than as a much-needed in-group critique. "The damn book is haunting," Kees admitted to Getty. "I am deeply concerned, almost as though it was something I had written myself, as to how it will be received." Indeed his distance from the book could be measured with the cardboard ruler he had invented for locating typographical errors, which he called "the Kees Patented Handy Line-Finder," like a tool manufactured by the F. D. Kees Manufacturing Company.

While Kees proofed Tony Myrer's book, he balanced the acid his friend poured on the Cape by volunteering to curate an exhibition for "Arts in Action," an event sponsored by the Temple Sinai in Oakland that included sculptors, weavers, filmmakers, ceramists, and others. The opportunity came after members of the Reform congregation discovered that the *Nation*'s former art critic now lived in nearby Point Richmond. Sometime in early February, the director of the event had phoned and asked him to jury a show of paintings. Without realizing it, however, Kees had really agreed to go out and find paintings for the show. This onerous duty and the idea of a cultural fair sponsored by a "joosh" church group grew into a series of misadventures that featured paintings that were not dry, a temple board that would not allow the paintings to hang, and the volunteer from the temple who came to pick them up:

Mrs. Horwitz, a smartly-tailored thirtyish lady showed up here in a station wagon, seeming distraught, muttering about not knowing "What she was getting into" and taking, I thought, a rather dim view of the work I had selected & crabbing mightily about the size of some of the paintings. I helped her get the ones I had here into the station wagon and off she went, with her additional puzzled questions about "What is the subject matter of these things anyway" ringing in my ears ... phone ringing, a few days later. It is Mrs. Ziegler, the prime mover, with the stimulating intelligence that Mrs. Horowitz had come back to the Temple in a thalo green rage at having to lug around such shocking kulturbolschewismus and would not even bring the paintings in from the street.

In the calm that followed the Temple Sinai affair—after a strong protest, the temple board let all the paintings hang—Kees felt that he and Ann deserved a trip down the coast via Highway 101 to Los Angeles. A week of jazz-clubbing would be one way to make up for the Cape. But they were "feeling the pinch" in May. Tony Myrer, knowing that his friend needed a summer getaway and good friends nearby, found a piece of property on Bixby Creek in Big Sur. Kees felt tempted, but he did not like the idea of having property that was not an "immediate necessity." He could still not see himself—and Ann—living in such a remote place without the amenities of a city. Again, the "lack of cash" ruled out any other consideration—and he could not ask his parents for outlays too close together.

From Myrer, he also learned that *Evil under the Sun* had become "the center of acrimony and controversy" at Random House. After a tempest over the house policy of substituting ellipses for em dashes, Albert Erskine's colleagues began to really read the novel and take issue with the book's overt judgmentalism instead of the $21.78 it cost to reverse the changes the copyeditor had made. Kees advised keeping in mind that Random House had "a very sizable investment" in *Evil under the Sun*. If there was to be a showdown over content, he also felt it prudent that Myrer have his agent and attorney review his contract in the event that the novel was pulled. Naturally, Kees wanted to be helpful, but he also felt responsible for the way Myrer's book had turned out. Certainly, the harsh caricatures of the Cape's habitués—and the harsher light to which they had been held up—must have seemed like a delicious joke to Kees. More than once he must have lapsed into the part of the student editor of the humor page of a Midwestern college paper instead of playing the part of the seasoned, published poet looking out for a friend's interests. He let many passages stand—and lent himself to others—in the spirit of a big send-up of Provincetown without realizing that the readership the book was intended for would not be entertained by being its butt. Still, the novel had not been released. Proofs had, as yet, not been sent to reviewers. And Kees, in his letters to Myrer, avoided creating a chill between him and his friend by changing the subject to the latest undeserving bestseller, *From Here to Eternity,* and deflating its author, James Jones. In Point Richmond, Kees brought home copies of the works of the English philosopher and aesthetician R. G. Collingwood, borrowed from the library of Gregory Bateson. He also practiced "Grandpa's Spells," "Chimes Blues," "The Pearls," and "Riverboat Shuffle" on his piano—and helped Ann learn "King Porter Stomp." No poems came during this time, save for a few odd limericks.

In the middle of May, the tactful letter from Robert Giroux bringing the sad news that Harcourt, Brace would pass on *A Breaking and a Death* pushed both Keeses into a long depression during which they kept to themselves for nearly eight weeks. Kees even ceased corresponding with his closest friends. The imaginary illness he glibly called "harcourtbraceitis" turned out not to be imaginary. The short list of its symptoms, which included mucous colitis and dyspepsia, were very real stress disorders suffered by him—and by Ann, as the enormity of her husband's setback accelerated the somatic effects of her drinking. The delicate balancing act that she performed between her denial of her husband's failure and her devotion to his art may have come undone as the summer loomed without a vacation, when all they had to show for security was a new fire-insurance policy. Within a few weeks they had helped to launch the career of one man—Tony Myrer—while the career they had so carefully cultivated for over ten years suddenly seemed to fade before their eyes.

Kees cut out a clipping from the *Chronicle* that advertised how, for thirteen dollars a day, two people could "vacation in a kingly style on a piggy bank budget" at the Hotel del Coronado with "*everything*" included: meals, room, dancing, tennis, and swimming. He pasted it in a letter to Tony Myrer to show the tawdriness of middle-class pathos. It was a kind of self-criticism, too, for Kees could hardly afford to pay even this budget rate.

In July, Kees and Bateson were between grants. The funds for the filmmaking project at Langley Porter had started to run out. They still needed money to do the technical work on their film, such as the final editing, titling, and sound recording. As Kees's take-home pay lessened, he tried to ration out what he spent on food and liquor—the gin Ann now used to numb her pain.

By way of solution to their financial straits, Kees applied to the Huntington Hartford Foundation, the new "super-Yaddo" in Los Angeles, in the hope that a long stay there might hold him and Ann over until "new methods of securing dough" were in place—or provide them with the vacation that they had to forgo. He also wrote his father, now living in Lincoln, Nebraska, asking him for an advance of money. Kees couched his request, in all probability, as one aimed at yet another crucial investment for the good of his reputation as a painter, for he wanted to ship back the paintings he had shown in New York earlier in the year for a possible one-man show in San Francisco in the autumn.

Ann underwent surgery in late July. After Kees brought her home from the hospital, he had a better reason not to write his friends or see anyone. In a short note to Tony Myrer, he admitted that he was "decidedly down in the dumps of late—pretty despairing and dismayed." He had been "intimately" acquainted with this kind of enervating depression before—and the bouts of sickness that often came with it in the form of sinus headaches and flu, for which he took a constant prophylaxis of aspirin and Enterol. Hearing that Myrer was well into his second novel, he wrote, "It is damn good to know that you, at least, are pushing the stone up to the top of the hill." To Kees, however, it seemed that he had done nothing with his own poetry or painting. He and Ann had to get by on a little good news coming from what was now another life to them. A letter from James Broughton reported that *Adventures of Jimmy* had been well-received at its New York press review and that the film would be shown in the fall at Cinema 16, the avant-garde New York cinema and distribution company. The score for the film had won much praise, Broughton wrote, and he realized "the great debt" he owed Kees.

The Keeses limited their evenings to sitting around their new Motorola radio, listening to Jack Webb's new show, *Pete Kelly's Blues,* a gritty drama that combined gangsters and jazz musicians. It featured a band that, in one episode, played "Louisiana," which Kees learned to play from memory. When Ann felt well enough to socialize, they drove to the Jug Club in the company of Douglas and Jermayne MacAgy. The latter, realizing that Weldon had not, as yet, mounted a one-man show in San Francisco, offered him gallery space in the Palace of the Legion of Honor, where she was director. Her offer and the return to some kind of normal life "on the ill-health front" helped raise the spirits of both Keeses in August and September. A six-page letter Weldon typed at work to the Myrers made up for weeks of silence and revealed that his sense of humor was still sharp as ever. Interpolating his regular narrative with the caps-lock key on and typing random "asides" from the psychological literature he had read, Kees assured the Myrers that "Weldon was his old self." He also found that his work at Langley Porter could offer him other perspectives and keep him from being so self-absorbed by his health and setbacks. While filming schizophrenic children for a new documentary, he found that "kids who are off their rockers are heartbreaking; and after a few hrs. with them I am reduced to a pulp."

One evening in August, the Keeses and the MacAgys sat around a table at the Jug Club and listened to Paul Lingle play a Wurlitzer electric organ. For Kees, the performance was conclusive proof, for his money, that Western civilization was in "firmer shape" than anyone had guessed.

In Point Richmond, the McChesneys loaded their furniture and canvases inside a former mail truck and took off for Mexico. Before they left, they staged a series of farewell parties that, Kees observed, were notable for their noise, duration, and intensity, with "addle-pated and leather-lunged stalinoids, mad with red wine, staggering, vomiting, and huggin and a chalkin all over the great outdoors." During this time, 204 Western Drive was sold to the Keeses' new landlord, Herbert Wheeler, a young architect who, with his wife, moved in with the "inevitable young baby."

As the publication date of *Evil under the Sun* approached, Kees began to psychologically prepare himself—and the Myrers, too—for its reception, taking into account everything from the most practical considerations to philosophical speculations about the bestseller. For the advance reviews, which would come out in September, he suggested that Tony write Dorothy M. Brandt, the proprietor of Literary Clipping Service in Walton, New York. For only five dollars, she would cut out and send fifty clippings from journals, magazines, and newspapers from all over the country.

Kees received a review copy of *Evil under the Sun* in the first week of September. He did not care for the black and yellow dust jacket, illustrated with ankh symbols and a hermit crab. Such packaging, to him, was out of keeping with the novel's content. "I have a feeling that Max Spivak, Jimmy Ernst, and Barney Newman," he wrote, "all blind drunk and working on a high wire without a net, and equipped only with stubs of soapstone, cd. have collectively knocked out, in twenty minutes, something more appetizing." The solution he arrived at was to remove the jacket, "thus leaving what's left in fine shape." Yet what troubled Kees more about the novel's packaging was the lack of any quotes from reviewers on the jacket. This silence ("Funny you don't hear from Nat Halper"), and his impatience with the fact that Miss Brandt's scissors had nothing to clip yet, compelled him to imagine a couple of reviews to go with the one that Tony Myrer obtained from the *Provincetown Advocate* (Random House had arranged for the novel to "premiere" where its action took place). These fictitious critiques were not only concocted so that the Myrers could enjoy a foretaste of the sensibilities the book might offend in certain quarters. They also would serve as psychological protection should *Evil under the Sun* be panned. Kees also imagined for the Myrers how the novel might be discussed at one of the Cape's watering holes that served a clientele that was not as visible in the novel as their male counterparts: "I can just see the 'Weathering Heights gang' (led by kindly, goiterous Alice King) sitting around the bony remains of a fish dinner, swilling glasses of warm gin, while a Back Bay lesbian in fishnet blouse inquires, 'What characters in *Evil Under the Sun,* have you, Mary Ellen, identified in the last twenty seconds?'"

༈

John Kees wired his son money in September to cover his expenses for mounting an exhibition at the Palace of the Legion of Honor the following month. There was enough to crate and ship back the work he had shown at his last Peridot show and to frame his latest paintings and collages. There was even enough to put a deposit down on the rental of a house in Big Sur. Weldon and Ann hoped this getaway could be tied to a trip to Los Angeles before Christmas. They wanted to see their friends there and hear Kid Ory and Red Nichols again. But a series of "strange and accusatory" letters from Kees's parents in Lincoln put a chill on the couple's plans. The elder Keeses felt that their son had made a very grave mistake by leaving New York. They felt he had damaged his chances at publishing another book of poetry. They felt he was wasting his time by painting. They may have reminded him that he was no longer writing for *Time* or the newsreels, once a source of special pride to them. Now they found it hard to explain—to themselves and their elderly friends—that their grown son worked in a psychiatric clinic, a kind of stigma for them. It seemed to John and Sarah a coming down in the world, which was more than proved by the fact that their son needed money at a time when everyone seemed to have a job and there was so much prosperity. Kees's straits just did not make sense, and both his mother and father felt that there was enough time for him to change, even to drop poetry and painting altogether—or to suspend such pursuits until he had made a *real* career for himself.

To Kees, who had been reading the R. G. Collingwood that Bateson had lent him, his parents were simply part of the impatient crowd needing amusement. They had confused art with entertainment. They wanted their gifted son to entertain them the way he had back in Beatrice. Sarah Kees wanted to read about her son in newspapers and slick magazines, which is why he wrote a response in the second week of October to a series of letters he had received from his parents throughout September. There is no evidence that he posted this letter, but he may have written it just as much to defend himself from his own doubts. Collingwood promised in his *Principles of Art* that "long afterwards, a few people, looking back, begin to see that [good art] has happened." This thought may have made Kees comfortable with the idea that he did not have to live to see his poetry take on value. Instead of feeling that he had accomplished nothing in his mother's world, he took the position that his life's work could already be considered a finished thing in itself:

[I thought] that both you and John took pride in my accomplishments— and that what I have been able to do in both my writing and painting was a source of satisfaction and pride to you. Up until now, I have never had any indication that you thought otherwise. I gather from your letter you feel I have been wasting my time. [...] I don't speak out of any conceit, but with a certain amount of pride in the fact that I have to my credit a body of work as creditable and sizeable as anyone my age. And if you know of anyone else, of any age, who had made something of a reputation for himself in both literature and art, I would like to know who it is. I remember how pleased both John and you were when I got in "Who's Who." How do you think I got there? You know as well as I the praise my work has had. For instance, I have written 150 poems—all of which have been published and alone would be considered a lifetime's work for most individuals. My new book of poems will eventually find a publisher. I believe in my work, and I even believe in the eventual success and acceptance of my work in painting. I have seen how long men like Hofmann and Knaths and Tobey have had to wait. I have seen how Cézanne and Van Gogh, whose lives you should read, have had to wait. [...] I would never have taken a cent from you if I hadn't believed it was given freely and with faith in my abilities and beliefs. There is no question of my gratitude. [...] I have demonstrated on a number of occasions my ability to take on any job that comes along and make a success of it; and if that becomes necessary again, I will be, I think, fully capable of

dealing with the situation. I shall certainly, however, try to arrange my existence so that I can devote as much of my time as I am able to the work in which I believe, either one of which is actually a full-time job. It has not been easy to try to do a number of things and try to do them well—to hold jobs to bring in money and to write and paint—when I have often been tired and worn out and discouraged. But I have gone ahead anyhow. I never for a moment until now, doubted that you and John shared my sympathies. It has been, and still is, hard to realize that you do not.

Mrs. MacAgy [...] is planning a beautiful and unusual installation.

I have been commissioned to write an introductory article on the art of this region, which the U. of California press will publish. I am to be paid $150 for the piece.

I can't write any more.

Kees kept this letter or a copy, perhaps because he was working at Langley Porter, where psychopathology was shoptalk, where a clinical fascination with the self was part of the job. This self-confession of an out-of-print Prodigal Son must have been as interesting to him as the suicide notes were that he found in case histories.

Nevertheless, Kees's words reveal that Sarah and John had scored hits, that his mother had backed him into a corner. Little in Collingwood could justify his letting *A Breaking and a Death* drift from one publisher to the next—or his lack of interest in writing new poems. Within days—or even hours—of Kees's writing his mother, her admonishments had the desired effect. He typed another kind of desperate letter and sent it to Allen Tate:

Forgive this imposition, but you are about the only person to whom I feel I can turn about this matter. I'm enclosing the manuscript of a new book of poems which I want to publish. I wonder if you know of anyone who might be interested, or for that matter any publisher at all interested in this kind of thing these days. I had a contract with Harcourt for the book; Giroux [...] rejected it on the basis of its 'salable qualities,' [...] the new yardstick. Since then it has been seen by a raft of outfits. [...]

Would you please read it and drop me a line? I think it's a better book than my other two (both now out of print) and still persist in the belief that, however bleak the situation, you may know of someone who might want to take it on.

Taking his setbacks on the waterfront of Point Richmond made it somewhat easier. Weldon and Ann could blame the rejections on the mercenary madness that they knew had taken possession of the East Coast. It was not his fault. It was not his poetry. It was something bigger than they were. Several days after writing Tate, Kees heard from Willy Poster, who confirmed that not much had changed since he and Ann had left. Money did not go very far. The kinds of jobs to be had that left one with the stamina to do creative work were even harder to come by. It was not the happy time that it had been during the war years. Working for the revived *American Mercury* entailed putting up with "no morals, no manners and damned little money," Poster complained—the "same mood," he told Kees, "you felt when you left." He described a New York peopled with restless individuals with some form of "nuttiness, reputation, sex, political or other kind of manias in exaggerated form, singly or combined." The city, to Poster, who possessed the latest manuscript of *A Breaking and a Death,* seemed to emit the sound of distant drums. Indeed, it seemed to "echo your poetry," he told Kees, unintentionally broaching the subject of the vital context that New York had been for his best work. Then he turned to news about a Greenberg "pick" named Larry Rivers and about how Mark Rothko had accosted Manny Farber, fiercely asking the art reviewer, "How's your ulcers?" before stalking off.

Poster's praise for the new manuscript helped revive in Kees the desire to write new poems. So did the invitation to read at the Poetry Guild Festival with Rexroth, Robert Duncan, Madeline Gleason, and other poets on the evening of November 1 at the Museum of Art in San Francisco. There Kees recovered some more of his self-esteem in the wake of his parents' doubts. His one-man show at the Legion of Honor lifted his spirits too:

This show is the best I've had, helped no end by an installation job by Mrs. Douglas MacAgy that beats anything I've seen along such lines. I wasn't permitted to come into the gallery until the show was completely installed. The [...] walls, against which the paintings [...] are hung, are black. In the center of the room is a stockade-shaped screen, about seven feet high, constructed of a heavy steel mesh (black), broken by panels about 2 feet wide and the same height as the whole stockade. The panels are brilliantly painted beaver board—an intense red, a fuchsia, green and black. Eleven collages reside in this enclosure, matted on theatrical gauze and bound in black tape. Two of the larger oils are hung very high, almost to the ceiling. A knockout, I'd say.

Instead of a review of the show, Helga Voigt, an arts reporter for the *San Francisco Examiner,* arranged an interview with Kees at his home in early November. She brought a camera, too, and took pictures of Kees in his studio. His being discovered in Point Richmond, as in Brooklyn four years earlier, provided a newspaper clipping at last for the elder Keeses' scrapbook—and a chance for their son to explain himself less defensively. Voigt wrote that Kees, with a reading on one side of the city and an exhibition on the other, could almost be in two places at once, was not bound by the "modern penchant for specialization" or how "modern society pushes people in one groove": "I just went ahead and started oils. And I didn't give up my writing—one did not exclude the other."

He went on to say that he and Ann intended to stay in California. He compared Point Richmond to Provincetown, where they had "got used to being near the sea." He told the reporter about his books of poetry and the Blumenthal prize he had won. When asked about the poets he read, he mentioned Rilke. He admitted to being influenced by the Elizabethans and the seventeenth-century poets he had read at Nebraska, as well as Eliot and Allen Tate. In defining his conception of good poetry, Kees reminded Voigt of Unamuno. His "gentle voice," she wrote, "became serious. 'In order for poetry to be good it must be rooted in a tragic sense of life ... achieved by the process of growing up in the modern world.' Then Kees paused and brushed his words aside with a quick gesture. 'Oh, let's throw out that stuff,' he said and laughed. 'Art rises from mysterious springs of action ... we should not question its sources,' he continued. 'All I know is I'm miserably unhappy when I'm not working.'"

That autumn, the lukewarm reviews of *Evil under the Sun* forced Kees to quietly divest himself of the psychological investment he had placed in the book. The critics were not even hostile enough for him. Certainly Getty could not have been as wrong about *Evil* as he had been about *Fall Quarter.* (He even went so far as to say that Myrer, in his jacket photograph, looked far more authentic than James Jones did in his "dirty T-shirt and three-day beard" or than Truman Capote with his "bangs and gay vest.") Yet other friends, such as Willy Poster, "didn't much care for it." Malcolm Cowley, in his review, stated that *Evil under the Sun* was just not evil enough.

Kees also felt some disassociation from his own writing. "I don't know what happened to my muse," he wrote Getty in September. "At least the condition does not stimulate a state of anguish as it sometimes used to." For months, the only words he put on paper that even resembled poetry were scraps of the *Richmond Independent* that he glued into his collages, which he intended to show next spring in New York. Their cryptic messages, however, could not be read in any conventional way. They freed him from the heuristics of poetry—and from painting, too, for making collages released him from yet another label he had grown uncomfortable with. As he told Helen Voigt, he no longer considered himself an abstract painter. He wanted a "freer situation than oils," and the feeling he enjoyed with collages had all the freedom of clear, unadulterated vision, turned as much inward as outward. "It might be something you glimpsed somewhere," he said, "like the nostalgia of a peeling billboard ... or it might be a dream—something you would like to have glimpsed somewhere."

Indulging himself in this way of seeing, Kees finished his Peridot consignment during late November and December. This milestone left him with time to relax and read other things besides the ironic headlines and columns he cut from the newspaper. He purchased the new Hogarth Press translation of the poems of Constantine Cavafy, a book that he found "wonderful." Kees had in his poem "The Umbrella" broached the same Hellenic world that Cavafy reinvented in his lyrical poems. Cavafy had worked virtually unpublished, virtually unknown—in a vacuum, almost in secret, in the neglect that Kees believed had formed around him—in Alexandria, a cosmopolitan outpost not unlike San Francisco. Kees saw in the decaying civilization that the Greek poet portrayed a parallel to the American one of his own work. This encounter had a good effect, for Kees started writing new poems, quickly, one after another in the week before Christmas.

At first, they were reworkings of earlier themes, with their scenes, sets, props, and narrations variations on those in older poems, going against what he had said in the late summer, when he had last tried to write poems and felt that he was repeating himself: "Sometimes I incline to the F. Scott Fitzgerald theory of emotional exhaustion, the idea that one has only so large an account to draw on, and once you've drawn on it, that's all there is."

The harsh, New York winters returned in "The End of the Library":

> When the coal
> Gave out, we began
> Burning the books, one by one.

Again, he imagined himself and Ann, joined by one of the surviving cats that they had inherited from the departing McChesneys, Lonesome or Pulque, "huddled, shivering, / against the stove." This time first, tentative lines did not spin off as false starts. Kees put aside his earlier resistance, and the new drafts almost took on a life of their own, following not so much a formula as a personal style that he had to accept as fixed, despite his impatience, his need to have things new and different. After months of disappointment, months that had seen the rejection of his book and his parents' dispraise, months in which his reputation seemed to come down to occupying little more space than his furnished rooms in Point Richmond, Kees found his voice. These rooms contained him, after all, like the other rooms in which he had lived, in Lincoln, Denver, and New York. As in "Xantha Street" and other older poems written in the previous decade, he felt "nailed up" in yet another of the enclosures from which he had projected his wronged worlds. So he returned to his own subgenre of "room poems." He even revisited this Denver street that fascinated him with the rooming houses, bars, and trapped lives—and reinvented it nearby his current lodgings in a new poem, "The Testimony of James Apthorp." Though he had wanted to take a new direction for his work, this showed how it borrowed from the old.

The effect Kees wanted to achieve in "Apthorp" seems to be that of the new *noir* films that he saw in the theaters. He also drew from the movie he had promised all his poems would be, with lines and scenes having a feeling of déjà vu, of having taken place earlier, in other poems. The hallucination of the pygmies, the bridge suicide, the disintegrating family, the black seeds seem familiar and strange at the same time, and all drive Apthorp to beat the druggist over the head with a jar. Kees even brought back the daughter in another form:

A girl of eight, with cancer, sick
For months and newly dusted with the snow.
I used to walk there. Now the vacant places
Fill with ice, and break. They found
Her older sister trying on her clothes at home; her mother
At a bar on Xantha Street.

When Norris Getty read the first draft, it was from his new teaching post at the Groton School, where he was now the Latin instructor. He had settled into his role as one of the masters and found the school an idyllic place, with the look and much of the feeling of a pleasant old army post. Among his students were Cabots, Coolidges, Higginsons, Morgans, Roosevelts, and others with important American names. "The smell of money is pretty strong in all the backgrounds of most of the boys," he wrote Kees, but "the snobbery that shows up later in college doesn't get much chance to operate here. Still, there are always little things to remind a person that this isn't Waco Public H.S."

Getty received the new poems a few days after Christmas, and he saw a new kind of work in "The Testimony of James Apthorp," one with a "real nightmare effect." "After a first rather startled reading," he wrote back, "I went on to realize that the poem is a natural further step in a certain line of development—so natural that you seem not to have broken your stride at all, in spite of your long verseless interlude."

While Getty was reading his new poems, Kees rewarded himself by seeing Kirk Douglas and Lauren Bacall in *Young Man with a Horn* at a Market Street "grind house." He had fun, too, pasting pictures of Santa Claus torn from magazines, newspapers, and greeting cards into some of the Christmas letters that he sent to his "Freudian-inclined friends." These were spin-offs from the collages that he had been making for his next Peridot exhibition, as were the amusing snippets and pictures interpolated between paragraphs of earlier letters, written during the months when he could not write poetry. They had the same tactile quality, too, which seemed necessary when he could rely on the more unfixed art of words. Now that he was writing poems again—he had started yet another ambitious piece, "A Guide to the Symphony"—he was hardly down in the dumps. He looked forward to 1952 with his "Sigmund Claus" letter to the Myrers, in which he pasted a Coca-Cola–

style Santa cheerfully wishing, "Noël! Here's wishing you all an oral Christmas and an anal New Year."

Weldon and Ann made their long-delayed trip to Los Angeles during the second week of January. Depending on the weather and the state of the roads, they intended to visit the Myrers as well on the way back. The trip gave Kees "a new lease on life." He could now take advantage of a standing invitation to stay at the Huntington Hartford Foundation in Pacific Palisades. Not only would it benefit his ego to be treated as one of the creative elite again, but the foundation would help house them and pay for the vacation that he and Ann could no longer afford. They needed this escape, too, for Kees had been suffering from sinus headaches and colitis again. The Lincoln needed engine work and new tires. And because he kept putting off seeing the dentist, Kees complained that his left jaw felt like it was falling. He needed a "good bicuspid man."

Before leaving Point Richmond and driving down the coast, Kees also spent some time in his studio. He tidied up, cleaned brushes, emptied coffee cans filled with spirits. He touched up his latest collage and mentally leafed through the ones that he had already sent Lou Pollack. What he thought surfaced as he later wrote Fritz Bultman: "After a long stretch on the collage pile, I now have 18 of them with Lou for a show in March. [...] I am glad about this work, and the protracted application opened up a lot of new vistas and taught me something. Collage, since Schwitters, has turned into an occasional occupation, when it actually needs to be given the same severe and drawn-out devotion one would give to oils, a novel, a long poem, or a symphonic work."

The revelation made it easier for Kees to let himself believe that the collages had, after all, needed the time he had lost for his poems in 1951. Amazingly, when his Peridot consignment seemed near completion, the poems had come again. With this sense that he had accomplished much in a difficult year of adjustment to his new life and city, Kees hardly noticed the constant back-and-forth of the Lincoln's wiper blades as he and Ann neared Los Angeles during its rainy season. In a letter, he imagined their approach to the city with a mock cinematic quality, with more of the *noir* color that now came when he felt better, when he was writing poems: "Segue into mood music—'Where the Sweet Forgetmenots Remember,' sounds of breaking beer bottles, call of a timber wolf to its mate, quick shots of Thomas Mann opening the front door and getting the milk and the A.M. edition of the Los Angeles *Mirror,* series of dissolve shots of a beat-up 1946 Lincoln sedan headed south on U.S. #101. Quick shots of the Muses, wearing glum and constipated expressions; several of them are reading the *Hollywood Reporter.*"

The Huntington Hartford Foundation consisted of some hundred acres of swank estate tucked away at the bottom of a ravine on Rustic Canyon Road, a private drive off of Sunset Boulevard. Kees had been told the foundation was an easy thirty minutes from Hollywood, but, as he realized, this meant in dry weather, in a movie star's Bugatti, and with a police escort. At the wheel of their Lincoln, he pointed out to Ann that the area around the foundation was remote enough to feature cougars as well as wolves. The houses in which Thomas Mann and another celebrated resident of the area, Aldous Huxley, might live had given way to something close to wilderness.

At the foundation's entrance, Kees nosed the Lincoln up to a huge iron gate. It seemed right out of a Norma Shearer movie from the 1920s and, as it turned out, opened automatically ("by radar, or something") on the exit approach. He used the key that the foundation had given him to open the gate. The final approach to the spot involved going over a narrow road with a deep canyon on one side and what looked like none too secure shale on the other. The road had, by his count, fifty-eight hairpin curves.

The grounds struck Kees as a kind of "Jumbo West Coast Yaddo" and comprised a main building that had evolved from a Frank Lloyd Wright–designed resort, many stables, and about fifteen cabin studios built by Wright's son Lloyd. These were "very snazzy affairs" to Kees, with wall-to-wall carpeting, enormous fireplaces, terraces, kitchenettes, and other amenities, which, he felt, could easily rent for five hundred dollars a month in New York's East Sixties if placed on top of a building. Some of these were now off-limits because of the flooding that came with the rains. There was also the "inevitable" kidney-shaped swimming pool, a feature he pointed out to Ann, to other guests, and to his correspondents in descriptions of the foundation, which he repeated in several letters. He could see more in the pool's biomorphic shape than just the trickle-down influence of avant-garde painting and sculpture. It was more insidious than that. Watching, for a moment, raindrops pelting the still, blue water, he saw those high ideas his painter friends—Baziotes, Gottlieb, Hoffman, Bultman—had being utterly coopted by the American preoccupation with "good living."

Quite unexpectedly, he and Ann encountered a number of people they had known in the East. Among them was Hubert Creekmore, the poet-translator and author of the novel *The Fingers of Night.* He had worked for James Laughlin and New Directions. Now he was busily translating Mallarmé. The poet Howard Griffin was also in residence. Kees detested him for constantly defending Auden's reputation and reminding anyone who listened that Auden was the "Major poet." There was also "a boy from the South, a novelist" from Allen Tate's circle whom Kees had met once before. His name, however, always escaped them. The "group feedings" revealed other coteries and "the inevitable young painter, ex-GI, who has a bad case of interminable Parisian reminiscences," and the "wonderful young writer," who looked like "a chorus boy in a show that failed to open," writing a novel about "elves in Latin America."

Also present was Sy Krim, who found being in Kees's orbit again a bracing experience because Kees was not intimidated by anybody (a quality appreciated by another young writer Kees more suffered than really liked, Norman Mailer, who saw this as a Midwestern or Canadian trait). The Keeses in turn were warm to Krim, even though he was too much under the influence of his friend Milton Klonsky and was playing his "usual well-conceived part as the Existentialist high school boy." Krim did not know whether he liked being "penned" in the foundation or being driven into Hollywood, given that what he knew of the place came from Nathanael West. During the week that the Keeses were there, he kept to his Lloyd Wright cabin and read Tolstoy. Later Krim showed Kees a poem that his friend Klonsky had sent him. It had "all the shattering impact of ten nights" in New York's San Remo Bar and "wd. probably look well in graffiti on a lavatory wall in a New Jersey filling station. The sort of spleen that makes Celine look like a scout leader of Troop Number #10." Krim also let Kees know that Klonsky was working on his autobiography—and presently flying into Los Angeles via TWA.

The foundation's guests quickly bored Kees, and the setting had all the languor of southern California. It was hard, he thought, to be expected to churn out the serious work for which the foundation had been established. The languor even affected the food, of a "rather middle-ground boarding-house type" that hardly rose to the "festive board spread at Yaddo." The foundation had that "nice place to visit, etc.," appeal, but little more. Like the rest of Hollywood, it seemed vaguely make-believe, a feeling reinforced by the knowledge that it had been created for a real Cinderella by Huntington Hartford, the thirty-nine-year-old heir to the A & P Tea Company. He had recently remarried, and his second wife, Marjorie Steele, a former cigarette girl from Reno, as Kees reported, "(a) wants to be a movie star, (b) wants to be a Great Stage Actress, (c) wants to 'do' something" about 'struggling artists.'"

The way her husband met desire (c) seemed to also be an "income-tax dodge" to Kees, an impression that made him feel all the more innocent about not working and using the place as a motor inn from which to make forays into Los Angeles. Unlike Krim and the other disoriented New Yorkers, the Keeses could forgo the foundation's station wagon, which ferried guests to and from the colony like the famous Yaddo station wagon.

In Los Angeles, the Keeses saw Kid Ory play. He had aged noticeably, yet he played his horn well despite a sore throat. His band, however, sounded dispirited to Kees. The sight of an old man trying to live up to his past performances and the Firehouse Five seemed depressing to Kees. He did not like the idea that his brand of music had become a tired exercise. The same mood struck Kees when he saw Red Nichols and his band.

On another evening away from the foundation, Weldon and Ann had dinner with Jim Agee. He seemed in good form after his heart attack. He said he was unhappy in Hollywood and homesick for New York, even with his family now moved out to southern California. But Kees also noted that he was successful. With John Huston, Agee had written the screenplay for *The African Queen,* which the Keeses had just seen in Los Angeles. They told Agee that the movie was certain to win more than one Academy Award. "Katherine Hepburn is better than ever before," Kees said, "and Bogart was his best since *The Maltese Falcon.*"

During the evening, the conversation turned to future plans. Agee told the Keeses about his new script, based on Stephen Crane's short story "The Bride Came to Yellow Sky," a whimsical piece about newly-weds out West. This new project would be a novelty, a *duodrama,* or two films in one, called *Face to Face,* the other feature being Joseph Conrad's *The Secret Sharer.* To their surprise, the Keeses learned that this was the movie that Huntington Hartford wanted to produce for his wife. She would play the bride in the Crane story alongside lead-ing man Robert Preston. "I have a small role in the film, too," Agee casually mentioned—a role he had written for himself. Taking liberty with Crane's story, he had invented a new character, a town drunk who could let himself in and out of jail at will.

As it turned out, the chance to reenter Hollywood offered itself to Kees that same week, and where he might have once resisted the temp-tation, with ideas for "a new kind of movie," there was now no resis-tance. All of a sudden, he put honest art and documentary films out of his mind. Agee's success played into this, as did the proximity to Hollywood and money.

A Turkish film producer, a friend of Nesuhi Ertegun, had interested Douglas Fairbanks Jr. in doing a picture in Istanbul. The aging leading man was "hot" to do it, as Kees pointed out. Studios were no longer offering Fairbanks the roles that had made him famous in Hollywood. Like other fading stars, the actor now looked abroad for a second chance. Ertegun and his producer friend took up most of Kees's time in Los Angeles. They had him read different plot lines and script ideas, which Kees took back to his studio at the foundation. They wanted Kees to help them decide on a story and to collaborate on the screen-play. Ertegun, with "a bee in his bonnet," promised his friend that there was "a fair chance of turning a fast dollar"—an idea that appealed to Kees as he and Ertegun went to work on the first rough treatment: "So: with Ann at the shorthand trick, we managed to dream up a 30-or-so page thriller a la Eric Ambler, which I must say ought to make a picture even the most exacting can sit through. We even managed to ring a few changes on the chase-through-the-streets-of-Istanbul rou-tine, and our false identity devices must be seen to be appreciated. If Fairbanks doesn't bite, perhaps we can sell it elsewhere. [...] Hope something comes of this: cd. certainly use some moola at the moment to take care of my gambling debts, this month's payment on the Bent-ley, etc."

Kees and Ertegun eventually titled their screenplay *Assignment to Peril*. For the hero, Kees invented a debonair academic who moonlights for the government as a secret agent. This would be in keeping with the character of the American doctor Douglas Fairbanks Jr. had recently played in the 1950 British spy thriller *State Secret*.

Kees returned to the foundation with his film ideas and Hollywood gossip, sometimes real and sometimes Keesian make-believe, like the Roberto Rossellini script he imagined in a letter to the Myrers: a modern version of the Sisyphus business planned as a vehicle for Rory Calhoun. It had the working title of *Keep 'em Rolling*, but Kees thought *A Good Stone Uphill Is Hard to Find* sounded better, with the important role of Mrs. Sisyphus going to "Ma Kettle," Marjorie Main. He gave little thought to doing anything more creative, but he found this strange artists' retreat getting stranger and less conducive to work as news spread of Huntington Hartford's rambling, twenty-one-page pamphlet against abstract expressionism, modern novels such as James Jones's *From Here to Eternity*, and contemporary classical music. This letter had been sent to various newspapers around the country with, as Kees noted, circulations of five hundred or more.

The appearance of Milton Klonsky, who showed up for breakfast in the main dining room on the day before the Keeses were to leave the foundation, also had its bad effect. If he knew that Kees detested him, the Village intellectual did not let that get in the way of sitting down with the Keeses and Seymour Krim, for he apprehended that Weldon had a car and knew where the parties were. Then after breakfast he pushed himself back in his chair, stood up with great show, and zipped up his fly with an "Old World charm," as Kees noted in a letter to Conrad Aiken. "It was a ritual he had neglected to perform earlier and lest anyone miss this attention to his toilette, he vocally called the attention of the breakfasting guests to his oversight."

The Keeses came back home to Point Richmond on January 19, finding a cold house, their cats scarred up from various battles during their absence, and stacks of second-class mail. Tired and frustrated, Kees felt like he was still "driving around in the L.A. floods." The California winter rains had washed out stretches of Highway 1 along the way back, forcing him to bypass Big Sur and the Myrers—whose company would have made up for the Klonskys, the Krims, and all the others he loathed at the Huntington Hartford Foundation. This "visitus inter-ruptus," he wrote them, "gave me somewhat the feeling that I'd gone to a double feature & they only showed the Fox newsreel & the D. Duck."

He soon returned to his job at the Langley Porter Clinic—and to another project he had started in December, when, between poems and collages, he had composed a rag on his piano. He liked it enough to give it a title, "Holiday Rag." He even took some of the poster board and glue for his collages and made a portfolio in which to protect the sheet music he had written. For the front cover, he glued down a blank sheet of manuscript paper and brushed it with a bright yellow wash. Then he illustrated it with a color cutout of a stem glass filled with sherry. With large red and black letters, scissored from newspaper ad-vertisements, he labeled the folder HOLIDAY RAG. Underneath the title, he pasted his name, cut from a gallery announcement. When he took his portfolio and new composition to Paul Lingle's house, the pianist played it about seven or eight times and decided he liked it. Lingle said he "could do something with" the piece. By an accident of tim-ing, Lingle was selecting the tunes he wanted to record for Les Koenig, the owner-producer of Good Time Jazz Records in Los Angeles. One of them would have to be Kees's "Holiday Rag." "Whether Koenig will pick it up as one to release is something else," Kees wrote Tony Myrer. "At any rate, I shld. be able to get an acetate for myself of Lingle playing it, which has its charms."

Kees so enjoyed composing a song and collaborating with a profes-sional musician that he began to work on new songs. From this point on, his new vocation took its place in the mix of screenplays, collages, and poems, all running contrary to the focused life and career his par-ents wanted from him now that he was approaching thirty-eight. This, however, was being focused for him. Songs were yet another response to the cultural life that San Francisco made possible, a phenomenon he tried to explain ambivalently in "A Note on Climate and Culture," the piece he wrote for the book *Painting and Sculpture.* Artists in the city benefited from the city's "equable climate" and beauty, its "mea-sure of serenity." But they were not the ones through whom to see these "benisons" transformed into art, into fetish. Kees pointed in-stead to the many architects, designers, ceramists, interior decorators, landscape gardeners, and entrepreneurs of modern furniture densely populating California. He saw their presence as a response to a society preoccupied with "good living" and with the "surface appearance of existence." These makers, from a "solidly entrenched craft tradition," were not too far removed, in a deft turn of social commentary, from other people Kees saw: "Sundays, off highways, in parking lots, in front of the clean angular houses, thousands of men, gripping Simonize containers, polish their gleaming, swollen automobiles; their eyes glow; they seem as intent and devoted as lapidaries polishing old and precious stones."

In February, Kees worked a few days a week at Langley Porter to bring in money, for Ann did not have a regular job. In the afternoons, he played his piano until the new downstairs neighbor, a Swedish exchange student named Brita, came home and started to practice her clarinet. The young woman had a knack for playing Mozart on a solo clarinet that always made it sound like "Three Blind Mice" to the Keeses. When it was quiet again, Kees wrote his fourth new poem since December, tentatively called "A Distance from Macedonia." For him, it was a longer poem, with the "slow revelation of a situation" in which he wanted "a certain amount of mystification." He mentioned it in a letter to Tony Myrer so as to show that he was mortal—and to take the sting out of his strong objections to a short story that Myrer had sent. "Just a shade too much [revelation or mystification]," Kees wrote, "& the whole poem is sunk. Dr. Getty is helping me on this case, as usual, and as usual is just the man to call in."

Strangely enough, Huntington Hartford's pamphlet, *Has God Been Insulted Here?*, had made Kees think about God—and art—and how there was a relationship among a miracle, a divine act, and a work of art. The main impetus behind the new poem, however, was some reading he was doing on biblical scholarship, particularly on a group of nineteenth-century German religious historians who attempted a completely literal account of the life of Christ. On a certain level, he wanted the poem to be a satire of the realism expounded by these religious historians. "From that," he wrote Getty, "it was only a question of carrying this sort of thing one step further." There was also an element of showmanship, stage direction, light and sound, the business, which Kees had brought with him all the way from the puppet shows in Beatrice—and fresh from Hollywood:

That raft we rigged up, under the water,
Was just the item: when he walked,

With his robes blowing, dark against the sky,
It was as though the unsubstantial waves held up
His slender and inviolate feet. The gulls flew over,
Dropping, crying alone; thin ragged lengths of cloud
Drifted in bars across the sun. There on the shore
The crowd's response was instantaneous. He
Handled it well, I thought—the gait, the tilt of the head, just right.

"I stuck pretty close to the Jesus story," Kees later admitted to Getty, "but used the walking-on-water business in the daytime because I wanted the poem to move from sunlight-daytime imagery to the nightfall at the end. As it is fixed up now, in accordance with yr. suggestions, I think it now has the proper tone of 'clear ambiguity.'" The poem, as he pointed out to Tony Myrer, was "about" the nature of art. "That is, to be down-to-earth as possible, even though art comes about through such mundane methods as building rafts under water," Kees wrote, "it is art in the end and we do experience the ecstasy." For the disciple in the poem, the ecstasy comes from "our making" the raft, "the summit of the whole experience."

"There is nothing like it, Weldon, that I have read anywhere," Willy Poster wrote Kees after reading the poem under its new title, "A Distance from the Sea." "Everything about it, its language, feelings, could only have emerged out of very special experiences, experiences so important and so complex, I don't think anybody has understood them and nobody else has at all utilized them as you have." He wondered if anyone was capable of responding to the poem fully. Yet he was certain the poem deserved to be published and could be published despite the most obtuse editors, responsible for the "ruck of the magazines." "There is a vibration, a controlled originality about it that I think even the hemmed-in litterateurs who control things these days should get."

The winter rains let up in late February, and the roads opened to Big Sur, allowing the Keeses to spend several days with the Myrers. The visit was strained, however, for Tony had taken Kees's remarks about the short story "Weep for Memory" too personally, and it was hard for Kees to soften his real feelings or blame himself. ("This is a bad problem of mine," he wrote Myrer, "that the boys on the fourth floor of the Langley Porter Clinic are now working on.") While Kees believed the quality of his friend's fiction had slid, Myrer wanted out from under Kees's influence, which had led to the problems the critics had found in *Evil under the Sun*. Still, in the name of fair play, Kees had sent his new poems down to Big Sur in advance of the visit, giving Myrer the chance to give "as good as he got."

Kees, however, felt confident about his new poems. He was waiting to hear from *Partisan Review*, having sent "The Testimony of James Apthorp" directly to Philip Rahv rather than to Delmore Schwartz, the poetry editor. Kees asked Rahv to make a "quick decision" on the poem and to bypass Schwartz, who had the habit of holding onto Kees's submissions until "the paper had grown yellow." He also knew that Schwartz was paranoid enough to consider him a rival, given what Willy Poster reported on Schwartz's mental state: "Delmore Schwitz [*sic*] has taken residence twenty miles outside Princeton where he is about to do some teaching or be poet-in-residence. His house is a shambles of no plumbing, broken walls etc which he cannot cope with. Phil sold him a car which broke down promptly. Shortly afterwards his lawn-mower was stolen and then passing through town cops picked him up and grilled him for three hours about a kidnapping! He then got two parking tickets (twenty-dollars each) and then the cops arrived in his house to question him about the theft of the lawn-mower and Delmore burst into tears and screamed 'You're persecuting me!' "

Instead of making a decision on the poem himself, however, Rahv sent it on to Schwartz, probably without opening the envelope or screening the cover letter. This, unfortunately, elicited more than just the expediency that Kees had requested. Obviously annoyed at him, Schwartz rejected the Apthorp poem. There were fine passages, he wrote, but the poem "did not come off as a narrative whole." Schwartz then went on to apologize for his "dilatory habits as an editor," which irritated Kees. "Since I don't get paid any longer as an editor of P.R., I have had to take on three part-time jobs which do pay me," Schwartz complained.

This should have wounded Kees, but he took the news mildly as other setbacks—of a nonliterary order—accumulated. The mechanic's prognosis for the Lincoln was not good. It needed an engine overhaul, and this would be "a fearful blow to the Kees exchequer." Douglas Fairbanks now wanted to do a movie in India, putting the Turkish movie in "limbo." Paul Lingle had recorded thirty-five thousand feet of tape for Good Time Jazz, but the producer, somewhat dissatisfied, had cut many of the tunes, including "Holiday Rag."

To keep from dwelling on his disappointments, Kees read new novels throughout March and April. He liked *Swanson* by Timothy Pember for its "heavy influence on the woof side by E. M. Forster, and on the warp side by Thos. Hardy." An Avon reprint of *How Brave We Live*, Paul Monash's first novel, brought the contemporary Village scene back to life. He also enjoyed Mary McCarthy's new book, *The Groves of Academe*, but not enough to make him, as Henry Volkening hoped, rework *Fall Quarter*. (The literary agent refused to follow the "drastic advice" that he should throw it away. Instead he asked Kees to look it over: "There's just a chance that you will still see in it what you once saw, and what I still see.")

Ann and Weldon, as before, kept to a social schedule that permitted them a balance of friendship and privacy.

The Keeses also looked forward to getting into the city to have dinner, as they did with Marie Rexroth, Kenneth's first wife, in March. During the course of the evening's conversation, as the three discussed the poetry scene in San Francisco and who was popular on college campuses (Dylan Thomas, et al.), Marie revealed some news about a rival that she knew would get an amusing response from Kees: "Hold tight! Guess who's in town? Yep, Kenneth Patchen, no less, along with devoted, fun-loving helpmate Miriam, recipient of many a dedication of a noble vol. Seems the P.'s have been living right here in SF for a good three months, all unbeknownst to us. Out of the 'Save Kenny at All Costs' campaign of poetry-reading, with Sister Edith Sitwell rattling the tambourines."

Underneath the amusement Kees took in Kenneth Patchen was some resentment. Patchen was popular on American campuses, and Kees's book, with the title *A Breaking and a Death*, was not what a college man would give his girl even if it were published now and not soldiering on at the trade houses. His manuscript was back at Farrar, Straus, and Young, thanks to the intervention of the poet Hugh Chisholm, soon earning another of the kind of rejection letters Kees had been receiving, which said the rejection was not his fault but the fault of "the economics of publishing." Kees's book also ran counter to another kind of economics. Given "what your poetry costs to produce," Willy Poster told him, seeing it neglected amid all the second-rate poetry rising around it, getting it published was "not worth the candle."

"What you say about my poems was very good to hear," Kees wrote back. "I get a bit sunk at times."

Kees took his Bell and Howell movie camera virtually everywhere he went. It was stored in the Lincoln's trunk, with other equipment, so that he had ready access to it when he left Langley Porter to work in the field with Gregory Bateson. It did not take Kees long to realize that the camera's presence made it equally convenient for putting to some better use. After his collaboration on *Adventures of Jimmy*, he felt the urge to make an experimental film of his own. This urge took its course in April, when Kees, driving home from Berkeley to Point Richmond, noticed that a whole district had been slated for demolition for a super-highway; it was leaving a ghost city of the past almost lifted from his poems: "avenues you saw demolished years before."

One day, he parked his car, got out, and began to explore the vacant buildings. One of them caught his eye, a two-story boardinghouse called Hotel Apex. The irony of such a simple building, which had probably been home to workers from the nearby oil refinery and the whores who serviced them, was all the more striking given its setting. Inside, he must have been struck by the interiors of the rooms. They were very much like the interiors he had imagined for certain poems. They almost seemed to whisper, as bits of glass and debris crunched under his shoes, the first of his "Five Villanelles":

> The crack is moving down the wall.
> Defective plaster isn't all the cause.
> We must remain until the roof falls in.

Kees brought back his camera and filmed cracks, piles of paper, peeling wallpaper, windows, and stairwells. Without giving away the location of the hotel, as Manny Farber would later write in the *Nation,* he let the camera "crawl" down a steampipe "at the pace of a half-dead bug," rest on a broken light socket, stare down a toilet bowl, and study an old newspaper's headline and the word "MacArthur." Kees had to work quickly, for the Hotel Apex was next in line for the wrecking ball. There were already gaping holes in the building that let in enough light for him to shoot eight hundred feet of film. The project consumed him for a time. By the third week of April, he was ready to add sound, but he could not make the film short enough to harmonize with the 78 that he wanted to use for the score: a George Lewis recording of New Orleans funeral-march music. The building's "starker" personality did not go with Lewis's clarinet. The architectural debris, with its many shapes, lines, and textures, came together in a way that reminded him of another kind of music: "Then repeated viewings convinced me it needed something astringent, nostalgic, woebegone and marked by many changes of rhythm & beat. [...] I showed it to a friend of ours [...] & she suggested something of Alban Berg's—Concerto for Violin, Piano, and 13 Wind Instruments. We played it against the picture & it was damned spooky: almost scene for scene it was right; one might have thought the picture had been cut to fit the music."

The first people to see *Hotel Apex* praised it for the primitive quality of Kees's camera work and cutting. Manny Farber compared it to the drawings of the *Moon Mullins* comic strips. But Kees's pattern of being both the throwback and the forerunner is present in his little film, too. Other critics saw his film as an advance in technique. Ernest Callenbach saw *Hotel Apex* as a return to the "embryonic years of the cinema"; however, instead of keeping the camera stationary, Kees moves with it and gives the impression of walking through a gallery of photographs:

The camera wanders around a deserted and disintegrating building, up stairs and along corridors, peering at the interesting and the trivial with impartial, insatiable curiosity. Not a cockroach stirs—only, along toward the end of the film, a sparrow hops a few paces, a startling revelation and almost the sole moving thing shown in the entire film.

But the camera's own movement emphasizes, in an uncanny way, the non-movement, the decay and death, of what it sees. The very uncertainty of its movement is a constant reminder of the uncertainty, casualness and improvisation of our real perceptions; it is a sign of life in the midst of things which are uniformly still.

In early May, Kees showed the picture with the music to Brant Sloan and Robert Greensfelder, the founders of Kinesis, Incorporated, a company in San Francisco that distributed experimental films. They liked *Hotel Apex* enough to offer to pay for the scoring and a print as an advance on royalties.

Not long after his little success, Kees woke urgently one morning, having nearly wet his bed. As he relieved himself in the bathroom, he saw a cloud of blood forming in his urine. Despite being badly frightened, he went to Langley Porter, thinking the symptoms were from cheap liquor. At work, however, the bleeding continued with each trip to the lavatory. Unable to endure the sight of his own blood in the toilet bowl, the burning sensation, and the thought that he had something fatal, Kees phoned a urologist and made an appointment. The doctor immediately had him admitted to Saint Luke's Hospital. There, in an unappealing ward, the bleeding cleared up before his medication took effect. Nevertheless, the urologist wanted to make sure his patient did not have prostate cancer, and Kees was ordered to stay in the hospital for a week. The fifteen dollars a day soon obsessed him more than "pissing blood." It was another sign that the ennobled, loft-rat subsistence that had worked in New York and Provincetown after the war no longer worked. Increasingly, he and Ann felt they were being "jumped on, pummeled, and put through the wringer by financial ogres."

The cost of the hospital stay, the lost time at work, and the rebuilding of the car's engine had to be absorbed by savings—and cashing in an insurance policy, which meant going through Weldon's parents. This time some of the money he needed would be covered by his and Ann's own efforts. A check had just arrived from Peridot, the result of the first sales of his art in over a year: a collage and a large oil. And Ann had taken a job at the psychiatric division of the University of California Hospital, handling the admission papers of students "with mental woes."

∾

In May 1952, Kees began the month by telling one friend, "Things have momentarily taken a turn for the better." A few weeks later, however, Karl Shapiro of *Poetry* returned "A Distance from the Sea" as "too long" and as reminiscent of Eliot's "Journey of the Magi." More depressing mail filled the letterbox—and some of the old pastimes that the Keeses had used to forget these things were no longer there. Paul Lingle had left San Francisco for Honolulu, where he now performed in a hotel for one hundred dollars a week and taught piano lessons to a beautiful Japanese girl, the daughter of a sugar planter. Kees did not envy his friend so much as he kept working on his own technique and composition, letting himself go, imagining himself entertaining the tourists in some exotic port of call, café, or cantina, no longer the washed-up poet, the stillborn painter.

In June, Kees learned from Hugh Chisholm that *A Breaking and a Death* could not be published: "It's a world of money, for money, by money. And though your poems will outlast any financial balances, I guess patience is the only answer."

In Chisholm's letter was a copy of a memo from Stanley Young, in which he reported to his partner, John Farrar, that he had taken Kees's manuscript with him to England and shown it to publishers there. Young had shown it to five publishers in London: Lehman, Warburg, Gollancz, Hart-Davis, and Cresset. Young and Farrar hoped that if one of the English houses took *A Breaking and a Death,* sheets could be imported for an American edition—a measure that had been used before to avoid the production costs for unprofitable literary titles. In his own letter, John Farrar even apologized for not being able to publish *A Breaking and a Death* and then sent the manuscript back by express, prepaid.

Fortunately, in June Kees's friend John Pauker of *Furioso* accepted "A Distance from the Sea," the Apthorp poem, and "A Guide to the Symphony" in what would be the next-to-last issue of a magazine that had long been Kees's "dependable market."

The Mills of the Kavanaughs and, later, *Homage to Mistress Bradstreet* denoted the new fashion for the longer poem. Kees could not see himself writing to such lengths, but he now seemed to realize that *A Breaking and a Death* needed more depth, and he pushed himself through the torpor of the summer of 1952. He had long been fascinated with existentialism; that, and his reading Conrad Aiken's new book, *Ushant,* fed his idea for an ambitious poem about time as the facilitator and trap of selfhood, an enormity that Aiken must have inspired with his own vision of the universe: "The stars, suns, moons, comets, nebulae, are the burning jewels of that majestic mechanism, into which, perhaps, the great horologist is this very minute gazing fixedly through his inquisitorial eye-piece. Is it going as it should?"

Norris Getty had asked his friend for a long poem the year before. Kees drew on his past to begin the poem, which he tentatively called "The Hours," beginning the first part, as he had "1926," in Nebraska, where his disillusionment and disappointment had begun, small and personal, before growing ever outward. He ended the first part with a monstrous vision of America, a vision that Allen Ginsberg and the Beats would later take on, in keeping with the inflated promise of the election year of 1952, which would pit Adlai Stevenson, the governor of Illinois, against General Eisenhower:

For in the violent stream, a thing is observed
And carried away, and another comes in place,
And it too will be carried away. A plume of steam
Hisses above the factory, and a thousand
Ham sandwiches come out of the lunch pails.

The poem continued to gestate in late July while Kees worked on a "daffy" project at Langley Porter, partly inspired by a film about Michelangelo painting the ceiling of the Sistine Chapel that Jurgen Ruesch had seen. Ruesch felt that the interiors of people's homes contained plenty of nonverbal communication in how furnishings were arranged. He asked Kees and Gregory Bateson to begin photographing the interiors of different kinds of houses from top to bottom. The work bored them.

A paid vacation in August gave Kees the chance to spend his time at home, "more or less holed up, writing, playing the piano, reading" such books as *Witness* by Whittaker Chambers. Chambers's Christian justification for his transformation from communist to conservative, his betrayals, and his cooperation with Congressman Nixon sickened Kees once again, as it had when the story had first been in the newspapers, several years before. The latest issue of *Partisan Review* fed Kees's revulsion, for Philip Rahv, in a review of *Witness*, had drawn a comparison between the editor of *Time*'s back pages and *Sports Illustrated* and Dostoyevsky and his religiosity. "To such stuff as this," Kees wrote of using Christ in place of secular truth, "I say, resoundingly, loudly, and with spirit, No."

During his vacation, the Keeses' relationship with their downstairs neighbor became a war of nerves. Brita complained about the noise from the Kees apartment at every opportunity, forcing Kees to play his piano when she was not at home. One day, however, she deviated from the "normal schedule" that he had become attuned to and started banging on the ceiling underneath the floor. She screamed at Kees to stop playing and continued to scream even long after he had stopped. After several days of this behavior, which included banging garbage-can lids together like cymbals, the police had to be called: "The screaming, chanting, denunciation whatever, with the decibel quality of Wild Bill Davison, went on without letup. It may well have been heard in neighboring cities. — Pretty soon an ossifer came groping through the bamboo & we had a hushed conversation with him.

He first wanted to know if she was on the hard stuff or something & we said we thought not. Then he inquired, 'Having a fight with the boy friend?' I said that she was of the lizzie persuasion."

Hearing this, the policeman called for backup. Soon a prowl car pulled up to the house, and Brita "assumed the role of the astonished, hurt, and ever-peace-loving citizen." She claimed that she had only been reading Swedish poetry aloud.

Brita was at last evicted, and the Keeses' life got back to normal with watching their cats in the yard, listening to the breeze in the eucalyptus trees, going down to the beach, and typing the new installments of "The Hours." In the poem, this ambiance filters in, Kees remembering the spirit that left New York when he did two years before. The poem also plays on fear of the atom bomb, the vulnerability that Kees and his friends felt living in cities that had become bull's-eyes in Moscow and Washington.

Through much of September and early October, Weldon and Ann drove down to Berkeley in their shabby Lincoln either to their jobs or to search for an apartment. The night of Brita inspired a "powerful urge to move" in them, and they wanted to be closer to their jobs and not have to drive to work. The classifieds led them to one depressing house after another, with "wallpaper out of the later novels of Frank Norris, enough light green walls to divide the Stevens Hotel, neighborhoods of a Gogol-like cast, dead ends, deadlocks and dead centers, peeling bathrooms with colored pictures of chickens and rosy children by way of decalcomania."

After all this, they found a small but "delightful" duplex apartment near the Berkeley campus, at 2713 Dana Street, which had room for the piano and generous built-in bookshelves. Having such a new home raised their spirits—almost as much as the presidential candidacy of Adlai Stevenson, something Weldon had started to count on, like many of his peers.

It was one thing to count oneself among the tiny readership of the *Nation*, reading its "ammunition" on what would happen if there were a Republican victory. Now the polls, though, were beginning to point to a Stevenson victory. The network commentators had even picked him to win by a good margin. This even seemed possible to Kees:

Caught S. on his appearance here in Berkeley at the West Gate of the UC campus. Bogart, Bacall, Fred Clark, Mercedes McCambridge & some local politicos also appeared. Stevenson had a remarkable sense of his audience & the speech cd. scarcely be construed to be a vote-getting one in the ordinary sense of campaigning activity. The charm is enormous & the wit, combined with an ad lib ability scarcely second to Fred Allen's, is a bit breathtaking. There seems to be such intelligence here that he scarcely needs to try: just scoops out little bits & these suffice. I cannot say I was moved, but enormously impressed & touched by the man; anyway, considering a lot of things, I'd just as soon not be moved by politicians.

As Kees tried hard to remain upbeat about his candidate, on another front he had to once again swallow yet another rejection of *A Breaking and a Death,* this time by the twentieth publisher. The poet Louis Simpson, then an editor at Bobbs-Merrill, admitted it was ironic that he should have to reject Kees's poems: "I have always admired your work and think that this is a truly excellent collection." This disappointment was added to the one that came from his vain hope that he could get "The Hours," now finished, into *Partisan Review:* "It came back (a bit smudged and wrinkled & thumbmarked) with a note from Just Plain Delmore saying that they 'can't see that it justifies its length. It has a good many beautiful perceptions, but weak formulations also, particularly those about Becoming.' Thus spake the editor who has recently printed such strongly formulated lines as 'The swollenest dream can't bulge beyond / the circular realm.'"

Kees, Schwartz, poets, and much of the rest of America's intelligentsia awoke after Election Day expecting their candidate to have won. Kees had even put a small wager on a Stevenson victory. John Berryman was so high on Stevenson that he did not want his liberal hero and champion to be merely president, but king. Instead of a coronation, though, Stevenson's supporters discovered a Republican landslide. Eisenhower's victory, which had developed during the early-morning hours, ended the hoped-for chance of an administration that would be generous to writers, painters, and intellectuals. Stevenson's defeat now assured a more banal Dark Age than the one they had already imagined around them. For Kees, this setback was another thing he would have to wait out, like the circumstances preventing his book from being published: "To me it was a fairly graphic demonstration of Gresham's law all over again, a triumph for the soap-opera &

singing commercial boys; and the campaign was probably the last one within our lifetimes that a Presidential candidate will conduct himself with even a modicum of honor & intelligence. Even so, I think I have steeled myself sufficiently to take it for the next forty-eight months, although I hope people won't hold it against me if I gag a little now & then at Dick & Pat."

While Kees reconciled himself to a Republican Dark Age, he received a letter from his old champion Malcolm Cowley on Viking Press stationery. Even Cowley knew that this was the same letter his friend had received too many times. However, unlike the others, Cowley was perceptive and honest enough to tell his younger friend things that might have been repressed for too long. *A Breaking and a Death* was not a book yet, Cowley said: "The style has more weight than the subjects and I am not sure that this particular book of yours justifies the quotation from the *Marble Faun*—I mean that the poems descend into a lot of little caves instead of one dark cavern."

In a way, Cowley was gently telling his younger friend that he had not gone all the way as a poet, whereas Kees believed he had made the full descent more than once—even as he spread himself out into painting, filmmaking, and making music. He left his book little changed and sent it on to a friend from his Denver days, Alan Swallow, who had an arrangement with William Morrow to print limited editions and pamphlets of poetry.

Everything was new and clean in the Dana Street apartment, with good colors on the walls. Ann repainted much of their furniture and tastefully decorated the rooms. The centerpiece was still the piano. Kees had to trade his beloved old Melville Clark upright for a small piano that fit through the apartment's door. But the new piano did have a "raggier" sound—and he now lived near one of the largest university libraries in the country and could find whatever book or journal he wanted. The only real disadvantages were the rent, which was higher than what the Keeses had paid before, and the lack of a place to set up a studio. For the present, Kees had to paint in the basement, where the landlord, who lived in the front of the house, always seemed to be passing through and stopping to watch. What little painting he did now was like "trying to take a bath at a D.A.R. meeting."

In November, the pleasure Kees derived from observing his own pets was counterpointed at Langley Porter, where Gregory Bateson started working with him on a new film about the nature of "play" with funds from a Rockefeller grant. For one day a week, Kees and Bateson filmed children interacting with animals. They visited the local zoos, too, and shot otters, raccoons, and bears. This work and the data photographs and films he had been making for Dr. Ruesch's ambitious study of nonverbal communication provided Kees with a paycheck. The Keeses' money problems, however, did not go away. And the Lincoln needed a new gear for its increasingly unreliable transmission.

Fortunately, money was scraped together to fix the car in time to drive down to Monterey at the end of November. There Weldon and Ann spent a relaxing weekend with the Myers, who had moved from the wilds of Big Sur. Kees brought his Rolliflex and Leica and took photographs of his friends, as well as many photographs of the Monterey Wharf—and the roadside attractions that could not be passed by. The diners and bars, each with some variation of a nautical setting applied to its storefront, authenticated their place, purpose, and promise of some simulacrum of the maritime life. If you drank a beer here or ate seafood there, you would enjoy them *like* a real sailor. If you purchased your bait from the store with a carved fish sign, you would catch fish *like* a fisherman. All of this was accomplished through intentional and accidental tableaus that, to Kees, were like found works of art and poetry, albeit primitive. They seemed to offer possibilities for illustrating what was fast becoming his book as much as Ruesch's.

Kees filled a roll of film on the way back. In the town of Gilroy, he took a photograph of a palm reader's sign with two giant pink palms groping toward a vacant lot. He thought up captions for the photographs that might work in the book and tested them out on Ann. A hotdog stand that serviced its customers from a sheet-metal wiener seemed to communicate the "philosophy of the common man." A defaced billboard advertising a career as an Air Force cadet: "nihilism." The photograph of the building with the pink hands: "translation." He was learning "how damned difficult it is to take a first-rate picture."

Back home, Kees read from a pile of *Provincetown Advocates* that the Myers had given him. He said he would not mind catching up on the Cape scene, even as he neglected his own painting downstairs in the basement of the Dana Street apartment. He had little enthusiasm for the newest gallery in San Francisco, Area Arts, which had offered to show his work. He felt that he should not exhibit there given how little he had finished—two paintings since the Legion show the year before. Despite this, the owner of Area Arts, Robert Nack, still wanted to sell his work if an arrangement could be made with Peridot Gallery, which still represented him. "Only tourists go to the Legion," Nack said as a way of convincing Kees. Having an entirely new one-man show in the Bay Area would bring in people who would buy paintings.

Kees relented, but he passed on writing reviews for *Art Digest*. The ten dollars a column seemed "horrendously substandard." Belle Krasne, the editor, also would not give Kees carte blanche to write about whatever shows and issues were important to him, an arrangement he had enjoyed at the *Nation*. It would be like "having Mama picking out the things you're to eat from the restaurant menu."

At this time, painting and writing about art had been pushed aside by Kees's passion for jazz. He could even see himself giving up his poetry to pursue a second career as a jazz pianist in the smoky clubs of San Francisco and Los Angeles, like his friend Paul Lingle. On Kees's part, there was now almost a quiet escape, a segue from being too much the poet. The jazz, the photographs, were all signs of this escape, as was a blurb he approved for the Kinesis catalog, which stated that *Hotel Apex* was "the first motion picture which has not a trace of any attempt to lend literary meaning to its material." He could not escape, however, the expectations of his parents. They were thinking of him. They had sent him a package for Christmas. He opened it and found warm clothes.

Someone must have told Kees that his dry wit and ironic poems reminded him or her of *New Yorker* cartoons. This or something like it encouraged him to write down cartoon ideas and send them out to the *New Yorker* cartoonists he had befriended while living in the East. The first batch, from which Kees had hoped to make some money, had come back from Charles Addams, whose "family" cartoons were not far removed from some of the personalities Kees had invented for his poems. (The critic Joseph Warren Beach, in *Obsessive Images* [1960], noted the similarity between the poems in *The Fall of the Magicians* and the macabre cartoons of Addams.) The material, according to Addams, was too shocking for the editors, and more than a few of the gags closely resembled something Addams had already done.

"I've tried the rumpus room before with no success," Addams tactfully wrote back on one occasion; "the snarl I did do for the New Yorker a year or so ago, 'All right children, sneer.'"

Kees persisted. He sent new ideas back to Addams—and other cartoonists at the *New Yorker*. Whitney Darrow Jr. returned an envelope filled with gags to Kees in late January 1953, which Kees sent back to Peter De Vries, hoping that the editor who had published the Robinson poems might show the gags to yet another *New Yorker* cartoonist.

Despite the burst of interest and energy that Kees used on this sideshow, nothing came of it. He would have to depend on the income he made from making films with Bateson "at fair pay," funded by a thirty-thousand-dollar Rockefeller Foundation grant that, he said triumphantly, "Alfred Kazin curiously did not manage to snag on." Kees also worked three days a week on the communications project with Jurgen Ruesch, making documentary films using the hidden-camera technique borrowed from Helen Levitt and producing "a photographic book on communication that," he guaranteed, "will be unlike any book heretofore."

That he was still considered a painter and a member of the "club" reminded Kees that he needed to service this role with at least more than a token gesture. His painter friends still wrote him. One of the first letters he had received in the new year was Adolph Gottlieb's, filled with news about his newest paintings ("radical departures"), shows, and the gallery Sam Kootz had opened in Provincetown. This was followed by a letter from Lou Pollack informing Kees that he needed a piece for a watercolor, drawing, and collage show to open on March 2. He wrote Kees again to tell him that an executive at Columbia Records wanted contemporary artists to design album covers for jazz releases. Pollack had shown the executive some of Kees's collages and explained that Kees was not only a painter but also a jazz critic and a poet of considerable reputation. With such a background, Pollack had little trouble getting terms that would pay Kees $275 for each album illustration. "Once the music were decided on," Pollack wrote from New York, "you would be given a free hand to design as you saw fit. This indicates that they'd work with you if you agree. The prestige involved would also be great since they are conducting a big publicity campaign on the covers."

Kees's one-man show at Area Arts opened on January 6 and ran through January 31. It went much less painfully than his openings in New York, which had always been underattended because of rain and snowstorms of "Jack London proportions." A good crowd turned out, and he even sold a painting, an oil titled *Zed*.

Kees sent a mixed-media work—ink and collage—to Peridot. He also had some pieces in a traveling show that Peridot sponsored in the Midwest and some collages with the art-lending service of the Museum of Modern Art. (Museum members could rent works of modern art, with a modest fee going to the artist—a plan, Pollack reported, that had yet to make a profit.) Kees had to beg off committing himself to any oil show for the next art season, even though Pollack wanted him to benefit from the gallery's growing reputation and its move to be near Fifty-seventh Street, a commercial necessity Kees found hard to approve ("Peridot is so closely identified in my mind with East 12th Street that I can't conceive of it uptown").

Two days before his thirty-ninth birthday, he wrote Bill and Ethel Baziotes. Studying a photograph of Baziotes on a printed announcement from the Kootz Gallery had reminded him that he had been delinquent: "Bill's expression seemed to convey a message to me, viz.: 'That bastard Weldon is later than usual with his annual letter.'" The reason for this was that he had little to do with the art scene of the West Coast. Instead he and Ann "hobnob mostly with jazz musicians of the SF–New Orleans revival persuasion."

From this circle, Kees had befriended the San Francisco clarinetist Bob Helm, whom he first encountered on jazz records by Lu Watters and Turk Murphy. Now both men were collaborating on a growing pile of sheet music, an endeavor that had grown from Turk Murphy's request that Kees write some lyrics for one of the band's songs.

"This association is most pleasant, productive, and may eventually be profitable," Kees wrote hopefully in February about his new venture, to which he contributed the words and Helm, typically, the music. "Our conscious intent is to fly in the face of the current dreck & our watchword is 'Back to the Twenties!' Or even further."

The whole experience of writing songs helped Kees to skirt the tepid support of his parents ("Of course we hope that some of your songs will click"). His sessions with Helm were always well lubricated with bottles of Jack Daniels Old Time Sour Mash to "enliven our labors" and act as a "splendid catalyst." It was now "Helm & me composing madly" on new material or improving the rags, blues ballads, and torch songs from his "Holiday Rag" folder, like "Why Are You Telling Me about the Moon?" and "You've Gone," which sounded nothing like the death-blow lines of his poems:

> The Poets write about enchanting graces,
> Romantic places they've known.
> But all I want is to be where your face is,
> Coming close to my own.

The song that Helm and Kees felt would be their best, indeed, the one that might *sell*, came after they had been working together for nearly three months. "Pick Up the Pieces" had the right balance of tastefulness, wit, and the bittersweet. It also had a little of the color of Kees's poetry under its smart surface, a kind of brittle chill, playing, as it did, on the notion of the fragmented being of existentialism, of clinical psychology. It was something Robinson would have played at "tempo di schitzi," as annotated in Kees's hand on the music's manu-script:

> Pick up the pieces; that's all that's left of me now.
> I'm like a cocktail glass that shattered in your hand.
> [. . . . .]
> [P]ick up the pieces; throw them away, say amen,
> because like Humpty Dumpty I can't be put together again.

The songwriting went on through much of early 1953, with Kees and Helm getting together at least once or twice a week. Not since he was a boy had Kees had as much fun as he now enjoyed, living out some-thing that was part second childhood and part serious business ven-ture. It even had a place for Ann, since Helm's pretty wife, Kay, was often present at her husband's sessions, and her company brought Ann out of her natural reserve and helped her form a new circle of friends. Kees found his new collaborator to be "a highly sensitive & aware sort of person, and unlike any jazz musician I've known before."

In early April, Kees received a brutally frank rejection letter from Ed-mund Nash of McGraw-Hill. It followed a rather auspicious communi-cation from the editor, who had received *A Breaking and a Death* upon the recommendation of Bill Roth. Nash had promised Kees that he would do everything in his power to handle the book once he got over "the shock of seeing some good poetry." The suddenness of Nash's letdown compelled Kees to put his book of poems in a drawer, rather than follow Nash's advice to send it to New Directions.

As Kees tried to forget about his poetry, he hardly noticed the interest that Dylan Thomas was bringing, as Nemerov reported from the Bennington campus, where the Welsh poet had just read. Kees was now temporarily removed from this other world, where coeds and college men flocked to hear poets read their verse and then sought their heroes out in the off-campus pubs. Thomas's drinking bout at the White Horse Tavern in New York and his subsequent death left Kees unfazed. Instead, he felt the approach of forty. He felt all of the significance placed on that age as a signpost of personal success—or failure. "The lacerating effects of middle age are dreadful," he wrote Norris Getty. "What the routes to wisdom along this particular terrain are I wish I knew. The trick of repeating, 'It can't get any worse,' is certainly no good, when all the evidence points to quite the opposite."

Near the end of April, Kees and Ann visited his parents in Santa Barbara, where they were staying until the end of May. It was more of an obligation—"the better to have us in their power"—than a getaway. Strolling behind his silver-haired parents at the International Cymbidium Orchid Show and visiting such sights as the old mission church in Santa Barbara, Kees felt as if he were in tow, the apocalyptic poet and jazzman trapped in his mother's orbit and slumming in reverse among the curious Catholic artifacts, like a comic-book life of Christ and a "Pray for Peace While You Drive" Recording Rosary order blank, which he pasted in a letter to the Myrers. He felt "tired, very tired," when he and Ann returned to Berkeley with his parents, who stayed for a short time until they seemed "disenchanted" and left for "huggable, lovable Lincoln."

He had enough energy, however, to lecture on jazz at San Francisco State College in late May and June, using his Forum 49 notes and his aging record player, which, like the Lincoln's dangling muffler, had recently been "in the hospital." And he must have been reminded that he was still a poet, even encouraged, by a letter from Countess Caetani in Rome. She wanted to buy "The Hours" for *Botteghe Oscure*.

༄

During the summer of 1953, Kees worked with Bateson on the last of their films as their grant money ran out. The work on the nonverbal-communication book, however, with the working title *Message through Object*, continued. For the past six months, Kees had sorted through nearly three thousand photographs with his coauthor, Dr. Ruesch, using their data to "find out what people are really saying through the arrangement of things," as he told Getty. The text consisted of a word-by-word collaboration between himself and Ruesch, making it clear that he had not simply cleaned up for Ruesch, a Swiss émigré whose native tongue was German and whose prose had been affected by years of writing clinical reports. For his part, Kees was responsible for the book's cultural editorializing, and he sometimes reworked this imper-sonal monograph in a personal way:

The specialists in mass communication, recruited largely from radio and television, advertising, propaganda, and the big circulation magazines, seem to gear their operations to a single end: capturing an audience and controlling its thought. Often the advertisers share with the popularizers the intent to shape a world in which the principle of least effort is sup-posed to pay off: a world in which everyone will smile without letup and where every problem has a solution, where every ache and worry—even loneliness and despair—can be speedily and painlessly dispelled. The ad-vertisers project the idea that despair may be hidden and loneliness may wear a mask; actually a contorted smile may be more alarming than a sober expression of preoccupation, and an assumed gaiety more distress-ing than an honest statement of disappointment.

Ann had settled into her job at the University of California's Cowell Hospital. She had also cut back on her drinking when she came home and found more relaxation in doing needlepoint on small pillowcases based on paintings by Matisse, Stuart Davis, and other artists or re-creating figures from the Bayeux tapestry and Pennsylvania Dutch de-signs. Kees found these pieces wonderful. They decorated the sofa and chairs, complementing his paintings on the walls, his collages. Some were given to friends as gifts. Since it was hard to match the colors exactly, Ann changed the chromatic structure of the originals she found in art books, a compromise that in the words of her husband made her into "a formidable colorist" in her own right.

Through June, July, and August, Kees worked on his own songs and

new collaborations with Helm. He contributed a number of love ballads to his pile of Parchment Brand music paper. In "Haunting," a lover
confesses that if "I couldn't be near you, you might disappear." In "Not
Even the Ghost of You," Kees played on the same theme, but here the
lover vanishes without a trace:

Thought I heard your footsteps on the stair,
Opened up the door, but there was no one there
Just the same old shadows in the summer air,
Not even the ghost of you.

Turk Murphy liked much of the music that Helm and Kees were
writing and promised he would try to fit a song on his next recording. To Kees, it was only a matter of time before he saw his name on a
record label.

In August 1953, Kees reached the midpoint of "a state of vague meta-
physical depression" that had lasted for weeks. "While this isn't exactly
uncommon," he wrote, "it's gone on far too long without some kind
of a break." Kees was as bored as the sea otters he and Bateson had recently filmed at the zoo. (They would not play—the behavior Bateson
wanted to observe—until Kees dangled a wad of paper on a string.)
Still, Langley Porter had advantages for him, such as his and Ann's enrollment in the state employees' retirement system. "So I string along
with it," he admitted in a letter, "all the time sensing I ought to make
some kind of a break."

But while Ann's job was secure, Kees's position at Langley Porter
was slated to run out in October, and he was still resistant to getting
a "real job" that would interfere with his songwriting and its promise of fast money. When the local nonprofit FM station, KPFA, offered
him the position of program director in late August, he gave it serious consideration but turned the offer down. Being program director would have taken up too much of his time in "frequent fourteen-
hour days"—and he distrusted the station's noncommercial status and
"how frighteningly avant-garde" it seemed in its intent. Kees did agree
to help out on a series of poetry programs that the station had con-
tracted for with the National Association of Educational Broadcast-
ers. The tapes would be heard on a few other nonprofit stations, and
they kept him interested in poetry when all he thought about were his

songs — and recording acetates and a demo tape for Nesuhi Ertegun in Hollywood.

With Ertegun's job with the Good Time Jazz label and his editorship of the *Record Changer,* a trade journal, it seemed that Kees and Helm had an insider who could help them get their songs in front of music publishers and A&R men. But late in September, Ertegun had to tell Kees the sound quality of their recordings was too poor. He had had no success with the songs. Most people did not listen to them after the first few bars. Ertegun suggested that Kees come down to Los Angeles to push the songs himself and see what Ertegun was up against.

Kees used a vacation in early October for this and drove with Ann down to Los Angeles in the battered Lincoln. Though both really wanted to relax and visit the jazz clubs, the trip soon became a harried attempt to break into the music business — which Kees learned he knew nothing about. He had also arrived on the scene when record producers and radio stations were looking for white talent to break through in rhythm-and-blues-inspired music, or what was already being called "rock 'n' roll." New Orleans–revival jazz, outside of a few small markets, hardly appealed to teenagers, whose tastes were now influencing the recording industry. The search for an Elvis Presley had begun, and no one he talked to was going back to the 1920s with Kees.

While the songs he recorded were running into dead ends in Los Angeles, the poetry he taped on KPFA's reel-to-reel recorder at least found an audience in the Bay Area. Though he dismissively called his listeners the Kenneth Patchen Fan Club, Kees still segued from the frustrated jazz composer to the elegant poet-intellectual, finding time to prepare provocative notes on the "awesome topic of reading poetry aloud": "The poem on the page occupies space and is so grasped by the reader. The poem read aloud occupies time. What I am saying now is being recorded on tape, and I think of the words as being squeezed out on a long, rolled-up line. But when they are unrolled against the recorder's head for broadcasting, they have come a long way from their look on the page."

November was the month when Kees had once had one-man shows at Peridot. He could hardly call himself an active painter now, even though Lou Pollack was still thinking of him when he put together a show for his move to Madison Avenue. "After all old man I couldn't very well open a new gallery without including a Kees," he wrote, mentioning an orangish collage left over from his last show. "It did remind visitors that you were still alive."

Pollack tried to entice him with a scene from the art world Kees had left behind, with "mobs of people" and two French bartenders serving martinis in a main room with cork walls, an inlaid floor, and a bank of windows that provided natural light muted by floor-to-ceiling chiffon curtains. "Get out of that depression, boy," Pollack suggested. "You should start painting. It would probably do you a lot of good."

The immediate problem of finding a job, however, made it impossible for Kees to think about Peridot or ever painting again. He had been to libraries. He had tried to find new film work. "Unless one is a CPA or a TV mechanic or a time-study man," he wrote, "things are rough." He turned down a job for a publicity man "with wide experience in fund-raising."

Forces smaller than the slowdown of the post–Korean War economy further undermined Kees's well-being. He could no longer afford to repair his big Lincoln roadster, which no longer shifted out of first. With a musician friend who had once sold cars between bands, Kees found a dealership on the San Francisco side of the Bay Bridge that would take his Lincoln in trade. In its place, he bought a new but unstylish 1954 Plymouth Savoy, a practical choice that may have been necessitated by the loan's being partly underwritten by his father, for the elder Keeses had just moved to Santa Barbara. They were close enough to expect their son and daughter-in-law down for Christmas and for more frequent visits, which required a reliable car—one their son now expected to be paying for "from here to Eternity," a complaint that would have been good news to Sarah and John.

The Lincoln's final journey came on Thanksgiving Day as Kees drove it across the Bay Bridge. The bathos of this moment became the inspiration for his first satirical poem in some years, "Weather for Pilgrims"; he achieved the visual poignancy of a drowning man as the Lincoln's ball bearings

> Oozed like the eggs of a carp
> At the end of Thanksgiving Day,
> Bounced on the trafficked stone.·
> Oil poured over the hood
> And the Chevrolets swam home
>
> To turkeys stuff with squares.

Kees projected his low feelings onto the old Lincoln, barely making it across the "longest bridge in the world." But the poem closed "on firm cement" as a metaphor for survival, even as 1953 began to close on him and he believed he had accomplished "next to nothing" that year.

He wrote a few more poems in December. It was the first real run of verse he had experienced in months.

Two weeks into 1954, on a Sunday night, as he and Ann drove from Berkeley to San Francisco, Kees made a left turn, and another driver collided with his new car, smashing the right front door.

Ann was badly bruised and shaken up. Kees had to swallow bromide pills to get back his composure. But they soon recovered, and the damage to their car was quickly repaired at a body shop. What almost seemed like an inauspicious start to the new year was smoothed over for Kees when he received a nice check from Countess Caetani for "The Hours," which now appeared in the new issue of *Botteghe Oscure*. He also learned that he no longer needed to find a new job. Jurgen Ruesch had secured new funding for revising the communications book. And as he took up his "frantic" schedule at Langley Porter again, Kees renewed his partnership with Gregory Bateson as well. The anthropologist had gone to New York City to meet with Dean Rusk, the chairman of the Rockefeller Foundation, who promised to find new funding for Bateson's research, which could include some novel project for Kees to guarantee him an income for the next year.

The afterglow of being gainfully employed, however, faded for Kees throughout February, March, and April. He complained about his workload. He was involved in three different projects at Langley Porter. He had to work weekends. Nevertheless, he found he could use much of the night and early morning to write songs and turn out a few new poems. He planned to write an exposé titled "What's Happened to Popular Music?" and interview Hoagy Carmichael so as to get him to agree that "a deterioration [had] set in, [...] an all-time low in taste." Such an association, he knew as he queried the bandleader, could lead to a fair hearing for the Kees-Helm songs, but it also must have been hard to play himself as "formerly on the staff of *Time* magazine" after not having worked there for ten years.

To stay awake through the night and for the workday, Kees used psychoactive drugs, such as Dexedrine. He took pills from his musi-

cian friends, and he may have obtained a prescription through someone at Langley Porter. Since Kees enjoyed the "high" of his work, "ben-
nies" and "dexies" gave him something like a new lease on life. As a
consequence, however, his speed and Ann's alcohol increasingly put
them out of synch with each other, and she rarely enjoyed her husband
the way the girl did in one of his newest songs:

> *Who's that man with the big brown eyes?*
> *Never sleeps so there's no good-byes*
> *That wide-a-wake baby of mine.*
> *Others falter along the way.*
> *My man's a midnight matinee.*
> *[. . . . .]*
> *He's the answer to all my ills*
> *Lives on air and those little pills.*

In a mood of a "rather ordinary kind of melancholia, much milder,"
Kees studied the watercolors of a Turkish boy who painted mysterious
figures in a Byzantine-like style and words that spelled out "Kill and
destroy" and the like. Then he wrote a chapter on schizophrenic art for
the nonverbal-communication book. With Bob Helm, he wrote some
"satirical hillbilly numbers" and told the radio announcer Vincent
Connolly, a friend from his days at Paramount, that his songs needed
"the context of a Broadway musical or revue, and possibly that is the
next step." At a Chinese restaurant on Telegraph Avenue, he opened a
cookie and found a fortune that read, "He who can handle a writing-
brush will never have to beg." And in the April 11 *New Yorker,* he read
John Cheever's story "The Five-Forty-Eight."

While putting together poetry programs at KPFA-FM, Kees had a
brief encounter with Kenneth Patchen and Yvor Winters. "There is
really not enough money to make up for such encounters," he told a
friend, going on to say that it was a relief to be with jazz musicians and
"their benzedrine & alcoholism & relatively pure devotion." Though it
seemed he had no time for literary men, Kees befriended the poet and
novelist Vincent McHugh in May. Ten years older than Kees, McHugh
was on the downside of a reputation that, for a time, had been on the
rise with the publication of his novel, *I Am Thinking of My Darling,*
which Kees had reviewed anonymously in *Time.*

McHugh had served in the Pacific. While aboard a Navy ship, he had drunk a concoction made from antifreeze that ruined the lining of his stomach and forced him to take his nourishment from milkshakes. His having survived this misadventure and a number of other personal setbacks must have buoyed Kees and given him someone to make up "for the Patchens and Dahlbergs and such that the East has recently disgorged." That McHugh knew Jelly Roll Morton and was a fervent admirer of "the early & middle Pound" counted in his favor, too.

Kees also liked McHugh because he was a good listener and enjoyed thinking of ways out of the predicament they shared, "the terrible weight of our time" and "the need to earn one's bread." The scheme Kees had in mind at this time was a project that would be an offshoot of Bateson's investigations into "the paradoxes of play," for which the anthropologist might receive more backing from the Rockefeller Foundation: a critical look at ventriloquism.

"Major items of data" would be prints of *The Great Gabbo,* a 1929 motion picture Kees had seen in Beatrice, with Erich von Stroheim playing the part of an egomaniacal ventriloquist, and the 1945 British production *Dead of Night,* with Michael Redgrave in a similar role. Kees's research, however, soon became centered on an amateur ventriloquist whose name came up from time to time at Langley Porter: Dr. Gerald Feigen, already a colorful San Francisco "character" who made his living as a proctologist and sometimes performed with his dummy for the young patients at Mt. Zion and Maimonides hospitals and Little Jim Ward Children's Hospital.

Through the weeks of May and June, Kees brought a tape recorder to the Feigen home and recorded the doctor—and "Becky," whom Feigen described for Kees: "She's 44 years old. She's female. According to tradition she's been married seven times. Four of her husbands died. Two were divorced. And the last one just couldn't keep up with her. The implication is sexually. She's a rather sexy kind of person. She's an iconoclast."

Kees learned that Feigen's method was very different from radio and television ventriloquists such as Edgar Bergen and Jerry Mahoney. "A sloppy technician," Feigen said of Bergen, who had to have his gags and patter written for him by others. Feigen, instead, improvised by letting a "conversation" develop between the dummy and her audience, who, of course, became players in a performance in which they might learn more about themselves than about Becky. Kees discovered this when she "apprehended" via Feigen that Kees was talking to her because he badly needed foundation money to keep his job:

BECKY: *What do you do, sonny?*
WELDON: *Well, right now we're trying to find out something about ventriloquism. Do you know something about ventriloquism?*
BECKY: *(interrupting) What do you do for a living?*
WELDON: *That's what I do for a living at the moment.*
BECKY: *Parasite.*

Through Becky, the ever playful Feigen acted as the foil to Kees's unflappable clinician. That Kees persisted for days of taping shows that he did not think his work lacked scientific value even as it became increasingly bizarre and seemingly out of control. He probably believed his experiment would contribute to Bateson's work on play.

WELDON: *I'm not a Westerner, Becky.*
BECKY: *No kidding! Where you from?*
WELDON: *I'm a Middlewesterner.*
BECKY: *Oh well.*
WELDON: *I was born in Nebraska. You know anything about the Great Plains region?*
BECKY: *Yes I do, and it's sure plain.*
WELDON: *It stinks, doesn't it?*
BECKY: *It does. Those kids with their goddamn poke-eyes. Milkshakes —everybody likes milkshakes.*
FEIGEN: *I guess it's a national drink back there, isn't it?*

On the next series of tapes, Kees wanted other people to interact with Becky. So he asked Ann if she would accompany him to the next session—and to his surprise found her in terror of revealing herself to a life-size puppet. He tried playing some of the tapes to allay her fears, to show her that it would be harmless to converse with the dummy. Ann's suspicions of the dummy baffled and disappointed him, but Becky pried too much:

BECKY: *What does your wife do?*
WELDON: *My wife, she—*
BECKY: *Does she take Nembutal?*
WELDON: *No, she doesn't take Nembutal, huhn-huh.*
BECKY: *How does she stand you?*

WELDON: *Oh, I don't know. She manages to bear it some how. Think she has a lot of stamina.*

BECKY: *What do you do when you're home at night? In the evenings, that is? Do you talk with her?*

Kees told Ann that some of their friends were going to meet Becky, that it would be fun, but she was as anxious and vociferous as she was about watching the Army–McCarthy hearings that were now on television. The mental connection she made between the hearings and an "interview" with Becky became a dangerous mix, which Kees at first did not see. He too found the hearings fascinating, addictive, and could not turn them off, even when Ann started drinking more than ever to calm herself of fears she had not felt this strongly since discovering her husband's involvement with the Nisei. She drank gin to the point that it was hard to keep a bottle on hand in the house, hard to keep the quinine water from running low.

For the time being, Kees assumed she would drink her way back to her old self and left her alone. He continued taping Becky. He brought klieg lights and a camera to create a publicity still of the dummy and the ventriloquist. He also invited Vincent McHugh to converse with Becky, along with Gregory Bateson, Janet Richards, and her new husband, Charles Richards. The project resulted in seven tapes and as many typed transcripts, which Kees finished over the next twelve months—too late for him to edit them into the serious data that he thought was there, that he thought would sound convincing and utterly original to the Rockefeller Foundation. He thus left Becky unsilenced, accusing Bateson of being out to "get grants" and "waste money" ("I'm sure he wastes it in prodigious sums," Kees replied) and interjecting all kinds of uncomfortable truths about her interlocutor:

BECKY: *You know he could be a Hollywood character, if he tried.*

I've thought of locking you
In a closet or cell.
　　—Weldon Kees song

Near the end of May, Ann and Weldon spent a pleasant Sunday afternoon at Bob and Kay Helm's country place in Marin County. Janet and Charles Richards came too. The weather was warm and sunny.

In one snapshot taken that day, Kees sits in a wicker chair. He holds up his glass of liquor. His legs are crossed. He smiles at Kay Helm, who took the picture. In another, he sits with his arms resting on the chair's backrest, a lit cigarette in his right hand. In yet another, he sits in profile, facing the hill. Inside the house, at the "bar" that divided the kitchen and the main room, he looks like any suburban Californian.

For a portrait of the songwriters, he held open the sheet music for "San Francisco Blues" and sat next to Bob, who in turn held his clarinet. Kees sent this photograph to Norris Getty. He also sent one of Ann.

She had been photographed relaxing in a deck chair, with her arms behind her head, squinting because of the bright sun. In other images, she sits beside Kay, talking and reaching for a drink — or laughing at an amusing snapshot Kay is showing her in a picture album. In these photographs, a cigarette burns in Ann's left hand.

The photograph that Kees thought Norris would like shows Ann without a drink in easy reach. Instead she holds a washboard for a prop, like the one Kees sometimes played on stage when he sat in with the Turk Murphy Band. Even though her eyes and face look a little puffy, her plain, unopened-mouth smile and demure figure, set off by a dress that shows her hips and slim waist, would dissuade one from thinking her unattractive. Weldon crouches down a little to make Ann appear taller, for her heels did not give her much height. A new cigarette burns in her hand.

"I think it is the best picture of her," he wrote Getty, "since the one you shot (in color) in Brooklyn Heights, a long time ago." Nothing seemed wrong with her, but it was hard for Kees to deny that she was no longer herself. Over about eight or nine months, he had watched her become a full-blown alcoholic. As he told Conrad Aiken, Ann drank "more than you, me, Malcolm Lowry and Tallulah Bankhead put together."

Not long after that day at the Helms' getaway, Ann's drinking and unpredictable behavior made having people over risky. An evening with the Myrers at the end of May turned into a disaster when Weldon made the error of playing the Feigen and Becky tapes for amusement. Both Judith and Tony were plainly bored and uncomfortable — and Ann was very outspoken and drunk. In the past, her outbursts had often been droll. That night, this quality was missing.

The events of late June can be traced with the notes that Kees made later at the request of Ann's doctor—"Notes on the past: before the break," a collection of loose-leaf diary notes, some dated, some undated, in which he recorded observations of his wife. Written at random moments over many days, the notes are almost impressionistic rather than a narrative. Kees intended to show them to Ann's doctor and keep them for his own analysis:

Tender with Lonesome, with the little girl in front.
Often tender with me
Wanting to be tender?
Later: "The piano sounded different"
"Different from what?" [...]
I went out in the yard and found her wandering around. Said she was
going to go up to the Clinic to work for a while. First said she wanted to
be alone, then that she had some work she had to finish if she was going
to type for me (the JR-WK book) on Tuesday.

To maintain the appearance of normalcy, Kees claimed to be too busy, to be suffering from a frantic schedule. He had no time to see people. Ann, who was drinking more than ever, no longer took care of how she looked. She did not pick up after herself around the house. She worried about her job and told him about strange things that went on at the "annex," that part of the student health clinic where she worked. Insistently, she cautioned him not to say anything to anyone else. Her imagination was now fired by television broadcasts filled with black-and-white images of Senator Joseph R. McCarthy. The Senate–Army hearings reached a climax in June as McCarthy and his aides verbally sparred with the Army's counsel, Joseph N. Welch, who at one point gave Ann some hope as he exposed the banality and cruelty of McCarthy's attack: "Have you no sense of decency, sir? At long last, have you left no sense of decency?"

She soon crossed over the line that Kees had seen after her surreal encounter with the stray dogs in Denver. This time, he tried to empathize with her and found that what had made his light-schedule life possible, her job, held her with a sort of fascination that he could not pinpoint, save to say that it bordered on the pathological:

She said, "But I like it there."
I said that as more and more of us are under strains and pressures,
the only out is to get some kind of part-time job that will not bring on

*so much worry and sense of responsibility. I talked about how there was
nothing I wd. like better than to have some time to paint and write
poetry; instead of having to think continually about projects that would
bring in money. I tried to talk about attitudes and codes—about working
out ways of looking at things and ways of behaving that would make life
easier. I mentioned trying to set up clear-cut lives between a job and one's
life outside, of cultivating new ways of looking at people and "things." All
during this time, she was drinking her drink and looking at pictures in
one of the books on her lap.*

There had been other episodes in the past when Ann's drinking "got
the better" of her. Kees had waited them out, and he intended to do the
same during this bout of drinking. He would just keep to his program
of intense work. He borrowed five books from the library about Hawaii
for an article he wanted to write. He made notes on Kenneth Rexroth
for a radio program he wanted to do. He wrote Philip Rahv about reviewing Marshall Stearns's *Main Currents in Jazz* for *Partisan Review.*
"Our fondest wish to you & Nathalie," he said for himself and Ann.
"Why don't you wangle a summer teaching job out here sometime?"

Kees received Sigmund Gottfried Spaeth's *A History of Popular Music in America* from Tony Myrer, who now worked in a bookstore
and discounted his friend's special requests. Its seven hundred pages
would last Kees until he received his next order, *The Limits of Poetry* by
Allen Tate. He proofed the manuscript of the retitled *Language of Nonverbal Communication* one more time, as did Ann, even as she drank
heavily. During this time, she was still the "first-rate editor" her husband had relied on, excellent at catching non sequiturs, grammatical
errors, typos, and the like. He noted that the manuscript moved her
and concerned her very deeply. One night, reading a chapter on dis-
tortions of communication when he knew she was very tired, she sat
for long periods, as long as half an hour, staring at or studying an individual page. Many times, when she was reading, often in a sober and
attentive mood, Weldon watched her staring into space. He asked why,
and she said, "Well, this book, it's like Proust. It makes me think of so
many things, it touches off so much. I have to stop and think about it."
There were other times, however, when she saw the book and all the
effort behind it differently:

*When I came out from my bath, asked, "How long has Ruesch's project
been going on." I said 8 yrs and I'd been on it for over 3 years.*

"And how long have I been the subject of a study?"
I said she had never been the subject of a study. She said she didn't believe it.

Despite such accusations, Ann returned to working on the book, hurrying now in a "race against the Waltham," as Kees said—and against Ann's deterioration—for his collaborator, Jurgen Ruesch, would leave the country on July 1. At the same time, Kees had to keep working with Bateson on the otter film and undertake the chairmanship of a benefit concert for KPFA. It was scheduled for September, with many of the Bay Area's jazz musicians taking part. Kees believed he could raise fifteen hundred dollars for the station. His old friends Bob Helm and Turk Murphy and his new contacts in San Francisco's music world, the folksinger Barbara Dane and the legendary blues artist Jesse Fuller, would be on the program.

"In between convulsions," he wrote Myrer, "I'm working away at poems." The ice in which Kees had so often felt frozen as a poet had been broken by the encouragement of Howard Moss ("Do send us others soon"; "I have a great fondness for your Thanksgiving poem"), who purchased one of the newer poems, "Colloquy," for the *New Yorker.*

Near the end of June, Kees noticed that he was waking up at dawn again "with a maddening regularity." Each morning, he felt wide-awake, as "alert as Anatole Broyard at a showing of pornographic movies. My mind is batting an all eight & there's nothing to do but get up & work." By the afternoon, he admitted, he was now always "slavering for a Spansule" filled with Dexedrine.

Scenes from the Keeses' life now seemed torn from Weldon's old short stories. "She cried frequently and told him repeatedly how ashamed she was and that from then on she would be a good wife to him," he had written of Gloria Peate in "The Life of the Mind." For Kees, this was his personal sideshow, to be added to all the others under the belief that "99 percent of the human race had gone nuts," a belief he shared with Willy Poster, who wrote back that there was much evidence of this in the East, with Delmore Schwartz leading the way in Princeton, getting so drunk his wife jumped out of the car they were in. "After going a few miles," Poster reported, "he returned to look for her and wrapped the car around a lamppost. They put him in the hoosegow and scared him near witless."

In very early July, Kees received a letter from Henry Volkening in which the agent suggested that he consider trying to publish *Fall Quarter* again. "It would make *you* feel younger too," Volkening promised. "You know I've always *liked* this book and thought someone should take it." Volkening wanted to restore Kees to his "active list." He believed the "atmosphere" was now right for a "satirically sad-gay novel" like *Fall Quarter* or another book that Kees might enjoy writing. It seemed *Fall Quarter* had a chance. After all, Randall Jarrell had just published an academic comedy, *Pictures from an Institution*. But Kees could not enjoy the compliment. Even if he wanted to, he could not think about the novel. Ann's condition had worsened as the holiday weekend approached.

Her paranoia had increased over the FBI harassment of liberals and independent spirits on the campus and at Langley Porter. At one point, just before Saturday, July 3, Kees had been talking on the phone to Charles Richards. He mentioned something about the skullduggery that was going on in the administration of federal public-health projects. Suddenly Ann came running into the room, her eyes flashing at her husband. Then she wrote "monitored" on the pad beside the telephone. After he hung up, he asked her if she *really* felt their phone was tapped. She said she didn't know, but she thought it might be, and she thought the telephones at her office were being tapped. Joseph McCarthy and the Rosenbergs made her think that such things were possible in this country, that the government had enormous powers and could reach all the way onto the Berkeley campus if it wanted to. Kees's flirtation with communism, his connection to the Nisei, his association with Yaddo and Whittaker Chambers could matter, and Ann mixed these with the rest of her fears like the tonic she mixed with her gin.

Kees tried to defuse his wife. "The way things are going today," he said, "is enough to make us all a bit paranoid." He reminded Ann of how silly they had found another couple, some years back, who thought people were listening secretly to their conversations. "You have to fight it," he told her. After wandering outside, fixing herself a new drink, after listening to her husband play things down, Ann seemed to go along with this.

Later that Saturday, Kees heard Ann talking coherently and pleasantly with a woman who brought her some Avon products. She accompanied him when he drove to a piano store in Oakland. As he picked out a new piano, Ann, noticing some black customers, whispered to her husband that there would be a "race riot." Other than this remark, he thought she had turned the corner. "Maybe I needed something like this," Ann said at dinner. But when Kees asked her what she meant, she did not go on. He noticed her trying to twist apart her vitamin pill as if it were one of his time capsules. When he came out from his bath that evening, he found his wife laughing at some of the crazy things she had been saying.

"What a day! I thought it was wonderful!" Ann said as she watched a movie on television. She seemed dazed and doped to Kees. Before he went to bed, she seemed "pretty tight" and extremely sleepy. Her eyes scarcely stayed open. He went over to her and kissed her goodnight. It was a long kiss. Then he asked her to come to bed. "I have to wait for the 4th of July," she answered bizarrely. "I'll come to bed at midnight." He took a Nembutal and never heard her come to bed.

When he woke up Sunday morning, Kees cleaned house while Ann slept. When she got up, she angrily asked him, "You still here?" Then she made herself some coffee. She had no other breakfast. At some point after that, Ann began to drink continuously, and Kees realized it was time to call a doctor. But everyone he tried was out of town, either at the seashore or up in the mountains for the lovely weekend, including Dr. Saxton Pope, the psychiatrist and renowned bow hunter, whom he knew and trusted. So he talked Ann into getting in the Plymouth. They then drove to the clinic and entered the building, where they experienced a strong sense of revulsion, as if it had been a mistake to come. No one was there that they knew. "Sensitized by their wounding experiences of the past days," Janet Richards wrote later (influenced by her own views as much as Kees's version of events), "they felt only that they had put themselves into the hands of a huge machine, manned by robots, where everything they believed in, everything that made Weldon a poet, might be in peril from careless nurses and callous doctors, all of whom seemed to them to be hurrying about grimly pursuing abstractions."

More to the point, Kees could not risk hospitalizing her without involving a long stay in a state sanitarium and shock therapy. He knew that would be destructive to Ann given the patients he had seen. Ann looked at him and asked, "Do we have to stay here?" "No," he said. He had worked at Langley Porter for four years and had developed an incredible rapport with many of its administrators. They only needed to wait out the horrible, interminably long holiday.

Kees took Ann back outside to the car and returned to their apartment on Dana Street. To keep her from drinking any more, he persuaded the young MD who lived next door to "pump" her full of sodium amytal so that she could sleep. Deeply afraid that some kind of trick was being played on her, Ann refused to cooperate. She kicked and screamed the whole time as her husband held her down so that the doctor could administer his syringe, a service he performed on Monday evening, too, at Kees's request.

Occasionally Ann had lucid moments. Most of the time, however, she was not sure who she was or who her husband was. Sometimes she thought he was one of her brothers.

In the meantime, Kees made arrangements for the delivery of the new piano the next day, while Ann remained certain that FBI agents waited outside the house.

Kees finally succeeded in reaching Dr. Pope on Tuesday. The urgency in his voice and his description of Ann's condition compelled Pope to cancel his appointments for the day and come right over. He talked to Ann for about two hours and managed to communicate with her as no one else had. He put her on vitamin B and phenobarbital and ordered her "to stay off the booze." Later, sitting in his car, Kees spoke to Pope at some length about having Ann committed.

When he returned, Ann requested a ham sandwich and a pickle. It was the first thing she had eaten in four days.

The piano, which had been delivered at 8:30 that morning, while she slept, had obsessed Ann most of the day. She kept stopping to stare at it and make remarks about how it seemed different from the old piano. "The baseboard doesn't fit," she said. She wanted to know whether the legs were hand carved or not. All of this seemed to be leading somewhere, for Ann seemed very quick at picking up her husband's verbal slips. She knew he was thinking about what to do for her next, what to do *with* her.

During the day, Ann said she didn't like the "little girl in front," the landlord's daughter. "She looks too much like you," she said to her husband as if baiting him. The Miró prints, one above the sofa and the other above the new piano, bothered Ann, too. She asked Kees to take them down. He put up a de Bonnard poster to replace the Miró above the sofa. She said she liked it at first, but once it was up, she objected to it and asked that it be taken down.

Ann did not like Lucky Strikes anymore. She asked Kees where the words "a time to" came from, and she volunteered some of the quotation she could barely remember: "to heal ... to break down."

"Ecclesiastes," he said and asked her if she wanted to hear the whole passage. He found his bible and read, "a time to embrace, and a time to refrain from embracing." He looked up at her every now and then before he finished. She was sitting in a chair across from him. Her head nodded as her pills took effect again. "A time to love," Kees continued.

After he read to her, he waited for Ann to fall asleep in her chair. She sat in silence for a long time after making some remark to end some of his attempts at small talk. Finally, she stumbled to bed. He sat up for ten minutes or so, smoking a cigarette and writing his notes. Then he heard her calling for him plaintively, "Weld, aren't you coming to bed?" He marked his place in the bible, got up, and walked into the bedroom, where Ann waited to return his kindness for reading to her: "She was very tender. Played with my penis. Did not seem at all groggy. Went down on me. I said I was too tired but discovered that I wasn't. I asked her if she wanted to fuck. We had intercourse. She said she was going to get a diaphragm again because she wanted me to come inside of her."

In a letter to the poet and lawyer Melville Cane, Kees apologized: "Serious illness in my family and pressure of other work has prevented me from writing you before this about the Shelley Memorial Award." Two weeks had passed before Kees could respond to being named to a jury of three poets who would choose the winner of the award given annually by the Poetry Society of America. At first, he was mystified by the honor. He had not published a book since 1947. In the past five years, he had published fitfully in the magazines. His name had nearly disappeared from every avenue of America's literary life. Now he had been picked as judge for an award of money and recognition that he hardly had himself. And the man who had suggested him was the president of the University of California, Robert Gordon Sproul, who had given the commencement address that Kees had missed in 1935. The honor itself was surreal enough, but he also had to think about nominating a poet—in concert with Cane and the other judge, Harry Levin of Harvard University—in the aftermath of Ann's breakdown.

"He had her put away in the Woodlawn Hospital for Mental Cases," Kees had written in "The Life of the Mind." On the day after Dr. Pope's visit, he took Ann to Langley Porter, where she signed herself in, and he stayed there overnight on the advice of the doctor. The next morning, still suffering from nervous exhaustion, he phoned Charles Richards at work and asked to be picked up at the clinic. Kees said he was too shaken to make the drive himself. He asked Richards if he could stay with him and Janet for a little while. He just needed to pick up some fresh clothes and things from Dana Street. In the car, while being driven across the Bay Bridge, Kees wildly talked himself into leaving Ann, saving himself at the cost of hurting her. He stayed at the Richardses' apartment on Clay Street for the next two weeks.

"A person on speed is very hard to be with," Janet Richards would later observe, remembering Kees expertly using a pocket knife to separate the capsules Dr. Pope had prescribed for him and push the granules into two piles. The red ones, he claimed, contained Dexedrine. He discarded the yellow ones. "The hell with those other little babies," he said. On the drug, he hardly felt depressed about Ann. After Charles and Janet could no longer stay awake with him and listen to his plans for a new life, he took the guitar he had brought from Dana Street and strummed softly, singing bits and pieces of blues songs and popular tunes from the 1920s. If he went to sleep, he would be up again at dawn. He crept through Janet and Charles's bedroom and into the kitchen to make coffee. At the table, he wrote his notes about Ann, notes that he soon lost interest in, as if they were a poem or a chapter that was a false start, ending with an undated entry about a violin and a horn in a shop window he wanted to see—and nothing about Ann.

During the three weeks she spent at Langley Porter, Kees went to see her often. He wanted to make sure that she received the best treatment—and he wanted her sufficiently recovered so that, with her doctor present, he could convince her that parting ways would be a good thing for both of them. At first, she resisted ending their sixteen-year marriage. Against the advice of Dr. Pope, she left the hospital in hopes

evenings spent performing in her eagle-filled bedroom went by with "great tiredness," as Kees wrote in his notebook.

Jerry found she was losing him. She imagined he was being unfaithful with the younger, prettier women of the Interplayers and the young married woman who came over to his apartment to transcribe his ventriloquist tapes and retype his manuscript of poems. As Jerry tried to possess him, Kees ruthlessly analyzed her in his diary-notebook, much as he had Ann. There he demonized Jerry. She became for him utterly childish and demanding, devious and scheming, and subject to playing "games" with him. He did not like that she was so role conscious, that she wore, and admitted to wearing, a false face. He hated the way she called mutual friends "sick" and the garbage can the "poo-poo."

One morning, not long after Labor Day, he found a note from Jerry left on his door: "You are the one to straighten me out. Would you?" But he could not. He had told his notebook the day before that he had lived with himself for forty years and did not understand himself very well at all. He tried persuading her to see an analyst and let things seem like they were getting better between them. He even let her drive him to the airport to catch a plane to see his parents in Santa Barbara, where he at last began to build some distance between them that would last.

∾

Three days before Kees flew out of San Francisco on September 21, Lonesome ran away. The cat was still missing on the evening before he left for Santa Barbara, when Jerry came over, as did the Richardses and Vincent McHugh and his girlfriend, Alice. They had drinks and listened to him play his new song, "Culture Vulture Lucy," and heard a tape of McHugh reading his favorite poems about animals, which, coincidentally, included Kees's poem about a stray, "Dog," and one that Kees liked too, Christopher Smart's "My Cat Jeoffrey."

Jerry's behavior, strangely enough, made being around his mother almost a pleasant experience for Kees after an uncomfortable ride on the evening "milk route plane" to Santa Barbara. "Sadie," as he still called her in his diary, even went with him to the college library to help him compile a list of names from the New York phonebook and the PMLA membership for the handsome prospectus that Adrian Wilson would print. She also found him a clinic on his first day in Santa Barbara where he could see a doctor and "get a shot of penicillin" for a bad sore throat that smoking Pall Malls did not help.

On Friday, September 24, Kees wrote Adrian Wilson in the morning, letting him know when he expected to be back to resume work on the book and where to reach him "should you want to change the title of book to *My Gun Is Quick* or *Quietly My Understudy Waits.*" Then he and his parents drove to Los Angeles in their car, which they lent him for the duration of his stay. He dropped them off at the downtown hotel where they were staying and drove on to Bettie and Nesuhi Ertegun's house on North Orlando. Nursing his sore throat and exhausted from travel, Kees asked the Erteguns if he could sleep in their garage. The unusual arrangement would save his hosts the trouble of making up the couch—and of seeing him not really sleep at all. He would simply rest in his parents' car, while going over in his head what he wanted to do during his busy weekend.

Kees wanted to see Christopher Isherwood and Jim Agee. He wanted to dine with the artist Luchita Hurtado, whom he had met in New York, where she made her living making fashion sketches for *Vogue.* Now married to the "dynaton" painter Wolfgang Paalen, a contemporary and friend of Hans Hofmann, Luchita would have wonderful stories of working in Mexico, where she and her husband belonged to the circle of Diego Rivera and Frida Kahlo. He also wanted to contact the Los Angeles gallery owner Earl Stendahl, who knew Walter and Louise Arensburg. Jerry had done Kees the favor of sending a letter of introduction to Stendahl, in which she vouched for Kees and the article and book he wanted to write about the couple and their art collecting.

Saturday afternoon had been reserved for meeting the songwriter Harry Barris, one of the original Rhythm Boys, whom Kees had listened to on his family's phonograph during his Beatrice days.

On Sunday, Kees drove his parents back home. He had dinner with them and spent the latter part of the evening with Hugh Kenner, who taught at the University of California in Santa Barbara. They had in common their meetings with Ezra Pound in Saint Elizabeth's, and Kees had war stories about *Time*—the famous review of *Four Quartets* and the "psychopathology" of working there that Kenner's fellow Canadian Marshal McLuhan had written about in *Partisan Review.* What more interested Kees, however, was talking about the Interplayers. He asked Kenner if he wanted to take a break from teaching English literature and write a sketch for *The Seven Deadly Arts.* It would be a lot more fun.

Kees flew back to San Francisco on Monday afternoon with a basket-
ful of freshly baked cookies from his mother—and found Lonesome
waiting for him on the doorstep. He also returned with a new fountain
pen for addressing the envelopes in which he would mail the printed
announcements for *Poems 1947–1954*. These were decorated with a distinctive red hourglass and featured a facsimile page with "Wet Thursday" and a note that declared him "one of the few poets of his generation" "who has continued to produce, slowly and with growing
authority, poems that communicate directly to the reader who values
work of permanent stature."

In addition to sending his prospectus to men and women of letters,
librarians, old friends, and others, Kees found novel ways to promote
his book. He thanked the *New Yorker* for permission to reprint the
Robinson poems and "Colloquy"—and suggested that the magazine
include *Poems, 1947–1954* on its Christmas list of books by contributors. He promised a review copy for Louise Bogan, adding in a tone his
father might have used in a card to a valued customer of the F. D. Kees
Manufacturing Company: "May I say that, over the years, The New
Yorker is the only publication in this country with which it is a pleasure
for a writer to do business? I have never submitted a manuscript that
wasn't either accepted or rejected promptly, intelligently dealt with in
every way; and no other magazine, so far as I know, can make this
statement." He could write this. He knew from Adrian Wilson that he
had been recommended to the National Institute of Arts and Letters
as a possible recipient of a grant that October.

Getting *Poems* ready for publication raised Kees's spirits. He was
"just getting by financially," and life had improved over what it had
been in Berkeley. "On the whole, I couldn't be better, and things are
looking up," he wrote Bob Helm, who was visiting Boston and staying
at Norris Getty's apartment. "Almost any place is a breeze after New
York," he continued more colorfully, "and Boston isn't bad at times,
when the wind is from the right direction and it isn't one of those times
when there have been three hard snows and the local Maffia hasn't even
taken the trouble to scrape the ninth layer of frozen dogturds off."

Kees also had the distance he wanted from Jerry—and if he wanted
her, she made herself available to be his date, as on the October evening
they went to see the singer Claire Austin perform at the Aluminum
Cherubim in the Embarcadero district. There they shared a table with

the former silent-film actor Walter McGrail (who Kees had seen rescue Pearl White in *The Perils of Pauline* back in Beatrice) and his wife,
Marian, now the proprietors of the Old Book Shop. They also sat with
another couple Kees recognized: "Isherwood is a nice fellow, though
I wish he wdn't write such bad novels as his last, but Auden kept saying, 'Mister Kees, is theh eny explahnation *why* the music has to be
so laoud?"

"I want to write for the stage: to combine music, decor, words, and
people," Kees wrote Allen Tate in early November. After mailing out
over fifteen hundred announcements for his new book—in time to
benefit from the appearance of "Colloquy" in the *New Yorker*—he had
shored up his role as the poet for now. Four or five blurbs were still
needed for the unusual paper band that would serve as the book's dust
jacket. In letters to Aiken, Tate, Malcolm Cowley, and Wallace Stevens,
Kees asked for ten to twenty-five words about his work as a poet.
Tate and Cowley obliged with their praise, though neither man expressed remarks as felt as those from an outsider, Norris Getty: "These
poems are vastly more engaging to eye, ear, & mind—and more con-
sistently so—than any new collection of verse that I've seen published
in quite a while. I wish that somehow—waving a wand or something—
I could come to these poems for the first time, without knowing their
author, just to check this impression; I think my judgment would still
be the same."

The ink drawings for twenty-five copies of the book became a small
reprise of Kees as an artist. He brushed them on large sheets that would
be cut up and bound into the special edition. Some resembled Franz
Kline's work. Some were based on subscription orders and personal-
ized, such as the bold calligraphic HH executed for Hans Hoffman's
copy.

Where Kees's contemporaries among poets would have planned for
a reading tour, made themselves and their book visible to award juries
and English departments hiring poets for writing workshops, Kees
used *Poems 1947–1954* as a departure point for new plans. He used as
its epigraph the "dark caverns" revelation from Hawthorne's *Marble
Faun*. Now he would make an orphic ascent from these caverns to a
theater stage.

He waited impatiently for the Interplayers to open their production of *Strange Bedfellows* so that more actors and dancers could be freed for his revue. He befriended an eighteen-year-old woman he had originally met in June, when she heard him talk about jazz music at San Francisco State College. Originally from Hope, Arkansas, the attractive coed had renamed herself Ketty Frierson and now sang torch songs at the Purple Onion, where Kees often went to see her. Though Ketty claimed to be older, Kees knew she was "jailbait" as she became part of his circle. But he wanted a black woman to sing his songs in a range between Bessie Smith and Billie Holiday.

He began sketching out a television show in which he imagined himself, Bob Helm, and his closest friends among the Interplayers playing roles little different from their own lives as struggling entertainers. The show would be easy, like turning a camera on themselves. He would be the Piano Player.

In late October, the Macy Foundation had awarded a grant to Gregory Bateson. He hoped that his friend and partner, with the new funding, would work full-time. Kees, however, had "too many irons steaming at the moment." This phrase was his mantra now, the very opposite of "being pigeonholed." It did not matter to him that he filled his days with plans, meetings, and projects that paid nothing and paid for nothing. His conduct, to him, was not some grown-up version of the play that he and Bateson studied. It was not this double-bind business of Bateson's, in which he was trapped by his parents' manic expectations that he could be an artist only if he had a nice day job. He was moving on, changing, "pushing the elevator bell," as he wrote in an early poem. This was freedom, free fall, and he wanted to enjoy it while it lasted. And he had something for John and Sarah to talk about, to put in their scrapbook. The editor Robert Evett, of the *New Republic,* wanted him to review books on a regular basis.

Taking up Bateson's offer of an expanded role at Langley Porter would have pulled Kees away from *Pick Up the Pieces,* the new name he had given his revue after Vincent McHugh said having "deadly" in the title would "not be good for any show." Rehearsals took up two nights of the week, and he needed to put the book for the show together. He worked only enough hours to earn "eating money" — and he made use of his friends. They did not mind having him over for dinner so often, for they enjoyed his talk and plans. They did not mind when he tagged along for the ride, sometimes in the Richardses' new Volkswagen, one of the first on the streets of San Francisco ("I guess those cars are up to snuff at running over people," he said in a letter, "along with having other valuable assets").

Other friends, however, did not like how he "used" them and even felt embarrassed to be associated with him. This was the case with the Myrers. Since his divorce, their friendship with Kees had cooled. It did not help that he disapproved of the commercial direction of Tony's new fiction, of his trying to write a war novel like Norman Mailer and James Jones. When Kees wanted Judith's help ("fave lingua") in seeking a favor from her friend John Marshall, the assistant humanities director of the Rockefeller Foundation, she warned that he was unstable given his manner on the phone and his schemes, which had become "pretty grandiose and frenetic in the last six months." Even though these were "parlous times for poets," she did not want Kees reflecting badly on her and Tony: "All this explanation is simply to say in advance that I'm sorry if this turns out to be any sort of bother for you at all."

Even as he was alienating old friends, Kees met the kind of best friend he had not had since his student days in Lincoln, the San Francisco reporter Michael Grieg.

A native of New York City, Grieg had tried a number of vocations, including poet, short-story writer, playwright, film scenarist, and narrator. He had worked as a sportswriter for United Press covering the Negro Leagues and as a theatrical and radio publicist for Fred Allen, Jimmy Durante, and Lily Pons. In 1948, he had moved to Potrero Hill in San Francisco with his wife, Sally. He had held a number of jobs, such as writing for *Look* and *Redbook* and hosting local television shows. He was now the director of the San Francisco Cinema Guild at the Green Street Theatre, where he showed European and American film classics. It was during the intermissions that he found he had much in common with Kees, especially when it came to being critical of Hollywood. In early November, after several evenings of drinks and long talks about the state of movies and filmmaking, the two men started doing a weekly radio program for KPFA, *Behind the Movie Camera*, the first of their several joint ventures.

Despite KPFA's weak transmitter, which hardly made it outside of Berkeley and across the bay, Kees and Grieg made their new venue sound influential in their press releases. Kees even stretched his and his friend's backgrounds a bit to lend them authority: "Out of their wide background in vaudeville, revues and direct experience in Hollywood musicals, they speak frankly and with no holds barred on how the popular musical has changed from an alive and vital phase of popular culture into a machine-made, juke-box operation controlled by a handful of recording executives and Hollywood producers."

BTMC, as Kees liked to abbreviate it in his program notes, became best known for its lively panel discussions. For the show on *The Barefoot Contessa,* Kees invited Vincent McHugh and Pauline Kael, who had recently started writing movie reviews for *City Lights Magazine.* Her rapport with Kees and acid repartee with Grieg (whom she called Kees's "evil genius without the genius") made the program KPFA's most popular—and prepared her for her later role as the film critic of *Partisan Review* and the *New Yorker.*

Having written their own film criticism and having read and absorbed that of Manny Farber, Jim Agee, and other friends, the hosts of *Behind the Movie Camera* decided it was time for critics to respond to Hollywood in a real way. Kees took on the task of drafting a prospectus for a new kind of studio, San Francisco Films.

The purpose of the company would be the production of experimental shorts and full-length features for art-house distribution in the United States. Kees hoped that the films the company produced would also derive income from foreign markets and that some feature-length films might be released nationally for general B-movie distribution.

Kees also recognized there might be money in such a venture. Columbia had announced an allocation of ten million dollars to finance independent production of films such as *On the Waterfront.* The Theater Owners of America, at a convention held in November 1954, had authorized the formation of a corporation to be capitalized at ten million dollars for financing independent productions.

It hardly seemed unreasonable to Kees, who had once published a pretend movie magazine as a boy in Beatrice and had only worked for the newsreels and made 16mm scientific documentaries and one art film, to think in terms of offering Class A stock for such a company. His enthusiasm and absolute seriousness regarding this project were enough to recruit a "small staff nucleus," as he described them in his prospectus, with thinner credentials than his. In a second draft, he listed himself as the company's production manager. Vincent McHugh would be in charge of script and direction because he had done some script work for Paramount Pictures. Michael Grieg would be manager of publicity and distribution given his experience as a minor theatrical agent and his management of a theater. As general manager, Kees volunteered Wallace Hamilton, the director of KPFA's public-affairs programming, because he had once produced a few short documentaries for the World Council of Churches. For financial officer, Kees put down Horace Schwartz, the business manager of Brooks Cameras and Supplies, where Kees had become a regular buying film and camera equipment. Kees, feeling it might help, added that Schwartz had been a timpanist for the Cleveland Symphony Orchestra. Save for Bill Heick and himself, only Frank Stauffacher, of the San Francisco Museum of Art's film division, had any real experience in filmmaking. Stauffacher had edited a volume of essays with pieces by Man Ray and Luis Buñuel and had made a number of short subjects, including *Notes on the Port of Saint Francis,* with Vincent Price narrating from Robert Louis Stevenson's essay. Kees asked Stauffacher to be chief cameraman and director.

That neither Kees nor any of his friends had the money to start even the groundwork for such a company was no reason to hold back the prospectus, which sounded reasonable, which had a businesslike and seemingly well-researched rationale. He cast the venture in terms of an utterly sound investment that had about as much risk as investing in Nebraska wheat:

San Francisco Films is being formed as a producing unit to meet certain needs in the field of motion picture production.

The company, to be incorporated in the state of California, plans to concentrate on the production of full-length features and shorts for mature American audiences.

San Francisco Films would meet a demand created by the shortage of films that had resulted from Hollywood's response to the competition of the television networks, which were "carrying an increasing share of the routine entertainment load" and forcing more and more of the "14,000 motion picture theaters, and 4,000 drive-ins in the USA" out of business. As far as the kinds of movies the company would make, Kees had in mind a cross between art-house foreign films and *noir* American B-movies, none of which was even on paper yet.

In early December, Adrian Wilson held a party for Kees on the publication day of *Poems, 1947–1954* at his loft near the waterfront. There was plenty to eat and drink. In Wilson's office, Bill Heick had poet and publisher pose together. Being the taller, Wilson sat, holding one of the brochures, and Kees stood, dressed in dark slacks and his favorite tweed sport coat. In Heick's other shots, he caught Kees mixing with the guests, typically in a listening profile, hearing the praise of his friends, while holding his cigarette as if he were an actor in a Van Huesen ad. "Like Tyrone Power," Heick thought to himself.

Late in the evening, word spread that it might be fun to continue the party at a jazz club. Soon Kees, Jerry MacAgy, Charles and Janet Richards, the Wilsons, and about fifteen other guests had crowded onto the freight elevator so that they could all leave together. Overloaded, the elevator refused to stop on the ground floor and descended down to the basement of the warehouse, coming to rest at the bottom of the elevator shaft with a hard thump. In the silence that followed, the revelers could see the threshold of the first floor above their heads. It looked unreachable. Then Kees, in a deep, commanding voice, ordered the person nearest to the elevator's control panel to push the "Assistance" button. Some of the people trapped, perhaps even Kees himself, may have realized the irony of their predicament, that it resembled the traps he set in the poems printed upstairs:

So walk through rain and drop into this hell
Where steam is rising and a bell
Rings like a phone.

Far above, somewhere in the building, a bell did ring until the building's caretaker, an old man, arrived to open the top of the elevator car.

During the last weeks of 1954, Kees devoted much time to *Gadabout,* the spy movie he and McHugh were scripting together. Like *Assignment to Peril,* the new project bore the influence of *The Third Man* and such detective films as *The Big Heat.* It would be the first motion pictures to be made by San Francisco Films, shot in black-and-white and on location in San Francisco.

The plot was simple and timely, for Alger Hiss and the Rosenberg spy ring were still fresh in the public's mind. A young woman reporter, with paranoid tendencies, has the persistent feeling she is being pursued, which she is. She in turn is searching for a scientist missing from her father's research laboratory. To develop the story, the poets taped their brainstorming sessions in Kees's living room and tossed ideas back and forth. Then they played the tape back to write down the best material, in which their city became a nightmare world as strange and threatening as postwar Vienna. Kees wrote down "Lysergic acid," "CIA," and "Gaypayoo Man" (a Soviet spy) on the first page of the screenplay's working typescript—a combination of elements that suggests Kees was anecdotally aware of covert LSD doping and mind control being employed by rival intelligence services. He was, after all, present in San Francisco at the height of the CIA's MK-Ultra project, which involved Barbary Coast prostitutes giving unsuspecting clients LSD. His work at Langley Porter also exposed him to research on and therapeutic use of LSD, for the drug was then a common topic among the professional community at the clinic. Connecting the CIA to the drug, of course, could have been just as much the result of Kees's fertile imagination.

LSD, however, is not the only thing tormenting the hero of *Gadabout*, a man very much made in Kees's own image, for Helwig Ennis comes from the world of the big government-funded research institutes in which his creator worked. "He is a worried man," Kees imagined for McHugh. Ennis is a man who "can't get away. This is a security job. This is such a top security job, you know they won't let you quit." Ennis is "running away from himself," obsessed with fleeing San Francisco for Port Moresby or a place even more remote, where he can assume a new identity and hide with his knowledge, an equation for a top-secret formula. The motivation to disappear, as Kees argued on the tape, comes from his unfulfilled and unrecognized genius: "This guy really wants power. He's really jealous as hell. He's done most of the work."

Kees also penciled "Hot Jazz," "Liquor," and "Dames" beside Ennis's name. He gave Ennis a "wife from whom he's separated," "several girlfriend Nurses"—and a taste for San Francisco's demimonde. He made Ennis as much a fallen poet, too, as a fallen scientist:

Camera pans to the other side of the Embarcadero. We see a man rather dumpy, 35, shambling, a bit drunk, across the street. He comes into the Tin Angel. The place is almost deserted. The musicians are putting away their instruments. He climbs up to the bar and the bartender says "How are you Helwig?" Helwig looks at the bartender, and past the bartender,

to his face in the mirror, and says "give me a double rye." The bartender
says, "this is the last one." He pours him a drink. Helwig looks at the bar-
tender and says, "Eddie, have you ever wanted to take the world and just,"
and at this point he cups his hands and presses them together. "Have you
ever wanted to squeeze the world into a little tiny ball?" At the table be-
hind, Chas. E. Forward [a Soviet agent] is sitting, staring at the mirror.
The light is reflected off his glasses—sinister.

Kees set aside *Gadabout*, with its role for Robert Ryan, its racetrack
scene at Pebble Beach ("about reel seven"), its chase through a new
southern California subdivision composed of identical houses ("I
don't think anything like that has ever been done!"). After the broadcast of a well-received *Behind the Movie Camera* program on the Japanese film *Ugetsu*, Kees used Christmas to visit his parents and as an
opportunity to line up new guests for BTMC.

From Santa Barbara, he drove his father's car to Los Angeles, where
he hoped to meet Buster Keaton, Robert Ryan, Fritz Lang, and others.
Most, however, were out of town for the holidays. Jim Agee was in New
York. So was Vincent Price. He tried to get Gloria Grahame for the
radio program, but her agent demanded to know what "was in it for
the performer." All he could do was promise to mail a brochure and
return to Santa Barbara, where he tried to make up for these setbacks
by having lunch with Hugh Kenner and listening to Kenner's idea for
a script based on Wyndham Lewis's novel *The Vulgar Streak*.

The lead could be played by Melvyn Douglas or Vincent Price. It
would be "a very fat role," the story of an English "gentleman" who
leaves the impression that he is a successful artist, a dress designer, or
a decorator. In reality, however, he is the son of a railway porter whose
wealth comes from being a sophisticated front for passing off counter-
feit five-pound notes engraved by his accomplice. Forced to confront
himself as a fraud, the man hangs himself in his empty apartment during the Blitz, wearing a placard on his chest: "Whoever finds this body,
may do what they like with it. I don't want it. Signed: its Former In-
habitant."

Kees promised to talk to people in Hollywood about the project and
about other books both men wanted to bring to the screen. For a time,
Kenner caught Kees's enthusiasm. After their meeting, he could not
get film ideas out of his head. He even imagined writing a screenplay

for one of the short stories from *Dubliners*. "You put me in touch with John Huston to help him dream up a Joyce picture," he wrote Kees a few weeks later, "and on the proceeds I'll buy all your books and attend all your openings and teach my little children to bless your name."

ov

When you've got poets on stools, you've practically got cats in trees.
　　　　　　　　　　　　　　　　　　　　　　　　—R. H. Hagan

Kees flew back to San Francisco to spend New Year's Eve with his friends. He had a cough and chest pain. Bronchitis, he thought. Nevertheless he lit another one of his unfiltered cigarettes.

He knew about cancer. Becky had even warned him about cancer when she saw him smoking in her presence. That and the drinking, pills, bad diet, and sleeplessness made him look haggard and old for his age. He was less perfectly groomed, too. Ann used to trim his mustache and cut and comb his hair, but those days were gone. He had tried to check up on her since the divorce and had seen her for one evening. All he could remember was how depressed she was and how helpless he felt.

In his wallet, he had a check from his father that would pay for some personal expenses and for printing *Poems 1947–1954*, which he had given copies of to his parents as a Christmas gift. It did not take them long to find, much to their surprise, that he had dedicated the book to them.

Looking down on the California landscape rolling under the silver wing of the airliner, he covered his mouth as another cough rose and looked forward to 1955. In a few days, with Pauline Kael, he would tape a *Behind the Movie Camera* devoted to the films of the previous year. Bob and Kay Helm would soon return from the East. They had talked about finding a shack in the country where they could all spend weekends together drinking whiskey and composing new songs. Maybe a new girlfriend would be a healthy change. He was more tired of Jerry than ever. Mentally he pictured prospects: Interplayer actresses, women at Langley Porter, Ketty.

In the first week of January, Kees, with Michael Grieg in tow, attended Jimmy Broughton's reading at San Francisco State College's new Poetry Center. The center had just been founded back in October by Ruth Witt-Diament, a teacher at the college, and dedicated by W. H. Auden, who, for the event, gave his seminal lecture, "The Hero in Modern Literature." That affair, to Kees, had been woefully stilted. He knew stories about Mrs. Witt-Diament's heroes, such as "Little Farfel" Spender and the "late Welsh rarebit" Dylan Thomas and Auden. He liked to tell how she had opened her home to "Ole Wyst," only to find out that he "wets the bed every night out of sheer spite." "So, if he ever wants to hit the hay at your place," he warned Conrad Aiken and others, "get out the baby's rubber sheeting, or, better yet, send him over to the corner of the hen-house."

As Kees and Grieg had coffee with Broughton shortly before the reading, Kees began to put down the whole idea of the mannered poetry recital. "Why not enliven the readings by dramatizing them?" he asked. "Why not make an evening of poetry lively?" As he and Grieg left the Poetry Center, they realized they had enough talented friends and friends of friends to mount just such a foil to the "literary evening." They decided on a name for the idea, *Poets' Follies*, a stage show that was part poetry, part theater, ballet, minstrel show, and chautauqua. It would also be a foil for Kees, a foil to the American poet manqué leaving his newly published dark poems behind for the Hollywood solution to life's troubles: *C'mon gang, let's put on a show!*

Three weeks later, most of the cast had been assembled. There would be four poets: Kees, Grieg, Vincent McHugh—and Lawrence Ferling, whose debut in the *Follies* would convince him to adopt a "real" poet's name, Ferlinghetti. As they read, the dancers Dick Martin and Jayne Nesmyth would perform modern-dance interpretations of the texts. Luther Nichols, the fired film critic of the *San Francisco Chronicle*, agreed to emcee the event, which would premiere Saturday, January 22, at the Theatre Arts Colony, a beautiful Maybeck building at 1725 Washington Street that had recently served as a Chinese Lutheran church, with additional performances at Berkeley's Little Theatre the following week.

For the musical entertainment, Kees put together a jazz band, the Barbary Coast Five, consisting of Horace Schwartz on his tympani, the actress Carol Leigh, billed as the "Queen of the Washboard," Adrian Wilson on clarinet, and Kees on standup piano. (The fifth member would depend on who was available.) They would play tunes once intended for *Pick Up the Pieces*, tunes that would be "Compositions of a Lowdown & Traditional Nature, Emphasizing Ragtime & the Blues," as Kees promised in the broadsides Wilson printed for the show.

The theater had a Steinway on which Kees could play interludes that linked the pieces in the show, which kept being added as the opening night approached. Grieg contributed a set of plays, *The Three Bottles; or, Poison in the Poetry,* with scenes in Wimbledon, Paris, and Telegraph Hill "dealing with angst and poets in three cultures." The first, "Quaff, Quaff," would feature an English poet who tries to poison his wife to get at her money for his "poetic growth" and an American butler who talks like Marlon Brando. To play the part of the wife, Lania, he chose an aspiring comedian, a housewife from Sausalito named Phyllis Diller looking for her first break. Grieg also wanted to read passages from *A Field of Broken Stones,* a work by the World War II draft resister Lowell Naeve. Vincent McHugh wanted to show off his new play, *The Women of Lemnos,* from which he planned to read extracts with one of the chief characters, Aphrodite. Her role would be nonspeaking, so McHugh decided on a wire dressmaker's dummy to play the part since he could not find a replica of the Venus de Milo.

To further remove *Poets' Follies* from the conventional poetry recital —and to parody the post-Kinsey men's-magazine culture of libido, intellect, and lifestyle—Kees and Grieg added another kind of love goddess to their literary evening. They visited the El Rey, a burlesque theater in Oakland, to recruit its most celebrated stripper, Lily Ayers.

At first, she laughed them off as Kees described how a stripper could help people read more poetry by reciting works by her "favorite" poets, such as Sara *Teas*dale and T. S. Eliot. An ecdysiast reading "The Waste Land" would "expose" that poem, as Kees put it. "Or you could explain the relationship between your art and the art of poetry." The platinum blonde, who could pass for Marilyn Monroe, began to say no in her husky voice. Leaning over, Lily's publicity man whispered in her ear and urged her to accept the invitation because it would make good copy. She did like the "biography" Kees made up to explain her "taste for poetry" as something she had acquired as a Berkeley coed who learned that taking off her clothes could pay her way through school. That was a good one. The only problem was fitting her into *Poets' Follies* between her two Saturday-night performances at the El Rey. "How can you get me over and back across the Oakland Bridge in time?" she asked. Kees told her not to worry. "We'll send a car with a motorcycle escort."

For the next week, leading up to the event, Kees was often seen with Ayers as he prepared her for her reading. They were even photographed together in front of the billboard for the *Poets' Follies of 1955.* Smiling, holding open a book of poems, he stands very close to her as she looks on in her furs. Their resemblance to a Hollywood couple going over a script in a publicity shot seems intentional.

The San Francisco artist William Mayo designed the billboard, which featured an abstract tribute to Miss Ayers's nude torso. Her portrait, painted in Mayo's studio, provided another chance for Kees to be seen near her, this time for R. H. Hagan of the *San Francisco Chronicle* (who had replaced Luther Nichols as emcee), Mike Grieg, and Bill Heick. In the snapshots Heick took that afternoon, Kees looks like he is in love with the elegant stripper in her black dress, diamond earrings, and pearls.

A few days before *Poets' Follies* opened, a letter from New York forced Kees to look back at his past. Lou Pollack thanked him for an inscribed copy of *Poems 1947–1954* and mentioned that everyone—Bultman, Gottlieb, the Hofmanns—wanted to know when he was coming back to New York. He was not interested in any of the San Francisco painters that Kees had recommended. As far as the photographs of Bill Heick went, he would only take a few on consignment—and with "return postage." As Kees read on, he would have had every reason to think that his friends in New York's art scene saw his being out in San Francisco as temporary, as an experiment that had gone on too long. All the exciting things he had told Pollack he was doing meant only to the gallery owner that he was not giving himself any time to paint. Pollock wrote back: "I really thought (and think) you have great possibilities." But he was painting—helping to paint the backdrop for the *Follies* poets. It showed San Francisco on the same map as Paris, New York, and London. This was what he was trying to tell Pollack and his friends, and they just could not see it.

The rehearsals for *Poets' Follies* took place on the Saturday afternoon of the opening. R. H. Hagan had had barely one day to prepare and soon realized, when he walked on stage for the first time, that he would have to be a little drunk to improvise that evening, to segue from one act to another.

The doors to the Theatre Arts Colony opened at 7:30. The tickets, at $1.00 for general admission and $2.50 for the privilege of sitting on one of the folding metal chairs in the dress circle, quickly sold out to an audience that consisted of people who generally knew each other and the cast from San Francisco's close-knit bohemia. At approximately 8:30, Horace Schwartz began to play a magisterial drum solo on his kettledrum. Bemused, blinking under the lights and the periodic flash of Bill Heick's camera, Hagan walked out onto center stage as Kees, below, in the open area serving as the "orchestra pit," adjusted the microphone of his tape recorder: "Oh! You're all here, aren't you? Well, ladies and gentlemen, I have a slight apology to make before the per- formance begins. In spite of the fact that I'm in a tuxedo and in spite of the fact of this lovely overture you've just heard, this is not the open- ing of the San Francisco Opera season. And also, I might add, that in spite of this tuxedo (at $5 an hour), I am really wearing this tuxedo to distinguish me from certain other people around here. I am the only non-Existentialist on this side of the footlights!"

The actress Penny Vieregge ran up and handed Hagan a list of names. "First of all," he continued, "I want to introduce Mr. Weldon Kees, poet, painter, artist, etcetera, composer, critic, etcetera, etcetera, ad infinatum." The audience clapped and cheered as Kees took a bow, for he really was all of those things in one.

The rest of the cast then received their introductions. Michael Grieg, Hagan assured the audience, was not a relict of "that well-known Scandinavian composer," but an actor and journalist "best known in most dental parlors as a ghostwriter for *The Autobiography of Pain- less Parker*." Carol Leigh was "a kind of animated version of washday in a Chas. Addams' cartoon." Bill Ackridge and Phyllis Diller, Hagan said, were "drama stars," with Miss Diller being the only one in Ber- muda shorts. After Vincent McHugh was introduced as a playwright, he walked from the line and stood beside the emcee, for he, too, had something to read to the audience that further set the *Follies'* tone of understatement, a telegram: "I have brought up a communication, Bob, that I think that the audience should know about. This is serious, by the way, or reasonably serious. Mr. Ezra Pound has sent us greet- ings. They have been relayed by Mr. C. H. Kwak of the *Chinese World*, our good friend and a good friend of all poets, and Mr. Pound's con- tact in San Francisco who may, by the way, soon be the publisher of a great bilingual edition of Mr. Pound's translations from the Chinese classics anthology. There is a little catch about this. Mr. Pound sends his greetings, by kind of a twist usual to Mr. Pound, in Swedish. I will read them phonetically. I have no choice."

The *Follies* got under way with Weldon Kees and the other musicians playing "I Ain't Gonna Give You None (of My Jelly Roll)," which had been retitled "Joseph Henry Jackson, You Made the Night Too Long" for the *Follies*, satirizing the *Chronicle*'s book reviewer—and the author of *Mexican Interlude*, an automobile travel guide to Mexico.

As promised, the poets read. They did so in two rounds, and the verse was supposed be light. Kees chose one of his limericks and "Crime Club," which was a strange choice given the merry atmosphere that he wanted:

> *Small wonder that the case remains unsolved,*
> *Or that the sleuth, Le Roux, is now incurably insane,*
> *And sits alone in a white room in a white gown,*
> *Screaming that all the world is mad, that clues*
> *Lead nowhere, or to walls so high their tops cannot be seen;*
> *Screaming all day of war, screaming that nothing can be solved.*

There was more jazz, satire, and poetry. Lily Ayers arrived with much fanfare, removed her mink stole, and, in a dress that revealed her bare shoulders, read Teasdale, Wylie, and Eliot, with one of the poet's stools serving as her impromptu lectern. "I'm a little nervous," she explained. "After all, this is not my forte. I hope you'll stand still for it." (She later felt miffed by the packed hall and the "cheapskate poets' club," as she called Kees and his friends. They were obviously making money after she had agreed to appear without charging her usual fee. She also felt tricked into buying a copy of Kees's book.)

"Well I might say that was well projected," Hagan said after Lily Ayers left the stage to a standing ovation. He then explained that the next entertainment would be pantomime and dancing to poetry by Dick Martin and Jayne Nesmyth. This marked the return of the four poets. Vincent McHugh read "The Waitress," by William Carlos Williams. Kees appeared dressed in an army uniform. He stood on a raised platform and recited "Unarmed Combat," by Henry Reed, a war poem by an obscure British poet that was out of place in the evening's gaiety.

Michael Grieg took his turn reading for the dancers. For his text, he chose Pound's moving translation of "The River-Merchant's Wife: A

Letter," by Rihaku. Lawrence Ferling appeared next and read from his translations of Jacques Prévert.

The finale was Grieg's play *The Three Bottles*. Kees, on the Steinway, tinkled out a little "British music" to start the first scene, which included a throwaway line that made him laugh as much as he wanted the audience to laugh at his poems that night: "They always forgive poets—once they're dead."

The *Follies* ended with the cast lined across the narrow stage of the Theatre Arts Colony in two rows. Hand in hand, they took their bows before the cheering, sold-out crowd. As the smiling Kees tipped his derby, he was already thinking ahead to the Berkeley performances at the Little Theatre on Sunday, January 30. He wanted the *Follies* to be more rehearsed and polished, even while preserving its improvisational charm, its having "all the forethought of a game of charades," as one reporter noted. The playful talk of taking the *Follies* on tour, of names in lights, of steady money, and the idea that the *Follies* could be shaped into a Broadway show did not seem farfetched.

Bill Mayo's new billboards and the broadside that Adrian Wilson's "Steam Press" printed for the second *Follies* promised more, while the *Follies* themselves lost little from their original venue. Lily Ayers, who had agreed to only one engagement, was replaced by her statuesque colleague at the El Rey, Rikki Corvette, a six-foot-six stripper with the added distinction of having been voted Miss Burlesk of 1955. Additions included the actress and coloratura soprano Tamara Lindovna and her offering of "Songs That Touch the Heart." Eric Vaughn built a wonderful mechanical prop for the premiere presentation of his "GIANT POETIC BRAIN." In his act, where Boob-McNutt cybernetics met iambic pentameter, Vaughn fed the "brain" the works of Alexander Pope, John Masefield, and Yvor Winters on one side and delivered poetic clichés on the other, to be read with great wonder and appreciation for the benefit of the Berkeley audience.

Bill Heick took a photograph of the line that formed outside the theater, with college men dressed in tweed jackets and their dates dressed in long, ankle-length skirts. One couple looks at a hastily written cardboard sign: the evening show had sold out and a second show had been added for 10:15. From all accounts, both performances brought the house down with applause and calls for more.

Kees and friends followed the same formula as the week before, save for the additions and minor changes made in deference to the many Berkeley students in the audience. The title of the Barbary Coast Five's opening number was changed to honor—and send up—the ultra-conservative president of the University of California—and Rikki Corvette lisped her way through the poetry of Dylan Thomas in "homage" to the late Welsh poet's campus readings in 1952.

The next day, Kees rewarded himself with a purchase from Saint Francis Liquors, which also helped him to savor the *Follies'* first press clipping. Under the headline "Poets Expose *Follies*—Public Asks for More," Kevin Wallace of the *Chronicle* praised the *Follies* for reviving the old straw-hat variety show with the sophistication of literature and dance. The survival of the *Follies* could be a worthwhile project for the community: "The poets and the peasants, or public, who separated the year beer went up from a nickel, are making overtures in public places that have started a lot of talk. [...] [T]he hostile parties made googley eyes across the footlights during the mad and headlong course of '*The Poets' Follies* of 1955,' a bouillabaisse of literate ambiguities, pratfalls, dixieland and just horsing around."

Even with the demanding work of putting on the *Poets' Follies*, keeping the idea of San Francisco Films going, and showing up to work at Langley Porter, Kees reviewed a book for the *New Republic* and praised and panned movies on *Behind the Movie Camera*. In reviewing the films of 1954, he remarked that the "exceptionally hammy acting" of Marlon Brando had ruined *On the Waterfront* for him. Yet he liked Roger Corman's first film, a B-movie called *Highway Dragnet*. He also liked *Naked Alibi*, and he liked *Dial M for Murder* quite a lot.

During the taping of the February 12 show, Kees sounded light-headed from the glass of whiskey and ice his listeners could hear him set down near the microphone. He sounded sleep deprived as he spoke: "It is frequently said of this program that we don't like movies. But I can heartily recommend up until the last ten minutes of *Bad Day at Black Rock* that it is an excellent picture and by all means see it."

The *Poets' Follies* reopened at the Theatre Arts Colony on Thursday evening, February 10. The printed flier, though cheaper and less descriptive than the ones Adrian Wilson had printed at his Steam Press, now featured blurbs from the newspapers. Kees scheduled shows for every Thursday and Sunday at 8:00 P.M. until the end of February. The cast changed a little for each performance. Ketty Frierson sang at one. A Chinese actress performed at another. And T. S. Eliot continued to hold a special place in the *Follies.* Instead of stretching the talents of strippers this time, the *Follies'* actors performed *Sweeney Agonistes,* with Eliot's songs "Under the Bamboo Tree" and "My Little Island Girl" set to the music that Kees had specially written for them. Kees also played the part of Wauchope, sang baritone to Bill Ackridge's tenor, and played the piano.

Kees called his parents on the Sunday after the reopening. He told them that the Thursday show had sold out again and that he expected the next one to sell out too. He had John on the line and inquired after the new apartment that he and Sarah had recently moved into. He also asked about their health. Sarah had broken a hip. John, in a guarded voice, said that she was healing slowly. On Monday, she hoped to play a foursome of bridge with her friends again, even though this meant suffering through the burning in "her old sitter." John tried to look on the bright side, however, knowing that his son could get impatient with his parents' troubles. It was nice to be away from Nebraska's "dreadful weather." The new apartment had a "wonderful furnace," too. It was situated up higher than in their old apartment. From the balcony, John and Sarah had a view out over the mesa. They could even see, in the distance, patches of the Pacific Ocean. *The Country Girl* would be showing in Santa Barbara next week, and they promised Weldon they would see it since he had enjoyed Grace Kelly as the wife of the alcoholic songwriter played by Bing Crosby.

For his forty-first birthday on February 24, after that evening's *Follies,* some of Kees's friends gathered at his home on Filbert Street to give him a party. Bob and Kay Helm were there, now back from the East, as were the Wilsons, the Richardses, the Griegs, the McGrails, Bill Ackridge, Vincent McHugh, and some musician friends. They put a reel of tape on the Ampex and recorded the party, where people sang covers and some of Kees's songs, including ones he had been working on with the blind pianist of the Castle Jazz Band, Freddie Crews, who had come to the party. Some care was taken in making the tape, preserving the moment for Kees. His friends spoke with a poignancy that seemed more suited to a wake than to a party for a man entering his forties. This feeling also extended to some of his songs: "There'll be no next time, not the way that I feel."

The idea that the *Follies* should continue stayed with Kees after the show closed on March 20, a Sunday he would not forget. The *Sweeney Agonistes* had been especially good. The lighting by Frank and Marge Craig had been remarkable. Burgess Meredith, in the city to perform the stage play *Teahouse of the August Moon,* had been in the audience.

Though the *Follies* had left him virtually broke, Kees needed to replace it with something like it. He enjoyed the acclaim, the newspaper reporters, the sense of purpose that came from working with other talented people. He hardly felt depressed. He knew he would miss the high of the *Follies.* None of the pills he took to stay awake was like that. He wanted the cast parties and the after-show nightclubbing and drinking. He liked filling his small, brown-leather address book with new names and telephone numbers. Its binding had started to crack, and its pages had loosened from being opened so much. He was filling the margins.

What was needed was a permanent home for the spirits he had raised with the *Follies,* not only his, but Grieg's and his other friends'. He wanted to finish *Pick Up the Pieces* and have a place to stage it along with all the other ideas he had. He wanted his own theater as much as he had once wanted the puppet theater he had as a boy.

The Showplace began as an empty pre-earthquake building at 2528 Folsom Street. It resembled—and may actually have been—an unfinished sailing ship that had been turned over and stranded far from water. The present owner, a neighborhood housewife named Esther Gewirtz, only knew that it had been a boys' club once. Its wooden floors were still painted with the markings of a basketball court. It had also been the home of an archery club. Its stage, however, made Kees think the old hall had a different and far richer past, one he and his friends might revive.

After some negotiating with Mrs. Gewirtz's lawyer, Kees and Grieg signed a five-year lease on March 26 that stated they would use the hall for "Club Rooms or any lawful undertaking." The rent would be sixty dollars a month—and a strain on the finances of both men. So getting the wood-frame structure ready for occupancy and paying for itself had to be done in a hurry.

Before signing the lease, Kees had already planned a fundraiser for the Saturday evening of April 2 that would feature the "entire cast of *Poets' Follies*" at their new headquarters, music by three jazz bands, and a sampling of material from *Pick Up the Pieces*. The money, Kees promised, would be used exclusively to restore the Showplace to its Barbary Coast days' grandeur, which he liberally invented for the folderol invitations that Adrian Wilson printed: "It is rumored to have been a hideout for such notables as Ambrose Bierce, Judge Crater, and Geronimo (though not all at the same time). For a time, during the early part of this century, it served as a retreat for 'Big Sid' Proust, eccentric gold miner millionaire and patron of the arts. The building is said to have figured in the shooting of Von Stroheim's masterpiece, *Greed* (1924) but the 80,000-odd feet allegedly photographed in its lofty auditorium all wound up, apparently, on the cutting room floor. The widespread rumor that Jack London bred wolves on its massive balconies would seem to be without foundation."

Esther Gewirtz was more down to earth in what she thought of the building: "A Polish barn, like the ones I saw when I was a little girl."

Leasing the Showplace did not fully occupy Kees. With the renowned stride pianist Don Ewell and Ketty Frierson, he rehearsed and recorded demo tapes on the evenings when Ketty was free from the Purple Onion. The tapes might lead to a record deal with Cavalier Records or Label X, where the famous producer Orin Keepnews would hear them. Ketty's interpretations, Kees hoped, would give his songs the commercial sound they had lacked when he took them down to Los Angeles the year before. He now kept the new arrangements in a special folder, "Tunes for Ketty." Some were even dedicated to her.

Ketty never adopted the Bessie Smith style that Kees had once wanted from her. Instead, in her own voice, his songs came off as sophisticated, contemporary, especially his new torch song, "Too Cool to Care." He had started it back in October, and if any of his songs could be a personal anthem, it was this one:

> *I'm so listless and torpid and bugged,*
> *Facing this life with a shrug.*
> *I'm so cool — 'cause that's the rule — too cool to care.*
> *I'm so mixed up and weary and gone,*
> *Taking it all with a yawn —*
> *I'm so cool — 'cause that's the rule — too cool to care.*

At one of Ketty's weekly sessions in early April, Kees leaned on his piano and wrote down the lyrics to a new song as Don Ewell played. In the photographs Bill Heick took that evening, Kees appears to be listening intently to the tempo. He holds a Pall Mall in his left hand and a pencil in his right. A brushed aluminum tumbler, filled with water for the singer, is leaving a ring on the folder of her songs.

During this time, San Francisco Films had reached a turning point rather than the post-*Follies* milestones that Kees had set for the company. He wanted to get moving on his new documentary *The Bridge.* It was still just the raw footage that he and Bill Heick had taken of the Golden Gate Bridge but was beginning to come together as a tribute both to the bridge and to Hart Crane, whose poem about the Brooklyn Bridge seemed to Kees to fit the Golden Gate as well. They also planned to film a schizophrenic woman artist at Langley Porter with funding from a drug company. These projects, however, were overshadowed by Frank Stauffacher, now terminally ill with a brain tumor.

The cameraman had left unfinished *The Scavengers,* a two-reel documentary about a day in the remarkable and opulent life of San Francisco's garbage contractors. They were a culture unto themselves, arriving in the early morning with the din of trashcans in the streets to salvage whatever they fancied before discarding the rest in dumps by the ocean swarming with harpylike seagulls. Stark images such as this echo again and again in Kees's poems and may have been as much an impetus to complete the film for the dying man as was the need to bring in money to get the film company up and running.

Kees put together a budget and made plans for the film's production and musical score. He began writing letters to solicit as much as one thousand dollars from Stauffacher's wealthy friends and other prominent people and organizations that might have an interest in the project. Even the actor and dancer Gene Kelly received a solicitation via the Screen Actors Guild and, though pleading ignorance of the San Francisco scavengers, asked for more information. The letters stated that Kees, Michael Grieg, and the other members of San Francisco Films looked "on the project as a tribute to Frank." This approach, however, did not have the intended effect on Stauffacher's wife, who found Kees and Grieg's solicitations to be not only exploiting her husband's illness but making it seem as if he were already dead. Taking on the power of attorney for her husband, she had her lawyer write a cease-and-desist letter to Kees and Grieg ordering them to stop using Stauffacher's name in connection with the film for the solicitation of funds.

The threat of a lawsuit nearly drained Kees of any enthusiasm for continuing the film company, and he might have walked away from the venture had it not been for the formation of a new division in March: the Film Workshop.

It began as a new partnership, with Kees as director and Grieg as associate director. They convinced Bill Heick to be an associate and brought in two other local filmmakers, Denver Sutton and Ernest Snazelle. Like Heick, these men made short industrial and training films for a living, but they too had the kind of unfulfilled creative ambitions that Kees could draw upon. Sutton produced a bimonthly television program for the San Francisco Museum of Art and had made a number of abstract films. Snazelle, a pioneer of early live television in San Francisco, came from a show-business family. He had connections that Kees needed for his own aspirations in the medium, such as producing an Omnibus "teleplay" of the *Follies'* version of *Sweeney Agonistes* with Ford Foundation backing.

Its founders had thin credentials for offering the kind of training the workshop promised in its half-printed and half-handmade announcement, decorated with San Francisco Films' distinctive and volunteer logo, a Steam Press engraving of a man with a box camera on a tripod. Such a presentation, however, revealed that the mind behind the project was no less resourceful than that of the boy who had loved movies in Nebraska: "Although there is an ever-increasing concern on the part of film enthusiasts, artists, still photographers, and students of the motion picture for an opportunity to learn all phases of film production from professional craftsmen of national reputation, until now there has been no center or school for such instruction in the Bay Area." Kees promised that "visiting Hollywood directors, writers, cameramen, and actors, when they are in the area, will take part in the courses."

The faculty posed for an official photograph, probably intended for illustrating a more professional-looking printed brochure or press release. They posed with klieg lights, cameras, and Hollywood-style director's chairs. In one of these chairs, Kees sits with a pencil and clipboard, looking intense, as if he had just been working on a script.

The *Chronicle* ran an article about the workshop, but very few prospective students signed up for the course, and even fewer sent in checks for tuition. As March 21 approached, a two-inch column appeared in San Francisco's newspapers advertising that the first class would be free, with a showing of rushes from films by Bill Heick, Kees, and Denver Sutton. When this failed to generate interest, the workshop was delayed for several weeks until there were students.

One check arrived—a partial payment from a young man who could not spare more since the "tax collector [had] caught up" with him. By April's end, the workshop existed as a pile of unpaid bills—and a memo from a clearly disillusioned partner asking Kees what percentage of the profits his firm would receive.

ᎧᏩ

April had really been a month of progress for Kees despite what had gone wrong with his movie company and film school. He still had his little salary from Langley Porter. The fundraising for the Showplace had collected enough money to start rehabbing the building. He had attracted plenty of volunteers, too. The broadcasts of *Behind the Movie Camera* had been especially interesting and fun to do in the "cruelest month."

Kees had even convinced Burgess Meredith to appear. The actor had also promised to lend his name and sponsorship to the Showplace. With a new friend and collaborator, Byron Bryant, who had performed in the later *Follies* and taught drama at Saint Mary's College, Kees had taped a passionate discussion for a philosophical documentary about Trappist monks that explored the need for faith and meaning—and the difficulty in achieving these. And for the second year, Kees had been made a Shelley Memorial Award judge and had again successfully convinced the other judges to accept one of his favorites: Robert Fitzgerald.

Also that April, Kees drafted and sent in the first of his "San Francisco Letters," reporting on San Francisco gallery and museum exhibitions for *Art News*, a job offered to him by the magazine's editor, Alfred Frankfurter, in March. Though he had been asked to restrict himself to brief reports on local art events without going "into long analysis of the work," Kees was allowed to interpret the news from San Francisco in as broad a way as possible. To achieve the right tone, he wrote a trial piece based on a long walk and conversation with Allen Tate, then in the city to read at the Poetry Center. In the fragment that survives, Kees, in a way, imparts what made him live in San Francisco:

Tate had never visited here before. We had lunch at a restaurant near the ocean, not far from Cliff House, and then walked for a while on China Beach, a little-frequented spot in the Presidio and only a short distance from downtown. It offers a remarkable view of Golden Gate Bridge and the Pacific, with gulls and lighthouses and an appalling brilliance of sunshine and, on that day, a small, shy dachshund with whom Tate and I attempted to strike up an acquaintanceship. [...]

Everyone who comes here wants, apparently, to stay; at least they say so. And more and more are arriving, thousands and thousands of them. The city spreads and grows down the Peninsula as smog-dazed refugees from Los Angeles and nervous émigrés from New York and other Eastern points pull in. Among them are increasing numbers of painters, writers, and educators. Something of this sort needs to be said in order to talk about the atmosphere of this city, where so much art activity, good, bad, and indifferent, is carried on.

It is possible to avoid here the narrowness of role into which one is cast in other towns I have known; I am thinking of places where painters speak only to painters, and where some of them merely talk to themselves. Novelists, poets, painters, sculptors, film-makers, printers and designers, composers, musicians and actors find it easy to meet on common ground, to become friends, and even to work together. Art galleries are springing up like so many ice plants; some of the blocks on Fillmore Street, in the Marina, are beginning to resemble a more sunlit version of 57th Street.

The managing editor of *Art News* did not use this copy. She strongly advised Kees to seek out the shows that would be up during the summer for the travel issue. She wanted, she told Kees, "descriptions of events that would benefit the tourist."

In his new résumé, prepared for the California School of Fine Arts, where Kees had been asked to teach an art seminar course in 1956, he did not list himself as a poet and made no mention of being a judge for the Shelley Memorial Award. He buried his three books of poetry in a paragraph that also fudged about his writings for the *New Yorker,* leaving the impression that they had been essays on "films, music, literature, etc."

That day spent with Allen Tate, to whom Kees once looked for help in getting published, had not rekindled his interest in the poetry "business." He thought of "fiddling" with a long poem again, but he was "tired of that particular struggle at the moment." He knew how well some poets made out nowadays. He had recently heard that his old friend Ted Roethke earned eighteen thousand dollars a year teaching at the University of Washington, lived in the painter Morris Graves's swank house, lectured, gave readings, and received prizes. For now, however, Kees accepted the modest nobility of being counted among the other good writers, musicians, composers, and teachers who were, as he said, "driving Yellow Cabs or tending bar."

When it seemed that he was only interested in writing for the movies, for television, for his music hall, Kees wrote a serious play, a literary play. *The Waiting Room* is first mentioned in a flier for the Showplace that Kees circulated in late April, which advertised "the first of a series of musical, dramatic and artistic events." The evening of April 23 would feature the Bay City Jazz Band. On May 1, Don Ewell would give his first San Francisco piano concert. Later in May, on dates to be announced, four one-act plays had been scheduled for a limited engagement. These dramatic evenings, titled *Four Times One*, included *Sweeney Agonistes* and three new productions: *The Gallant Cassian* by Arthur Schnitzler, *The Tenor* by Frank Wedekind, and the new play by Weldon Kees.

Kees wrote *The Waiting Room* for three actresses from the Interplayers. Penny Vieregge had appeared in several performances of the *Poets' Follies*, as had Jan Davis and Nina Boas, a young married woman Kees had become attracted to. He wanted her to play Nancy, a disturbed child-woman tormented by her father fixation, his suicide, a domineering mother in the mold of Sarah Kees, and the death of a beloved young husband who had protected her from the real world. Kees knew about such damaged young women from working at Langley Porter.

Mike Grieg, Byron Bryant, J. Padgett Payne, and other San Francisco theater directors were involved in *Four Times One*. Yet it is not hard to detect Kees's hand guiding the choice of the plays by Schnitzler and Wedekind. Kees, for his part, must have known about Schnitzler's play from his student-acting days, when a Little Blue Book translation was widely available. *The Gallant Cassian* anticipated the German Expressionist theater and cinema of the 1920s, which Kees enjoyed and counted as an influence on his own artistic development; Schnitzler had called this work his "puppet play." *The Tenor* exploited the lofty, Romantic conception of art and the artist-prince once held by the German middle classes and taken up by prosperous Americans in the postwar years. Kees, given that he was nearly broke all the time, would turn that notion inside out, for he was certainly and ironically the fallen artist-prince, especially to his parents. There was a certain truth in Wedekind's play that he—and his younger friends, too—needed to hear more often: "The measure of a man's worth is the world's opinion of him, not the inner belief which one finally adopts after brooding over it for years. Don't imagine that you are a misunderstood genius. There are no misunderstood geniuses."

Nina, in readings and rehearsals, did "everything but fly a kite," and this encouraged Kees to perfect his play throughout the first two weeks of May. He was doing it for her. She would make an entrance and encounter two other, older women, sitting across from each other on long wooden benches. The premise that time has stopped is quickly established in the waiting room of what could be a railroad station or bus terminal. The uncertainty of where the three women are shows the influence of Sartre's *No Exit*. That they are waiting for people who never appear and things that never happen suggests the influence of *Waiting for Godot,* as well, for Grove Press had published the English text of Beckett's play in 1954.

The play progresses through a number of surreal and even horrific interludes. The principal characters could be fragments of Kees in female form. Patricia, forty, is like a woman Robinson or his sister, another Kees alter ego, another one of the show-business personas through which Kees saw himself. Patricia's New York years, described to Nancy, seem a deflated stand-in for Kees's own time in that city. Jill had been married to a drunken grotesque, like the one Ann became: "'Jill,' he'd say—I remember he used to lean forward as though it was a matter of life and death, and he'd point his finger at me ... God, he *never* cleaned his fingernails ... and he'd say, 'In this culture'—he was always using that phrase."

The dialogue given over to Nina-Nancy, however, drives the play toward moments that gave Kees an opportunity to see himself stripped of being the tough-guy construct—a reason why he must hold a mirror up in female *and* child form — indeed, the vulnerable and "cherished" daughter in his poems, of the little-girl murals painted on the walls of a New York restaurant, and so on. Nancy's parents live in Santa Barbara, and her alcoholic father is remote and helpless to change the course of the madness that the mother set in motion for her child. He is still her intercessor, her last hope, and when Nancy reveals his fate, it could almost be the playwright pathologizing his own situation, what it would be like not to have his own father:

PATRICIA: *Poor man.*
NANCY: *He's dead now.* (Dissolve out on *Father.*)
PATRICIA: *(*Touched *) Oh, I'm sorry.*
NANCY: (Rapidly*) You know? After one of those phone calls one day, he hung up the receiver and ... shot himself.*
(A long pause)
JILL: *(*Anxious, tense*) Listen, did you hear that sound?*
PATRICIA: *I didn't hear anything.*
JILL: *(*To Nancy*) Didn't you hear it?*
NANCY: *No.*
JILL: *It was like ... something falling.*

Nancy is profoundly acute in her madness. She is Kees's Electra. She intuits what is wrong with a world of disappointments and of being a disappointment herself. Kees could observe himself at various angles in Nancy that were not otherwise visible in his mustached face. And he may have done so in an especially harsh light, observing that he had spent his life doing over what he did in Beatrice, that his plans and projects, his books and paintings, were what he and Bateson studied in humans and otters: forms of play:

NANCY: *Why did you let me grow up? (Patricia* alert; *Jill* nervous and annoyed*)*
NANCY: *(*Toneless*) I said: why did you let me grow up?*

The image of the child victim runs throughout the play. Kees made it impossible to miss when he replaced the poem Nancy recites early in the play, Edna St. Vincent Millay's "The Hardy Garden," with an unattributed poem that he may have supplied himself ("I am a child or the pale ghost of a child, / Strangely withdrawn and apart").

The toy balloon Nancy carries on a stick is part of this sublimated image, too. It is a gift for her little boy, who never appears in the play, who may not be alive or even real. It is inflated at the beginning of *The Waiting Room* and deflated at the end, when the women decide to leave and Nancy hesitates. "Sometimes," she says to Patricia, "nothing turns up and you have to live with that, too. I can still pretend." She smiles as the other women go, and she takes up the balloon that is now clearly a symbol of the world, life, dreams, and all the sublimated things Kees knew an audience would read into it. She blows the balloon up and holds it out admiringly. "I want to be happy!" she cries three times. Then Nancy breaks the balloon, though it is uncertain how: with her hands, with a stickpin, with too much air. The play ends with a drum roll.

It is also uncertain whether Kees or one of his friends added the quotation from "Aristophanes' Apology," by Robert Browning, as the play's epilogue. It is even uncertain when this quotation was slipped into the "Director's Copy." It lacks the annotations for lighting, sound, and other stage directions, made in Kees's hand. Though not formally incorporated, the epigraph fits. It makes *The Waiting Room* into another "Aristophanic fragment," as Eliot called his *Sweeney Agonistes,* and more of a companion piece in the setting of *Four Times One.* Its poet's curse would have been to Kees's taste, too; it could almost be his finger pointing at the guilty party:

> And the home I scatter, and house I batter,
> Having first of all made the children fall,
> And he who felled them is never to know,
> He gave birth to each child that received the blow,
> Till, Madness, I am, have let him go.

Around this time, Kees started dating Virginia Patterson, an attractive thirty-one-year-old clinical psychologist who lived across the bridge in Sausalito and worked at Langley Porter. She was much sought after by the men there, and she was known to have a taste for the strong type, which Kees seemed to be with his deep voice and dark good looks. He first came on to her that spring, asking her out to the Purple Onion to see Ketty sing or to dances at the Showplace. He had wanted a new relationship and had left himself open to one around the workplace.

It must have been deliciously ironic to him to find himself in the company of Virginia. She was the antithesis of Ann and Jerry, a healer as opposed to the sick, who now chided him for his overdrinking. With her background in analysis, she could listen and respond to his feelings about the rise of psychiatrists and self-help Freud. To her, he would have sounded very much like he did in the review of Vernon Duke's autobiography he was now writing for a June issue of the *New Republic:* "I suppose that everyone thinks that his life is interesting to some extent or the suicide rate would be even higher than it is; consider the number of persons who keep journals, diaries, write their autobiographies or talk about the most humdrum aspects of their lives to each other or even pay for the privilege of doing so in the company of such professional listeners as psychiatrists." Such sardonic remarks were pure Kees to his friends during this time of rehearsals and rebuilding the Showplace—nothing to worry about. This was his world-view, and to them he seemed utterly comfortable living with it, their "Papa Wel."

The Vernon Duke review was his because Bob Evett knew Kees understood songwriting. He also knew that Kees was a researcher at the Langley Porter Clinic and had the gimlet eye to expose the fraud in the latest "self-analysis-can-be-fun" manual: *Love and Hate in Human Nature,* by Arnold A. Hutschnecker, M.D. It was the sequel to his best-seller, *The Will to Live.*

The doctor, who practiced Freudian analysis on wealthy and celebrity patients, believed that if people could understand their emotional upsets, they would avoid physical and mental illness and contribute to world peace.[2] Naturally incredulous, Kees probably enjoyed the Jungian synchronicity of reading Hutschnecker while writing and rehearsing *The Waiting Room.* The play countered the idea that happiness came through self-knowledge. Kees's Nancy would have been unable to reach the doctor's nine easy steps. In writing his review, with the parodic title "How to Be Happy: Installment 1053," Kees took such self-improvement plans to task and made the point that Dr. Hutschnecker had ignored what artists "of the order of Sophocles and Shakespeare, or any poet with a tragic sense," had been saying since well before Freud had been canned and sold: "Socrates, Proust, and Coleridge, for instance, had more 'self-knowledge' and knew more at first hand of love and hate than the Doctor will ever know; they also wrote very well indeed, unlike the Doctor, and with greater reverence and humility; and they never believed for a moment that 'self-knowledge' could, in the long run, save them—or us. [...] The liberal assumption that self-knowledge will lead to 'adjustment' and 'happiness' is a curious one."

A "New York offer" to Ray Higgins, who had the title role in *The Tenor*, forced Kees and the other directors and players of *Four Times One* to change the opening date of the first performance to Friday, May 27. Higgins's departure also entailed the hasty replacement of *The Tenor* with an equally hasty substitution, *The Brimstone Butterfly*, by Michael Grieg. This "lighter" entertainment, more of a divertimento than a play, would be directed by its chief prop, "Leo the Butterfly," who, in turn, also played "himself" in the lead role. Though Grieg now had equal billing as one of the Showplace playwrights, the original "scheme" of plays had been compromised. Nevertheless, with Grieg's play inserted after the intermission and before *The Waiting Room*, the climax of the evening now belonged to Kees; *Four Times One* would end with Nina Boas's desperate plea and an exploding toy balloon that would resonate through the Showplace, with all kinds of interpretations about what *that* might mean, including the atom bomb.

This was not to be, however. The rehearsals for *The Waiting Room* seemed undisciplined and chaotic to some of the actors, due in part to Kees's hectic and inky rewrites on his director's copy. Nina's pantomime scene, in which she transforms herself from a little girl to a ballroom dancer to a secretary in a law firm, had not been resolved. Kees had typed "QUICK BUSINESS TO BE WORKED OUT WITH NINA," as if the urgency of the capital letters would fix things. He had to somehow get the balloon discreetly deflated, Jill's shoes back on after she took them off, and other details sorted out. To the three women, he at once looked terribly driven and devoted to their art and less and less the theater professional they had mistaken him for.

On Monday, May 23, Kevin Wallace's profile of the Showplace, "'Longhair Vaudeville' Goes to Folsom St.," appeared in the *Chronicle*. A three-column-wide photograph of the Showplace's interior illustrated the article, with a barefooted and ponytailed Nina Boas and Penny Vieregge leaning on their mop handles, taking a break from cleaning the wooden floors. They listened to Kees, Grieg, and the reporter talking on stage about the *Follies* for next year and about *Four Times One*, due to open that week.

The free publicity, however, had the unfortunate effect of attracting the attention of the fire department. After a routine inspection of the Showplace, an inspector declared the building unsafe and ordered it closed.

Kees had new fliers overprinted with an announcement that *Four Times One* had been postponed. Then he waited for the fire marshal to make a further inspection to assess what needed to be done to bring the Showplace up to code. He knew there was no money for that. The theater had yet to turn a profit. The money from the housewarming concert and dance was gone. The Don Ewell show had been poorly attended.

Kees had to come to a painful decision about the Showplace. *Pick Up the Pieces* was still ideas on paper, as it had been for months. The Showplace, though, was where he would show off the persona he preferred above all others. He had even scripted a trailer for his musical that Bill Heick would shoot, that would be shown on a small screen during the intermission of *Four Times One,* in which he would sit before an upright piano with its front off so that its hammers could be seen, the Piano Player, Papa Wel: "He wears a derby hat, has a chewed butt of cigar in corner of mouth and pencil behind his ear. There is a bottle of gin on top of the piano. He holds up a folio with 'Shuman' on the cover. He studies a phrase of music, takes a pencil from behind his ear and writes notes on a piece of manuscript paper."

He would have to let the Showplace go, and let go of its piano player, if *Pick Up the Pieces* was not finished enough. He would have no choice. With June's rent due, the San Francisco Fire Department inspector came and gave him the "final dicta." All the wood walls would have to be covered with sheetrock. "I wanted to cry, 'Enough!' So I did," he wrote Byron Bryant. "The towel, clutched compulsively for so long, has now been thrown in."

Kees was forced to leave the theater seats he had found and the piano inside the building. He returned the props and lighting equipment to their owners, including an antique clock and candelabra borrowed from the Legion of Honor with Jerry's blessing. As for the lease, it remained to be seen if he and Grieg could get back their deposit and get out of paying any penalty for breaking it, which, for the moment, could be the whole five-years' rent.

The debt, from his perspective, seemed crushing. He looked to Santa Barbara again.

Leaving Langley Porter one day, not long after the closing of the Show-place, Kees took a long look at the Campanile on the Berkeley campus. From the top, he could have seen the students walking to and from their classes: young men with crew cuts, girls in long, pleated skirts and white blouses, clasping books over their breasts. He had filmed them once for one of Bateson's films.

He took a deep breath, walked back down the stairs, and joined his old life again. He purchased a new wiper blade for his car. He took his phonograph to Pardini's Radio and TV to get a new tube installed. He wrote a check for $34.50 to pay the premium for another year of theft insurance on his apartment. He saw Deborah Kerr in *Tea and Sympathy* and looked forward to seeing another touring Broadway play, *Dear Charles,* with Tallulah Bankhead.

With the last of their Rockefeller money, he and Gregory Bateson finished the river-otter film. Kees even picked up *The Waiting Room* again and began revising the stage version into a teleplay, still thinking he could break into television.

Kees, though not an outdoorsman like his friend Kenneth Rexroth, took Virginia camping at Big Basin and Big Sur on the second weekend of June. This put some color and movement back into a relationship that he had pushed for, not her. And he would not have the expenses of dinner and drinks that came from going to restaurants and bars. The entertainment would come from the car radio instead of a Los Angeles nightclub. The wildlife would be supplied by an encounter with a raccoon and a snake during their hiking.

The following weekend provided another low-budget outing, during which they attended an opening at the San Francisco Museum of Art. There the punch, Kees thought, was better than the modern art. The exhibition had been mounted for the visiting dignitaries gathered in San Francisco for the tenth anniversary of the signing of the United Nations charter. Their presence in the museum reminded Kees of the Showplace, for he had hoped that some of them would fill the seats for *Four Times One* and give it international exposure.

For the rest of June, Kees tried to resume his old routine. Orin Keepnews sent him an urgent telegram requesting that he and Ketty come down to Los Angeles. Keepnews wanted to record some of the songs they had been rehearsing. But Ketty's manager interfered, insisting that she not be limited to just singing Kees's originals, that she have some songs in the "pop category" and some union musicians (whom Kees could pick). Keepnews never wired the money. Kees continued work on his color documentary about the schizophrenic woman painter at Langley Porter and learned that there would not be any money coming for a feature-length version. Horace Schwartz and Bill Ackridge asked him to help produce a *Poets' Follies*-style revue for the United Nations celebration, but he begged off.

He wanted to get away again, and an opportunity came when one of Nina's friends offered him and Byron Bryant the use of a cabin seventy miles north in Sonoma County, on the banks of the Russian River. Bryant, however, was recuperating from an illness in the Marin County countryside.

Kees did travel north in the last week of June to appear on the stage of the Napa County Fair, playing piano, with Jesse Fuller on Footdella and Penny Vieregge on vocals. The show should have left him feeling better about things, yet that same week his affair with Virginia hit a low point. There had been a feeling between them since the camping trip that they were breaking up. For her part, Virginia was overwhelmed by him. He wanted something more from her than she could give, and she did not like how depressed he became and how he explained it away as worry over his mother's health. She especially felt uncomfortable with him when he talked about suicide statistics, particularly in reference to the Golden Gate Bridge, when he drove her home to Sausalito. He said he was working on a book about suicides, but she wondered. Nevertheless, she held onto the copy of Fitzgerald's *The Crack-Up* that he had lent her. She assumed she would see him again.

The anniversary of Ann's breakdown came and went on July 4, which may have been one reason why Kees wanted some kind of commitment from Virginia. He felt more tired as he kept to his routine. He returned to his radio show on Saturday night. It now had a new name, *Behind the Scenes,* and a new location on the radio dial, KRE-AM/FM. His friend Maury Schwartz, the owner of two movie theaters, the Bridge and the Rio, sponsored the program, which had been widened to include books, plays, art, and music for a "heavy culture-minded, book-buying audience" that Kees estimated to include twenty-five thousand listeners. He tried to believe that San Francisco wanted this and him.

He had received a wonderful letter praising him for the Garbo show he had done in April, and Virginia loved the rapport in his May interview with Jerome Cowan, the character actor who had starred in two of his favorite movies, *The Maltese Falcon* and *Young Man with a Horn*. He still made remarks with plenty of acid, like his dig at Robert Taylor for a "fearfully inept performance" in *Camille*.

The summer, however, seemed as disappointing and boring as the art scene he described in *Art News*, in a column that had been edited down to a list of shows. Anyone could have written it.

But no one else could have written so calmly about "our present atmosphere of distrust, violence, and irrationality, with so many human beings murdering themselves—either literally or symbolically." Kees could look ahead to this rather signature observation in his review of *Love and Hate in Human Nature* in the *New Republic*. It would come out on July 18 and keep his name in print for a little while. Then there would be nothing until *Nonverbal Communication* came out— and he still had no idea when that would be. He kept reading his novel.

By now he had taken to heart the passages in *The Devils* in which Kirolov, the engineer, the bridge builder, is revealed to be "collecting observations" about "the causes of the increasing number of suicides in Russia." It sounded like *Famous Suicides*, that book Kees had talked about writing or that Lowry Wimberly, back in Lincoln, had never got around to writing.

As Kees read further, he came to Kirolov's rationalization that full freedom would only come when it made no difference whether one lived or not. Such a state would be the arrival of a new life, a new man. Everything would be new, transformed: "Deception will be killed. Everyone who desires supreme freedom must dare to kill himself. He who dares to kill himself is a god. He who dares to kill himself has learnt the secret of the deception. Beyond that there is no freedom; that's all, and beyond that there is nothing. He who dares to kill himself is a god."

Kees could savor the idea that he knew there really were people like Kirolov. He was one. And as his dark thoughts ran parallel to the text for that brief time, he could more *author* his last days than simply get through them. His death would have a style. He could stand back and enjoy his despair as if it were something he might want to read next.

In those days that felt like his last, Kees went to the Rincon Annex and retrieved his mail as before. He kept a few more appointments. He purchased a new bottle of Jack Daniels and poured Lonesome a fresh dish of milk. He reread passages from *The Tragic Sense of Life*. He took other books from his shelves and read or reread certain pages, certain poems that would have read differently in his current state.

Kees met friends, often for dinner. He drove to Mill Valley to see Nathan and Carol Asch, whom he had gotten to know well again after those happy days spent at Yaddo in 1942. Though they thought he seemed down on the suburbs, Kees seemed to make himself at home. He took off his necktie, opened his collar, and really seemed to relax and talk.

He visited his parents in Santa Barbara and even left on good terms with his mother — and without any money.

Not long after getting back, he met Grieg over the course of several evenings. Grieg thought they would discuss the idea of converting an old movie theater into a revival house. But Kees, with his bottles of Jack Daniels, was not loosening himself up to talk about business. In the harrowing conversations that followed, he told Grieg about his plan to either jump from the Golden Gate Bridge or go to Mexico. He talked long enough and hard enough to work up an appetite. The two men had supper together at the Italian Village on the last night they saw each other, Sunday, July 17.

Kees took most of the following Monday to make his final decision. He was still undecided when he made a last phone call to the Richardses in the afternoon. He caught Janet just as she and Charles were leaving for the airport to pick up her elderly aunt:

"I may go to Mexico. To stay."
"Right away?"
"I don't know."
"Weldon, for God's sake don't go without seeing us."
"I won't," he said, and then he hung up.

He did not keep his promise. Probably during the evening, he drove across the Golden Gate for the last time. It is not possible to know his thoughts, to know what he now apprehended after reading Rilke's "Archaic Torso of Apollo" on the previous evening, but it is possible to see that the bridge was where he might have confronted himself as a poet easily and naturally. He had been coming out to it so often during the past months to film his combined homage to Hart Crane and the Golden Gate. Here he could feel the air and the height that had inspired Crane's masterpiece "The Bridge" the same way that he had in New York. He could really feel what it was like to be Crane's "bedlamite speeding to the parapets, / Tilting there momently, shrill shirt ballooning."

The fog may have already been rolling in when Kees arrived. It was so thick that evening that it enveloped the bridge, as some of his friends would later remember. He parked in the sightseers' lot on the Marin County side. From there, he knew well the footpath that led to the bridge and the railing and how long it took to walk until there was no land below.

Epilogue / Ellipsis

*There was scarcely anyone
whom I thought more likely
or better fit to survive.*
　　　　　—Willy Poster

Two days after they learned of his disappearance, Kees's parents checked into the Saint Francis Hotel. They had come up the coast from Santa Barbara. To Kees's San Francisco friends, though, who were received in their room, the elderly couple might as well have come all the way from that small town in Nebraska that Kees said he was from. Though he physically resembled his mother, the friends could also see how much of the father had been passed on to the son. Weldon's ironic voice and impeccable taste in clothes had come from him.

"And would he leave Lonesome alone in his apartment for days?" John asked, remembering his son's beloved cat, speculating hopefully out of consideration for his wife, Sarah. She wondered aloud if it was possible that her son would turn up. The police had not found a body, she said. Then, thinking that he had, like a little boy, been neglectful, she said that he probably had forgotten to tell anyone he was leaving town. Perhaps Ann, she said, had come back to haunt him?

The police had already talked to John—and because of them he was already speaking of his son in the past tense. He did not let on to his wife, however, that Weldon was not coming back. Nor did he say anything to contradict the Richardses, Michael Grieg, and the few others who came and kept resuscitating the possibility that their friend would return.

John had not forgotten the last time he saw his son in Santa Barbara, a few weeks before. The problem of money had come up between them, and so had other things. Both had read Malcolm Cowley's *The Literary Situation,* and both had been moved by the chapter that describes the change of life a writer experiences when he turns forty and must confront what he has or has not achieved. The younger Kees at last seemed to be ready to break the manic pattern that always led him back to his father with debts and little to show to his mother. He had to take into account his parents' age and health. They both had illnesses. They had doctor bills. They might not be able to live independently. They might need his help. He was all they had, too. Something had to change, John knew, after Weldon went back to San Francisco, and something did.

"After all," he heard his wife cry as she clutched someone's hand, "they haven't found his body in the bay."

When it was time for the friends to leave, John escorted them to the elevator. While holding the door to the car, he asked if anyone would take Weldon's cat.

Janet Richards said she could not. She had a parakeet.

"I never thought of Lonesome as much of a hunter," the elder Kees said with a restrained smile. Then he let the elevator go.

On Saturday, July 23, Pauline Kael wrote the editor of *Partisan Review,* Philip Rahv. In her letter, she wondered if the Eastern papers had carried news of Weldon Kees. Surely the Eastern papers would print something about him, since his name had been in the news. She reported how depressed and guilty she and Kees's other friends had felt: "All of us—the 30 or 40 people—who saw Weldon frequently & who were used to being yanked out of bed by his fantastically early telephone calls—knew that he was miserable, he had been telling us all how slack & lethargic & miserable he was."

Kael blamed herself and the rest of Kees's circle for how they could not reach him or do anything to help: "It was as if a dynamo had suddenly run down—& we couldn't think of any way to help start it up." She felt she had failed, along with the other friends. There had been visible signs of isolation, she wrote. The last time Kees had visited, he spent the entire evening clutching Kael's little daughter. He mentioned that his parents were ill and that this concerned him. He felt everything was slipping away. "He had been talking for weeks about nobody giving a damn for him & his not giving a damn for anybody either."

Michael Grieg taped *Behind the Scenes* without his co-host, Weldon Kees. The program aired one week after the disappearance. Grieg opened with a recording of Ketty Frierson singing "Daybreak Blues," which he had discovered the day before in Kees's apartment. The torch song had taken on a new meaning as Ketty sang, "Got the bad news." Now it no longer simply lamented being abandoned by a lover. Its giveaway lines, in which Phyllis Diller and other friends now thought they heard Kees predicting his own death, had become more haunting.

Grieg described the song's composer as one of the "most distinguished poets writing in this country, though not as recognized as he, I think, should be."

Nathan Asch, Grieg's guest on the program, warmly described meeting and befriending Kees at Yaddo during the war years. To him Weldon stood out from the other summer residents. He was a strange figure for a poet and did not look the part, "if that means anything to anybody who tries to imagine what a poet looks like. I always thought he looked more like a Broadway character. He was always very well dressed, right in a Brooks Brothers' style. And he always had a slightly confidential look about him, leaning forwards towards you, as if he was about to buttonhole you and impart to you something of extreme importance."

"I always felt the man was somebody I knew well," Asch continued, "even though I really didn't know him very well."

Grieg steered the conversation back to Kees the poet as he seemed to reassure his listeners that Kees's cat, Lonesome, would be taken care of by friends. He recited the last serious poem that Kees had published in a magazine, "Colloquy," which had appeared in the *New Yorker*. In a halting voice, Asch responded. In the shadow of Kees's disappearance, one could now really hear him for the first time. One could really apprehend fully what he meant by "the customary torments / And usual wonder why we live":

I have a feeling, without wanting to presume anything at all. It would be a terrible thing to presume, to tell what exactly has happened to Weldon. At this moment, we his friends are waiting, just as the newspapers, just as the police are waiting. And we don't know what has happened to him. But all of his friends have agreed that Weldon was essentially a sad person, and that for all the fact that he was interested in some of the more or less joyous aspects of, let's say, theatrical life, he was essentially a person who was melancholy. And almost everything he writes, there is a great melancholy in it. Whether it was a condition of his or whether he had an unhappy time, we don't know. No real artist has ever a happy time of it, really. But he may have been particularly predisposed to unhappiness.

On this the two men agreed. Then Grieg read another poem, "Travels in North America," which touched on how deeply Kees felt about being separated from his friends. For Asch, the poem revealed the dispossessed American artist Kees had become since their Yaddo summer of 1942. He waited for Grieg to finish and then said: "It is a beautiful evocation of America, [an] *Under the Road* of America, the description, the observation, he saw these things and makes us see them now. I would *hate,* absolutely hate to think that this particular giftedness, such a rare gift and a gift which is often neglected in this America of ours, for bringing back America to us poignantly, be lost. I am hoping that it isn't."

As the news of Kees's disappearance spread, some of his friends could not believe that he had simply vanished. Virginia Pauker was certain she and her husband, John, had had supper with him *before* his car was found. This would have been on Monday, or on Tuesday, July 19. The Paukers were in town and had not seen Weldon in some time. They drove to the restaurant. Then they took Kees back home to his apartment near the Marina. The Paukers kept tactfully silent about Ann all evening, even though they had all been friends, close friends, during the war years in New York. Then, unprompted by anything that had been said that evening at dinner or in the car, as they pulled up to Kees's apartment, he muttered from behind them something that sounded like, "Ann's not here anymore."

When Hugh Kenner learned in August that Kees had vanished the month before, he too found it hard to believe. He was sure he had seen his friend in the Santa Barbara Library in late July. He had practically just talked to Kees about those films they had wanted to script—and it was not unusual to see him in Santa Barbara unannounced during one of the visits he paid his parents.

Kenner had not talked long in the library with Kees, who seemed preoccupied by something. He left him alone, assuming there would be more occasions to talk.

Norris Getty learned about the disappearance from Kees's father in late August. A month had passed. There was still no word from Weldon, no new information about him. In his letter, however, John tried to give his son's best friend from his Nebraska and Colorado days a little hope. He reported that Kees's bank balance was just over eight hundred dollars. His son should have had no pressing "financial worries." All he needed to do was wire for the money from somewhere. The

California Highway Patrol believed that he had not leaped from the bridge. His wallet, watch, sleeping bag, and savings-account bankbook had not been found. These were things that suicides did not take with them. And then there was Weldon's tidiness, which extended to taking care of personal responsibilities. The detective assigned to the case had discovered that one of the last things Weldon did was make the final payment on the Plymouth.

Weldon, John admitted, was certainly depressed and discouraged, but his closest friends in San Francisco thought he was no more depressed than he had been at other times. He should have at least left some note to allay his mother's anxiety. John felt that his son should have been courteous in this regard. This was so "out of character for him." Perhaps his depression had turned into amnesia. "I know so little about that," the elder Kees wrote, "but hope that he will recover and return. The uncertainty is hard to bear."

When Ann Kees learned about her former husband's disappearance and the car left on the north end of the bridge, she was certain he had not only jumped but done something cleverer. The state patrol, she would write Norris Getty, "simply couldn't know that Weldon was an expert on suicide and would do exactly the things that a policeman wouldn't expect." She was also still bitter and at one point told the psychologist Dr. Joseph Wheelwright, her supervisor at the student health center, that Kees had run off with a male lover.

As the person who volunteered to be the caretaker of Kees's belongings, Michael Grieg found this role uncomfortable from the very beginning. When he met with Ann to discuss her getting back some of the things she had once held in common with Kees, she could not bear to talk about him. She said she wanted nothing of his except any letters from her.

Her very coldness was probably reason enough for Grieg to avoid seeing her again and to return the letters she had sent to Kees at Yaddo. However, he probably rightly assumed that she wanted to destroy something her ex-husband had intended to keep, and this ran counter to another possible motivation for Grieg's actions and inaction in protecting not only Kees's things but, perhaps, Kees's memory itself.

This is borne out in the way Grieg tried to get the *New Republic* to run a notice of Kees's disappearance and a request that if readers possessed manuscripts or paintings belonging to Kees, they should return them to his care at Kees's Filbert Street address.

Grieg also contacted Lou Pollack of the Peridot Gallery in order to get Kees's inventory of paintings and collages shipped back to him. His doing this made the elder Kees suspicious of the inordinate interest Grieg had taken. John Kees wanted his son's artworks returned to him or kept in New York, but Grieg ignored or only partly fulfilled this request. He had heard that John did not consider his son's painting important. He had seen John give the paintings and collages away for nothing to almost anyone calling themselves Weldon's friend; it might be impossible to find them again and gather them together so as to see what Kees had achieved as a painter.

Instead of doing what John asked when it came to giving away Kees's art or selling his first editions, Grieg remained their protector. He tried to disarm the father with news of ventures to keep Kees's name alive or of Lonesome, who had finally gotten used to Grieg's presence in Kees's apartment, for which John continued to pay the rent until the end of 1955.

Malcolm Cowley, like other friends in the East, found it hard to get news about Kees's fate. In a November letter, writing to Conrad Aiken, he could only report a disdainful comment about Kees from his only source of information, Kenneth Rexroth. Cowley knew, of course, that they had been rivals, that "Kenneth rides his own hobbie horse" when it came to Kees. He also reported that there was still no word from Ann. He repeated the rumor that Kees had lost his job because of security reasons.

The *Poets' Follies of 1956* opened on January 26 at the Cellar Stage. This time, Michael Grieg assumed much of the role Kees had, including "Has Tux, Will Travel."

Many of the same performers appeared, among them Phyllis Diller, "Uncovered by Last Year's *Follies*" and now the Purple Onion's comedian, and Jan Davis as Molly Bloom, reading from *Ulysses*. On a new *Follies* broadside, Adrian Wilson's Steam Press listed these and other entertainments, which included the world premiere of *The Bridge*, a film by William Heick and Weldon Kees, and a lobby exhibition of the Kees paintings and collages that Grieg had moved from Kees's old apartment to his basement.

After buying a broiling chicken and a bottle of gin for her dinner, Ann, one evening in late May 1957, typed out a reply to an old letter from Conrad Aiken asking for some explanation of Weldon's disappearance. She had only seen him twice after signing their divorce papers: a brief, unpleasant meeting in January 1955 and an accidental encounter at a restaurant in the spring. He struck her as manic then. She could see that he was obviously driving himself, and there had to be a letdown. It must have been during this most trying period of all that he disappeared. On his calendar, he had even circled the date, she had learned from friends, on which he would kill himself: "I think his friends and his family hoped against hope that he would reappear—from the hills of Mexico or the wilds of Schweitzer's Africa, or wherever. I accepted his disappearance as a suicide from the beginning because it was something he had talked about ever since I've known him—and that goes a long way back."

In the aftermath, Ann felt she had started to "flourish a little." She still had her job. The Berkeley students looked to her as a kind of mother figure. And she looked forward to going back to Wyoming for a visit—in time to see the state fair, with its parades of palominos and Indians, its rodeos, flower shows, canned carrots, and spun taffy. "I think I am trying to say," she admitted, "that it took more than the court's sayso to divorce me from Weldon, but that had finally come about."

The gathering and printing of *The Collected Poems of Weldon Kees* began as a strange letter that the poet and teacher Donald Justice received from John Kees. John Kees had learned that the spring 1957 issue of the *Hudson Review* featured a sestina by Justice in which he responded to lines in Weldon Kees's own sestina, "Travel Notes," using the same words: *others, voyage, silence, away, burden,* and *harm.* "Please tell me how you happened to write the poem," the elder Kees wrote, for it seemed that Justice was having a kind of secret conversation with Weldon. "Did you know Weldon? It is now two years since he went away. We still cling to the hope that he is still living and that one day he will return."

John received a reply from the young poet and an explanation for the poem. Justice told him how he had written the sestina in the summer of 1955, not long after earning his Ph.D. from the University of Iowa, where he had studied in the Iowa Poetry Workshop. Justice thought his poem was good enough to show the man who had inspired him to work in such a difficult form and that doing so might be the right gesture since he had used Kees's name in the title. After getting over some initial reticence about forcing himself and his poem on Kees, Justice tried to look up his address. He thought of asking Ray West, from whom he was renting a house in Iowa City that summer. After all, West had known Kees in Denver and was just now getting back from a trip to San Francisco. It seemed only natural to think the two friends had gotten together. But this had not happened. When West tried to look Kees up, he learned instead that he was missing.

At this news, Justice felt something like disappointment trailing off into shock. His new poem could now be read quite differently, and the six borrowed words resonated with more than just Kees's poem, especially the words *silence* and *away*. (A concordance reveals that of the six words, Kees used these two the most.) Now the sestina was an unintended elegy as news of Kees's disappearance slowly circulated in the poetry world. (*Western Review* and *Poetry* printed notices in 1956. Their belatedness only gave the strange story the unreality and remoteness more often associated with a lost expedition or a famous mountain climber who had not returned.)

Justice exchanged a number of friendly letters with John Kees. A year later, he offered to edit a limited edition of Weldon's poems. John hoped that a piece of his son's artwork might be used for the frontispiece. Then he changed his mind and suggested a portrait or photograph—probably at the behest of his wife—to "help find him if he is living." Two hundred copies were printed by the Stone Wall Press in 1960 and bound in black leather. It was reviewed in the *New York Times* by Kenneth Rexroth in a piece called "A Stranger on Madison Avenue," which John Kees got to savor before he died and his son's name vanished from the stage of American poetry.

The public-television station in Lincoln, Nebraska, aired a documentary entitled *The World of Weldon Kees* in the winter of 1961. John Hull, who would later become the director of the Program Fund for the Corporation for Public Broadcasting, met John and Sarah Kees at their home on South Twenty-seventh Street to interview them and collect some photographs and manuscripts for the program, which featured a University of Nebraska professor discussing Weldon's poetry and short stories and the curator of the university's art gallery showing some of Weldon's paintings, photographs, and his film *Hotel Apex*.

Hull could tell that the elderly couple had not fully recovered from the loss of their son. He never forgot the poignancy of the moment when Sarah Kees began to talk about the cruise she and John had recently taken to Hawaii and Australia. As their ship sailed into Sydney's harbor, it passed another ship leaving port. It came close, and among the passengers standing on deck, Sarah could see a man who looked like Weldon. She and John waved and called, but their voices did not carry.

In August 1962, Eleanor Barrett's daughter Toni, now fourteen, visited New Orleans in order to spend a week with her father. One evening, still warm from a day on which the temperature had reached over one hundred degrees, her father took her to Preservation Hall on Bourbon Street. Outside a crowd had lined up to see and hear the great clarinet player George Lewis.

Toni's father found a place to stand against the wall of the club, but close to the stage. Across the room, Toni could see the entrance and the people coming in and paying a man at the door. Just before the eight o'clock performance began, the handsome man she had seen as a little girl, her stepfather's friend, who came over to dinner so often, the man with the mustache and the dark piercing eyes, paid his cover charge. On his arm was a willowy young woman with blond hair.

Her mother had said he was not dead. He could not have taken his life the way it was reported. He was too fastidious, and he would not have liked his neat clothes getting wet. He was strange in that way, she said, he was a strange man.

For a brief moment, Toni's eyes and the man's locked, and she felt a rush of mutual and instant recognition pass between them. He had been kind to her when she was a little girl. He had once said she looked pretty. She turned to her father and, without realizing that he would not know the name, whispered loudly, "Daddy, it's Weldon Kees!" Then Toni looked back across the room and pointed. But the man and his companion were gone.

Notes

1. In 1941, Kees would make Gable the model of a small-town man of letters and the author of *The Boy's Book of Camera Craft* in the novel *Fall Quarter.*
2. Kees even entertained the notion of becoming a "medicine-man of the left-press" at the behest of the socialist writer Paul Corey, who proposed that labor-union locals and farmers' organizations have "some live person" present at their meetings to sell the works of leftist authors in order to intercept "massamerica" before it spent its money on Hearst publications, a movie, or "five gallons of gas for just running about."
3. See "The Chaotic Age: Twentieth Century," in *The Western Canon,* by Harold Bloom (New York: Harcourt Brace, 1994).

DENVER, 1937–1942

1. Vilfredo Pareto (1848–1923) was an economist adopted by the Italian fascists—and in Kees's mind their American counterparts—whose theories were considered both an antidote to the Depression and a counterargument against Communists.
2. Kees refers here to the best-selling Scottish novelist A. J. Cronin.
3. Tess Slesinger was the author of the screenplay for *A Tree Grows in Brooklyn.*
4. In one of her Yaddo letters, Ann brings up Kees's need to appear masculine and does so suggestively by comparing him to his best friend. "Your Yaddo is black and white and gray," she wrote. "You have a good color sense but you don't use it nearly enough. I think you're afraid of becoming fruity. As an example: the immediacy of Norris' description of Huachuca by giving colors of mountains, shadows, sky, desert."

NEW YORK, 1943–1948

1. *See Here, Private Hargrove,* by Marion Hargrove, was a humorous account of army life.
2. During this time Kees adopted a vegetarian diet and gave away his meat-ration cards to Malcolm Cowley and other friends he encountered on the street. Conceivably, he did so to affect his red-blood-cell count.

3. The painters Bob and Virginia di Nero were the parents of the actor Robert DeNiro.
4. "Flents" refers to the Swedish brand of earplugs indispensable for sleeping near the El.
5. Borglum was the sculptor of Mount Rushmore.

PROVINCETOWN, 1948–1950
1. Excerpted from "Reviews and Previews," Weldon Kees by M.G., Copyright © 1949, *ARTnews LLC, November.*

SAN FRANCISCO, 1950–1955
1. Kees refers here to Edward de Vere, the Earl of Oxford, who, in the 1848 edition of John Thomas Looney's *"Shakespeare" Identified,* was once again asserted to be the real author of Shakespeare's works. That de Vere had been dead for nearly 350 years may be the intended humor—not Giroux's later Shakespeare scholarship, which was unknown to Kees.
2. As an advisor to the Nixon administration, Hutschnecker authored a program for detaining children with a potential for violence in concentration camps.

Sources

The bulk of Weldon Kees's papers and other materials such as films and recordings exist in two depositories, namely The Heritage Room of the Bennett Martin Public Library in Lincoln, Nebraska, and the Gertrude Stein Gallery in New York City. The latter source comprises papers, manuscripts, paintings, films, recordings, photographs, and books from Kees's library entrusted to the care of his friend Michael Grieg by the poet's father, John Kees. After the death of Michael Grieg, these materials came into the possession of Gertrude Stein. Smaller depositories exist, such as the one that I have gathered during my research. Much of this book is based on this material, and readers may assume that any unattributed evidence has been drawn or inferred from there, from the selected sources listed below, and from the information made available by the individuals and institutions noted in the acknowledgments.

PRIMARY

Babb, Sanora. 1992. Letter to the author. January 20.

Bellow, Saul. 1992. Letter to the author. October 21.

Broughton, James. 1997. Letter to the author. September 30.

Bryant, Byron R. 1983. Letter to the author. August 29.

Bultman, Fritz. 1982–83. Conversations with the author.

Carlson, Bernice Wells. 1991. Letter to the author. July 15.

————. 1991. Letter to the author. July 23.

Federal Bureau of Investigation. 1942. Communist Infiltration at Yaddo, Saratoga Springs NY. File No. AL. 100–11391. Document made available through the Freedom of Information Act.

Getty, Norris. Correspondence, 1941–56. Weldon Kees Papers. The Bennett Martin Public Library, Lincoln NE.

Hoffman, Paul. 1941. Memoranda to Alfred A. Knopf, February 21 and December 8. Alfred A. Knopf, Inc. Records, 1914–61. Manuscripts and Archives Division, The New York Public Library, Astor, Lenox and Tilden Foundation.

Hull, Ron. 1983. Letter to the author. August 3.

Johnson, Maurice. Correspondence, 1935–48. Weldon Kees Papers. The Bennett Martin Public Library, Lincoln NE.

Kael, Pauline. 1955. Letter to Philip Rahv. July 23.

Keeley, Mary Paxton. n.d. Weldon Kees on the Missouri Campus. Mary Paxton Keeley Papers, 1830–1983. Western Historical Manuscript Collection—Columbia, University of Missouri/State Historical Society of Missouri.

Kees, Ann Swan. Correspondence, 1942. Weldon Kees Papers. Gertrude Stein Gallery, New York NY.

———. Correspondence, 1943–50. Weldon Kees Papers. The Bennett Martin Public Library, Lincoln NE.

Kees, Weldon. 1932. The Percy Poggle Incident. Weldon Kees Papers. The Bennett Martin Public Library, Lincoln NE.

———. Correspondence, 1934–55. Weldon Kees Papers. The Bennett Martin Public Library, Lincoln NE.

———. 1949. American Jazz Music. Weldon Kees Papers. Gertrude Stein Gallery, New York NY. (An edited version was published in *Dark Horse* 4 [winter 1996–97]: 50–53.)

———. Song lyrics, 1952–55. Weldon Kees–Bob Helm archive. Caliban Bookshop, Pittsburgh PA.

———. 1953. KPFA broadcast, fall 1953. Weldon Kees Papers. Gertrude Stein Gallery, New York NY. (Transcript of a discussion on the nature of reading poetry.)

———. 1954. Notes on the Past: Before the Break. Weldon Kees Papers. Gertrude Stein Gallery, New York NY. (Informal diary concerning Ann Kees, June–July 1954.)

———. 1954. San Francisco Films: A Prospectus for Motion Picture Production in the Bay Area. Weldon Kees Papers. The Bennett Martin Public Library, Lincoln NE.

———. 1954. Transcripts of "Becky" tapes. Weldon Kees Papers. The Bennett Martin Public Library, Lincoln NE. (Interviews with ventriloquist Dr. Gerald Feigen and "Becky," his dummy.)

———. 1955. Prospectus note from an announcement for The Film Workshop: A Division of San Francisco Films. Weldon Kees Papers. Gertrude Stein Gallery, New York NY.

———. [1955]. San Francisco Letter. Weldon Kees Papers. Gertrude Stein Gallery, New York NY. (Fragment of an unpublished trial essay written for *Art News*, c. March 1955.)

———. 1955. *The Waiting Room*. Director's copy. Weldon Kees Papers. The Bennett Martin Public Library, Lincoln NE. (No complete version of Kees's one-act play is known to exist at this writing. A seven-page fragment of the later teleplay version exists [Weldon Kees Papers, Gertrude

Stein Gallery, New York NY] that was probably drafted in June 1955. It should be known that previous publications of *The Waiting Room,* most notably the text published in *Prairie Schooner* [spring 1986], are based on the flawed transcript made by John Kees. A reconstruction of the teleplay has been prepared by the author.)

————. n.d. *Word and Act: A Film about How People Understand Each Other.* Weldon Kees Papers. The Bennett Martin Public Library, Lincoln NE. (Script for a film about nonverbal communication by Weldon Kees and Gregory Bateson.)

Kees, Weldon, and Nesuhi Ertegun. 1954. *Assignment to Peril: An Original Screenplay.* Weldon Kees Papers. The Bennett Martin Public Library, Lincoln NE.

Kees, Weldon, Pauline Kael, and Michael Grieg. 1955. Tape-recorded broadcast of *Behind the Movie Camera: The Films of 1954.* KPFA-FM (Berkeley CA), January 8. Weldon Kees Papers. Gertrude Stein Gallery, New York NY.

Kees, Weldon, and Vincent McHugh. 1954. *Gadabout: An Original Screen Story.* Weldon Kees Papers. Gertrude Stein Gallery, New York NY. (Incomplete typescript of screenplay.)

————. 1954. Tape-recorded discussion of *Gadabout* screenplay. Weldon Kees Papers. Gertrude Stein Gallery, New York NY.

Kees, Weldon, et al. 1955. Tape-recorded dialogue from *Poets' Follies.* Weldon Kees Papers. Gertrude Stein Gallery, New York NY.

Kenner, Hugh. 1993. Letter to the author. October 18.

————. 1993. Letter to the author. November 18.

————. 1993. Letter to the author. November 19.

————. 1993. Letter to the author. December 6.

————. 1993. Letter to the author. December 29.

Krecek, Vicki Elliott. 1964. Weldon Kees. (Unpublished paper written for a high-school composition class based on interviews with Sarah Kees and other relatives and supplied to the author.)

Krim, Seymour. 1984. Letter to the author. November 17.

Laughlin, James, IV. 1992. Letter to the author. April 2.

Lowry, Robert. 1983. Letter to the author. June 21.

Marvin, Robert. 1977. Letter to John McKernan. December 6.

————. 1979. Letter to Leonard Thompson. November 21.

————. 1979. Letter to John McKernan. December 6.

————. 1980. Letter to Leonard Thompson. January 16.

————. 1980. Letter to John McKernan. January 24.

————. 1984. Letter to the author. March 9.

———. 1984. Letter to the author. June 15.

———. 1985. Letter to the author. January 16.

———. n.d. Letter to Richard Brengle.

Myrer, Anton. 1983. Letter to the author. November 17.

———. 1984. Letter to the author. February 9.

———. 1984. Letter to the author. February 26.

———. 1984. Letter to the author. March 19.

———. 1984. Letter to the author. April 18.

———. 1984. Letter to the author. July 16.

Poster, Constance H. 1984. Letter to the author. December 30.

Richards, Janet. 1983. Letter to the author. January 22.

Rothschild, Judith. 1982–84. Conversations with the author.

———. 1984. Letter to the author. April.

Ruesch, Jurgen. 1986. Letter to the author. March 26.

———. 1986. Letter to the author. April 17.

———. 1986. Letter to the author. May 7.

———. 1986. Letter to the author. May 16.

———. 1986. Letter to the author. August 7.

Strauss, Harold. 1941. Memoranda to Alfred A. Knopf, March 6 and December 9. Alfred A. Knopf, Inc. Records, 1914–61. Manuscripts and Archives Division, The New York Public Library, Astor, Lenox and Tilden Foundation.

Umland, Rudolph. 1984. Letter to the author. September 19.

———. 1984. Letter to the author. October 16.

West, Ray B. 1984. Letter to the author. August 4.

———. 1984. Letter to the author. September 7.

———. 1984. Letter to the author. September 13.

SECONDARY

Abbott, Craig S. 1989. The Guidebook Source for Weldon Kees' "Travels in North America." *Notes on Contemporary Literature* 19:8–9.

Ashton, Dore. 1973. *The New York School: A Cultural Reckoning.* New York: The Viking Press.

Beatrice Daily Sun. 1931. Club and Social Affairs: Weldon Kees as Player. *Beatrice Daily Sun,* December 27, 6.

———. 1946. Weldon Kees Author of Bikini Newsreel Script. *Beatrice Daily Sun,* August 12, 1.

Brooklyn Eagle. 1948. Boro Writer Makes Mark as Painter. *Brooklyn Eagle,* November 7, 12.

Broughton, James. 1993. *Coming Unbuttoned.* San Francisco: City Lights Books.

Bultman, Fritz. 1987. Weldon Kees: Enemy of Mediocrity. *Provincetown Arts* 3:119.

Callenbach, Ernest. 1955. *Hotel Apex* (1952): Notes. (Unpublished supplement to Callenbach's course and textbook *Our Modern Art: The Movies* [Chicago: Center for the Study of Liberal Education for Adults, 1955]. Also intended as material for "program notes or publicity purposes.")

Cowley, Malcolm. 1941. "What Poets Are Saying." *Saturday Review of Literature,* May 3, 3, 10.

Crane, Milton. 1985. Three Recent Volumes of Verse. Review of *The Fall of the Magicians,* by Weldon Kees. In *Weldon Kees: A Critical Introduction,* ed. Jim Elledge, 144–45. Metuchen NJ and London: Scarecrow Press. Originally published in *New York Times Book Review,* June 8, 1947.

de Kooning, Elaine. 1949. Abstract Watercolors. Review of Weldon Kees in group show at Peridot Gallery, June 25 through July 25. *Art News* (summer): 54.

Deutsch, Babette. 1943. Some Recent Poetry. Review of *The Last Man,* by Weldon Kees. *Common Sense* (November): 419.

Gendel, Milton. 1949. Weldon Kees: Peridot to November 26. Review of one-man show by Weldon Kees. *ARTnews* (November): 51.

Getty, Norris. 1979. Weldon Kees. *Sequoia* 23:21–22.

———. 1989. Remembering Weldon Kees. *Boulevard* 4:143–56.

Gioia, Dana. 1989. The Afterlife of Weldon Kees. *Boulevard* 4:137–43.

Goodnough, Robert, ed. 1951. Artists' Sessions at Studio 35 (1950). In *Modern Artists in America: First Series,* ed. Robert Motherwell and Ad Reinhardt, 9–22. New York: Wittenborn, Schultz.

Gordon, Ambrose. 1985. New Verse. Review of *The Fall of the Magicians,* by Weldon Kees. In *Weldon Kees: A Critical Introduction,* ed. Jim Elledge, 145–47. Metuchen NJ and London: Scarecrow Press. Originally published in *Furioso* 2/4 (1947).

Gregory, Horace. 1985. Of Vitality, Regionalism, and Satire in Recent American Poetry. In *Weldon Kees: A Critical Introduction,* ed. Jim Elledge, 141. Metuchen NJ and London: Scarecrow Press. Originally published in *Sewanee Review* 52 (1944).

Grieg, Michael. 1956. Letter to the Editor. *Intro Bulletin* 1/8: 4. (Corrects some factual errors in an article by Helga Voigt Epstein, Speculation Growing on Strange Disappearance of Weldon Kees: Report of Poet's Suicide Remains Unconfirmed. *Intro Bulletin* [March–April 1956].)

Harper, Robert D. 1977. Weldon Kees: Nebraska's Versatile Artist. *The Periodical of Art in Nebraska* (winter): 2–4.

Hays, H. R. 1985. Mirror to Human Inadequacy. Review of *The Fall of the Magicians*, by Weldon Kees. In *Weldon Kees: A Critical Introduction*, ed. Jim Elledge, 147–49. Metuchen NJ and London: Scarecrow Press. Originally published in *Poetry* 70 (1947).

Kazin, Alfred. 1986. Untitled memoir. In *Six Decades at Yaddo*, 25–31. Saratoga Springs NY: Corporation of Yaddo.

Kees, Weldon. 1934. Saturday Rain. *Prairie Schooner* 7:179–83.

———. 1935. Frog in the Pool. *Prairie Schooner* 9:115–22.

———. 1936. Noon. *Manuscript* 3:41–44.

———. 1937. Homage: In the Library: Four Sketches. *Direction* 1:21–31.

———. 1938. Zuni Street Evenings. *Rocky Mountain Review* 3:7, 9–10.

———. 1940. The Life of the Mind. In *The State of the Nation: Eleven Interpretations*, ed. Robert Lowry, 31–46. Cincinnati: Little Man Press.

———. 1943. Uninhibited Ha-Ha. Unsigned review of *I Am Thinking of My Darling*, by Vincent McHugh. *Time*, August 16, 104.

———. 1975. *The Collected Poems of Weldon Kees.* Donald Justice, ed. 1960. Reprint, Lincoln: The University of Nebraska Press.

———. 1984. *The Ceremony and Other Stories.* Dana Gioia, ed. Port Townsend WA: Graywolf Press.

———. 1986. *Weldon Kees and the Midcentury Generation: Letters, 1935–1955.* Robert E. Knoll, ed. Lincoln: The University of Nebraska Press.

———. 1988. *Reviews and Essays, 1936–55.* James Reidel, ed. Ann Arbor: University of Michigan Press.

———. 1990. *Fall Quarter.* James Reidel, ed. Brownsville OR: Story Line Press.

Kees, Weldon, and Gregory Bateson. 1951. *Hand-Mouth Coordination.* (Data film dealing with communication and interaction. Collection of the author.)

Kees, Weldon, and Bob Helm. 1998. Holiday Rag. Trinidad CA: Badger Press. (CD compilation of demo recordings made by Kees and Helm from 1953 to 1955.)

Kees, Weldon, and Jurgen Ruesch. n.d. *Approaches and Leavetakings.* (Data film dealing with communication and interaction. Collection of the author.)

Laughlin, James, IV. 1944. Editor's Notes. In *New Directions 8*, xv–xx. Norfolk CN: New Directions.

Loeser, Katinka. 1985. Dismal Yew and Dismal Me. Review of *The Last Man*, by Weldon Kees. In *Weldon Kees: A Critical Introduction*, ed. Jim Elledge,

142–43. Metuchen NJ and London: Scarecrow Press. Originally published in *Poetry* 63 (1944).

Loudon, Michael. 1992. Weldon Kees. In *Critical Survey of Poetry (English Language Series)*, ed. Frank N. Magill, 1787–95. Englewood Cliffs NJ: Salem Press.

Marvin, Robert. 1948. The Upper Room. Editorial column. *Beatrice Daily Sun,* December 22, 2.

"Muskrat Ramble: Popular and Unpopular Music." *Partisan Review* 15 (May 1948): 614–22.

Myrer, Anton. 1951. *Evil under the Sun.* New York: Random House.

Nebraska State Journal. 1941. Dedication — Wendell Kees Winning High Recognition. *Nebraska State Journal,* June 15, 6.

Nelson, Raymond. 1989. The Fitful Life of Weldon Kees. *American Literary History* 1 (winter): 816–52.

Poster, William. 1985. Some Recent Verse. In *Weldon Kees: A Critical Introduction,* ed. Jim Elledge, 143–44. Metuchen NJ and London: Scarecrow Press. Originally published in *New Republic,* December 20, 1943.

—————. 1950–52. Correspondence. Weldon Kees Papers. The Bennett Martin Public Library, Lincoln NE.

[Preston, Stuart]. 1948. Three One-Man Shows Head Week's Art. Review of Weldon Kees's one-man exhibition at Peridot Gallery. *New York Times,* November 5, 23.

Rexroth, Kenneth. 1985. A Victim of Today. In *Weldon Kees: A Critical Introduction,* ed. Jim Elledge, 158. Metuchen NJ and London: Scarecrow Press. Originally published in *New York Times Book Review,* April 17, 1955.

Richards, Janet. 1979. *Common Soldiers.* San Francisco: The Archer Press.

Ruesch, Jurgen, and Weldon Kees. 1956. *Nonverbal Communication: Notes on the Visual Perception of Human Relations.* Berkeley: University of California Press.

Scott, Winfield Townley, and J. F. A. [Weldon Kees]. 1949. Bookman's Gallery. *Sunday Providence Journal,* September 25, sec. 6, p. 6. (Article about Forum 49.)

Shively, Steven B. 1992. Re-Claiming the Home Place for Weldon Kees. (Unpublished paper supplied to the author.)

Umland, Rudolph. 1977. Lowry Wimberly and Others: Recollections of a Beerdrinker. *Prairie Schooner* 51:17–50.

Voigt Epstein, Helga. 1956. Speculation Growing on Strange Disappearance of Weldon Kees: Report of Poet's Suicide Remains Unconfirmed. *Intro Bulletin* 1/6 and 7: 2.

—————. 1985. Point Richmond Artist Weldon Kees Devotes Time Evenly between Two Fields. In *Weldon Kees: A Critical Introduction,* ed. Jim Elledge, 104–6. Metuchen NJ and London: Scarecrow Press. Originally published in *San Francisco Examiner,* November 1951.

Yazoo/Kees Power Equipment. 2001. About Us: Company History. Available at <http://www.yazookees.com/about/index.html>. (This company Web site provides a history of the F. D. Kees Manufacturing Company and its various owners from 1874 to the present.)

Index

The abbreviation WK refers to Weldon Kees. Page numbers in italics refer to photographic inserts; the first number is that of the text page preceding the insert, the second, the illustration number.

art, of WK (*cont.*)
150–51, 158; painting in Provincetown, 173, 175, 203, 207, 210, 223, 226;
painting in San Francisco, 238, 282,
283–84; paintings given away, 151, 181;
painting style, 151; painting titles, 179;
Poets' Follies backdrop, 329; prices
of paintings, 178, 181; relationship of
painting and writing, 150–51, 179; sales
of works, 181, 224, 277, 286; sculpture,
242; titles of paintings, 179. *See also* art
exhibitions, WK's work; Kees, Weldon,
Works
art criticism: of Farber, 138, 259; of
Rosenberg, 138, 162. *See also* Greenberg, Clement
art criticism, of WK: on Baziotes, 174,
216; Cézanne project, 179; for Kootz
gallery, 151; for the *Nation,* 207–08,
210, 212–13, 216, 218, 219–20, 222, 227,
251, 284; profile of Motherwell, 162–63
Art Digest, 284
art exhibitions: Gallery 200 (Provincetown), 197, 199, *192–14;* Guggenheim
Gallery of Non-Objective Art, 78;
in Provincetown, 197, 199, 223, 225;
Whitney annual, 212, 238, 241–42. *See
also* Peridot Gallery
art exhibitions, WK's work: at Kootz
Gallery, 219; at Palace of the Legion
of Honor, 254, 256, 259–60, 308; in
Provincetown, 200; reviews of, 180,
211–12; in San Francisco, 283–84, 285–
86, 360–61; Whitney annual, 212, 238,
241–42. *See also* Peridot Gallery
Art News, 203, 211–12, 339, 350
art of schizophrenics, 294, *192–30*
"Arts in Action," WK as curator, 251
Arvin, Newton, 102, 104, 105, 111, 161
Asch, Carol, 351
Asch, Nathan, 102, 351, 357–58
Ashton, Dore, 138, 236
Aswell, Edward, 100
Atlantic Records, 234
atomic bombs: anxiety about, 167, 215–
16, 280; Hiroshima bombing, 148; tests
of, 148
Auden, W. H., 79; defenders of, 266;

influence seen on WK, 130; lectures
of, 327; poetry of, 139, 183, 213; Rhoda
Klonsky and, 232; WK and, 318; at
writers' conferences, 81, 91
Austin, Claire, 317
avant-garde. *See* abstract art; little magazines; modernism; New Directions
Ayers, Lily, 328–29, 331, 332, *192–24,
192–25*

Babb, Dorothy, 47–48
Babb, Sanora, 47–48
Balanchine, George, 196
Balcon, Sir Michael, 313
Ballard, Fred, 30
Barbary Coast Five, 327–28, 331, 333,
192–27
Barker, George, 118
Barr, Alfred, 220
Barrett, Eleanor, 307, 309, 363
Barrett, Jim, 307, 309
Barris, Harry, 316
Bateson, Gregory: relationship with WK,
252, 256–57, 297; research on schizo-
phrenia, 308; view of psychoanalysis,
240
Bateson film projects: data film on
mothers and children, 239–40, 245–
46, 253; equipment, 275; funding,
253, 289, 293, 295, 297, 319; on play,
283, 290, 295, 296, 301, 348; students
filmed, 348; on ventriloquism, 295–97.
See also nonverbal communication
Baudelaire, Charles, 119, 130
Bauhaus, 206
Baur, Rudolf, 78
Baziotes, Ethel, 171, 286
Baziotes, William: boycott of Metropolitan Museum exhibit, 222; and Eighth
Street Club, 191; financial problems of,
176; paintings of, 138, 174, 180; radio
programs with WK, 192; relationship
with WK, 156, 171, 173–74, 208; WK's
letters to, 201, 286; WK's reviews of
paintings of, 174, 216
Beach, Joseph Warren, 284
Bearden, Romare, 150, 197, 210, 222–23
Beatrice NE: and Buffalo Bill Show

parade, 17; Carnegie Library in, 13, 21; cultural life in, 13; described in WK's short stories, 10, 16, 37; economy of, 12–13, 22; First Presbyterian Church, 12, 22; high school, 23, 27–28; Institution for Feeble-Minded Youth, 13, 28; Kees family in, 11–12, 233; Mennonite Deaconess Hospital, 11; and name of town, 13; weather of, 10–11; WK's view of, 23; WK's visits to parents in, 57, 58, 93, 108, 171, 177

Beatrice *Daily Sun,* 14, 16, 21, 23, 30, 88, 155

Beats, 278

Beckett, Samuel, 342

Becky (ventriloquist's dummy), 295–97, 298, 326

Beddoes, Thomas Lovell, 90, 91

Beekman, Gerardus, 206

Behind the Movie Camera, 320–21, 325, 326, 333, 339

Behind the Scenes, 349–50, 356–58

Beiderbecke, Bix, 23, 104

Bellow, Saul, 106, 108, 115

Bemelmans, Ludwig, 131

Berg, Alban, 276

Berger, Arthur, 118, 119

Berkeley CA: Ann Kees's secretarial work in, 239; Keeses' apartment in, 280, 282; *Poets' Follies* performances in, 332–33. *See also* Langley Porter Psychiatric Clinic; University of California, Berkeley

Berkman, Alexander, 3

Berryman, John, 141, 149, 185, 281

Best Short Stories, 41, 88

Biddle, Francis, 195–96, 203, 205, 227, 237

Biddle, George, 67, 193, 195–96, 197, 200–201

Bierce, Ambrose, 48

Big Sur CA: Myrers in, 234–35, 251–52, 264, 269, 272–73; visits to, 256, 272–73, 348

Bill (homosexual textbook salesman), 34–35

Bischoff, Elmer, 244

Bishop, Elizabeth, 141, 154, 217–18

Blake, Peter, 197

Blesh, Rudi, 202

Bloom, Harold, 53

Bloomberg, Wilfred, 206

Boas, Nina, 341, 342–43, 346, 349, *192–31*

Bobbs-Merrill, 281

Bogan, Louise, 73, 117, 134, 317

Bogart, Humphrey, 46, 246, 267, 281

Bolender, Todd, 196

book reviews. *See* Kees, Weldon, Works

Borglum, Gutzon, 161, 366 n.5

Born, Max, 142

Born, Wolfgang, 142

Botteghe Oscure: publicity by WK, 227, 237, 243; WK's poetry published in, 288, 293

Bourgeois, Louise, 191, 223

Bourne, Randolph, 15, 71, 82, 106, 134

Bowles, Paul, 215

Boyle, Kay, 73

Brace, Ernest, 139–40

Bradford, Charles, 219

Brando, Marlon, 184, 333

Brandt, Dorothy M., 255

A Breaking and a Death (Kees): rejections of, 246–47, 252, 258–59, 277–78, 281, 282, 287–88; submission to publishers, 233, 247, 250, 274, 277–78. *See also Poems 1947–1954*

Breit, Harvey, 121, 123, 125, 128

Breuer, Marcel, 193, 196–97, 206

Brita (neighbor), 271, 279–80

Brooklyn Bridge, 181, 337, *192–12*

Brooklyn Heights NY, 149–50, 158, 175, 181, 189–90, 192

Brooks, Cleanth, 81, 160

Brooks, James, 178, 223

Brossard, Chandler, 231–32

Broughton, James, 243–45, 254, 326–27

Browne, Byron, 151, 180, 238

Browning, Robert, 344

Broyard, Anatole, 231–32

Brugh, Spangler Arlington. *See* Taylor, Robert

Bryant, Byron, 339, 341, 347, 349

Bultman, Fritz, 240; exhibitions organized by, 223; family of, 199; Forum 50, 225; and paintings, 238; photographs, *192–14;* posters, *192–15;* re-

Bultman, Fritz (*cont.*)
   lationship with wk, 173, 191, 192, 198,
   204, 223, 225, 227, 329; withdrawal
   from Forum 49, 206, 223; wk's letters
   to, 264. *See also* Forum 49
Bultman, Jeanne, 173, 175, 192, 198, 199
Busa, Peter, 102

Caetani, Marguerite, Countess, 227, 288,
   293
Calas, Nicolas, 79
Caldwell, Erskine, 63, 85
California: articles on, 238; compared to
   East Coast, 237; decision to move to,
   226. *See also* Big Sur ca; Los Angeles;
   San Francisco; Santa Barbara ca
California Highway Patrol, 5
California School of Fine Arts, 235, 236,
   340
Callenbach, Ernest, 276
Camper, Art, 106
Cane, Melville, 305, 306, 314
Cantwell, Robert, 64, 122, 123
Cape Cod. *See* Provincetown
Capote, Truman, 161–62, 186, 260
Carlson, Bernice Wells, 19
Carmichael, Hoagy, 293
Carnegie Foundation, 82, 83
cars: Lincoln Zephyr, 221, 224, 226, 231,
   232, 264, 273, 283, 292–93, *192–16;*
   Plymouth Savoy, 5, 292, 293, 352, 359;
   Plymouth ("Tiresias"), 189, 192, 198,
   211
cartoons, *New Yorker,* 284–85
Castle, Ted, 238
Cather, Willa, 11, 38, 88
cats: Flowerface, 108; Lonesome, 307,
   308, 315, 317, 355, 356, 357, 360, *192–23;*
   poems about, 315; in Point Rich-
   mond, 238, 239, 262, 269, 280; wk's
   preference for, 9
Cavafy, Constantine, 261
Céline, Louis Ferdinand, 145–46
Cézanne, Paul, 179
Chaffee, Oliver, 200
Chambers, Whittaker, 302; testimony to
   House Un-American Activities Sub-
   committee, 181–82; at *Time,* 122, 123,

125, 126, 127, 128; and *Witness,* 123, 182,
   279
Chapin, Katherine, 196, 227
Chaplin, Charlie, 203
Chapman, Eulalia, 82–83, 108
Cheever, John: "The Five-Forty-Eight,"
   294; military service, 101; relationship
   with wk, 93, 98; in Saratoga Springs,
   101, 103; *The Way Some People Live,* 93,
   119, 120; wk's review of book, 93, 119,
   120
Cheever, Mary, 93
Chermayeff, Serge, 193, 196, 200
Chiang Kai-shek, 123
Chicago Roller Skate Company, 157–58
Chinese Nationalists, 123
Chinese poetry, 73
Chisholm, Hugh, 274, 277–78
Christian College, 32
cia (Central Intelligence Agency), 324
Clair, René, 143
Clapton, Eric, 311
Cocteau, Jean, 61, 143, 189
Cohl, Emil, 203
cold war, 167, 183–84, 194, 216
Cole, Sidney, 313
collages, 261, 263, 264, 286, 292
Collingwood, R. G., 252, 256–57
Colman, Bunky, 244
Colorado: family cabin, 41–42. *See also*
   Denver
Colorado Springs Fine Arts Center, 86
Colt Press, 90, 91, 97, 101, 108, 109,
   124–25, 129, 310
Columbia mo, 32–35, 232–33
Columbia Pictures, 321
Columbia Records, 285
Columbia University, English Institute
   Conferences, 78, 81, 84, 91
Common Sense, 130, 134
communism: Chinese Nationalists and,
   123; investigations in United States, 45,
   123, 181–82, 208, 220; wk's views of,
   40, 44, 45, 47, 51, 60, 185, 302
Connolly, Vincent, 294
Conrad, Joseph, 268
Copland, Aaron, 184
Corbett, Edward, 236

Corey, Paul, 365 n.2
Cornell, Joseph, 73, 203
Corvette, Rikki, 332, 333
Cowan, Jerome, 349–50
Cowell Hospital, University of California, 277, 289, 290, 299–300, 359, 361
Cowley, Malcolm: *The Literary Situation,* 314, 355; opinions of WK's poems, 318; political activities, 73; reaction to WK's disappearance, 360; relationship with WK, 87, 92, 93, 98, 121, 128, 365 n.2; review of *Evil Under the Sun,* 261; on WK's poetry, 87, 89, 282; on Yaddo, 102
Craig, Frank, 335
Craig, Marge, 335
Crane, Hart: film tribute to, 337, 351; in Greenwich Village, 115; in Mexico, 4; poetry, 52, 53, 337, 351–52; residences in New York, 78, 149, 181; suicide, 3, 52; Tate and, 81; WK's view of, 130, 231
Crane, Milton, 152–53
Crane, Stephen, 237, 267–68
Creekmore, Hubert, 266
Crews, Freddie, 334
Crosby, Bing, 23, 334
Cultural and Scientific Conference for World Peace, 183–84, 185, 191, 201
Cummington Press, 310

dance: ballet, 140, 196; in *Poets' Follies,* 327, 331–32
Dane, Barbara, 301
Dante, 213
Darensbourg, Joe, 234
Darrow, Whitney, Jr., 285
Davis, George, 151, 161
Davis, Jan, 341, 360
Davis, Stuart, 151, 197
Decker, James, 148
de Corsia, Ted, 246
de Kooning, Elaine, 203, 207
de Kooning, Willem, 138, 178, 191, 219, 220, 221
DeNiro, Robert, 365 n.3
Denney, Reuel, 121
Dennis, Nigel, 121, 123, 142

Denver: during approach of World War II, 76, 83; draft board, 108; Keeses' apartments in, 59–60; radio programs in, 63–64; Xantha Street in, 262
Denver Public Library: collection, 64; Rocky Mountain Bibliographic Center for Research, 82–83, 84, 108–09, 112; WK's employment, 58, 62, 64, 65, 66–67
Derrière le miroir, 183
detective fiction: read by WK, 97, 120, 173; by WK, 120, 137–38, 144
Deutsch, Babette, 130, 134
Devree, Howard, 227, 236, 239
De Vries, Peter, 164, 285
Dewey, Thomas, 102
Diamond, David, 102–03, 104, 107
Dickinson, Emily, 188–89
Diers, Harry E., 16–17
Dietrich, Marlene, 131
Diller, Phyllis, 328, 330, 356, 360
di Nero, Bob, 141, 365 n.3
di Nero, Virginia, 141, 365 n.3
Diogenes, 87
Directions, 62
Doane College, 28–32, 44
Döblin, Alfred, 43
dogs, 9, 315
Dondero, George A., 208, 210, 212, 220
Dos Passos, John, 29, 41, 51, 71
Dostoyevsky, Fyodor, 279; *The Devils,* 5, 350
Doubleday Doran, 45
draft: efforts to avoid, 87, 108, 112, 115–16, 117–18, 121, 128–29, 365 n.2; WK's classification, 89, 116, 127, 128–29; of writers, 115–16
Duke, Vernon, 345
Duncan, Robert, 259

Eberhart, Richard, 204
Egan, Charles, 178
Eighth Street Club, 191
Eiseley, Loren, 36
Eisenhower, Dwight D., 278, 281, 308
Elder, Donald, 45, 65, 69, 79
Eliot, T. S., 195; Auden's poem to, 183; *The Cocktail Party,* 216–17; discussion

Eliot, T. S. (*cont.*)
    at Forum 49, 206; *Family Reunion,*
    246; *The Four Quartets,* 124; influ-
    ence on WK, 130, 260; "Journey of
    the Magi," 277; poetry read in *Poets'
    Follies,* 328, 331, 334; Pound on, 218;
    publicity for *Botteghe Oscure,* 227, 237;
    read by WK, 29; *Sweeney Agonistes,*
    334, 341, 344; Tate and, 81; *Waste Land,*
    71; WK on, 42, 135, 163
Eppler, Joseph R., 5
Erickson, Bill, 244
Erskine, Albert, 148–49, 152, 214, 225–26,
    250, 252
Ertegun, Ahmet, 233, 234
Ertegun, Bettie, 316
Ertegun, Nesuhi, 233–34, 268–69, 273,
    291, 316
Evans, Walker, 84, 121
Evett, Robert, 319, 345
Evil Under the Sun (Myrer): Getty's
    editing, 247–48, 260; Kees persona,
    248–49; Mexico reference, 4; pub-
    lication, 255–56; publisher, 225–26;
    reviews, 260–61, 272; satire in, 225;
    song lyrics by WK, 248, 252; WK's
    editing, 247–51, 253, 272
Ewell, Don, 336–37, 341, 347, *192–29*
exhibitions. *See* art exhibitions
existentialism, 146, 278, 287

Fadayev, Aleksandr A., 184
Fairbanks, Douglas, Jr., 268, 269, 273
The Fall of the Magicians (Kees): dedi-
    cation, 147, 154; poems, 146, 153, 154,
    172, 190; publication, 152, 214; reviews,
    152–54, 284; submission to publishers,
    148–49; success, 154, 191, 247
Fall Quarter (Kees): attempts to inter-
    est publishers, 97, 100, 107, 109, 120;
    characters, 32, 33, 93–94, 128, 365 n.1;
    discussions of war in, 89; Getty's com-
    ments, 94–95, 260; Knopf contract,
    85–86, 95–96; rejection of, 96–97;
    revisions, 308; Volkening's support of,
    246, 274, 302; writing of, 77, 83–86, 87,
    90–91
Farber, Janet. *See* Richards, Janet Farber

Farber, Manny: as art critic, 138, 259; film
    criticism, 321; friends, 235; relation-
    ship with WK, 132, 133, 233; review of
    Hotel Apex, 275, 276; separation from
    Janet, 147; social life, 141
Farrar, John, 278
Farrar, Straus, and Young, 274, 277–78
Farrell, Hortense, 101, 116
Farrell, James T.: Ann as secretary, 124;
    anthology dedicated to, 88; Guggen-
    heim fellowship, 47; political activi-
    ties, 73; relationship with WK, 80–81,
    93, 97, 101, 116, 133, 142; writing of, 63
Faulkner, William, 42, 44, 46, 224
FBI (Federal Bureau of Investigation):
    Ann's fear of, 302, 304; Chambers
    and, 123; investigations of leftists, 123,
    302; surveillance of Yaddo, 101; visas
    denied to artists, 184
F. D. Kees Manufacturing Company:
    factory, 13–14, 27; history, 11–12; John
    Kees's work at, 22, 23, 27; products,
    11–12, 14, 19, 49; sale of, 157–58, 176;
    WK's interest in working for, 28
Fearing, Kenneth, 47, 51, 53, 101, 130, 154
Federal Bureau of Investigation. *See* FBI
Federal Writers' Project: *The American
    Guide,* 232; *Nebraska: A Guide to the
    Cornhusker State,* 13–14, 49–52, 57–58;
    WK's employment, 49–52, 57–58
Feigen, Gerald, 295–97, 298
Ferling, Lawrence (Ferlinghetti), 327, 332
Ferrell, Sylvia Green, 15, 18
Ferril, Thomas Hornsby, 68
Fields, W. C., 199
Filler, Louis, 134
films: *Adventures of Jimmy,* 243–45, 254,
    275; documentary on WK, 362–63; ex-
    perimental, 203, 243–45, 254, 275–76,
    321; Forum 49 program, 196, 202–
    03; French, 12, 65; by Heick, 312–13;
    noir, 224, 262; *104th Street,* 196, 203;
    Paramount newsreels, 131–32, 143, 148;
    radio programs on, 320–21, 325, 326,
    333, 339, 349–50, 356–58; reviews for
    Time, 126–27; San Francisco Films,
    321–22, 323, 333, 337–38, *192–21; The
    Scavengers,* 337–38; school, 338–39;

Ginsberg, Allen, 278
Giroux, Robert, 191, 246–47, 252, 258
Gleason, Madeline, 259
Gnosticism, 165
Golden Gate Bridge: film project, 337, 351–52, 360; suicides, 349; WK's car found near, 5, 352; WK's plan to jump from, 3, 351; WK's visits to, 72, 351–52, *192–33*
Goldwater, Robert, 162–63
Golffing, Francis, 209
Goll, Ivan, 92
Goodman, Paul, 118
Goodnough, Robert, 220, 221
Gordon, Ambrose, 153–54
Gorky, Arshile, 138, 173, 220
Gosse, Edmund, 90
Gottlieb, Adolph: apartment in Provincetown, 209; artists' panel at Studio 35, 220; boycott of Metropolitan Museum exhibit, 221–22, 226–27; exhibitions, 212; paintings, 150; participation in Forum 49, 193, 197, 200, 206; participation in Forum 50, 225; relationship with WK, 285, 329; writing on art, 138
Gottlieb, Esther, 197, 209
Grabhorn, Jane, 90, 91, 108, 109, 124–25, 310
Graham, John, 151
Grahame, Gloria, 325
Grateful Dead, 311
Green, Edward, 17
Green, Mary Weldon Odell (grandmother), 15
Green, Stephen Warren (grandfather), 15
Greenberg, Clement: art criticism, 138, 162, 174, 177, 216, 259; on *Life* magazine, 241; military service, 116; as *Nation* art critic, 180, 181, 207; paintings, 185; political activities, 73; on Pound, 194; in Provincetown, 201; relationship with WK, 80, 133, 193, 197, 201, 207, 208, 220; social life, 141; on WK's paintings, 180, 181
Greensfelder, Robert, 276
Gregory, Horace, 79, 130; relationship

with WK, 80, 90, 93; review of *The Last Man,* 130; WK's letters to, 128
Grieg, Michael: career, 320; Film Workshop, 338; *Four Times One,* 341; photographs of, *192–24;* plays by, 328, 332, 346; in *Poets' Follies,* 327, 329, 330, 331–32, 360; radio programs, 320–21, 349–50, 356–58; reaction to WK's disappearance, 4–5, 355; relationship with WK, 3–4, 320, 326, 327, 334, 351; at San Francisco Films, 322; Showplace and, 335, 347; WK's belongings kept by, 359–60
Grieg, Sally, 320, 334
Griffin, Howard, 266
Griggs, L. S., 99
Gropius, Walter, 206
Gross, Chaim, 207
Groton School, 263
Guggenheim, Hazel, 84
Guggenheim fellowships, 47, 93, 98, 176
Guggenheim Gallery of Non-Objective Art, 78
Guston, Philip, 178

Haarus, Agatha, 11
Hagan, R. H., 329, 330, 331
Haggin, B. H., 80
Haines, John, 224
Halper, Nathan, 206
Hamilton, Wallace, 321
Harcourt, Brace, and World: Ernest Brace and, 140; *A Breaking and a Death* and, 233, 246–47, 252, 258; *A Late History* submitted to, 190, 191, 203–04, 209, 210; purchase of Reynal and Hitchcock, 154, 190
Hare, David, 220
Harper's, 107, 217
Harper's, 209
Harper's Bazaar, 237–38, 313
Hartford, Huntington, 267, 268, 269, 271. *See also* Huntington Hartford Foundation
Harvard University, 155, 167, 195
Haverstraf, Alex, 207
Hawthorne, Nathaniel, 191, 318
Hayakawa, S. I., 307

jazz (*cont.*)

202; in Los Angeles, 233–34, 238, 256, 267, 291; New Orleans-style, 23, 159, 160, 234, 275; radio broadcasts, 23; recordings, 201, 210, 234, 270; in San Francisco, 236–37, 238, 244–45, 255, 286, 301; white musicians, 202; WK's interest in, 23, 284; WK's lectures on, 201–02, 220, 288, 307, 319; WK's writing on, 126, 159–61, 202. *See also* music, of WK

Jazz Man Record Shop, 233–34

Johns, Jasper, 220

Johnson, Jean, 111

Johnson, Maurice: book dedicated to, 130; comments on *Fall Quarter,* 93–94; military service, 120; at Nebraska, 40; relationship with WK, 38–39, 43, 91; teaching career, 155; WK's letters to, 40–42, 44, 46–47, 94, 116, 147, 189, 227

Jones, James, 252, 260, 269

Joyce, James: discussion at Forum 49, 206; films based on works, 326; *Finnegans Wake,* 39, 206, 246; read by John Kees, 15; read by WK, 29, 39; scholars, 102; Stuart and, 59; *Ulysses,* 39, 360; WK on, 76

The Joy of Cooking (Rombauer), 125

Justice, Donald, 361–62

Kael, Pauline, 321, 326, 356

Kafka, Franz, 59, 62, 145–46

Kahlo, Frida, 316

Kanai, A. L., 100, 110

Kazin, Alfred, 102, 104–05, 107, 109, 117, 119, 285

Keeley, Mary Paxton, 32–35, 232–33

Keepnews, Orin, 336, 348–49

Kees, Ann Swan: attitude toward children, 199; Berkeley apartment, 282; Brooklyn Heights apartment, 189–90; clothing, 199, 213; cross-country trip (1950), 231, 232–33; dates with soldiers, 106; in Denver, 58, 64, 98–100, 105–07; depression, 326; editing skill, 300–301; encouragement of WK's writing, 90, 97; family, 37; friends in Denver, 67–68, 69, 86–87, 98–99, 106, 111; friends

in New York, 358; friends in Provincetown, 198, 199, 224–25; friends in San Francisco, 274, 287, 297–98; friends' views of, 245; health, 64, 182, 213, 253; injuries in car accident, 293; at Langley Porter, 303–04, 306; letters to Eleanor Scott, 211; letters to Getty, 79, 110–11, 179, 197, 198, 359; letters to WK, 42, 98, 105–07, 108, 359, 365 n.4; on life in New York, 82; Los Angeles visits, 264–69, 291; mental illness, 110–11, 252–54, 298–301, 302–05; move to California after college, 39, 42, 44, 48; move to New York, 124; music played by, 252; at Nebraska, 37–38, 40; needlepoint, 289; New York City vacations, 77–82, 91–93; photographs of, 298, *192–6, 192–16, 192–18, 192–20;* physical appearance, 38, 199; Provincetown vacations, 156, 171–75, 193, 198–99; publicity for *Botteghe Oscure,* 243; reaction to WK's disappearance, 359, 361; relationship with Sarah and John Kees, 107, 156; San Francisco vacation, 70–72; social life, 141–42, 198; typing of WK's manuscripts, 60, 94, 190; ventriloquist's dummy and, 296; view of Forum 49, 198; view of WK's painting, 139; WK's letters to, 105, 106. *See also* Kees, Weldon: relationship with Ann

Kees, Ann Swan, drinking of, 78, 156; alcoholism, 298, 303; in Denver, 64; in New York, 218; in Provincetown, 198–99; in San Francisco, 253, 289, 294, 297, 300

Kees, Ann Swan, employment: *Antiques* magazine, 132, 141, 142, 151, 157, 176, 213; in Denver, 60, 98; secretarial work in Berkeley, 239; as secretary to James Farrell, 124; University of California Hospital, 277, 289, 290, 299–300, 359, 361

Kees, Clara (aunt), 12, 233

Kees, Dan, Jr. (cousin), 157

Kees, Dan (uncle), 12, 27

Kees, Emma Zimmermann (grandmother), 11

Kees, Frederick Daniel (grandfather),

work published by, 64, 70. *See also* New Directions

Lazzell, Blanche, 200

League for Cultural Freedom and Socialism, 73–74

Leen, Nina, 226, 240–41

Leigh, Carol, 327, 330, *192–27*

lesbians, 131, 136; McCullers as, 103–04; novels, 66, 67; WK's view of, 12

Levin, Harry, 306, 314

Levitt, Helen, 141, 142, 196, 285

Levy, Julian, 173

Lewis, George, 275, 363

Lewis, Sinclair, 67

Lewis, Wyndham, 75–76, 109, 193, 325

Library of Congress, jazz recordings, 210

Life: coverage of contemporary art, 177–78, 219, 220; Irascible Eighteen photograph, 226–27, 240–42; Pollock story, 197, 200; stories on end of World War II, 155

lighthouses, 312, 314

Lincoln NE: jobs in, 43; public television station, 362–63; summers in, 40–41; visits to, 233; writers in, 36. *See also* Federal Writers' Project; University of Nebraska, Lincoln

Lindovna, Tamara, 332

Lingle, Paul: in Honolulu, 277; performances, 255; relationship with WK, 236, 284, 307; WK's music played by, 270, 273

Lin Yutang, 123

Lippold, Richard, 220

little magazines: book reviews by WK, 53; history of, 135; read by John Kees, 15; WK's work published in, 49, 62, 87. See also *Furioso; Prairie Schooner*

Little Man Press, 77–78

Lloyd, Harold, 13

Loeb, Janice, 196

Loeser, Katinka, 130

Los Angeles: communists in, 44–45; jazz in, 233–34, 238, 256, 267, 291; visits to, 233–34, 237, 264–69, 291, 316, 325; WK's stay in (1936), 44–49. *See also* Hollywood

Lowe, Jack, 244

Lowell, Robert: Capote on, 161; editors and, 191; mental illness, 186, 192, 204; poetry, 149, 154, 172; political views, 185

Lowry, Malcolm, 314; *Under the Volcano,* 4, 152, 214

Lowry, Robert, 77–78, 87, 151, 154, 185–86

LSD, 324

Luce, Henry, 121, 122–23, 128, 178

Luhan, Mabel Dodge, 84

Maas, Willard, 79, 118

MacAgy, Douglas: Bateson and, 239–40; as director of California School of Fine Arts, 236; divorce, 308; at Museum of Modern Art, 314; relationship with WK, 237, 239, 254, 255

MacAgy, Jermayne: affair with WK, 20, 308–09, 311, 314–15, 317–18, 323, 326; Andean art exhibition, 314; divorce, 308; exhibition of WK's work, 254, 256, 259–60, 308; friendship with WK, 243, 255, 347; photograph of, *192–22;* Stendahl and, 316

Macdonald, Dwight, 79, 136; apartment, 149; Forum 49 and, 192, 194–95, 197, 201, 207; friends, 84, 207; political activities, 73–74, 110, 185; in Provincetown, 205; relationship with WK, 80, 133, 196, 198; talk on Soviet Union, 194–95, 201

Macdonald, Nancy, 80, 133, 149, 196, 207

MacLeish, Archibald, 77, 92, 204

Macleod, Norman, 158

Macmillan, 217

Macy Foundation, 319

Magazine of Art, 162–63

Mailer, Norman, 184, 224, 248, 266

Malaquais, Jean, 161

Mann, Thomas, 80, 86, 93, 142, 184, 265

Manuscript, 49

March, William, 118, 133

Marie-Jeanne, 196

Marshall, John, 320

Marshall, Margaret, 141, 207, 223–24, 227

Martin, Dick, 327, 331–32

Marvin, Robert, 21, 29

Matthews, T. S., 121

29, 330, 332, 334, 339, 341, 360; plans, 327–29; rehearsals, 329; reviews, 333; San Francisco performances, 329–32, 333–34, *192–28*

Point Reyes Lighthouse, 312, 314

Point Richmond CA, Keeses' apartment, 235, 236, 238–39, 262, 264, 271, 279–80

Pollack, Lou, 151, 178, 329. *See also* Peridot Gallery

Pollock, Jackson: Irascible Eighteen photograph, 227; *Life* article, 197, 200; paintings, 138, 180, 185, 197, 200; sculpture, 242; WK on, 220

Pope, Saxton, 303, 304, 306

Porter, Katherine Anne, 64, 91, 102

Possibilities, 152

Poster, Connie, 181, 227

Poster, William: on *Evil Under the Sun,* 260–61; letters to WK, 238, 242, 259, 272, 274, 301–02; painting given to, 181; poems sent to, 247; relationship with WK, 130, 227; review of *The Last Man,* 130; on Schwartz, 273; WK's letters to, 232, 246

Pound, Dorothy, 217

Pound, Ezra: Bollingen Prize, 194, 217; letter read in *Poets' Follies,* 330–31; letters, 235; *Pisan Cantos,* 194; read by WK, 29; at St. Elizabeth's, 217–18, 316; "Sextus Propertius," 174; translations, 331–32; vorticist movement, 75

Pound, Louise, 38

Pousette-Dart, Richard, 220

Prairie Schooner, 35, 36; book reviews by WK, 53, 71; Winslow poems, 66; WK's work published in, 36–37, 39, 48

Prentice Hall, 147

Preston, Robert, 268

Preston, Stuart, 206

Prévert, Jacques, 332

Providence RI, 192

Providence Journal, 180, 205, 209–11

Provincetown MA: art exhibitions, 197, 199, 223, 225; artists, 127, 173, 200; Forum 50, 223, 225; galleries, 285; homosexuals in, 247; Myrer novel set in, 225–26, 247–51, 252; vacation (1942), 127; vacation (1947), 156; vaca-

tion (1948), 166–67, 171–75; vacation (1949), 192, 208–09; vacation (1950), 219, 221, 223–26. *See also* Forum 49

Provincetown Advocate, 283

Provincetown Art Association, 223, 225

Provincetown Players, 205, 209

psychoanalysis, 196, 206, 240

psychology: popular, 345; tests for draftees, 129

Purple Onion, 319, 336, 344, 360

radio programs: *Behind the Movie Camera,* 320–21, 325, 326, 333, 339; *Behind the Scenes,* 349–50, 356–58; in Denver, 63–64; on Forum 49, 192, 200; on poetry, 290, 291, 294, 300

Rahv, Natalie, 117, 136

Rahv, Philip: friends, 84; Greenberg and, 116; news of WK's disappearance, 356; parties, 136; relationship with WK, 79, 117, 273; review of Chambers's *Witness,* 279; WK's letters to, 300

Ramsay, Robert L., 32

Random House, 217, 225–26, 250, 252, 255–56

Ransom, John Crowe, 74, 93

Razaf, Andy, 126

Reed, Henry, 331

Reed, John, 66, 127

Reich, Wilhelm, 224

Reinhardt, Ad, 184, 220, 222, 236

Rexroth, Kenneth: assistance to Japanese Americans, 99, 100; as conscientious objector, 115, 143; poems, 141, 300; poetry readings, 243, 259; political activities, 73; radio programs, 313; relationship with WK, 70–71, 175, 185, 237, 360; review of *Collected Poems,* 362

Rexroth, Marie, 70–71, 99, 274

Reynal and Hitchcock: book proposal submitted to, 119; *The Fall of the Magicians* published by, 148–49, 152, 154, 214, 247; purchased by Harcourt, 154, 190

Richard, Albert J., 131

Richards, Charles: reaction to WK's disappearance, 355; relationship with

schizophrenics: art of, 294, *192–30;* films of, 246, 254, 337, 349, *192–30;* research on, 308

Schnitzler, Arthur, *The Gallant Cassian,* 341–42

Schwartz, Delmore: at *Partisan Review,* 273, 281; poems, 61, 141; political activities, 73; in Princeton, 273, 301–02; relations with other writers, 80; wartime activities, 143

Schwartz, Horace, 322, 327, 330, 349, *192–27*

Schwartz, Maury, 349

Scott, Eleanor, 190, 192, 211

Scott, Win, 180, 192, 204, 211

screenplays. *See* Kees, Weldon, Works

Scribner's, 119, 120

sculpture, 242

Seide, Michael, 102

Senate, Army-McCarthy hearings, 297, 299

Sergeant, Winthrop, 125–26

Sewanee Review, 130

Shapiro, Karl, 148, 277

Shapley, Harley, 183

Shaw, Irwin, 88

Sheets, Kermit, 245

Shelley Memorial Award, 305–06, 308, 314, 339

Sherwood, Marion, 21

Shostakovich, Dmitry, 184

Showplace, *192–31;* building rehab, 339, 345; closing of, 346–47; dances, 344; *Four Times One,* 341–44, 346–47, 348, *192–32;* fundraiser, 335–36, 339

Sills, Milton, 20, 23, 177

Simon, Ben, 43

Simpson, Louis, 281

Siqueiros, David, 184

Slesinger, Donald, 196, 206

Slesinger, Tess, 80, 365 n.3

Sloan, Brant, 276

Smart, Christopher, 315

Smedley, Agnes, 186

Smith, Anthony, 193

Smith, Dale: letters to WK, 219; novella, 109; photographs of, *192–5;* relation-ship with WK, 38, 49, 51, 58; WK's letters to, 45, 47, 60, 89

Smith, Hassell, 235

Smith, Margaret, 38

Smith College, 102, 105

Smits, Lee, 64

Snazelle, Ernest, 338

Snell, George, 70

Snow, John C., 198

Soby, James Thrall, 241–42

Solomon, Hyde, 224

Soviet Union, 183, 194–95, 201. *See also* cold war

Spaeth, Sigmund Gottfried, 300

Spender, Stephen, 156, 327

Spiegel, Leo, 206

Spring Quarter. See *Fall Quarter*

Sproul, Robert Gordon, 40, 305–06, 333

Stafford, Jean, 156

State Department, 123, 148, 184, 232, 237

The State of the Nation, 77–78

Stauffacher, Frank, 322, 337–38

Steam Press, 332, 360

Stearns, Marshall, 300

Steele, Marjorie, 267, 268

Steinbeck, John, 47, 69, 248

Stekel, Wilhelm, 156

Stendahl, Earl, 316

Stepanek, Orin, 39–40

Stern, Jimmy, 128

Sterne, Hedda, 220, 227, 238, 241

Stevens, Wallace: books owned by WK, 4; books reviewed by WK, 22; poetry, 139, 141, 154; Pound on, 218; publisher, 90; WK on, 135; WK's letters to, 318

Stevenson, Adlai, 278, 280–82

Still, Clyfford, 139, 227, 236

Stone Wall Press, 362

Story, 88

Strauss, Harold, 45, 85–86, 95–96

Stuart, Michael, 59

Studio 35, 220–21, 222, 236

suicide: stories collected by Wimberly, 36, 350; Williams on, 92. *See also* Kees, Weldon: suicide and

Sutton, Denver, 338, 339

Swados, Harvey, 63

Swallow, Alan, 282

Volkening, Henry: as Brace's agent, 139; *A Breaking and a Death* and, 246, 247; support of *Fall Quarter*, 246, 274, 302; as WK's agent, 109, 137, 313

Waley, Arthur, 73, 117, 130
Walker, Hudson D., 198
Wallace, Henry, 151, 183
Wallace, Kevin, 333, 346
Waller, Thomas "Fats," 40, 126, 159, 219
Wallis, Charles Glenn, 118–19
Washington DC, St. Elizabeth's Hospital, 217–18, 316
Webster, Ambrose, 200
Wedekind, Frank, *The Tenor*, 341, 342, 346
Weinrich, Agnes, 200
Welch, Joseph N., 299
Welty, Eudora, 102, 109
Wescott, Glenway, 91
West, Nathanael, 46, 64, 75, 84–85, 266
West, Ray B., 63, 70, 96, 167, 362
Western Review, 362
Wheeler, Herbert, 255
Wheelwright, Joseph, 359
Whitney Museum, 212, 238, 241–42
Wight, Frederick, 206
Wilbur, Lorraine, 224
Wilbur, Robert, 224
Wilde, Oscar, *The Importance of Being Earnest*, 28, 30
Wilder, Thornton, 174, 237
William Morrow, 282
Williams, Florence, 92, 98
Williams, Oscar, 74, 92, 93
Williams, Tennessee, 183
Williams, William Carlos: books in Denver Public Library, 64; books owned by WK, 4; influence on WK, 61; poetry, 92, 139, 141, 331; political activities, 73; read by WK, 29, 92; relationship with WK, 92, 98, 101, 133–34; WK on, 135; on WK's work, 92
Wilson, Adrian: in Barbary Coast Five, 327, *192–27*; broadsides for *Poets' Follies*, 328, 332, *192–26*; invitations to fundraiser, 336; publication of *Poems 1947–1954*, 310–11, 315–16, 317, 318, 323;

reaction to WK's disappearance, 5; relationship with WK, 310, 334; Steam Press, 332, 360
Wilson, Edmund: Myrer character based on, 225; novels, 116; poetry, 91, 174–75; in Provincetown, 127, 174–75; publicity for *Botteghe Oscure*, 237; relationship with WK, 116–17, 119, 136, 155–56, 310; view of New York, 231
Wimberly, Lowry Charles: relationship with WK, 35–37, 39, 40–41, 47, 52, 185, 233; students, 38, 50; suicide stories collected by, 36, 350; on WK's work, 88. *See also Prairie Schooner*
Windsor Quarterly, 43
Winslow, Walker, 66–69
Winters, Yvor, 163, 294, 332
Witherstine, Donald, 191, 197
Witt-Diament, Ruth, 327
Wittwer, John, 237
Wolfe, Thomas, 37, 42, 67, 88, 135
Wolfe, Tom, 212
women: female personas in WK's work, 74, 136–37, 342–43. *See also* Kees, Weldon: relationships with women; lesbians
Woodberry Poetry Room, Harvard, 167
Works Progress Administration. *See* Federal Writers' Project
The World of Weldon Kees, 362–63
World's Fair, 1939, 78
World War II: approach of, 71, 73–75, 83; effects on publishing industry, 84, 120; effects on writers, 143; end of, 143, 145, 146, 155; Holocaust, 194; internment camps for Japanese Americans, 99–100; news of, 88–89; newsreels, 131, 141, 143; Nuremberg war trials, 155, 195; pacifists' opposition to, 71, 73–74, 76–77, 110, 134; patriotism during, 75, 76; Pearl Harbor, 95–96; writers supporting, 77, 89. *See also* draft
Wright, Frank Lloyd, 265
Wright, Lloyd, 265
Wright, Richard, 88
writing, of WK: advantages of poetry over fiction, 53; agents, 69, 109; ambition, 61–62; in California, 237–38;